DAY BY DAY

PARADISE TO THE PROMISED LAND

Day by Day

Paradise to the Promised Land

Edited by
JOHN BENNETT

PRECIOUS SEED PUBLICATIONS

© Copyright Precious Seed Publications 2007
PO Box 573, Fareham, UK, PO14 9FB

First published September 2007

ISBN 978-1-871642-21-6

This is the eleventh book in the Day by Day series.

The others are:

Day by Day through the Old Testament
Day by Day through the New Testament
Day by Day in the Psalms
Day by Day Moments with the Master
Day by Day in Prayer
Day by Day with Bible Characters
Day by Day Christ Foreshadowed
Day by Day Bible Promises
Day by Day Divine Titles
Day by Day Bible Commands

Printed in China

Contents

Contents

Acknowledgements

The Day by Day series, *Paradise to the Promised Land* being the eleventh volume, has sought to encourage the daily reading of scripture and to provide a meditation derived from a particular passage. This latest volume continues that worthy tradition, focussing upon the seed-plot of the scriptures. As before, twenty-four of the Lord's servants have contributed of their time, effort, and obvious gift to enable its compilation. We would acknowledge the debt we owe to these brethren and our thanks are extended to them. We know their labours to be a demonstration of their love for the Lord and evidence of their desire for the blessing of the Lord's people.

Apart from the significant contribution of the authors, the production of the book would not have been possible without the work of other committee members. The list of readings, from which this book was derived, was developed by John Scarsbrook. He and Roy Hill rendered valuable service at the proof reading stage, offering helpful suggestions to the editor. Derek Hill assisted us by setting the type from which the pages are printed. The cover design is the work of Barney Trevivian, developed from an idea of John Scarsbrook. Once the book was complete, Roy Hill played his part at the printing stage. We would express our sincere thanks to all for their valuable assistance.

No one could read through the New Testament without appreciating how much of it is built upon and develops types and principles that are first revealed in the Old. One example was the Lord's use of the book of Deuteronomy to provide His answers to the testing by the devil. Yet, for many, a significant number of such passages are neglected. It is the desire of the committee that this book will encourage saints to explore the Pentateuch, to appreciate its types and to apply its lessons.

On behalf of the Precious Seed Committee
John Bennett
September 2007

The Contributors and their Contributions

Ian Campbell	England	January 1 – 16
Jeremy Holifield	Wales	January 17 – 31
John Bennett	England	February 1 – 15
Ian Affleck	Scotland	February 16 – 29
Jim Cochrane	Canada	March 1 – 15
Robert Thomson	Scotland	March 16 – 31
William Burnett	Canada	April 1 – 15
Roy Hill	England	April 16 – 30
Colin Lacey	England	May 1 – 15
Alex Wiseman	England	May 16 – 31
John Scarsbrook/ John Bennett	England	June 1 – 15
Lindsay Parks	USA	June 16 – 30
Jim Flanigan	Northern Ireland	July 1 – 15
Richard Catchpole	England	July 16 – 31
Jack Hay	Scotland	August 1 – 15
Ken Rudge	England	August 16 – 31
Douglas Mowat	Scotland	September 1 – 15
Ian Rees	England	September 16 – 30
John Scarsbrook	England	October 1 – 15
Howard Coles	England	October 16 – 31
David Newell	Scotland	November 1 – 15
David Wilson	Ireland	November 16 – 30
Tom Wilson	Scotland	December 1 – 15
Alan Gamble	Scotland	December 16 – 31

Biographies of the Contributors

Ian Campbell was commended to full-time service from the assembly at South Shields, England. A former teacher, his particular exercise has been children's work, including visits to schools, and this has taken him to all parts of the UK. He also does regular presentations on the truth of Creation in which he has a particular interest. Married to Bitten, he has two grown-up children.

Jeremy Holifield was born to parents in assembly fellowship in 1965. He was born again on 28th February 1974 and baptised on 18th March 1983, coming into fellowship with the saints at Deri, Wales, shortly after, where he remains in fellowship. He has worked exclusively in the construction industry. Helen became his wife in 1990 and they have three daughters and a son. He regularly ministers the word of God throughout the UK.

John Bennett is an elder in the Gospel Hall, Kirkby-in-Ashfield, Nottinghamshire, England. He is active in ministry in England and has written numerous articles for assembly magazines. He became a trustee of *Precious Seed* in 2002 and publications editor in 2004. He presently works as a teacher in a local College. He is married to Rachel and has three children.

Ian Affleck has been in fellowship in the Lossiemouth assembly, Scotland, for 36 years and has been an elder for almost 30 years. He retains an active interest in the proclamation of the gospel and has been privileged to minister to the Lord's people throughout the UK, Canada and India.

Jim Cochrane was born in Canada and was brought up in the warmth of a Christian home and in the happy fellowship of an assembly. In a Sunday School class he received the Lord Jesus as his Saviour. His Christian life was formed under the example and the regular teaching of the church elders and their wives. Commended in 1947 to the work of the Lord in the Dominican Republic, he moved into a cultural, language and social world that was new and different. He has spent most of his years in a teaching ministry primarily in the Dominican Republic and in recent years in many other areas. His written ministry has been published in Spanish and English.

Robert Thomson is in fellowship at Bishopton Gospel Hall, Renfrewshire, Scotland. He is busy in Bible teaching throughout the UK and, in the last four years, has had an interest in Canada. He is Director of a Scottish housing charity that has particular concern for older and disabled people.

William Burnett was born and raised in Scotland, and spent his professional life in the oil refining business. His employer seconded him to Canada in 1972, and he accepted early retirement in 1994. He has been a 'tentmaker' among the assemblies since his late teen years, and now ministers throughout North America, and abroad. He also sits on the board of *Counsel* Magazine, and contributes regularly to various assembly publications. He and his wife Beth reside in Oakville, Ontario, Canada, where they are in happy fellowship in Hopedale assembly. They have three married sons, and eight grandchildren.

Roy Hill is an elder in the assembly at Pensford Gospel Hall, near Bristol, and is well known as an international Bible teacher. He is married with five children and five grandchildren. Having spent his life in the printing trade he is currently chairman of *Precious Seed* and a board member of Gospel Folio Press in Canada. He also writes extensively for assembly magazines and heads up Christian Year Publications.

Colin Lacey was born into a Christian home in Sussex, saved at the age of fifteen, baptized, and received into the fellowship of the assembly at Haywards Heath. He was headteacher of a large secondary school in the West Midlands for fourteen years and currently works part-time, training and assessing aspiring head teachers for the National Headship Qualification. He is an elder in the assembly at Stourbridge, and travels widely throughout the UK teaching the word of God. He has a particular interest in working with and encouraging young people. He has written the commentary on Judges in the *What the Bible Teaches* series published by John Ritchie and has contributed to several volumes in the 'Day by Day' series.

Alex Wiseman was born in Gardenstown, North-East Scotland. He now lives in Bournemouth and is an elder in the Drummond Road Gospel Hall. Before retirement, he worked in Northampton for many years as Chief Internal Auditor to the Nationwide Building Society. His teaching ministry has taken him throughout the UK, and he also writes for assembly magazines. He and his wife Jean have two daughters and three grandchildren.

Lindsay Parks is an elder in the assembly meeting in the Gospel Hall, Indiana, PA, USA. He is a self-employed family physician, married to Diane, with three children, and eight grandchildren. He has preached the gospel and ministered the word in a number of assemblies in the USA, Canada, and Northern Ireland. He has also contributed regularly to *Truth and Tidings* and *Words in Season* magazines and the *Choice Gleanings* calendar. With his brother Alan, a full-time commended assembly preacher and teacher, he helped produce the albums of Believers Hymns.

Jim Flanigan was raised in a Christian home in Northern Ireland. He was saved as a young man and received into the Parkgate Assembly in Belfast in 1946. In 1972 he resigned from full-time employment in response to the call of God to give more time to the work of the Lord. Most of this has been in ministering the word of God. He has travelled widely in the British Isles, the USA, Canada, Australia and Israel. He is the author of three volumes in the *What the Bible Teaches* series published by John Ritchie – on the books of Hebrews, Song of Solomon and Ruth.

Richard Catchpole lives in South Norwood, London, with his wife Judith and their three daughters. He is in fellowship in Denmark Road Gospel Hall from where, in fellowship with the assembly at Bermondsey, he was commended in 1989 to the grace of God for the work of the Lord. He travels extensively in the U.K. in a Bible teaching ministry and engages in children's and school work in his home locality.

Jack Hay is in fellowship in the assembly at Perth, Scotland. He is a commended full-time worker preaching the gospel and teaching the word throughout the UK, North America and the Far East. He is also the author of numerous magazine articles.

Ken Rudge is retired after a life spent working in education. He was headteacher of two Primary schools in Cornwall where he now lives. Since his conversion at the age of sixteen, he has always been in fellowship in a local assembly and is convinced of the scriptural grounds upon which they meet. He has served as an elder for many years and devotes his time to evangelism in the county of Cornwall, editing the *Precious Seed* magazine and ministering the word of God to assemblies in the UK. He has contributed to several of the 'Day by Day' series in the past.

Douglas Mowat is an elder in the Culloden assembly in Inverness, Scotland. He and his wife Elisabeth spent several years in full-time service in Finland before returning to the UK. He is employed as a Chartered Surveyor in Inverness and is actively involved in preaching and teaching throughout the UK.

Ian Rees saw an assembly planted in Francistown, Botswana, having served the Lord there for 13 years. Now based in the UK, he continues in fellowship in Manvers Hall, Bath, one of his commending assemblies. He is currently editor of *Young Precious Seed*. He is married and has seven children.

John Scarsbrook is an elder in the Killamarsh assembly, Derbyshire, England. He is active in ministry throughout the UK and he became a trustee of the *Precious Seed* magazine in 2003. He is a self-employed financial advisor, married to Ruth, with four married sons and nine grandchildren.

Howard Coles is a trustee of *Precious Seed*. He is a qualified accountant, running a small manufacturing business. He is married with three grown-up children and is an elder in the Coleford, assembly, near Bath. His ministry is mainly amongst assemblies in the South West of England.

David Wilson and his wife are missionaries to Ireland, having been commended by their assembly in New Jersey, USA, in 1997. They were in fellowship in the assembly in Kilkenny but have now started a new work in Waterford. They have two young daughters. David is an elder in the assembly and involved in teaching, evangelism, and pastoral care.

Tom Wilson is an elder in the Springburn assembly in Glasgow and ministers the word throughout Scotland. For many years he was an editor of *Believer's Magazine* and is principal of a specialist college in Glasgow.

Alan Gamble is in fellowship in Bethesda, Linthouse, assembly in Glasgow, Scotland. He is active in Bible teaching in the UK and North America. He serves as a trustee of Interlink, a missionary service group. Married to Elizabeth, they have three children. His professional background is in law.

Introduction

It should not be surprising to any believer to know that few areas of scripture have come under such concerted attack as the books of the Pentateuch, particularly Genesis. The Darwinian theory of human origins has become so widely accepted in society as to provide a regular challenge to the faith of many. As leaders in Christendom accept the lie of evolution or offer the compromise of so-called theistic evolution, so the Bible-believing Christian becomes more isolated. Yet the biblical account of creation is fundamental to the whole book. To undermine the passages that deal with these early days of earth's history is to undermine the complete canon. How can we teach the divine inspiration of all scripture and believe that Genesis chapters 1 to 6 may be mere allegory or myth?

We believe in a God whose power is awesome. He is the architect, creator and sustainer of all things and He will bring all things to their given conclusion. The prophet reminds us, 'Thus saith God the Lord, he that created the heavens, and stretched them out; he that spread forth the earth, and that which cometh out of it; he that giveth breath unto the people upon it, and spirit to them that walk therein', Isa. 42. 5. We are not the outcome of some process of 'blind chance'! We are the handiwork of God, responsible to Him as the One in whose hand is our every breath.

Apart from challenging the power of God and our responsibility to Him as our creator, speculative human theories of origins also undermine the words of the Lord Himself. If God did not create, what credence could we give to the words of One who said, 'For in those days shall be affliction, such as was not from the beginning of the creation which God created unto this time, neither shall be', Mark 13. 19? However, we do not rely upon the views of atheistic scientists, we accept the word of One who was there, the One 'by whom also he made the worlds', Heb. 1. 2.

Human theories also seek to undermine the reality of Adam and Eve. To destroy our first parents is to destroy the headship of Adam in respect to humanity as a whole. To remove the record of Genesis chapters 2 and 3 is to remove the principle of sin as present in all our lives, to challenge the genealogy of Joseph in Luke chapter 3, and the teaching of Paul in Romans 5, 1 Corinthians 15, and 1 Timothy 2. Such truths that permeate the whole of scripture cannot be dispensed with lightly!

How do we explain destruction, disease and death? How can we reconcile the infamous events of history with our ideas of a God of love if we dispense with sin and the effects of the fall? The heartache of humanity is but part of a far wider malaise that was experienced as a consequence of Adam's transgression. Paul wrote, 'For we know that the whole creation groaneth and travaileth in pain together until now', Rom. 8. 22.

Sin has brought death, Rom. 5. 12. God made the consequences of disobedience very clear, 'But of the tree of the knowledge of good and evil, thou shalt not eat of it: for in the day that thou eatest thereof thou shalt surely die', Gen. 2. 17. And, again, 'Unto the woman he [God] said, I will greatly multiply thy sorrow and thy conception; in sorrow thou shalt bring forth children . . . And unto Adam he said . . . cursed is the ground for thy sake; in sorrow shalt thou eat of it all the days of thy life', Gen. 3. 16-17.

Far from the theory of the ascent of man, scripture records man's descent to the point where, 'God saw that the wickedness of man was great in the earth, and that every imagination of the thoughts of his heart was only evil continually', Gen. 6. 5. Sin brought spiritual death and physical death upon Adam and his descendents, and God's judgement upon a sin-tarnished world. Peter bore testimony to the comprehensive nature of the flood when he wrote, 'few, that is, eight souls were saved by water', 1 Pet. 3. 20.

The days of Noah and of Lot also prefigure days when God will intervene in world affairs again, 'in the days of the Son of man', Luke 17. 26. God's judgement will not be a flood but, 'the day of the Lord will come as a thief in the night; in the which the heavens shall pass away with a great noise, and the elements shall melt with fervent heat, the earth also and the works that are therein shall be burned up', 2 Pet. 3. 10. What a challenge comes with such truth! As believers we have a responsibility to live lives of holiness and godliness and to warn people of the judgement to come.

But apart from defending the truth of the word of God, we can also see in the Pentateuch pictures of the Person and work of Christ. Who could read of Mount Moriah without thinking of Calvary? So much has been written on that response of Abraham to Isaac, 'God will provide himself a lamb', Gen. 22. 8. How precious to meditate upon the Baptist's salutation, 'Behold the Lamb of God, which taketh away the sin of the world', John 1. 29.

In Exodus, we are told of the Passover lamb and its sacrifice, the means of Israel's protection from the destroying angel who passed through the land of Egypt. Paul provided the antitype when he wrote of 'Christ our passover . . . sacrificed for us', 1 Cor. 5. 7. Similarly, when Moses struck the rock in Horeb, Exod. 17. 6, we are told by Paul, 'they drank of that spiritual Rock that followed them: and that Rock was Christ', 1 Cor. 10. 4. Equally, the chapters that deal with the design and construction of the tabernacle and its vessels, as well as the priestly garments given to Aaron are all full of Christ.

To appreciate something of the fullness of the work of Christ we might turn to the Levitical offerings. There were the free-will offerings, indicators of the truth that 'Christ . . . offered himself without spot to God', Heb. 9. 14. In the burnt offering there was a reminder of what the Father saw in the sacrifice of Christ. In the meal offering there was that which prefigured the perfect life of the Lord laid down upon the altar of Calvary. Equally, there were those offerings that spoke of the impact of the work of Christ reminding us that 'he hath made him to be sin for us, who knew no sin; that we might be made the righteousness of God in him', 2 Cor. 5. 21. How essential to appreciate the importance of the work of Christ before reading the legal requirements of a righteous God and the penalties meted out upon the transgressor!

In Numbers there are pictures of Christ and practical lessons of import. The Lord provided the typical teaching of the fiery serpents sent among the nation when they 'spake against God', Num. 21. 5. The Lord instructed 'the teacher of Israel' that, 'as Moses lifted up the serpent in the wilderness, even so must the Son of man be lifted up', John 3. 14. In the sacrifice of Christ there is the only remedy for sin, an equally deadly foe.

The perusal of the Pentateuch will also bring us many practical lessons. We are introduced to Egypt in the life of Abram, Gen. 12. Apart from his folly of describing Sarai as his sister, we can also see the impact for evil upon the life choices of Lot. But how slow we are to learn! In Genesis chapter 20, Abraham presents the same half-truths to Abimelech in respect to Sarah his wife. When we think of Abraham's lack of faith on these occasions may we remind our hearts that, 'whatsoever things were written aforetime were written for our learning', Rom. 15. 4.

The lesson of patience was one that Jacob learned. A young man, impatient to receive his father's blessing and spurred on by the schemes of his mother, deceived his blind and ageing father. As a consequence, deceived by his uncle Laban, Jacob had to work fourteen years to receive Rachel as his bride. Paul reminds us, 'Be not deceived; God is not mocked: for whatsoever a man soweth, that shall he also reap', Gal. 6. 7.

So much of the Pentateuch is taken up with the journey of the children of Israel. At the commencement of that journey they came to the Marah. Parched after three days without water, they found the waters bitter. At such a crisis the Lord showed Moses a tree which, when cast into those waters, made them sweet. What a lesson for us in the bitter experiences of life! But the instruction came, 'If thou wilt diligently hearken to the voice of the Lord thy God, and wilt do . . . and keep all his statutes, I will put none of these diseases upon thee, which I have brought upon the Egyptians: for I am the Lord that healeth thee', Exod. 15. 26. Sadly, the instruction was not obeyed and the warnings were not heeded. As the writer of Hebrews reminds us, as a consequence of their continual disobedience, their 'carcases fell in the wilderness', Heb. 3. 17.

As being some of the earliest of the inspired writings it would be easy to think that the lessons of the Pentateuch are no longer relevant in the twenty-first century. Such complacency may well have marked the Corinthians, to whom Paul wrote, 'Now all these things happened unto them for ensamples: and they are written for our admonition, upon whom the ends of the world are come. Wherefore let him that thinketh he standeth take heed lest he fall', 1 Cor. 10. 11-12.

With such a wealth of typical and practical teaching before us, may the reader enjoy these meditations upon such a foundational section of holy scripture.

John Bennett

January 1st

Genesis 1. 1-8

IN THE BEGINNING GOD

The opening verse of our Bible introduces us to the creation of **time**, 'In the beginning'; **space**, 'the heavens'; and **matter**, 'the earth'. Earth, a pinprick in the immense vastness of those stretched out heavens, was, in the eternal hidden purposes of God, to be the platform for a greater work: the unfolding drama of redemption.

The details of day one afford us a lovely picture of the salvation of a soul. Firstly, the water-covered planet was engulfed in *darkness*. The apostle Paul reminds the believers that formerly they had been in bondage to 'the power of darkness', Col. 1. 13. Secondly, the Spirit of God was operating on that global ocean. Paul informs us that the same Spirit operates in salvation, 'And such were some of you . . . but ye are justified in the name of the Lord Jesus, and by the Spirit of our God', 1 Cor. 6. 11. Finally, by the command of God, light burst onto that scene. Paul states that the very same God, 'who spoke that out of darkness light should shine . . . has shone in our hearts for the shining forth of the knowledge of the glory of God in the face of Jesus Christ', 2 Cor. 4. 6 JND.

On day two, God divided the waters from the waters. He took water from the deep and placed it high above Earth to form what some call 'a vast vapour canopy'; no doubt an important factor in the longevity of the pre-flood generations.

The phrase 'the evening and the morning' would inform us that Earth was spinning. In contrast with Earth's divinely planned 24-hour spin, the planet Venus takes 243 Earth days to turn once on its axis! Had such been the case with Earth, the part facing the sun would be baked and burnt, and what life did survive would be frozen in the four-month-long night!

Sadly, the masses today reject creation and swallow the lie of evolution. Atheism is not a phenomenon peculiar to this century. Even in David's day he could speak of the fool who had said in his heart, 'There is no God', Ps. 14. 1. PROFESSOR ADAM SEDGWICK, a contemporary and friend of Darwin, described evolution as, 'a dish of rank materialism, cleverly cooked and served up *to make us independent of a Creator*'.

January 2nd
Genesis 1. 9-19

EARTH, SEAS AND, TWO GREAT LIGHTS

As the dawn broke on day three, angel hosts witnessed the laying of the 'foundations of the earth'. The 'corner-stone' was laid and 'the morning stars sang together, and all the sons of God shouted for joy', Job 38. 7. They were indeed privileged spectators as the awesome power of God caused the dry land to appear, suitably clothed in a blanket of fertile soil. Then, at the command of God, Earth was carpeted in lush verdure: 'grass', 'herbs', and 'trees'.

No doubt, as the Master Gardener was at work, He would be anticipating the coming of His own 'tender plant', the One who would 'grow up before him . . . as a root out of a dry ground', Isa. 53. 2. He would be considering that solitary 'corn of wheat' which must needs fall into the ground and die so that it would not abide alone, John 12. 24. He would be pondering the arrival of the 'true vine', John 15. 1, He who would bring eternal pleasure to His God, so unlike Israel which was to become a 'degenerate plant of a strange vine', Jer. 2. 21. As the first tree was planted, Jehovah would scan the future millennia to see His own Son 'bare our sins in his own body on the tree', 1 Pet. 2. 24. Then, penetrating centuries beyond the grandeur of Golgotha, the heart of God would rest, beholding His earthly people dwelling in safety under the rule of His 'plant of renown', Ezek. 34. 29.

The two great lights, namely the sun and the moon, were created on day four. Thus, the light source on day one could not have been the sun. What was that light source? Revelation chapter 21 verse 23 may help us here. Then, almost as an after-thought, the Spirit of God says, 'He made the stars also'. In 2003, Australian astronomers calculated the stars in the universe numbered 70,000,000,000,000,000,000,000 and the psalmist informs us, 'He calleth them all by their names', Ps. 147. 4. The Lord is called the 'Sun of righteousness', Mal. 4. 2, and 'the morning star', 2 Pet. 1. 19 JND, but nowhere is He ever likened to the moon. The reason being, the moon has no intrinsic light; it is merely a reflector. Christ, we are told, is 'the effulgence of his glory', Heb. 1. 3 JND.

January 3rd
Genesis 1. 20-25

EVERY LIVING CREATURE

Sadly, not every Christian accepts the literal interpretation of the Genesis account of creation. Such people, believing that the Bible needs to be interpreted in the light of current scientific thinking, hold out, what one has called, 'that cowardly white-flag of theological compromise', and adopt the position known as theistic evolution. They believe that God created the initial building blocks of life but then stepped back and allowed the process of evolution to run its course and turn primordial soup into sociable primates. The observant mind will immediately see that today's scripture throws out several problems for this position of compromise. Evolution teaches that the first life forms were microscopic; whereas the Bible informs us they were 'great whales'. Evolution has land mammals before sea mammals, and reptiles before birds. Evolution has sea life preceding plant life. In this case, compromise definitely leads to conflict. Lest the espouser of Darwinism should think there was some suggestion of evolutionary processes in v. 20, 'Let the waters bring forth', that is, the water produced life, it needs to be pointed out the better rendering would be, 'Let the waters swarm with swarms of living souls', JND. Scripture also answers once and for all the old conundrum, 'Which came first, the chicken or the egg?' 'God created . . . every winged fowl after its kind', v. 21, and they duly laid eggs!

Since all sea, air and land dwelling animals were created on days five and six, it follows that must include the creatures commonly known today as dinosaurs. The word dinosaur is not found in the Bible, for it was only coined in 1841 by the British Museum superintendent, Sir Richard Owen. The word literally means 'terrible lizard'. However, we do read occasionally in the Bible about 'dragons'. 'The frequent references to dragons in the Bible, as well as in the early records and traditions of most of the nations of antiquity, certainly cannot be shrugged off as mere fairy tales. Most probably they represent memories of dinosaurs handed down by tribal ancestors who encountered them before they became extinct', HENRY MORRIS.

AND GOD SAID, LET US MAKE MAN

That man is unique and distinct from the animal world around him is evident from the first occurrence of the expression found in verse 26, 'And God said, Let us'. We are made privy to the counsels of the Godhead! It is worth noting what scripture does not say. It does not say, 'And God said, Let **Me** make man in **my** image'. The words 'let us', speak of *plurality*. Some might suggest that in 'let us', God is speaking to angels. However, that cannot be, for the verse goes onto say 'our image'. Angels are never said be in 'the image of God'. So 'let us' speaks of *deity*. Further, it does not say, 'Let us make man in My image', but rather 'our image'. This would confirm *equality* within the Godhead.

The Hebrew word for man is *Adam* which simply means 'red'. This is no doubt a strong indication of the colour of our first parents. 'The first created man, Adam, from whom all other humans are descended, was created with the best possible combination of genes . . . As all the factors for skin "color" were present in Adam and Eve, they would most likely have been mid-brown' – *Where Did the Races Come From?* by *Answers in Genesis*.

The expression 'let us make man' obviously includes Eve too, for we read in verse 27, 'in the image of God created he him; male and female created he them'.

So God conferred on Adam the high dignity of being made 'in the image of God'. Many today make strenuous efforts and go to great lengths to gain the grand titles and plaudits of their fellow men, and in the process fail to see that the highest honour of all, already rests upon them – 'made in the image of God'. Some might ask, 'Does man still bear the image of God, for after all he is a fallen creature?' The answer comes in a most definite affirmation! 'Whoso sheddeth man's blood, by man shall his blood be shed: for in the image of God made he man', Gen. 9. 6. 'For a man indeed ought not to cover his head, forasmuch as he is the image and glory of God', 1 Cor. 11. 7.

Creation is completed and crowned with the forming of man, and, as God contemplates His handiwork, all is very good.

January 5th
Genesis 2. 1-7

ON THE SEVENTH DAY GOD RESTED

Many ask, 'Are the days of Genesis chapter 1, literal twenty-four hour days?' Some suggest that Psalm 90 verse 4 indicates the days could represent long periods of time, 'For a thousand years in thy sight are but as yesterday'. However, the verse does go on to say that 'a thousand years are . . . as a watch in the night', that is, three or four hours. All the psalmist is conveying is that God is totally beyond the scope and limits of time. Exodus chapter 20 verse 11 clearly states, 'For in six days the Lord made heaven and earth, the sea, and all that in them is, and rested the seventh day: wherefore the Lord blessed the sabbath day, and hallowed it'. Those who find a problem in accepting six literal twenty-four hour days, would do well to consider what one wise believer asked, 'I wonder why God took so long?' It appears this Christian had an understanding of the infinite power of God.

The keeping of the sabbath was not something that Moses brought in with the giving of the Law on Mount Sinai. The sabbath was certainly kept before the law was given. This is apparent from the instructions relating to the manna. 'The Lord hath given you the sabbath, therefore he giveth you on the sixth day the bread of two days; abide ye every man in his place, let no man go out of his place on the seventh day', Exod. 16. 29.

God formed Adam from the 'dust of the ground' and, preceding this grand event, we are told, 'a mist went up from the earth, and moistened the whole surface of the ground', JND. We can assume, therefore, that Adam was made from *moist* earth. The Lord, when healing the man who was born blind, 'spat on the ground, and made clay of the spittle', John 9. 6. It was moist earth He used: a beautiful touch that was so reminiscent of that time when He created Adam.

God also created animal life from the ground, Gen. 2. 19. However, the uniqueness of man is seen, not only in the fact that he is made in 'the image of God', but in the intimate detail of God breathing 'into his nostrils the breath of life; and man became a living soul'.

A GARDEN EASTWARD IN EDEN

Many disasters have scarred the history of mankind: the nuclear power accident at Chernobyl in 1986, or the tsunami in the Indian Ocean in 2005. However, the world's worst ever disaster took place in the unlikely surroundings of a garden bearing the name 'Pleasant' or 'Delight', for such is the meaning of Eden. Having created Adam outside the boundaries of this garden, God then placed our first-father in it, 'to dress it and to keep it'.

The two most notable trees found within Eden were 'the tree of knowledge of good and evil' and 'the tree of life', the latter of which was located 'in the midst' of the garden. It is clear that eating from this tree, would see even fallen, mortal man living 'for ever', Gen. 3. 22. It reminds us of another tree found 'in the midst' many centuries beyond Eden's disobedience and it is by partaking of the fruit of this tree that 'eternal life' in a far greater sense can be enjoyed, both presently and in the future. 'Golgotha: where they crucified him, and two other with him, on either side one, and Jesus **in the midst**', John 19. 17-18.

'And a river went out of Eden to water the garden; and from thence it was parted, and became into four heads . . . Pison . . . Gihon . . . Hiddekel . . . and the fourth river, is Euphrates', vv. 10-14. WILLIAM HOSTE speaks of another stream, 'If four rivers watered Eden, a fifth arose from it: the great stream of humanity, poisoned so effectively by sin at its very source that every drop is contaminated'.

One wonders too what Adam made of the stark warning given by God, 'For in the day that thou eatest thereof thou shalt surely die'. What did Adam know about death, for, up to that time, he lived in a deathless world? That his death was not to be instantaneous is apparent from the *Literal Translation* by ROBERT YOUNG, 'For in the day of thine eating of it – dying thou dost die'. Death for Adam was to be a process.

If this pleasant garden was to be the scene of tragedy for mankind, we can thank God for another garden that was to become a garden of delight for so many. 'Now in the place where he was crucified there was a garden; and in the garden a new sepulchre, wherein was never man yet laid', John 19. 41.

24

January 7th

Genesis 2. 18-25

AN HELP MEET FOR ADAM

The creation of Eve from a rib and flesh of Adam is considered by some Christians to be merely allegorical. It is not in doubt, as we shall see that there are several spiritual applications to be made from the 'building' of the rib into Eve, but that this event really did happen is confirmed by the Lord Jesus Himself. In Matthew chapter 19 the Pharisees come to the Lord asking, 'Is it lawful for a man to put away his wife for every cause?' He directs them to Genesis chapter 1 verse 27, 'male and female created he them', and then to Genesis chapter 2 verse 24, 'Therefore shall a man leave his father and his mother, and shall cleave unto his wife: and they shall be one flesh'. He challenges them by asking, 'Have ye not read?' The serious issue of marriage is not based on a myth or allegory, but on events that the Saviour accepted as fact!

The apostle Paul quoted from this section of scripture too when speaking about Christ's bride, the church. 'They two shall be one flesh. This is a great mystery: but I speak concerning Christ and the church', Eph. 5. 31-32. At the time of the creation of Eve as a bride for Adam, there was, hidden in the heart of God, another bride that would, in a future day, be 'built' for His Son. Having formed Eve, Jehovah Elohim presented her to Adam. In contrast to this, Paul informs us that Christ shall present the church to Himself, 'glorious . . . not having spot, or wrinkle, or any such thing', Eph. 5. 27.

Interestingly, the creation of Eve also has a bearing on two areas of church practice: namely the sister's head covering and the sister's silence. With reference to the former, Paul writes, 'For a man indeed ought not to cover his head . . . For the man is not of the woman; but the woman of the man. Neither was the man created for the woman; but the woman for the man', 1 Cor. 11. 7-9. With reference to the latter, Paul writes, 'But I suffer not a woman to teach, nor to usurp authority over the man, but to be in silence. For Adam was first formed, then Eve', 1 Tim. 2. 12-13. Many today say the above-mentioned practices are based on culture. Such thinking is wrong. They are based on the truth of creation: in particular the creation of Adam's bride.

January 8th

Genesis 3. 1-7

HATH GOD SAID?

Satan, having fallen at some earlier stage, evidently entered personally into the serpent, then a far finer creature than now, with the intention of carrying out his evil scheme of marring God's creation and terminating man's fellowship with his Creator. Using a three-pronged attack, he systematically set about beguiling the woman. The first recorded words of the adversary show that he first of all set about undermining Eve's confidence in the word of God, 'Yea, hath God said?' Eve should have stood her ground and proclaimed like the psalmist did centuries later, 'Thy word is very pure . . . thy word is true from the beginning', Ps. 119. 140, 160.

Next, the devil, in whom is 'no truth', the one who 'is a liar and its father', openly accuses the 'God who cannot lie', of speaking falsehood to the first couple, 'Ye shall not surely die'. In saying this he represented God's judgement as being nothing more than an idle threat. Eve should have known the absolute impossibility of God's word failing. 'For I am the Lord: I will speak, and the word that I shall speak shall come to pass', Ezek. 12. 25.

The devil's final tactic was to charge God with acting out of jealousy. The serpent then dangles the offer of deity to the weakening vessel, 'Ye will be as God' JND. This is all too much for Eve and, instead of saying, 'Get thee behind me, Satan: thou art an offence unto me', Matt. 16. 23, she succumbs to the temptation, and takes and eats!

Adam, with open eyes and in wilful disobedience, and possibly swayed by his affections for Eve, transgresses the divine prohibition and in so doing, brought 'sin . . . into the world, and death by sin', Rom. 5. 12.

A certain Christian was once asked by a seeking soul whether he needed to believe in the Genesis creation account before he could be saved. It was pointed out to him that he needed to get saved because he was a sinner, and he was a sinner because he was a descendant of Adam. Destroy Adam and original sin and you destroy the very reason for which the Son of God came. The two are linked inseparably!

January 9th

Genesis 3. 8-24

ADAM . . . WHERE ART THOU?

The ripples of Adam's wilful disobedience spread far beyond the boundaries of Eden's garden. The consequences of the fall were at least sevenfold. (1) **Personal**: The first couple were now estranged from God their Creator. 'Adam and his wife hid themselves from the presence of the Lord God', v. 8. (2) **Physical**: Adam was now to experience incessant toil. 'In the sweat of thy face shalt thou eat bread', v. 19. (3) **Physiological**: To Eve, God said, 'I will greatly increase thy travail and thy pregnancy; with pain thou shalt bear children', v. 16 JND. (4) **Botanical**: 'Cursed is the ground for thy sake . . . thorns also and thistles shall it bring forth to thee', vv. 17-18. (5) **Pathological**: Death must needs ensue. 'Dust thou art, and unto dust shalt thou return', v. 19. (6) **Zoological**: The Poet Laureate, Tennyson, aptly summed up this change in the animal kingdom with his immortal line, 'Nature, red in tooth and claw'. Only in the coming millennial reign of Christ will the wolf again 'dwell with the lamb, and the leopard shall lie down with the kid', Isa. 11. 6. (7) **Cosmological**: Adam's sin reached upward, and the decay process touched even the starry skies. 'The heavens are the works of thine hands . . . they all shall wax old as doth a garment', Heb. 1. vv. 10-11. This bleak state of affairs is concisely summed up by Paul: 'The whole creation groaneth and travaileth in pain together until now', Rom. 8. 22.

Against this depressingly dark backcloth three bright shafts of 'marvellous light' appear. Firstly, although the banishment was an act of judgement, it was also an expression of the love of God for man, for we read it was, 'lest he put forth his hand, and take also of the tree of life, and eat, and live for ever', v. 22. Eternally fallen! Irretrievably lost! How unimaginably solemn! Secondly, God demonstrated He was prepared to sacrifice in order that Adam and Eve might be clothed righteously in garments of skin: an early picture of the death of His own Son to cover the redeemed with 'garments of salvation'. Thirdly, God made the first direct promise relating to the advent of Christ: the 'seed of the woman', who, in coming, would 'crush' the serpent's head.

January 10th

Genesis 4. 1-16

CAIN ROSE UP AGAINST ABEL AND SLEW HIM

The promise that one day a coming male seed of the woman would crush the head of the wily serpent, would live on in the minds of Adam and Eve. When Cain was born, one can almost discern this expression of hope as Eve exclaims, 'I have gotten a man from the Lord'. Cain, however, was not to be the conqueror of the serpent, but instead, the killer of his brother.

The divine commentary on the two brothers is very revealing. The Saviour spoke of Abel as 'righteous Abel', Matt. 23. 35, whereas of Cain it is said, his 'works were evil', 1 John 3. 12. Both men had the desire to approach God. This was indeed a noble thing. No doubt both men had been told by their parents the sad story of their expulsion from Eden and of the way in which God, in His goodness, had slain a beast in order that they could be covered with skin. Abel in wisdom accepted this vital instruction, whilst Cain, in foolishness, ignored it. As WILLIAM KELLY points out, Cain 'makes a religion from his own mind, and brings of the fruit of the ground now under the curse; whilst Abel by faith offers the firstlings of the flock'.

W. W. FEREDAY makes an interesting observation. 'It is noticeable that the blood, of which so much was made in the sacrificial system of Israel at a later date, is not mentioned in connection with Abel's offering, nor indeed anywhere in the book of Genesis in connection with offerings to God. Not the blood, but the fat, is emphasized. The reason is this. It was a question, not so much of remission, as of acceptance. Not for some specific sin was the lamb brought, but as a means of approach to God'.

What instruction does this sad story have for us? The lesson is obvious: for although Abel has long been dead he still speaks today, Heb. 11. 4. It is God's abiding testimony that He will have all men forsake the 'way of Cain' and approach Him solely on the ground of a death, the death of His own dear Son. The tragedy, surely, is that the majority refuse to do so. 'For they being ignorant of God's righteousness, and going about to establish their own righteousness, have not submitted themselves unto the righteousness of God', Rom. 10. 3.

January 11th

Genesis 4. 17-26

ANOTHER SEED INSTEAD OF ABEL

At the time that Cain 'butchered' his brother Abel, we must not think that the world population totalled only three: Adam, Eve and Cain. This can be observed from Cain's dialogue with Jehovah following the murder: 'Every one that findeth me shall slay me', 4. 14. This fear would have been groundless if the potential threat on his life came only from his parents!

Destined now to be 'a wanderer and a fugitive on the earth', JND, and with his 'mark' upon him, Cain settled in 'the land of Nod', literally, 'the land of wandering'. It seems his wanderings were limited, for 'he builded a city'. How different to that great man of faith, Abraham, who 'dwelt in tents with Isaac and Jacob . . . for he waited for the city which has foundations, of which God is the artificer and constructor', Heb. 11. 9-10 JND. The verses before us today, trace the line of Cain and they furnish us with interesting details of pre-flood civilization. Far from being puny-brained primitives, they were capable of building the first city, forming the first musical instruments, v. 21, composing poetry, v. 23, and using forging techniques to create 'every kind of tool of brass and iron', v. 22 JND. Cain's progeny had certainly made massive technological advances since that time when Adam and Eve first 'sewed fig leaves together, and made themselves aprons', Gen. 3. 7. It has to be noted that had the fifth descendant in Cain's genealogy, Lamech, lived in the New Testament church age he would have fallen well short of what was expected of an 'overseer' in the local assembly, for he was the husband of two wives: this being the first recorded example of polygamy in the scriptures!

The birth of Seth must have taken place shortly after Abel's death, as Eve says, 'God hath appointed me another seed instead of Abel'. Seth, conscious of the 'feeble frame' of man, names his son Enosh, meaning, 'weak and mortal'. In the purposes of God, this genealogy would, after some millennia, culminate in Messiah. Though the line of Seth produced godly men such as Enoch and Noah, it, like the line of Cain, would degenerate to the point that God was obliged to obliterate it in the deluge. Salvation does not run in the blood!

January 12th

Genesis 5. 1-22

THE GENERATIONS OF ADAM

Genesis chapter 5 has been called one of the most solemn chapters in Holy Scripture, for it is a chapter over which the shadow of death hangs, apparent from the eight-times repeated expression, 'and he died'. This would confirm the great Bible doctrine expressed in the Epistle to the Romans: 'By one man sin entered into the world, and death by sin'. Death does indeed touch 'the generations of Adam'. It should therefore come as no surprise to see the final verse of Genesis, presenting us with a man in a coffin! How refreshing, then, that in this chapter of death we meet a man who did not die, 'for God took him', v. 24.

In 1925, in Tennessee, USA, a schoolteacher named John Scopes was charged with breaking a law which forbade the teaching of 'any theory that denies the story of the divine creation of man as taught in the Bible, and to teach instead that man has descended from a lower order of animals'. It became known as the 'Scopes Monkey Trial'. Defence lawyer Clarence Darrow put the prosecuting lawyer, William Jennings Bryan, on the spot when he asked him, 'Did you ever discover where Cain got his wife?' Sadly, Bryan's reply, 'No, sir; I leave the agnostics to hunt for her', did little to allay the scorn of the critics and sceptics. Had he stood unflinchingly upon the infallible word of God, he would have replied, 'Cain married one of his sisters!' The unambiguous statements of scripture teach that all races of men can trace their roots back to Adam and Eve. This being so, Cain **must** have married a sister. Verse 4 of today's reading tells us, 'Adam . . . begat sons and **daughters**'. The scoffer will immediately raise his voice in horror and object, appealing to the law against brother-sister intermarriage. However, this prohibition came at a much later date, during the ministry of Moses. 'None of you shall approach to any that is near of kin to him, to uncover their nakedness', Lev. 18. 6. 'Remember that Abraham married his half-sister and God blessed this union to produce the Hebrew people through Isaac and Jacob. It was not until some 400 years later that God gave Moses laws that forbade such marriages', *Answers in Genesis*.

30

January 13th

Genesis 5. 23-32

ENOCH WALKED WITH GOD

All men and women, and even Satan, are presented in the scriptures as 'walking'. The masses are said to 'walk in their own ways', Acts 14. 16, also described as walking 'after the flesh', 2 Pet. 2. 10. These features certainly characterized the pre-flood era when 'the wickedness of man was great in the earth', Gen. 6. 5. How refreshing then to read of two men who walked with God, even when living 'in the midst of a crooked and perverted generation', Phil. 2. 15 JND. These two are Enoch and Noah.

Enoch, 'the seventh from Adam', had a definite conversion experience as we read of his walk commencing at the age of 'sixty and five years', after he 'begat Methuselah'. He is mentioned three times in the New Testament and the reference in Jude would indicate he was surrounded by ungodliness, as the word 'ungodly' is found four times in the space of one verse, v. 15. It is to be noted that he was no recluse, he didn't shut himself away in a monastery to walk with God, for we are told he 'begat sons and daughters'. The Christian is often reminded that the race he runs is not a sprint but a marathon which calls for great endurance, Heb. 12. 1. We must applaud the amazing endurance and determined consistency of Enoch who walked with God for 300 years! This was much more than a marathon!

We know he had no grave and no headstone to adorn it, for he 'was translated that he should not see death', Heb. 11. 5. However, the Spirit of God gives to Enoch a commendation that every one of us should covet for our own headstone, 'he had this testimony, that he pleased God', Heb. 11. 5. What, we may ask, was the power behind such a God-glorifying life? The answer is **faith**! 'Without faith it is impossible to please him', Heb. 11. 6.

Enoch is a lovely type of the church, snatched away to heaven before the fearsome judgement of God descends on planet Earth. Noah, in the ark, is a picture of Israel, delivered safely, but only after passing through the intense period of trial. 'The translation of Enoch was the first formal testimony of the great divine secret, that man was to have a place and inheritance in the heavens', J. GIFFORD BELLETT.

January 14th
Genesis 6. 1-12

MY SPIRIT SHALL NOT ALWAYS STRIVE WITH MAN

The swelling stream of humanity, poisoned at its source by Adam's wilful disobedience, was now marked by such foul, moral lawlessness, that 'it repented the Lord that he had made man on the earth, and it grieved him at his heart', v. 6. Most grievous of all, was the fact that fallen angelic beings (the sons of God, v. 2) made physical, sexual union with the 'daughters of men': which expression is a Hebraism meaning simply 'human daughters'. This awful invasion from the realm of evil, having come 'in unto the daughters of men', produced offspring called 'giants', v. 4. This word, translated as 'fallen ones' by ROBERT YOUNG in his *Literal Translation*, comes from the Hebrew root which means 'to fall'. According to Psalm 8 verse 5, man was made 'a little lower than the angels', but this cohabitation of fallen angelic beings with 'human daughters' was blurring this divinely ordained distinction and God was compelled to destroy man from the face of the earth. 'Unless He had done so, the *entire* human race would have become a mongrel breed. Satan would have become triumphant. Only through a godly remnant and a new start would the human race be preserved so that Messiah eventually would come to identify Himself with the *human* race to redeem it', MERRILL UNGER.

It was in this depressingly dark, immoral scene that one bright light appears, 'And Noah walked with God', v. 9. The true greatness of this man of faith is seen in the fact that this walk was maintained for many decades, without any supporting fellowship other than his own immediate family and the God he served.

Peter's commentary on this shameless period in man's history is, 'the longsuffering of God waited in the days of Noah'. Though great, the longsuffering of God is not infinite, as is indicated by the direct phrase of warning, 'My spirit shall not always plead with man', v. 3 JND. The name *Methuselah* means 'when he is dead it shall be sent'. So the deluge would only come after the death of Methuselah, whose life was lengthened out beyond that of any other man who has ever walked the planet. Such is the longsuffering of God!

January 15th

Genesis 6. 13-22

MAKE THEE AN ARK

'By faith Noah, being warned of God of things not seen as yet, moved with fear, prepared an ark to the saving of his house', Heb. 11. 7. As with Moses in the construction of the Tabernacle, Noah was not left to guess at the dimensions of the vessel he was to build. They were divinely communicated. If the cubit of 18 inches is accepted, the ark would have been 450 feet long, 75 feet wide and 45 feet high. We might ask whether, in nautical terms, these dimensions make for a seaworthy vessel. It is interesting to note that when Brunel built the *S. S. Great Britain* in 1843, he built it using proportions that were virtually identical to those of the ark! PROFESSOR HENRY MORRIS calculated that the ark would be 'exceedingly stable, almost impossible to capsize. Even in a sea of gigantic waves, the ark could be tilted through any angle up to just short of 90° and would immediately thereafter right itself again'.

The apostle Peter, when writing his second letter, calls Noah 'a preacher of righteousness'. How tragic that from the masses of wicked mankind only seven individuals responded to his preaching. It appears the ark took 100 years to construct and we can imagine how discouraging it must have been to see so few converts in that period. However, in spite of the prevailing apathy, the man of faith pressed on, having 'the conviction of things not seen', Heb. 11. 1 JND. Should we not take Noah's conviction and faithfulness in the midst of gross indifference to his message as a lesson for us all in today's increasingly godless and secular society?

We are told that Noah prepared the ark for 'the saving of his house'. We observe from Genesis chapter 5 verse 30 that his wider family included brothers and sisters. It is apparent from their failure to enter through the one door of salvation that they too thought little of their brother's preaching.

Noah wanted to see his family saved and so he 'prepared an ark'. Christian parents find it no easy matter to bring up children in a Christ-rejecting society. However, let us 'prepare an ark' for our children, by exposing them to the scriptures, the fellowship of saints, prayer, and our own sanctified lives.

THE WINDOWS OF HEAVEN WERE OPENED

'The second month, the seventeenth day of the month' saw the longsuffering of God draw to a solemn, climactic conclusion as 'all the fountains of the great deep were broken up, and the windows of heaven were opened'. The expression 'windows of heaven' most likely refers to the water that had been separated from the global ocean on day two of the creation week and placed high above the earth's atmosphere to form what many call the 'vapour canopy'. It was the dissolution of this canopy that brought the rain 'upon the earth forty days and forty nights'. As well as descending from above, the wrath of God was seen in the breaking up of the earth's crust beneath the oceans. 'The Bible excludes the possibility of a mere fortuitous combination of natural geologic causes here, for we are told that this involved, "*all* the fountains of the great deep" and that they were all broken up "on the *same day*"', JOHN WHITCOMB, *The World that Perished*. Genesis chapter 1 verse 31 speaks about the finished work of creation satisfying the eye of God, 'And behold, it was very good'. And on each of the six days, with the exception of day two, we read, 'And God saw that it was good'. Why then this striking omission on day two? Could it be that God, in His foreknowledge, knew that the water canopy would descend in judgement in the coming days of Noah?

Was the flood local to the region of Mesopotamia as some suggest or was it global? Verse 19 strongly indicates it was the latter, 'And the waters prevailed exceedingly on the earth; and all the high mountains that are under all the heavens were covered', JND. The waters topped the highest peak by 15 cubits, which was half the height of the ark. This meant the ark could float freely over every mountain. Chapter 8 verse 4 speaks of the ark coming to rest on 'the mountains of Ararat', which scale the dizzy heights of 17,000 feet. 'A 17,000-foot Flood is not a *local* flood!', HENRY MORRIS. Further, observe that according to verse 14, Noah took on board 'every bird of every sort'. Had the flood been merely local, this would have been unnecessary, for the birds could have survived by flying, with just a little effort, to a region beyond the intended scene of judgement.

January 17th

Genesis 8. 1-14

THE ARK RESTED, THE WATERS DECREASED

Whilst we might pass over the introductory words to this chapter, 'and God remembered Noah', as declaring the inevitably obvious, for the man inside the ark the realization of this truth came as sweet release.

God is incapable of idle forgetfulness, although He does exercise Himself to forget wilfully in judgement, cf. Jer. 23. 39; Hos. 4. 6. Though the sense of relief must have been great for Noah in escaping judgement, being within the secure confines of the ark those long days and nights may have caused him to speculate regarding the timing of his release. After all, God had told him how long the rain would last but He had not given him a time when he would be released from the ark. He was able to count down the forty days and nights of deluge but could not anticipate how long it would be before he was set at liberty. His patience was stimulated, as ours should be, by the sure knowledge that his God was not 'slack concerning his promise', 2 Pet. 3. 9.

Noah was unaware of the speed with which 'the waters decreased continually', v. 5. In the event, it was a further 110 days after the rain ceased before the ark rested, v. 4, and a year and ten days since the rain started, he stepped out of the ark upon dry ground, v. 14. During this, to him, unknown period of time, he would be able to console himself with the thought 'now is our salvation nearer than when we believed', Rom. 13. 11.

Whilst awaiting release, the issuing of the birds from the ark presents an interesting picture. The raven going 'to and fro' portrays for us the incessantly restless adversary of man who similarly moves, 'seeking whom he may devour', 1 Pet. 5. 8; cf. Job 1. 7. The dove, representing the Holy Spirit, would not rest upon the carcases of men, hence, had to return to the ark. Only when the Lord appeared on earth do we see the dove resting upon man and residing.

It is not without significance that the word Ararat derives from a root meaning 'holy ground'. It was onto this ground that Noah stepped upon his liberation and to this environment we have right of access 'by the blood of Jesus', Heb. 10. 19.

January 18th
Genesis 8. 15-22

BE FRUITFUL AND MULTIPLY

In the new environment into which he stepped, enjoying the relief of deliverance, Noah was moved to express his appreciation and immediately made to realize his responsibility.

It is praiseworthy that as Noah 'went forth out of the ark'; his first thought was not to gratify himself, but to glorify his God. By building an altar and offering a sacrifice he demonstrated that sense of gratitude encapsulated by Paul when he viewed himself as 'enriched in every thing to all bountifulness, which causeth through us thanksgiving to God', 2 Cor. 9. 11. It is a mature mind that moves on from the mere enjoyment of ones blessings to question, 'What shall I render unto the Lord for all his benefits toward me?' Ps. 116. 12. This naturally moves us to express our gratitude.

It would have been delightful for the Lord to smell 'a sweet savour' in contrast to the corrupt stench that had formerly arisen from the moral decay of the world prior to the flood, Gen. 6. 12. We have the unique opportunity, amidst our similarly corrupt, secular society, of being 'unto God a sweet savour of Christ', 2 Cor. 2. 15.

As he was invited to inhabit a purged earth, Noah was also reminded of the burden of expectation that was upon him. God said, 'be fruitful and multiply'. In like manner, though we delight to dwell on the fact of our own salvation, we are duty bound to consider the purpose for which we have been delivered. We have the distinct privilege of being those who alone can and 'should bring fruit unto God', Rom. 7. 4; cf. Gal. 5. 22-23.

In placing the injunction upon Noah to be fruitful and multiply, God pledged to mankind the necessary conditions that would be conducive to productivity whilst at the same time reminding them of their dependence upon Himself for the increase. Though the harvest, heat, summer and day are to be enjoyed, the rigours of the seedtime, cold, winter and night are to be endured. This should cause us to be ever mindful of our need to rely upon Him who would have us bring forth 'much fruit', John 15. 5.

January 19th
Genesis 9. 1-19

I DO SET MY BOW IN THE CLOUD

The new environment into which Noah and his family stepped was to be characterized by a number of new conditions. There was instigated a new dominion recognizing the superiority of human life, a new diet for the sustenance of human life and a new discipline for those that would disregard the sanctity of human life. It is significant that these principles, though never revoked by God, are being challenged and overturned in today's society.

Increasingly there is evidence of the attempt to equate the value of animal life with that of human beings. This has been manifest with animal rights vigilantes even being prepared to commit atrocities to establish the claims of their cause. It is undoubtedly a devilish attempt to devalue the status given by God to man, who, uniquely among His creation, has been made in His image, Gen. 1. 27.

Furthermore, and energized by those who devalue human life, there is a developing trend towards a vegetarian diet. This is not only unnecessary according to the instruction in our portion today, but also bears undertones of new age philosophy which seeks to reintroduce primitive pagan principles. Paul associates this practice with 'latter times' conditions and warns against adopting it, 1 Tim. 4. 3.

More disturbing is the readiness in our day to take another's life with impunity. Such wanton violence, exhibited before the flood, provoked God to introduce to human administration the deterrent of capital punishment, a measure which has been ignored by many societies. Romans chapter 13 verse 4 indicates that it is incumbent upon man that he administers order in God's creation.

Besides these new conditions, God introduced a new covenant with all flesh – He would not judge universally by way of a flood again. God has given a visible reminder in the clouds of His promises, to counter man's tendency to forget them. It has been well said that whilst 'the bow in the hands of man was an instrument of battle, the bow bent by the hand of God has become a symbol of peace', WORDSWORTH.

January 20th

Genesis 9. 20-28

CURSED BE CANAAN

It is with sadness that we review this first recorded incident of life after the flood. Despite a new start and the best of conditions in which to develop, evidence is provided, if at all needed, that 'the heart is deceitful above all things, and desperately wicked', Jer. 17. 9.

This first appearance of the intoxicating drug alcohol establishes the unrivalled power it has to destroy both individuals and families. This incident proves that casual drinking within the confines of one's own home, can have catastrophic consequences. Noah, the man who demonstrated righteousness in public, failed to exercise self-control in private. Alcohol encourages excess, Prov. 23. 31-35, Eph. 5. 18. Logic would suggest, and prudence would demand, that if drunkenness is to be avoided then total abstinence is the safest stance to adopt.

If the shameful consequence to Noah were not bad enough, the effects on his family were devastating. By telling his two brothers of the event, it is implied that Ham delighted in reporting his father's shame. The wise man points out that the man who mocks sin is a fool, Prov. 14. 9.

It is significant that it was not Ham who was cursed, but his youngest son Canaan. Here is a glimpse of the truth expressed by Balaam that there cannot be a reversal of God's pronounced blessing, Num. 23. 20; Gen. 9. 1, 8-9. Thus, the curse was placed upon Canaan. How essential for parents to be always aware of the implications of their own actions upon impressionable offspring!

The attitude of the other brothers, Shem and Japheth, to their father's shame was commendable, and worthy of reward. They demonstrated, by not looking upon the sordid scene, an attitude that is characteristic of godliness, being of 'purer eyes than to behold evil', Hab. 1. 13. In today's libertarian society, this example is to be admired and imitated.

There is a solemn lesson in the fact that we have no comment on the last third of Noah's life. How precious to approach the latter end of one's life 'with joy', Acts. 20. 24, rather than with the haunting regrets caused by moments of weakness.

January 21st

Genesis 10. 1-32

THE GENERATIONS OF THE SONS OF NOAH

There is a pattern developed in the ordering of the historical detail in Genesis that reveals that God 'taketh away the first, that he may establish the second', Heb. 10. 9. Repeatedly, we have set before us the history of those who give place in importance to others. For example, the story of Cain and his family is documented before that of Seth and his descendents. This principle is here in chapters 10 and 11, where the family trees of Japheth and Ham precede the messianic line of Shem.

Without elaborating upon the individual nations that trace their origin to this genealogy, in general terms, Japheth is the ancestor of the Aryan nations, such as the Russians and Europeans, whilst Ham's descendents include Arabian and African peoples. Shem's lineage is that which develops into the people uniquely favoured by God, cf. Gen. 11. 10ff.

Amongst the long list of names, the man of principal interest is Nimrod. This man's name means 'we will revolt', KEIL and DELITZSCH, picturing for us the devil himself, the original leader of rebellion against God. His opposition was evidently to God's stated will, suggested by the fact that he became a mighty hunter, not so much 'before the Lord', v. 9, as 'in the face of' or 'against' God.

The nature of his revolt is inferred in the fact that he became a 'mighty hunter', which implies tyranny over his fellow men more than his skill in killing already fearful animals. Such oppression is in direction rebellion to God's command to observe the sanctity of human life, Gen. 9. 5-6.

The obsessive ambition of the man for power is witnessed by his founding of this world's first imperial kingdom, v. 10-12. Not content with the lower reaches of the Euphrates and Tigris rivers in the land of Shinar, he expanded his domain northwards and set up the Assyrian empire with its capital Nineveh. There he gave rise to idolatry which, even now, blights mankind.

We do well, in reviewing such a man as Nimrod, to guard against personal opposition to God's will, an oppressive attitude to our fellows and an obsessive desire to satisfy one's own thirst for power.

January 22nd
Genesis 11. 1-9

BABEL

The portion before us today for contemplation is a re-enactment of divine intervention in judgement upon humanity that was rapidly rising in rebellion against God. It was once again a dark scene that caused God to execute judgement with universal effect.

It is to be regretted that man employed those faculties that distinguish the human race from the animal kingdom, namely the ability to speak and convey intelligent thought, as an empowering tool in his resistance of God. In union, man settled down in the fruitful plain of Shinar and ignored the injunction to 'replenish the earth', Gen. 9. 1. We need to remind ourselves that we too have a commission to 'go . . . into all the world, and preach the gospel', Mark 16. 15, lest we settle into a life of ease.

There is rich imagery in the fact that man built with a mixture of the processed brick, and the natural, slime or asphalt. This is contrasted with our God who builds with spiritual material, cf. 1 Pet. 2. 5. Man, like the bricks, became simply hardened clay.

In the building of the city they provided for themselves a focal point for government. With the construction of the tower, they introduced a focal point for their worship. It appears that their intention was not to 'reach' into heaven, for the word is italicised in the King James Version. Rather, the thought being conveyed is that the top was 'unto heaven', in the sense of being dedicated to the heavens. Hence, man was beginning to worship the creation rather than God. This deviation is complete when we see man worshipping 'the creature more than the Creator', Rom. 1. 25.

Decisive action was required if this and future developments were to be thwarted. In confusing the speech of the people, the most potent deterrent to union was introduced to mankind. On this occasion, the execution of judgement furthered rather than frustrated the purposes of God, for in scattering the people abroad, the replenishing of the earth was guaranteed. God's will shall 'be done in earth, as it is in heaven', Matt. 6. 10.

Genesis 11. 10-32

THE GENERATIONS OF SHEM

Perhaps the most striking feature of this fifth of ten genealogies in the book of Genesis is the rapidly diminishing age expectancy. To generalize, the lifespan of those immediately following the deluge is approximately half of those who lived prior to the flood. The average age halves again subsequent to the Babel dispersion of the nations in Peleg's day. Whilst the initial drop might be influenced by climatic changes and effects of increased levels of radiation reaching the earth, the second is more likely to be due to the consequence of prevalent sin.

Mindful of the fact that He had promised not to issue universal judgement to eradicate increasing sinfulness, God's method in preserving a people for Himself is seen here as being the selection of a family to live for Him in a sinful world. With the introduction of Abram this intention was realized.

Acts chapter 7 verses 1-4 are explicit in stating that it was Abram who received the command to leave Ur of the Chaldees. From our verses it is evident that Terah was in measure sympathetic to the call and, as patriarch of the family, led them out with the intention of resettling them in Canaan. Not having received a call himself, however, he was able to bring them out but not in to Canaan itself. Separation is one thing, dedication is another matter altogether. We, like Terah, can disassociate ourselves from the world and yet fail to be dedicated to our Lord. The complete work of sanctification requires both aspects.

Terah's history is typical of so many who set out with good intentions only to have them thwarted by external factors. Haran appears to have been a desirable location insofar as Terah was concerned, sufficiently so for him to reside there. Often we can be content with that which is adequate, whereas God would have us go on further in order to enjoy that which is best. This often requires determination on our part.

We should also recognize that the extent of our ambition can have an effect upon others with whom we are associated. There is something of Terah's contentment reflected in the decision of his grandson Lot to choose the settled circumstances of Sodom rather than the life of separation pursued by Abraham.

January 24th

Genesis 12. 1-9

I WILL MAKE OF THEE A GREAT NATION

There is a hint of frustration introduced by the fact that 'the Lord *had* said' for Abram to leave his country and travel to a land that would be revealed. To have settled in Haran would not have fulfilled divine purpose. Though he had left Ur he had not yet severed the link with his kindred nor his father's house. The Lord is satisfied with completed undertakings, a principle which is endorsed by Paul, who says, 'he which hath begun a good work in you will perform it', Phil. 1. 6.

Accepting that the path of obedience is sometimes demanding, it should also be noted that it is undoubtedly rewarding. In verses 2-3 there are seven aspects of reward mentioned that more than recompense the price paid by Abram. Not only was he and his own going to be blessed, but others by association with Abram or his faith would experience God's favour.

In continuing his journey Abram left nothing behind to tempt him to retrace his steps and return to Haran. Such a break is required of us if we are to show true dedication to our Lord's direction, cf. Luke 9. 57-62. This determined separation is still to be seen in the old man Abraham, Gen. 24. 7.

When arriving in the land, the presence of the resident Canaanites would make Abram appreciate immediately that his reward was going to be hard won. Yet the swift appearance of the Lord surely served to encourage him. Likewise, though there are many factors that would prevent our present enjoyment of our inheritance, we can take heart from the fact that, 'greater is he that is in you, than he that is in the world', 1 John 4. 4.

The appearance of the Lord provoked the response of worship from Abram. To realize something of His august majesty will result in willingness to worship. A reluctance to express ourselves in worship betrays a poor appreciation of His worth.

From the behaviour of Abram we can deduce that the path to blessing is to walk according to the Lord's directives, be prepared to confront those forces which prevent us realizing our blessings and be keen to afford homage to the One upon whom all our blessings depend.

January 25th

Genesis 12. 10-20

A FAMINE IN THE LAND

Today's portion represents the most shameful moment in the life of Abram, who is otherwise rightly lauded for his faith. Repeatedly his judgement is seen to be flawed, with potentially devastating consequences.

Despite famine, it is never wise to move outside the boundaries of where God would have his people to reside. Though he did not go *back*, Abram did go *beyond* where God had led him. For us, both courses of action are similarly fraught with danger.

As he neared Egypt, his trepidation betrayed the fact that he had forgotten the assurances that God had given him in verses 2-3 of our chapter. Furthermore, by his suggestion to his wife, it is evident that he had taken his security into his own hands. It is the most stressful of situations to find ourselves where God's promises and protection are no longer our automatic resort.

Abram displays a reprehensible disregard for his wife, and also the Egyptians, in his request that Sarai present herself as his sister. Uppermost in his mind was his own welfare, to the exclusion of others. It reveals an attitude which is the exact opposite of that Christ-like disposition, considering not 'his own things' but having regard for 'the things of others', Phil. 2. 4.

Though he did not lie outright, for Sarai was his half-sister, cf. Gen. 20. 12, Abram exposed all parties to serious repercussions by not telling the whole truth. The man who recently had been told he would be a blessing to all families of the earth is seen to place at jeopardy those who became acquainted with him.

Despite the fact that he prospered shamelessly as a result of his excursion into Egypt, Abram's conscience must have smarted at the recollection. To experience an irresistible, stinging rebuke from an ungodly person is surely the most humiliating experience for those who have been given greater light.

The silence of a man whose cunning has been exposed is self condemning. Though the famine in the land had been grievous, Egypt had proved to be even more so. Yet from such events character can be developed if lessons are learned, for 'he that regardeth reproof is prudent', Prov. 15. 5.

January 26th
Genesis 13. 1-13

LOT CHOSE HIM ALL THE PLAIN OF JORDAN

There is great significance in the fact that Abram returned to the place where 'his tent had been at the beginning'. He had to retrace his steps to the point from which he began to go astray, for only there could true recovery be realized. Previously, he had arrived at Bethel showing courageous faith, now he comes conscious of his folly. Thankfully, the Lord is never slow to recognize genuine sincerity, cf. Ps. 145. 18.

It is sad to see, however, that the consequence of his actions did not end with his expulsion from Egypt. Both Abram and his nephew Lot had prospered from their visit to Egypt, and it was that which they had accumulated which caused the division between them and made it impossible for them to 'dwell together'. How often do we see that material matters have an effect upon our spiritual relationships?

Abram was concerned that confrontation with Lot would compromise their position before the Canaanites and Perizzites. The fact that they were brethren was a unique relationship in the land that noone else shared with them. What they had in common should have been enough to maintain unity. It is vital that we understand that when we bicker and fall out we are not strengthened as a result, but weakened.

Though it was an act of unselfishness on Abram's part to leave a man like Lot the choice of where to dwell, it was not the wisest thing to do. His nephew's appetite had been influenced by his experience and, though he tried to justify his choice by giving the plain some spiritual worth by likening it to Eden; it was its resemblance to what his own eye had seen in Egypt that allured him. We should guard against trying similarly to disguise what is our own desire by clothing it with a spiritual motive.

As well as being alike physically, Revelation chapter 11 verse 8 likens Sodom and Egypt spiritually. There, they are said to represent Jerusalem, where 'our Lord was crucified'. Such a place cannot be a wholesome environment in which to live and bring up a family for God. For Lot, the choice of the well-watered plain proved to be fatal rather than fruitful.

44

January 27th

Genesis 13. 14-18

LIFT UP NOW THINE EYES

When considering this incident it is apparent, having previously contemplated Abram's departure from Haran, that though separation is sometimes a painful experience, there is compensation from the Lord. Once again, the Lord speaks to Abram to expand upon the promises made in chapter 12 verse 7. The patriarch is thus encouraged not to dwell on his severance from Lot and be downcast but to preview his prospect.

How different was Abram's vision to that of Lot's. His nephew's eye fell only on the plain of Jordan and was seduced by it and looked no further. The Lord, however, encouraged Abram to have a wider vision in order to take in the full extent of his blessing. His prospect was all encompassing; as is ours in Christ Jesus, cf. Eph. 3. 18.

This is the first of four occasions where we read of Abram lifting up his eyes, cf. Gen.18. 2; 22. 4, 13. All four incidents are significant as Abram is drawn to consider his prospect, his progeny, his proving and God's provision.

Here we have the first mention of the promise, which has caused incessant wrangling ever since it was made, that of a land for Abram's seed. Throughout history the ownership of this small, seemingly insignificant tract of land has been bitterly disputed, and remains so today. This will be the case until the right of ownership to all land, northward, southward, eastward and westward, will be held by one of Abram's seed, cf. Gal. 3. 16.

Not only was Abram granted a great prospect but he was also encouraged to enter into the experience of it immediately. Despite the presence of the natural inhabitants of the land who denied him the full enjoyment of it, Abram lived his life 'persuaded by' his promises and 'embraced them', Heb. 11. 13. The Hebrew Epistle states that he was prepared to confess and 'declare plainly' his pursuit in life in a fashion that we do well to imitate.

There is little wonder that Hebron, meaning 'association', appears on the page of scripture for the first time here. In that place Abram began to realize true fellowship with his Lord.

January 28th
Genesis 14. 1-16

FOUR KINGS WITH FIVE

From the incidents detailed for us in today's reading we can draw instruction as to how we can avoid getting embroiled in the difficulties that arise in the world. We also discover how we might assist those that find themselves in such predicaments.

As we come into contact with Lot once again, we find that the man who had initially 'pitched his tent toward Sodom', Gen. 13. 12, was now resident in the vile city. There have been many who have followed such a course; tentatively flirting with the world only to find themselves sucked into the vortex of its society. John is particularly frank when he records that 'if any man love the world, the love of the Father is not in him', 1 John 2. 15.

It is to Lot's credit that he appears not to have taken up arms in the five king's conflict with the four warlords from the north-east. Nevertheless, because of his chosen life-style, he was enveloped in the consequences of the hostility. It is noticeable that the man who lived as a stranger and a pilgrim in relation to the society of his day, Abram, was not caught up in the clash.

It would be reasonable to assume that Lot did not share the sentiment of the Hebrew Christians who 'took joyfully the spoiling of their goods', Heb. 10. 34. His sorrow was caused by the fact that he had not sought 'a better and an enduring substance'. The pursuit of this world's bounty with an all consuming passion is ultimately an unrewarding occupation, cf. Col. 3. 2.

The attitude of Abram is commendable. His eagerness to respond to his nephew's predicament is one that suggests a large heart. A lesser man might have been reluctant to get involved and taken the stance 'he's made his bed; let him lie in it'. Such a stance does not 'fulfil the law of Christ', Gal. 6. 2.

Undoubtedly, Lot was thankful for his salvation. However, gratitude did not result in a change in his behaviour. The next time he appears on the page of scripture he is seen sat in the gate of Sodom, Gen. 19. 1. How appreciative he should have been of the one who cared for him, despite his tendency to live his life courting the world, cf. 1 John 2. 1.

MELCHIZEDEK KING OF SALEM

The contrast between the two kings who met with Abram after the battle is stark. Melchizedek brought refreshment, which provoked gratitude from Abraham, whereas the king of Sodom came with an unacceptable proposal and was looking to exploit the situation for his own benefit. How typical of the two who vie for the attention of men and women; our Lord and the devil!

In the definition of his name and that of his city, king of 'righteousness' and 'peace' respectively, Melchizedek is a fitting type of the One in whom these virtues are to be seen in fullest complement, cf. Ps. 85. 10. These attributes portray a well appointed character, characteristics which are similarly in evidence in the life of the Saviour who 'increased . . . in favour with God and man', Luke 2. 52. It behoves everyone who claims a relationship with God to develop such traits, cf. Heb. 12. 14.

Melchizedek's initial appearance on the page of scripture is as suggestive as it is dramatic. It was no mean feat to have cultivated a well developed relationship with the true God in an idolatrous, pagan society. The fact that Melchizedek could achieve this in his day provides us with an encouragement in our 'present evil world', Gal. 1. 4.

The meeting had a profound effect upon Abram. The blessing of Melchizedek gave rise to a spontaneous act of giving by Abram. A mature understanding of our blessing will have a similar impact upon us, as it did upon Noah previously, cf. Gen. 8. 20.

Furthermore, the fresh revelation of God that Abram received from the king of Salem stood him in good stead when it came to confronting the king of Sodom. An appreciation of the One who possesses heaven and earth throws a new light on the tawdry bounty of this world. The gain to be had from the king of Sodom's proposal was nothing in comparison with the price to be paid for compromising his position as a stranger and a pilgrim, cf. Heb. 11. 13. Abram shows commendable fortitude in resisting a 'get rich quick' opportunity that would have had long term, regrettable consequences.

January 30th

Genesis 15. 1-21

A SMOKING FURNACE AND A BURNING LAMP

The Lord's reassurance, coming quickly after 'the things' of the previous chapter, did not allow Abram to dwell upon the fact that he might have made new enemies by taking up arms to rescue Lot, or what might have been, had he taken the rewards offered by the king of Sodom. The Lord was both his shield and reward. Yet, notwithstanding this, Abram had a sense of being unfulfilled.

As he advanced in age, the fact that Abram was childless made it increasingly difficult for him to understand how God would keep His promise regarding his seed. To his credit, 'He staggered not at the promise of God through unbelief; but was strong in faith, giving glory to God', Rom. 4. 20. Little did he realize that God would wait until he was past the ability to reproduce before his heir would be born. Such is God's way at times that His greatness might be magnified.

Through a vision, God enabled Abram to appreciate that His promises would be honoured. It is significant that he was made to realize this through sacrifice and 'an horror of great darkness'. As we reflect upon our 'exceeding great and precious promises', 2 Pet. 1. 4, we recognize that they are ours because our Lord experienced the horrific darkness of Golgotha when He 'offered one sacrifice for sins', Heb. 10. 12.

Despite the consolation of a renewed pledge, Abram came to understand that the purposes of God were to be accomplished by strange means. Not only would Abram die before their fulfilment, but his descendants would suffer before coming into their inheritance. This pattern of suffering preceding glory, signified by 'a smoking furnace and a burning lamp', is repeated often in scripture, cf. Rom. 8. 18; Heb. 2. 10; 1 Pet. 1. 11; 4. 13; 5. 1.

The fact that Abram did not have to pass through the pieces of the sacrifice to ratify the contract indicates that it was not dependent upon him for execution. God's unconditional promise encourages us to 'believe in the Lord' for, in the Lord's own words to Habakkuk, 'though it tarry, wait for it; because it will surely come', Hab. 2. 3.

January 31st

Genesis 16. 1-16

AND HAGAR BARE ABRAM A SON

The incident before us today is one that has had lasting repercussions. The consequence of the illegitimate birth of Ishmael and the resulting animosity between his offspring and that of Isaac's is at the root of the irreconcilable differences in the Middle East today, cf. Gal. 4. 29. The lessons to be learned are therefore of highest import. The attempt of Sarai to force a fulfilment of the promise of God that Abram would be blessed through his progeny proved cataclysmic. Though the intention may have been good, the means employed to engineer the circumstances were shocking.

Sarai was evidently conscious that time was working against them insofar as Abram having an heir was concerned. Little did she realize that the One who is not governed by time was working for them. Being past the age of childbearing herself, Sarai concocted a scheme that would deliver the promised outcome. Knowing the will of God and seeing it executed are different issues. Sometimes, in our enthusiasm, we err, as did Sarai, in imposing means and methods upon God's stated aim that do not correspond with His ideal.

The selfish disregard of Sarai for Hagar rebounded on her in telling fashion. Our scheming can give rise to situations that develop beyond our control. Furthermore, it is possible that, in the events of this chapter, the effects of Abram's disastrous foray into Egypt were still being shown, even after such a long time. Hagar may have been one of the 'maidservants' given to Abram during his visit, cf. Gen. 12. 16. The results of a dalliance with the world are not always immediate.

It is touching to read that 'the angel of the Lord found' Hagar as she fled. In like manner, we are grateful that One sought us until He found us when we were in the wilderness, cf. Luke 15. The moment was literally a turning point in her experience.

Her willingness to 'return . . . and submit' was crucial to her realizing God's favour. The path to blessing is always along this route. In going back to a difficult situation, the fact that Hagar was conscious of being under God's gaze was both a challenge and a great comfort.

49

February 1st

Genesis 17. 1-14

AN EVERLASTING POSSESSION

Abram was ninety-nine years old. Thirteen years had elapsed since the birth of Ishmael, 16. 16, and those years of silence indicate Abram's folly in seeking his own solution to the problem of Sarai's barrenness. The cost of disobedience is great!

However, God now appears to Abram again and does so as 'the Almighty God', v. 1. Abram had to learn the lesson of the all-sufficient, all-powerful God, One who was in control of every situation and was sufficient for every crisis. Was Sarai barren? Yet God says, 'Thy name shall be Abraham; for a father of many nations have I made thee', v. 5; 'I will establish my covenant . . . and . . . be a God unto thee, and to thy seed after thee', v. 7; 'I will give unto thee, and to thy seed after thee', v. 8; 'thou, and thy seed after thee', v. 9. It was for Abraham to appreciate the answer to the question, 'Is any thing too hard for the Lord?', Gen. 18. 14.

But with this new revelation comes responsibility. The command is, 'Be thou perfect', v. 1. A relationship with God necessitates our sanctification: 'But like as he which called you is holy, be ye yourselves also holy in all manner of living', 1 Pet. 1. 15 RV. Linked with that command is the manifest token of Abraham's separation, 'Every man child among you shall be circumcised', v. 10. Its application was extensive, 'every man child in your generations . . . born in the house, or bought with money', v. 12. For us, that circumcision is in Christ, 'the circumcision made without hands, in putting off the body of the sins of the flesh', Col. 2. 11. No half-measures will do!

From those steps of obedience there comes the experience of God's blessings, 'I will make thee exceeding fruitful', v. 6; 'I will make nations of thee', v. 6; 'I will give unto thee, and to thy seed . . . all the land of Canaan, for an everlasting possession', v. 8. How extensive is the blessing. Yet, in contrast to the New Testament believer, it is, as Israel's blessings, material and earthly. Our blessings are on a higher plane, we have been 'blessed . . . with all spiritual blessings in heavenly places in Christ', Eph. 1. 3. What praise should emanate from our lips and what obedience should be manifest in our lives!

SARAH THY WIFE SHALL BEAR THEE A SON

As, again, we find Abraham on his face before God, vv. 3, 17, two little phrases are remarkable; 'and God talked with him', v. 3; and 'he left off talking with him', v. 22. It indicates to us what it meant for Abraham to be known as 'the Friend of God', Jas. 2. 23. There is no familiarity or lack of reverence as Abraham is upon his face, but there is a reality and openness about their exchange. Conscious of Sarah's age, there is a sense of incredulity when Abraham makes his request, 'O that Ishmael might live before thee!', v. 18. What wondrous grace, then, when God's reply is, 'As for Ishmael, I have heard thee: Behold, I have blessed him', v. 20. How precious is such intimate communion with God! How precious too that God hears and answers prayer!

But as there could be no communion without obedience it is important to see Abraham's response to God's command. The extent of his obedience was that he 'took Ishmael . . . and all that were born in his house, and all that were bought with his money . . . and circumcised (them)', v. 23. This was a ready response for we read that it was 'in the selfsame day, as God had said unto him', v. 23. Yet, in the name that Abraham was to give his son, 'Isaac' means 'to laugh', there is a reminder to Abraham that he doubted how the purposes of God could be accomplished in the way that He said.

It is interesting that the promise that God gave to Abraham in chapter 12, 'I will make of thee a great nation', v. 2, was expanded in chapter 15 when God stated that Abraham's heir would 'come forth out of thine own bowels', v. 4. Here in chapter 17, the timescale is revealed, 'Sarah shall bear unto thee at this set time in the next year', v. 21. But all of this progressive revelation took place over what could have been more than twenty years. Each revelation confirmed what had been said before and unfolded a little more of the purposes of God. Yet, all of it was to be accomplished through 'one, and him as good as dead', Heb. 11. 12. 'O the depth of the riches both of the wisdom and knowledge of God! how unsearchable are his judgments, and his ways past finding out!', Rom. 11. 33.

February 3rd

Genesis 18. 1-15

HE RAN AND BOWED HIMSELF

Although our verses for today do not mention the word worship, they are surely a sublime example of Abraham's recognition and appreciation of his heavenly Visitor. We can notice that the background of the previous chapter indicates Abraham's obedience and this is surely the prerequisite. Separated lives are a necessity if we are to worship.

The Character of Worship. Even though Abraham had 'flocks, and herds, and tents', Gen. 13. 5, and 318 trained servants, 14. 14, he 'bowed himself towards the ground', v. 2, addressed the Man as 'My Lord', v. 3, and described himself as the 'servant', v. 5. Abraham was a man of wealth and power. This was no act of simple eastern courtesy. His actions and his words demonstrated his recognition of the greatness of the One in whose presence he was found. This is true worship!

The Cost of Worship. To prepare something for his heavenly guest was costly to Abraham. Although at least 100 years old, he 'ran' to meet his guests, v. 2, and to fetch the calf from the herd, v. 7. All of this energy was expended 'in the heat of the day', v. 1. There was a commitment and zeal about his activity because of the importance he attached to this act of worship. We might also notice the level of his personal involvement, 'he ran', v. 2; 'I will fetch', v. 5; 'he took . . . and set it before them', v. 8; and 'he stood by them', v. 8. Apart from the personal cost there was also a financial cost. He used 'three measures of fine flour', v. 6, and brought 'a calf tender and good', v. 7. Only the best was good enough for this Visitor! What a challenge to our hearts! What personal preparation do we make in order that we might mention something before the Father as we gather to remember the Lord? What does it cost us?

The Co-operation in Worship. It is interesting to see how Abraham involved others in all that he did. He 'hastened . . . unto Sarah, and said', v. 6, he involved his wife. He 'gave it unto a young man', v. 7, and, in so doing, gave this young servant the opportunity to worship with his master. How important it is to encourage and draw out the appreciation of others as we are focused upon our remembrance of the Saviour.

SHALL NOT THE JUDGE OF ALL THE EARTH
DO RIGHT?

As two of the heavenly visitors move on, we are told, 'Abraham drew near', v. 23. What gave Abraham the liberty? It was that Abraham had already been in the presence of God that day. Abraham's words in verse 3 of the chapter are, 'My Lord, if now I have found favour in thy sight, pass not away . . . from thy servant'. Here was a man who had been in the presence of God in worship who could now enter the presence of God in supplication and intercession. The man that had given God His portion now seeks to plead on behalf of his nephew in Sodom.

In his pleas in the presence of God Abraham tells us something of his appreciation of God. In verse 25, he says, 'That be far from thee to do after this manner, to slay the righteous with the wicked'. The testimony of Abraham is to the righteousness of God. In the preceding verses, God said, 'I will go down now, and see whether they have done altogether according to the cry of it', v. 21. Did God really need to go and see the city for Himself? The testimony had already been recorded, 'the men of Sodom were wicked and sinners before the Lord exceedingly', 13. 13. Perhaps as many as twenty years had elapsed since that record was written. Even against the background of such heinous sins God is longsuffering, withholding His judgement until the time is ripe. But verse 21 also teaches us that the case for the judgement of the men of Sodom will be proven beyond doubt. Scripture will detail their crimes as the two angels go into Sodom. God will be seen to be right. His righteousness will be vindicated in His judgement of the cities of the plain.

But why did Abraham appeal to the righteousness of God? Would we not expect him to appeal to the mercy of God? What Abraham appreciated was that God's mercy does not enable Him to overlook sin! God, in His righteousness, must punish sin. But, for God to remain righteous, He cannot punish the just with the unjust. He cannot punish the innocent with the guilty. This is why Abraham appeals to the righteousness of God. These are the reasons that Abraham could acknowledge, 'Shall not the Judge of all the earth do right?'

February 5th

Genesis 19. 1-11

THERE CAME TWO ANGELS TO SODOM AT EVEN

One can only describe this chapter of Genesis as incredibly sad. To see what Peter describes as a 'righteous man' seeking to live in such a sinful city and prosper in its society is indicative of how far Lot had sunk. A few signs of spiritual life are present: 'unleavened bread', v. 3; 'do not so wickedly'; v. 7, and 'Lot went out, and spake unto his sons in law', v. 14. However, his testimony was lost and the grip of the city upon his life was significant, v. 16.

The record of Lot's movements towards Sodom started when Lot 'lifted up his eyes, and beheld all the plain of Jordan', 13. 10. From that initial impression Lot 'pitched his tent toward Sodom', 13. 12, and was later described as one that 'dwelt in Sodom', 14. 12. In our reading today we find Lot 'sat in the gate of Sodom', v. 1, having risen to a position of influence and government, v. 9. What lessons we need to learn from Lot's decisions and the consequences for his spiritual life!

The two angels came at evening and this indicates the gathering gloom before the storm of divine wrath. The city was ripe for judgement. Its streets were places of inherent danger where mob rule seemed the norm, vv. 2, 4. There was no respect for property or human life, vv. 5, 9. There was no respect for authority or the rule of law, v. 9. Sexual deviancy was rife, vv. 5, 8. How sad that Lot could not see the city for what it was, but the implications of continued compromise are evident in his willingness to sacrifice his daughters to the crowd.

But does this catalogue of problems not resonate with those issues afflicting our society today? Does this not teach us that the Rapture and the period of Tribulation are near? What should be our response? 'Seeing then that all these things shall be dissolved, what manner of persons ought ye to be in all holy conversation and godliness . . .?', 2 Pet. 3. 11. How important that our lives should be different! But, conscious of the implications for the unbeliever, Paul wrote, 'Redeeming the time, because the days are evil', Eph. 5. 16. We have a responsibility in an evangelistic sense. However, life and testimony must be in harmony otherwise, sadly, our testimony will be like Lot's, v. 14.

February 6th

Genesis 19. 12-29

ESCAPE FOR THY LIFE

In yesterday's meditation we commented upon Lot's spiritual weakness that led him to Sodom and caused him to remain in that city. The awful consequences for a carnal Christian are now brought before us – for his children, his own life and that of his wife.

In verse 13 the angels made their mission known to Lot and the reason for it. It is a further indictment of Lot that they should need to explain the reason why, 'Because the cry of them is waxen great before the face of the Lord', v. 13. But impending judgement galvanizes Lot into action and he seeks to convey the message to his family to 'flee from the wrath to come'. Concerned for his married daughters over whom he had no control he concentrated his efforts upon his sons-in-law. Was the message heeded? 'He seemed as one that mocked', v. 14. As the Lord indicated, the salt had lost its savour, Matt. 5. 13, and Lot's message made no impression. How important to realise that the spiritual condition of the messenger can have serious implications for the reception of the message.

What a dilemma for Lot! Judgement is imminent and he must now leave members of his family to face it! Sadly, the consequences of his lack of witness and weakened testimony are evident. 'While he lingered, the men laid hold upon his hand . . . and they brought him forth', v. 16. Of Lot's wife, H. E. MARSOM wrote, 'And on that road along which Lot fled for his life, there is that silent monument of salt. His wife became in her death what he should have been in his life'.

But against the background of this sad account of the failure of Lot, let us meditate upon a more positive phrase: 'God remembered Abraham', v. 29. As Abraham looked out upon the 'smoke of the country', v. 28, he did not know the fate of Lot but he did know that the Judge of all the earth would do right, 18. 25. He could rest in the double assurance that he had interceded on behalf of Lot and he knew and had a personal relationship with the God who would answer his prayer. May we be encouraged today to 'continue in prayer, and watch in the same with thanksgiving', Col. 4. 2.

February 7th
Genesis 19. 30-38

LET US MAKE OUR FATHER DRINK WINE

Our reading today brings to an end the sad history of Lot, and what an end! The impact upon his children of Lot's lifestyle was immense. His daughters clearly believed that the end, 'that we may preserve seed of our father', v. 32, justified the means! The outcome, Moab, v. 37, and Ammon, v. 38, teaches us that it does not.

It is noticeable that Lot comes back to the mountains but not the heights of fellowship that he had once experienced. He had left the mountains in chapter 13 and chosen the well-watered plains of Jordan. He had rejected the angelic command when told to 'escape to the mountain', v. 17, and feared that 'some evil take me', v. 19. Now, driven by fear, he chooses that pathway, but in unbelief. How depressing is the way of those who fail to obey the word of God! What a contrast with the experience of the psalmist, Ps. 23. 4!

In that cave in the mountain the private conversation of the two daughters is unfolded to us. What a wicked plan is conceived! But is their preoccupation with sexual matters not typical of life in society today? Is there not tremendous pressure upon young men and women to indulge in those things that scripture clearly forbids? This passage is a lesson in the folly of illicit and ungodly relationships. The miserable record of the progeny of this activity was that, as the 'children of Lot', Ps. 83. 8, they took counsel together 'that the name of Israel may be no more in remembrance', Ps. 83. 4.

But what was the method that the daughters used to ensnare their father? 'Let us make our father drink wine, and we will lie with him', v. 32. Lot must have been a regular drinker otherwise his daughters' plot would not have been accomplished so easily. Clearly, he did not appreciate the dangers and, like the incorrigible alcoholic, he thought he was in control. Sadly, he lost control of more than he knew. May we remember the words of the writer of Proverbs, 'Wine is a mocker, strong drink is raging: and whosoever is deceived thereby is not wise', Prov. 20. 1. For Lot, perhaps it was easier to take him out of the world than it was to take the world out of him!

Genesis 20. 1-18

HE SHALL PRAY FOR THEE, AND THOU SHALT LIVE

Abraham had been living in the 'plains of Mamre', 18. 1, but now 'journeyed . . . toward the south country', v. 1. What caused Abraham to make such a journey is not recorded but the consequences of the journey were significant. Why should he move to a place of which he could say, 'the fear of God is not in this place', v. 11?

It is strange that the man who had worshipped God with such commitment and had communed with God with such intimacy in chapter 18 should now say of Sarah his wife, 'She is my sister', v. 2. How quickly he had forgotten the lesson of Egypt, 12. 14-20. But how easy it is for us to have a shallow appreciation of the sin of lying, particularly when we can convince ourselves that there is an element of truth in what we say, v. 12. The Lord taught the disciples of this particular characteristic of the devil, 'When he speaketh a lie, he speaketh of his own: for he is a liar, and the father of it', John 8. 44. For this reason Paul emphasized, 'Lie not one to another, seeing that ye have put off the old man with his deeds', Col. 3. 9.

But there is in this chapter a testimony to the character of God. It was the righteousness of God that decreed that taking another man's wife is sin, vv. 3, 6. It was the mercy of God that withheld judgement from Abimelech because of the integrity of his heart and the 'innocency' of his hands, v. 5. It was the omnipotence of God that 'withheld (Abimelech) from sinning', v. 6, and that 'closed up all the wombs of the house of Abimelech', v. 18. It was the goodness and faithfulness of God that brought Abimelech to say to Abraham, 'My land is before thee: dwell where it pleaseth thee', v. 15. The covenant-keeping God, 15. 18; 17. 4, would not fail Abraham at this point in his life.

We, like Abraham, discover that the life of faith is not an easy one. There have been 'given unto us exceeding great and precious promises', 2 Pet. 1. 4. But sometimes we forget that the God who has promised will also fulfil. Today, may we rejoice with Paul that, 'all the promises of God in him are yea, and in him Amen, unto the glory of God', 2 Cor. 1. 20. He does not fail!

February 9th

Genesis 21. 1-8

SARAH BARE TO HIM ISAAC

As we closed yesterday's meditation we reminded ourselves that God does not fail – He keeps His promises. As this chapter opens it would appear that a year between the time God's promise was made and the point at which it was eventually fulfilled, had elapsed, cf. 17. 19-21; 18. 10; 21. 1. As Abraham grew older and his wife passed the age of child bearing, 18. 11, we can imagine the questions and doubts that must have arisen. Yet God is faithful, and He is also the God of miracles! It is significant that scripture records, 'the Lord visited Sarah *as he had said*, and the Lord did unto Sarah *as he had spoken*', v. 1. Not only was God's promise fulfilled but it was also *at the set time* of which God had spoken', v. 2. What was the reason for this long wait, for this test of faith? Perhaps it is that as the event unfolds a miracle is attested. The conception was a miracle. The period of gestation was a miracle. The safe delivery of a child to a woman close to 100 years old was a miracle. The feeding of the child was a miracle, for Sarah said, 'Who would have said unto Abraham, that Sarah should have given children suck?', v. 7.

But let us pause to think of the response from the hearts of Abraham and Sarah. Abraham moved in willing obedience and 'called the name of his son . . . Isaac', v. 3, cf. 17. 19. He also 'circumcised his son Isaac being eight days old, as God had commanded him', v. 4, cf. 17. 23. It was Sarah that testified, 'God hath made me to laugh', v. 6, partly a confession of her failure in chapter 18 verse 12, and partly an expression of her joy that God had removed the stigma of her barrenness and given her the son He had promised. The writer of Hebrews testifies, 'she judged him faithful who had promised', Heb. 11. 11. In that 'great feast', v. 8, there was a testimony to Abraham's belief in the God who sustains His people, 'Isaac was weaned'.

In simple terms it is easy to say that a year is not long to wait. What of those of us who 'through the Spirit wait for the hope of righteousness by faith', Gal. 5. 5? May we learn from Abraham that 'God is faithful', 1 Cor. 1. 9!

February 10th

Genesis 21. 9-21

THIS BONDWOMAN AND HER SON

In our reading today, the result of Abraham's relationship with Hagar becomes a serious problem. It is strange that Abraham should have listened to Sarai's unwise counsel in chapter 16 verse 2 but finds her counsel here 'very grievous', v. 11. What made the decision difficult was that it now involved a person, Ishmael, with whom Abraham was affectionately linked. However, it is noticeable that Ishmael is not named. He is called 'the son of Hagar', v. 9, 'the son of this bondwoman', vv. 10, 13, 'his son', v. 11, 'the lad', vv. 12, 17-20, and 'the child', vv. 14-16. How important that the principle of verse 12 should not be jeopardized by personalities and family ties! What an important lesson for us all to learn!

The key was that 'Isaac, the object of holy laughter, was made the butt of unholy wit or profane sport', HENGSTENBERG, quoted by KEIL & DELITZSCH. Applying the practical picture, the product of fleshly activity was 'at war' with the spiritual heir, Gal. 4. 23 – a war that continues today, Gal. 4. 29! We find this antipathy as we move amongst men and women of the world. We discover the same antagonism between the flesh and the 'inward man', Rom. 7. 22-23, in our day-to-day spiritual lives. What must we do? 'Cast out this bondwoman and her son', v. 10! But how can that be done, practically?

There are two aspects of truth here. On a personal level we can heed Paul's exhortation to the Romans, 'Put ye on the Lord Jesus Christ, and make not provision for the flesh, to fulfil the lusts thereof', Rom. 13. 14. In verse 12 of our chapter Abraham was reminded of the promise that God had made to him and that same principle applies to us, 'Having therefore these promises, dearly beloved, let us cleanse ourselves from all filthiness of the flesh . . . perfecting holiness in the fear of God', 2 Cor. 7. 1.

But there is a further line of truth that we need to develop and that is in respect to our lives in the world. Like Abraham, there will be times when we find it 'very grievous' but the message we need to obey remains the same, 'Come out from among them, and be ye separate, saith the Lord, and touch not the unclean thing', 2 Cor. 6. 17.

February 11th

Genesis 21. 22-34

A COVENANT AT BEER-SHEBA

'The ordinary uneventful days of a believer's life are usually a better test of his true character than an emergency or crisis. It is sometimes possible to face a great occasion with wisdom and courage, and yet to fail in some simple, average experiences of daily living', W. H. GRIFFITH THOMAS. It is in this passage that we see Abimelech's assessment of Abraham's life, 'God is with thee in all that thou doest', v. 22. 'His consistent walk of separation is admired, and God's personal blessings acknowledged', WARREN HENDERSON. This is quite a confession from Abimelech but also a testimony to Abraham's faith evident in his daily life.

The event described in the verses of today's reading surrounds what is little more than a disagreement between neighbours over a well, v. 25. This watering hole had been taken over by Abimelech's men without his knowledge and it was depriving Abraham and his flocks of their necessary water. How should this matter be resolved? It is clear from the comments of verse 22 that Abraham's testimony could have been damaged or lost if this matter were not handled sensitively. The fact that Abimelech sought peace gave Abraham the opportunity to resolve the matter and demonstrate his goodwill by setting 'seven ewe lambs of the flock by themselves', v. 28. How important to handle these 'simple' things with acumen: 'Walk in wisdom toward them that are without', Col. 4. 5. It was the Lord who taught His disciples, 'But let your communication be, Yea, yea; Nay, nay: for whatsoever is more than these cometh of evil', Matt. 5. 37. May we, in every way, 'walk reputably towards those without', 1 Thess. 4. 12 JND.

The results of the covenant that was sworn that day was peace between Abimelech and Abraham, v. 34, and the maintenance of Abraham's testimony. But, from verse 33, we might suggest that there was also a deepening of Abraham's relationship with his God. It was there that he 'called . . . on the name of the Lord'. It was there that he also came to know 'the everlasting God', one who changes not. Don't underestimate the importance of 'little things'!

February 12th

Genesis 22. 1-8

TAKE NOW THY SON

'By faith Abraham, when he was tried, offered up Isaac: and he that had received the promises offered up his only begotten son', Heb. 11. 17. Such is the Spirit's commentary upon this remarkable chapter before us today.

It is noticeable that so much is contained in the command that was issued. Isaac is named; there can be no confusion with Ishmael. His place in divine purpose is clearly stated, 'thine only son', v. 2, cf. Heb. 11. 18. The affection between father and son is emphasized, 'whom thou lovest'. How telling is every phrase!

What unquestioning obedience Abraham exhibited, for God gave no reason or explanation. **What devotion** Abraham displayed: 'Behold, here I am', v. 1; and 'Abraham rose up early in the morning . . . and went', v. 3, cf. Ps. 119. 60! **What faith** he exercised: 'I and the lad will go . . . and come again', v. 5, cf. Heb. 11. 19; and 'My son, God will provide himself a lamb', v. 8! **What fellowship** he experienced: 'they went both of them together', vv. 6, 8. **What agony** he must have felt: 'on the third day Abraham . . . saw the place afar off', v. 4; 'Abraham took the wood . . . and laid it upon Isaac', v. 6; 'Isaac spake unto Abraham . . . and said . . . where is the lamb?', v. 7! '*Reason* might have argued: If Isaac was offered up, those promises, which were all centred in him, would fail. *Nature* might have argued: It could not thus offer up the son of its love. But *Faith* had a more reasonable argument: Abraham had learned and proved that his God was entirely trustworthy and dependable, and that His word was absolutely reliable', H. E. MARSOM.

This passage presents a tremendous challenge to all our hearts. Abraham's experience is but a picture of a far greater sacrifice that God made; a sacrifice for which no substitute could be found. Paul reminds us, 'He . . . spared not his own Son, but delivered him up for us all', Rom. 8. 32.

'For this, O may we freely count
Whate'er we have but loss!
The dearest object of our love
Compared with Thee but dross.'

[JAMES HUTTON]

February 13th

Genesis 22. 9-14

A BURNT OFFERING IN THE STEAD OF HIS SON

The opening verse of our reading today is remarkable for the methodical and ordered way in which Abraham makes *preparation*, v. 9. All this activity took time but how important that everything should 'be done decently and in order', 1 Cor. 14. 40. However, it is notable for the submission of Isaac, remembering that he was probably a young man in his early twenties, as he allowed Abraham to bind him and lay him upon the altar.

What *pathos* there is in verse 10! 'God, and Abraham, and Isaac alone, know all that those awful moments meant to that affectionate father, and to that loved son. Abraham, in the obedience of faith, sacrificing the dearest object of his heart; Isaac, obedient unto death, bound there upon that altar, the knife upraised, the fire ready', H. E. MARSOM.

It is important to see the note of *praise* there is in verse 12. 'I know that thou fearest God, seeing thou hast not withheld thy son'. God interposed and stayed Abraham's hand for, as far as God was concerned, Abraham 'had offered Isaac his son upon the altar', Jas. 2. 21. As we shall see, this action of Abraham was to form the basis of a further revelation and blessing.

What *provision* there is in verse 13! 'And Abraham lifted up his eyes ... and behold ... a ram caught in a thicket by his horns'. A substitute was found! How perfect is the divine provision for, caught by its horns, the ram could not fight.

What a *picture* there is in verse 13! The ram was 'offered ... up for a burnt offering in the stead of his son', 'a beautiful fore-shadowing of Christ dying in the stead of sinners who are, as Isaac was, *already in the place of Death*, "bound," unable to help themselves, with the knife of Divine justice suspended over them', A. W. PINK.

What a *prophecy* there is in verse 14! The place was called 'Jehovah-jireh' for 'in the mount of the Lord it shall be seen'. Perhaps this was the place and event of which the Lord spoke when He said, 'Abraham rejoiced to see my day: and he saw it, and was glad', John. 8. 56.

There is much upon which to meditate in this most precious passage. May it draw from our hearts an appreciation of Christ.

February 14th

Genesis 22. 15-24

I WILL BLESS THEE

There was no mention at the beginning of chapter 22 of the blessing that would be brought to Abraham as a consequence of his obedience. When he rose early on that morning to take his journey to Moriah, he only knew where and what: 'one of the mountains . . . offer him there'. When 'the angel of the Lord called unto him out of heaven' to stay his hand and not to slay Isaac, Abraham was given only an instruction and a ram.

It is 'the second time' before the blessing that God had in mind is revealed and the promise is renewed to the patriarch. The revelation of chapter 12 is developed in chapter 15, and chapter 17, before reaching its climax here in chapter 22. The blessings are manifold, 'I will bless thee . . . I will multiply thy seed . . . thy seed shall possess the gate of his enemies' . . . in thy seed shall all the nations of the earth be blessed', vv. 17- 18. Although the blessings were conditional, 'because thou has done this thing', v. 16, they were also assured, 'by myself have I sworn'.

There is, in the short list of names that concludes our chapter, evidence of the first steps in the outworking of the divine purpose in blessing. We are told, simply, that 'Bethuel begat Rebekah', v. 23. Some fifteen years later Abraham's servant discovered 'Rebekah . . . who was born to Bethuel, son of Milcah, the wife of Nahor . . . and the damsel was very fair to look upon, a virgin', 24. 15, 16. Isaac's wife was already provided in order that seed as 'the stars of the heaven' might become possible! Similarly, we may not be able to see the future but we can rest with assurance that the purposes of God will be brought to fruition in His own time.

Before we close our meditation today, we might consider the impact of these events upon Abraham as he returned to Beersheba. The man that had 'called there on the name of the Lord, the everlasting God', 21. 33, was a different man now and his relationship with his God was deeper than it was when he left. How important that from the sphere of worship when we dwell upon the man of Calvary we should return changed and better developed, ready for His service.

February 15th

Genesis 23. 1-20

THE CAVE OF MACHPELAH

This passage contains the first occurrence of a man weeping and this silent act was a witness of the deep affection that Abraham felt for his wife. They had spent over sixty years together and, as they are often mentioned together, had been united in the things of God, cf. Gal. 4. 22-23; Heb. 11. 11; 1 Pet. 3. 6. That Sarah's death is afforded such a mention is also an indication of her spiritual stature. How fitting, then, that Abraham should come 'to mourn for Sarah, and to weep for her', v. 2. Though we 'sorrow not, even as others which have no hope', 1 Thess. 4. 13, we do sorrow for the loss of those we love and with whom we have laboured and it is appropriate that we should mourn.

We said in our meditation yesterday that in the birth of Rebekah there was the first simple step in the accomplishment of divine promise. Here, in Abraham's purchase of the cave of Machpelah, we have a further small step towards the nation dwelling in the land. Stephen reminded the Jewish leaders that God 'gave him (Abraham) none inheritance in it, no, not so much as to set his foot on: yet he promised that he would give it to him for a possession', Acts 7. 5. Yet, in this cave that was to be the burial place of Abraham, Sarah, Isaac, Rebekah, Jacob, Leah, and Joseph, Gen. 49. 30; 50. 13, we have the first parcel of the land that was later to become Israel.

The choice of this particular portion of land is not without significance. Abraham had no desire to return the body to Ur or any of the other places through which they had passed on their journey to the promised land. But why Machpelah? W. FERGUSON suggests an answer, 'This was an area connected with many of Abraham's most memorable experiences with God. The use of this burial place . . . declared a continuity of hope in the promises of God'.

Yet, though this was a small parcel of the land that Abraham's offspring would one day inherit, he did not receive it as a gift but purchased it. In the detail of the transaction we have a remarkable lesson in how a man of God conducts his business: openly, 'in the audience of the sons of Heth', vv. 10, 16; and courteously, 'Abraham . . . bowed himself', vv. 7, 12.

64

February 16th

Genesis 24. 1-16

TAKE A WIFE UNTO MY SON ISAAC

We see from our passage today that God has blessed Abraham in all things, that is, materially, physically and spiritually. He is now an old man who no doubt still feels keenly the loss of his wife Sarah and yet he has never lost sight of the promise of God, that in Isaac shall his seed be called. Therefore, his desire is that his servant would go to his own country and bring a wife for his son, for what God has promised He will fulfil.

It is quite obvious that Abraham's household is one where God is remembered and His word is revered, so he instructs his servant and commits the matter to the Lord. The simple obedience of the servant is challenging; he has no matters of his own that need attending to, he is ready to do what the master requires of him. Yes, he asks questions but merely to clarify the master's request. What a contrast with the would-be disciple of whom the Lord speaks in Matthew chapter 8 verse 21, who said, 'Lord, suffer me first to go and bury my father'.

What follows is very instructive in relation to divine guidance in all matters and sets out a simple pattern for all to follow. Firstly, we note that the servant goes to the place where women will be found and at the right time. Secondly, he makes request to God with no preconceived ideas; this allows God to make His will clear and plain. Finally, he will ensure that the answer received is in accordance with his master's word.

We turn from the practical to the typical teaching of this passage. We have seen in Genesis chapter 22 that Isaac is a type of the Lord Jesus, inasmuch as he was laid upon the altar and figuratively received back to life again. In this passage, Abraham is seen as a picture of God the Father who gave the church to be a bride for His Son, John 17. 24. Therefore, the servant must be a picture of the Holy Spirit who has been sent to bring the bride to the Lord Jesus, who loved her and gave Himself for her, Eph. 5. 25. It is noticeable that the servant is un-named although many would speculate that he is Eliezer of Damascus, 15. 2. If this be the case then we can note that there is no rivalry in Abraham's household, a reminder of the unity of the Godhead, Father, Son and Holy Spirit working in perfect harmony.

WHOSE DAUGHTER ART THOU?

In today's portion what is outstanding is the eager anticipation of the servant for a response to his prayer. He sees a young lady coming to the well and runs to meet her, what a challenge this is to us all. Sometimes we pray asking God for guidance in a matter but do we really expect Him to respond? In James chapter 1 verse 6 we are reminded that if we need guidance then we must ask in faith doubting not at all, for if we doubt then we should not expect an answer to our dilemma.

Rebekah's response was an answer to prayer, she was so kind and willing to help this stranger, and the servant must have thought, 'this is the wife for my master's son'. Yet, we read in verse 21, the servant wonders and holds his peace. How wise just to make sure that he is in the will of God for this is all important to him and should be the objective in our lives as well. It may be costly, for in the garden of Gethsemane the Lord bows His will to the Father's and it cost Him everything.

The response to his question, 'Whose daughter art thou?', confirms God has made his journey prosperous thus far, and he lifts up his heart in praise. What a joyful exclamation, 'I being in the way, the Lord led me', and how many of us can add 'Amen' to that? But it is strange that sometimes we become so taken up with the answer to our prayer that we forget to thank God for it and nothing saddens God more than an attitude of ungratefulness among His children.

Rebekah's brother ran to meet the servant and gave him a wonderful welcome, 'Come in, thou blessed of the Lord; wherefore standest thou without?' I wonder if Laban would have been quite so inviting if he had not seen something of Abraham's wealth? It is possible to give expecting something in return and to be taken up with what a man has rather than what he is. This attitude is very prevalent in the world today and sadly it can creep into the lives of believers as well. Let us remember the injunction found in James chapter 2 verse 5, 'Hearken, my beloved brethren, Hath not God chosen the poor of this world rich in faith, and heirs of the kingdom which he hath promised to them that love him?'

February 18th

Genesis 24. 32-60

WILT THOU GO WITH THIS MAN?

What a true servant this man is. His all consuming passion is to do what his master commanded him. He would not even eat until he had done all that was required. Shining through this chapter is the servant's love and respect for Abraham. Was this because of how well he was treated and what Abraham had done for him? What a challenge to those of us who claim to be the servants of a greater master than Abraham! We do well to think of what great things the Lord has done for us, and love and honour Him in return.

The servant now relates why he has been sent, confirming the greatness and glory of his master Abraham. He then speaks of how Sarah wonderfully conceived a son in her old age and how that son means everything to his master. All that Abraham has is for Isaac and his desire is that he should have a wife to share the inheritance. The servant confirms that he has been sent with the express purpose of finding a bride for his master's son. He also unashamedly declares the faithfulness of God who has led him thus far and how that He has made clear that Rebekah is the one he seeks.

The question now is will they agree to his proposal or not. Both father and brother accept that the matter proceeds from the Lord, nevertheless it is a big thing for a father to send his daughter so far away; I know this to be true from personal experience. But Bethuel knew that he could not argue with God. It is good for us all to have the same attitude when God makes His way plain.

When it is time to say their final farewells then naturally the brother longs for a few more days but Abraham's servant wisely rejects this. The choice is Rebekah's alone, 'Wilt thou go with this man?', to a man she has never seen. Her unhesitating reply is, 'I will go' and she does so with her family's full blessing.

We have seen previously how Abraham is a picture of God the Father who desires a bride for His Son, the heir of all things. How glad we all are that when asked the same question in relation to the Lord Jesus we replied in like manner for although we have never seen Him we do love Him, 1 Pet. 1. 8.

February 19th

Genesis 24. 61-67

WHAT MAN IS THIS?

Today's passage highlights two aspects of this beautiful love story, the journey of the bride and the meeting in the field. It goes without saying that the journey must have been wearisome and although we may never have taken this mode of transport we can imagine that it would not be the most comfortable in the world! Yet we never read of the distance or the difficulties of the way and we wonder why this is, but as the servant thrills her with details of her husband soon to be, the hours and days would soon pass. It is worth noting that Rebekah and her damsels followed the servant for he not only knew the master but he knew the way to him. Surely, we can relate to this as we journey heavenward and homeward, for as the Spirit reveals something of the love and beauty of our heavenly Bridegroom the days fly as we anticipate our meeting in the air.

In the meantime, Isaac goes out into the field to meditate at eventide. Of whom would he be thinking? Would he be anticipating a successful conclusion to the servant's mission, his heart taken up with the one who would be his wife? His exercise of meditation and prayer is a lesson to us all for we live in a busy world and we ought to take time to think about God and His will for us. When we are alone we realize that we are not alone for God is with us listening to the very thoughts of our hearts. Isaac's exercise is a reflection of the Lord who anticipates the moment He will come to claim His bride, for He says three times over in Revelation chapter 22, 'Behold, I come quickly'.

What a meeting it is when Rebekah sees Isaac for the very first time and the servant says, 'It is my master'. She modestly veils herself in a lovely spirit of humility and subjection. May this be our attitude to our Lord Jesus. Isaac is interested to hear everything about Rebekah but he longs to take her to himself and know her more intimately. As we think of this meeting we recall the words of PAUL GERHARDT,

'Who is this who comes to meet me on the desert way,
As the Morning Star foretelling God's unclouded day?
He it is who came to win me on the cross of shame;
In His glory well I know Him evermore the same.'

February 20th

Genesis 25. 1-11

AN OLD MAN, AND FULL OF YEARS

Perhaps it is only natural for Abraham to feel lonely after the death of his wife and the marriage of his son. He did therefore what many a man in his position has done, he married again. It is interesting to note that we now have three wives brought before us in chapters 24 and 25, Sarah who has died would speak of Israel's cutting off. Rebekah would be a type of the church and therefore Keturah would remind us of Israel being brought into blessing again.

Keturah was naturally fruitful and bore Abraham six children, none of whom had the place in his heart that Isaac had. When he makes his will it reflects his love for Isaac for he gave gifts to all the family but he could truly say to Isaac, like the father in Luke chapter 15 said to his elder son, 'All that I have is thine'. He also put a distance between Isaac and the rest of his sons for he sent them away from him. In the purpose of God we can understand his actions, for Isaac was the son of promise and is a beautiful picture of our Lord Jesus Christ. We are also the sons of God but He is absolutely unique and will be throughout the countless ages of eternity. It should be pointed out that in natural families it will always cause trouble to show favour to one member of the family over another and we do well to have the same love for all.

Abraham is now an old man and full of years. We read a lovely expression here and elsewhere in scripture, 'He was gathered to his people'. It suggests that he was with loved ones gone before and such a thought has encouraged many a saint.

If Abraham is united in death then his two sons are united in grief as they bury their old father. They had their differences, for Isaac was the son of promise, the answer to prayer, while Ishmael was the product of the flesh when Abram and Sarai took it into their own hands to speed up the purpose of God. But these differences are set aside as they comfort each other over the passing of their godly father. They lay him to rest beside their mother and no doubt they have fond memories of both, but their greatest comfort would be that they were buried in the sure and certain hope of resurrection.

February 21st

Genesis 25. 12-26

TWO NATIONS ARE IN THY WOMB

In this passage we are caused to wonder why Ishmael is blessed with twelve sons while Isaac's wife is barren. I have no doubt this caused much heartache and heart searching with this godly couple. They would be happy for every son born to Ishmael but what sorrow as they thought of Rebekah's unfruitfulness.

How considerate and wise of Isaac to pray to the Lord for her and, after twenty long years had run their course, God answered his prayer and his wife conceived. Is it not strange that in our society today many look on children as a burden they could do without? But not this couple, for they thought of a family as the blessing of the Lord. Oh that we all might look on our children in such a way! But is there another challenge for us in these days of spiritual barrenness? Does the fact that we see so little blessing of a spiritual nature drive us to our knees in supplication or are we content to know that our souls are bound for heaven and that is to us all that matters?

If Isaac has shown a godly example in his concern and prayer for his wife, then Rebekah teaches us a lovely lesson of how God speaks in the everyday issues of life. She feels the struggle in her womb and is sensitive to the fact that God is speaking to her through this experience. She asks Him what He is trying to tell her. What an answer she received! Not only was she about to give birth to twin boys but two nations were in her womb. How great is our God!

God stamps His sovereignty across this passage when He declares that the elder shall serve the younger. Why should God say this? Is He being unfair or unkind? The answer is No, He is simply being what He is, God, and He can and will do what pleases Him. However, it is good to remember He cannot make a mistake. We also note that God's rights of sovereignty did not infringe upon Jacob and Esau's responsibilities, for in the process of time they would both make choices which vindicated God. This is something that our finite minds cannot fully grasp but which we accept by faith and bow in adoring worship before Him. From birth, the boys are different in looks and outlook. Esau lived for the present, Jacob looked on to the inheritance.

SELL ME THIS DAY THY BIRTHRIGHT

We are considering today the growth of Esau and Jacob and have noted that though they are twins yet they are so different. For Esau was a hairy man and an expert hunter, preferring stalking animals in their environment to the quiet home life that Jacob enjoyed. One wonders how this could be and yet what parent has not looked at their own family and noticed differing traits peculiar to each one.

The Spirit's comment regarding father and mother is worthy of mention, for in verse 28 we read, 'Isaac loved Esau . . . but Rebekah loved Jacob'. We are left in no doubt as to why Isaac loved Esau, for his venison satisfied Isaac's fleshly appetite, but no reason in given for Rebekah's love of Jacob. Some have speculated that she was more spiritual than her husband. This may be the case but we should not overlook the potential danger to any family when favouritism is the order of the day. On that basis it is not difficult to envisage more than just normal family squabbles. In this situation it escalates to brother at war with brother. Could I therefore appeal to every parent to have the same love for every member of the family? There will be some characteristics that we might be unhappy about in each but we should not let that affect our love for them. Such impartial love should extend to the family of God as well, for Paul's example of this is seen in 1 Thessalonians 1 verse 2, 'We give thanks to God always for *you all*'.

The extent to which these boys differed in outlook is evident in these verses. Esau lived for today, simply to sustain and satisfy the flesh. He saw nothing beyond this life as is evidenced in his response to Jacob, 'I am at the point to die: and what profit shall this birthright do to me?' v. 32. He gave up something that had spiritual and eternal value for what could sustain only natural life, and the full consequence of his action is revealed in Hebrews chapter 12, for, though he sought the blessing with tears, he was rejected having found no place for repentance. It should also be noted that while Jacob had an appreciation of the true value of the birthright he used carnal means to gain it which is not commendable. What a challenge to our hearts today.

February 23rd

Genesis 26. 1-16

SHE IS MY SISTER

Isaac is faced with a great test, that of famine conditions. We are reminded that this famine is different from the one which Abraham faced, teaching us that trials are the common lot of those who seek after God. Famine conditions can be of a material or a spiritual nature and God will use such to make His people more dependent on Him. Some godly men, like Elijah, even prayed that the blessing of God would be withheld from the people of God because of their idolatry.

Sadly, many rely on self in such circumstances and, like Isaac, move outside the will of God. But while he was minded to follow his father's footsteps when in a similar situation, God spoke to him at the right moment, confirming the promise of blessing in relation to his seed and the land he was about to leave. It is always a good exercise to seek the mind of God in our trials lest we move outside the current of His will.

Isaac obeys the voice of God and stays in the land, albeit in its border. It is here he is asked concerning Rebekah and he lied, saying, 'She is my sister'. No doubt he feared for his life but by his action he put his wife in a dangerous position. What he would have done if someone had taken her to wife is mere speculation, but thankfully he was spared the problem in the providence of God. Have we not all been grateful for this providence, especially when the flesh is weak?

Perhaps we should not be surprised at Isaac's response when we recall how his father set him a bad example in chapter 12. Maybe what Abraham did was worse since he asked Sarah to lie on his behalf. May God spare us from putting those we love into dangerous situations because of our lack of faith.

Before leaving this point we note how sin found out Isaac, for he was 'sporting' with his wife. I take it he was being overly familiar with her and so the king reckoned she was his wife and has to rebuke him for his folly in lying to him. Also, we learn that conduct which is acceptable between a husband and his wife is unacceptable between unmarried persons.

The section closes with God greatly blessing Isaac. When we enjoy days of prosperity may the Lord keep us humble.

February 24th

Genesis 26. 17-35

A WELL OF SPRINGING WATER

From this passage we learn the importance of maintaining a fresh water supply, for Isaac and his servants dig four wells besides re-digging his father's wells which had been stopped by the Philistines. Fresh water is essential for life and wellbeing and is one factor that assures a harvest from the land. The Philistines showed a total disregard for this by stopping Abraham's wells so that neither they nor Isaac could drink of them.

Then Isaac's servants found water while digging in the valley and this time it was a well of springing water. The Philistines fight for this well, claiming it for themselves. Isaac simply moves on to the next place and again finds water and the response of the enemy is the same. At last he is left in peace to dig yet another well and is thankful to God for His goodness and grace.

Isaac comes to Beersheba and there the Lord appeared and spoke to Him confirming the promise He made to Abraham. His response is delightful, for he builds an altar calling upon the name of the Lord and then pitches his tent. We note that Isaac's heart was right with God for he wants to enjoy communion with God. The order is also suggestive, for he builds his altar then sets up his home. Sadly, we often work the other way round and make sure our job and home are secure before we seek a place to gather with the Lord's people.

All the while the Philistines have been taking note of everything that is happening with Isaac and have to admit that the Lord was blessing him. They were both afraid and envious and thought their interests would best be served by making a truce with Isaac. Sadly, he agrees to it and thus compromises his position and that of his family. We do well to be careful when the world extends the hand of friendship for usually there is an ulterior motive.

In conclusion, we consider the application of this to our lives today for as water is essential to life so the word of God is to the spiritual wellbeing of the people of God. It is to be our constant source of refreshment and will ensure our fruitfulness for God; but let us be careful not to allow the enemy to prevent us from enjoying it.

February 25th
Genesis 27. 1-29

ART THOU MY VERY SON ESAU?

We come now to a very sad episode in the life of Isaac. He is old, almost blind and death is approaching, but even more sad, is the fact that his physical condition mirrors what he is spiritually. Old age will come to us all, if the Lord be not come, and that makes us more dependent on others. How despicable, then, to read that Rebekah and Jacob conspire to deceive the old man and take the firstborn's birthright. They may have been well meaning, after all Rebekah had been told the elder would serve the younger, but the end does not justify the means. The same was true when Moses struck the rock for a second time, having been told by God to speak to it, nevertheless water flowed to the blessing of the people, Num. 20. 11.

Rebekah is the instigator of the deception and she seems to have no qualms about what effect this will have on either her husband or her elder son. She also must have had faith in her culinary ability since the plan involved making goat meat taste like venison, which is no mean feat, but it begs the question 'had she so deceived him before'? We must also ask another question, 'Why did she wish to deceive her husband'? It may be that she did not trust him to do what was right and how sad if that was the case. But what she did was inexcusable. Paul's exhortation was, 'let everyone of you in particular so love his wife even as himself; and the wife see that she reverence her husband', Eph. 5. 33.

Rebekah's plan would be difficult, but the hardest part would be to make Isaac believe that Jacob was Esau for, as we have noted, they were quite different. Jacob recognizes the problems and voices his misgivings but, in the light of his mother's forcefulness, fulfils the plan to the letter, even when Isaac asks who he was and how he had returned so quickly. We note that he claims his brother's name, 'I am Esau thy firstborn'. He also takes the Lord's name in vain saying the Lord had brought the animal to him. Isaac may take some convincing but when his fleshly appetite is satisfied he gives to Jacob the blessing of the firstborn, which surely was God's will, but how it was brought about was never God's way.

THY BROTHER
HATH TAKEN AWAY THY BLESSING

In today's passage, the full impact of what Jacob did is clear for all to see, for not only did his brother hate him but he caused himself much grief. We have an incident with remarkable similarities when the mother of James and John requested that her sons be granted the place of honour in the future kingdom of our Lord Jesus, Matt. 20. 20-28. No doubt she had her sons' best spiritual interests at heart but we read that the rest of the disciples were filled with indignation against the two brethren. The lesson is simple; it is easy to cause division.

Nevertheless, great lessons are to be learned from the character and life of Esau for he received the due rewards of his deeds. We gather much about **the person he was** both from this passage and the record in Hebrews chapter 12. 15-17.

He is called a fornicator, that is one who sells his body, and Esau, in a spiritual sense, sold his soul and spiritual birthright, for he lived only for 'today'. Then, we are told he was a profane person, for he crossed the dividing line between what is acceptable and unacceptable to God. Lastly, we read he was a bitter man and moved with hatred against his brother. As such, he was a sad character indeed.

Then, we might consider **the choice he made**. He sold his birthright when he thought it would be of no earthly use to him. How many spiritual wrecks are strewn on the sands of time having made the same wretched choice. What is our goal in life? Is it the things that this world has to offer and so please self? We should remember the words of the psalmist, for when the children of Israel 'lusted exceedingly', God 'gave them their request; but sent leanness into their soul', Ps. 106. 15.

Lastly, let us think of **the price he paid**, for it was very costly. He lost his right as the firstborn son of Isaac which was spiritual as well as physical and we read that Esau cried with an exceeding great and bitter cry. He sought the blessing and although both he and Isaac felt that Jacob took it away, Esau never sought the place of repentance. In this God is vindicated as to His promise that the elder would serve the younger.

February 27th

Genesis 27. 41-46

THEN I WILL SLAY MY BROTHER JACOB

We shall view the passage under the following headings:

Esau's murderous intent, v. 41;

Rebekah's motherly advice, vv. 42-45;

Rebekah's manipulative appeal, v. 46.

In the first section Esau is seen for what he is and the murderous intent of his heart; an evil man who cares for no one, not even his own brother. His brother had claimed his birthright but Esau had sold it to him and now realizes that he got the worst of the bargain. His evil plan is to slay his brother before he has the opportunity to produce seed then the blessing will be his again. Though he seems happy to wait until his old father has passed away yet nothing will stop him getting his own back. Although no true child of God could stoop so low as to actually murder a brother in the Lord, it is possible that we could have a grievance with someone and be waiting for the right moment to settle that perceived injustice. True love would save us from such an attitude for it covers a multitude of sins. It is much better to commit the matter to Him that judgeth righteously.

Now while scripture records that Esau only said these things in his heart he must have told someone of his evil intention for his mother was informed of it and she knew that he was capable of carrying it through. What a heartbreak for every mother when there is strife in the family. No doubt she will do anything to limit the damage. Rebekah is no different. She advises Jacob to flee to his uncle Laban for a few days till 'the dust settles'. Scripture does not say why she thought Esau's raging fury and anger would turn away or indeed how he would forget what Jacob had done to him. Perhaps, as others, she felt that time is a great healer. Whatever her thought she assured Jacob that he would come back again for she said, 'Why should I lose both sons in one day, one by murder and the other by the avenger?' Sadly, the few days stretched to twenty long years and we have no record that Rebekah saw Jacob again.

Finally, she appeals to Isaac to send away Jacob but she does not tell him the true reason why this must be. How sad that she has to indulge in further manipulation of her husband!

76

February 28th

Genesis 28. 1-9

ARISE, GO TO PADAN-ARAM

The reading for today is easily divided into two sections:

Isaac's blessing and charge to Jacob, vv. 1-5;

Esau's response, vv. 6-9.

It is instructive that Jacob receives the blessing of Abraham which assures the fruitfulness of his seed so that he is the father of a multitude and that the family would inherit of the land of Canaan. To Abraham and Isaac Canaan was the land of promise but Jacob would possess the land and enjoy the blessings of it. How wonderful to think of the promise of the Lord Jesus in relation to the Father's house for He promised to come again and receive us unto Himself. But how much more infinitely precious when He actually takes us there and we will be no more strangers but we shall be at home:

'There, no stranger, God shall greet thee!

Stranger thou in courts above;

He who to His rest shall greet thee,

Greets thee with a well known love'. *[J. N. Darby]*

We must remember that Jacob was charged not to take a wife from the daughters of Canaan but go to his mother's family in Syria. This would be very difficult for Jacob for he would leave home with mixed feelings. He would be happy to escape his brother's wrath and anger for he was afraid of him. To go with the full blessing of his father would mean a lot to him. This is not a deceived Isaac but a father who accepts the hand of God behind what has happened and deliberately blesses his younger son. Yet, what a wrench for him to leave the family home and especially a mother's love. He would not find it easy, nevertheless this was God's will. How many young Christians have the same mixed feelings when they leave home for university or employment? The best advice to give in such circumstances is to seek God's guidance for that will save from many a pitfall.

Esau does not seem upset at Jacob's quick departure. He seems prepared to wait the opportune time to settle his grievance. However, his wilful character is shown for, knowing that his wives displease Isaac because they are Canaanites, he marries a descendant of Ishmael and made matters worse!

February 29th

Genesis 28. 10-22

ANGELS OF GOD ASCENDING AND DESCENDING

As Jacob went towards Haran, which means dry and barren, it was there that he had the most wonderful dream of a ladder reaching from earth to heaven with the angels of God ascending and descending upon it. It is in the most unexpected of places that God speaks to us! Jacob called the place Bethel, House of God, such was the blessedness of the experience.

In verses 10-11, it was a place of **rest**, for Jacob took stones for his pillows and lay down to sleep. Surely this should mark every assembly today, where every believer enjoys peace with God and the peace of God. I wonder, do we promote this when we gather?

In verse 12, it was a place of **revelation**, where God spoke with Jacob. We too gather to enjoy communion with God and also to hear Him speak through His word. How often our souls have been refreshed by these collective exercises.

In verses 13-15, it was a place of **reassurance**, for God confirmed to Jacob the promise He made to Abraham in relation to His people and the prospect which lay before them. We too ought to be assured in relation to these things. How blessed to read in John chapter 14 verses 2-3, 'I go to prepare a place for you. And if I go . . . I will come again, and receive you unto myself; that where I am, there ye may be also'.

In verses 16-17, it was a place of **reverence**, for there Jacob realized the awesomeness and dreadfulness of the presence of God. This is something that we, as Christians, seem to be losing sight of today and many of us have to confess with Jacob, 'I knew it not'. When we gather together and claim the presence of God, never let us forget that reverence ought to mark us.

In verses 18-19, it was a place of **remembrance**, for there Jacob set up a pillar as a memorial to God. It is interesting to read that Paul described the local assembly as 'the pillar and ground of the truth', 1 Tim. 3. 15.

Lastly, in verses 20-22, it was a place of **responsibility**, where Jacob vowed to give a tenth of all he possessed to God. Should we not be more concerned with what we put into the assembly rather than what we are getting out of it?

March 1st

Genesis 29. 1-14

RACHEL CAME WITH HER FATHER'S SHEEP

'And Jacob lifteth up his feet, and goeth', v. 1 YLT. What does it mean? Because this is the only time the phrase appears in the Bible, scholars exercise caution as to its significance. Possibly the thought picks up the wonder of Jacob's encounter with God at Bethel. He now moves forward with joy. Undoubtedly, he still has many lessons to learn yet. Even so, in incomparable grace, God promised Jacob great blessings at Bethel. No wonder he lifts his feet and confidently moves onward!

Arriving at Haran, Jacob was now in 'the land of the people of the east'. The well and the flocks of sheep indicate a group of nomads or a nearby village. Jacob asks the shepherds four questions. The answers express no warmth, no sense of welcome as he is a stranger. Apparently a physically strong man – he may have rolled the stone from the well himself! – he projected a presence that could not be ignored. In spite of the cool welcome, Jacob was in for a surprise. Asking about his uncle, Laban, who lived nearby, the shepherds point to a young woman approaching with her father's sheep, probably indicating that she could answer his questions. Life has its beautiful surprises.

A man's wealth and social position would be appraised by the size of his flock and the calibre of the sheep. Rachel, a shepherdess caring for her father's flock, was evidently a responsible young woman. Jacob would never forget his first encounter with Rachel, his cousin. He broke the usual customs and simply rolled the stone from the well and watered his uncle's sheep. Then Jacob kissed Rachel, the accepted way of greeting relatives. We wonder what emotions filled Rachel's heart as she ran to tell her father that his nephew had arrived.

Having deceived his father and cheated his brother, Jacob will reap the consequences of his sin. He will know on the night of his wedding how cruel deception can be. Yet, at the well, near Haran where he met Rachel, Laban's daughter, Jacob would remember God's promises, 'I am with you, and will keep you . . . I will not leave you', Gen. 28. 15 NKJV. In spite of our failures, God remains true to His word. In His grace He will bless us and use us in His service.

March 2nd
Genesis 29. 15-35

JACOB LOVED RACHEL

In *A Midsummer Night's Dream*, Shakespeare writes, 'The course of true love never did run smooth'. Many disagree, yet the sad story of Jacob would appear to strengthen his case!

Sketching out the diverse characters before writing a novel, a writer could hardly do better than the individuals in this portion: two men, master deceivers, two women, one never really loved by her husband, the other deeply frustrated by not having children, and two maids. God holds it all together, for He is working out His purposes despite the fact that they revolve around such diverse and, in some cases, unsavoury individuals.

Jacob loved Rachel at first sight. She was physically attractive, yet there was nothing superficial about Jacob's love. It was a serious commitment. Jacob was in no hurry to return home to the father he deceived or to the brother he cheated. He will stay in Haran and work, not for money, but for Rachel's hand. The seven years passed quickly, like a few days.

Jacob's years of work may justify the command, 'Give me my wife', not 'my wife to be'. Some wonder if Jacob and Rachel had a relationship between them similar to that of Joseph and Mary, cf. Matt. 1. 24, 25. Either way, the moment had arrived for consummation, v. 21. Jacob loved Rachel.

By morning Jacob knew his bed partner was not Rachel. The consummation turned into bitter disillusionment. Jacob had recently pretended to be his brother, Esau. Now Leah had pretended to be her sister, Rachel. Jacob reaped what he had sown. Without hesitation, he pledges seven more years of work, so they could be married immediately. Jacob loved Rachel.

Laban may not have noted or cared that Leah was unloved. God knew and blessed her with sons. Priests would later come from one son and kings from another. In spite of all the unethical behaviour involved, God was working out His purposes. Is there a lesson here? Peter failed, but became a great leader. John Mark failed, yet later Paul recognized he was gifted. Nothing justifies improper actions, outright failures and sad mistakes. Thank God He carries on his work even when we fail. The glory always belongs to God, not to Jacob or to us.

March 3rd
Genesis 30. 1-24

GIVE ME CHILDREN, OR ELSE I DIE

A Christian parent reading this portion aloud to the family as part of a daily devotion might be asked some serious questions by any teenage children present. From a Christian perspective they are not easy to answer. But Jacob did not live in New Testament times, not even in the times of Moses, the lawgiver. His complicated, tension-filled marital life was perhaps not that much different than others in Haran at that time.

The situation comes to a climax with Rachel's bitter cry, 'Give me children, or else I die'! The cry expresses Rachel's persistent envy of Leah who had already given Jacob four sons. Outwardly beautiful, jealousy consumes Rachel. She may be Jacob's preferred wife, but to be childless is intolerable. To Jacob's shame, he shows no sympathy or understanding for Rachel's deep sorrow. His angry response to her demands does not help. This must be a very low point in their relationship.

Rachel is no saint. She gives Jacob her maid who bears him two sons, adopted sons for Rachel. Leah did the same and her maid bore two sons. The competition is fierce. Hearing that one of Leah's sons has discovered mandrakes, a plant believed to help a woman conceive, Rachel wants some whatever the price. And an ugly price it was! Leah 'hired' Jacob with her son's mandrakes and bore him two more sons and a daughter.

From the moment he first saw Rachel, Jacob no doubt believed she would be the mother of his children. God had other plans. Leah, with her maid, would mother most of his children. Yet God understood Rachel's pain and graciously answered her many prayers. After years of marriage, Rachel gave birth to a son and recognized that God had removed her deep sorrow. Her son, Joseph, would eventually be the most important man on the world scene, eclipsing by far all the other brothers.

Human weaknesses mar this story. While the details will not be the same, many Christians find themselves in situations today equally charged with tension. How wise to wait on the Lord and cast all our care upon Him, for He does care for his own, Isa. 40. 31; 1 Pet. 5. 7. Then, instead of working against the Lord, we will be working together with Him, 2 Cor. 6. 1.

March 4th

Genesis 30. 25-43

SPECKLED AND SPOTTED

How wrong was Jacob's mother! Because of Esau's plan to kill Jacob, Rebekah advised her son to journey quickly to her brother's home in Haran and to spend a few days with him, Gen. 27. 43-45. Days turned into long years. With the birth of Joseph, Jacob knew he must go home and face his family, especially his brother whom he had defrauded. Respectfully, Jacob asked Laban leave to go with his wives and children.

This sounds strange to us, but Rachel and Leah had not as yet moved away from Laban's home to Jacob's ancestral land. Laban does not respond to Jacob's request. He does acknowledge that his wealth comes from Jacob's God and asks how he can repay him. Jacob declines payment, but he does request that the striped, speckled and spotted, that is, the irregular animals, be given to him and the regular animals remain with Laban. The flocks were widely separated so there would be no confusion.

Scholars are at a loss to know just how Jacob increased the strength of the animals and the size of his flocks. If there was significance to the rods and reeds (some are not even sure what kind of shrubs or trees they were) the meaning has been lost in history. Rachel was sure the mandrakes would make her receptive to childbearing, yet when Joseph was born she acknowledged that it was God, not the mandrakes, who had taken away her reproach, v. 23. When Jacob's flocks increased in size with strong animals, he acknowledged to Rachel and Leah that it was God, not the reeds and rods, who had taken away Laban's livestock and had given it to him, Gen. 31. 9. In both cases, first Rachel and then Jacob, recognized that God had intervened on their behalf. As already noted, even Laban confessed that God, not Jacob, was the source of his increased wealth, v. 27.

To the Romans, Paul refers to those 'who are the called according to his (God's) purpose', Rom. 8. 28. Undoubtedly, there is evidence of this truth in ancient times. God called Abram and, by implication, Jacob, whose sons became the leaders of Israel. As in our case, God was 'in all things' working out His will in Jacob's life and doing so for His glory. Our challenge is to live a life in harmony with God's character and will.

March 5th

Genesis 31. 1-21

ARISE, GET THEE OUT FROM THIS LAND

When Rachel gave birth to Joseph, Jacob spoke to Laban and requested permission to leave for Canaan, Gen. 30. 25. Why did he bring up the subject at that time? Did motherhood confirm her as his wife? One thing is sure, whatever the reason was, this time he was in step with God. The time was coming to return to his ageing parents, to Esau, the brother he cheated, and to the land promised to Abraham. Directly and personally, God confirmed to Jacob that he would be with him all the way, v. 3.

Was Jacob surprised how quickly and enthusiastically Leah and Rachel embraced the idea of leaving Haran for Canaan? He delivered quite a speech and had hardly finished when they confessed they were strangers to Laban and were ready to leave. And leave they did – secretly. Jacob, his family, his servants and great herds of goats and sheep 'stole away', v. 20.

As in many stories about Jacob, there is a jarring note in this one. Before leaving, Rachel stole her father's idols. Why? Various suggestions have been made, but we really are not sure why she did this. We do know there would be serious consequences.

Haran would not be a place of happy memories for Jacob. Yet at Bethel, before he even arrived in Haran, God said to him, 'I am with you and will keep you wherever you go', Gen. 28. 15 NKJV. To Isaac, Jacob's father, and to his grandfather, Abraham, God promised to be with them, Gen. 12. 1-3; 26. 24. On the eve of entering Canaan, Moses powerfully affirms to all Israel that God would be with them, Deut. 31. 6-8. Joshua takes Israel into a whole new experience reaffirming this truth, Josh. 1. 5. The same message, in the same words, is part of the New Testament, Heb. 13. 5. This does not condone the sad things that happened in the lives of the patriarchs, or in Israel, or in church history. However, it does establish that God's promise to His own is unconditional. He will be with them and help them.

Jacob starts a journey. We also are travellers, for our Lord said, 'Go'. In familiar or in very different environments, we are on a journey of service and witness for Him. We travel with confidence, for He said, 'I am with you always, even to the end of the age', Matt. 28. 20 NKJV.

March 6th

Genesis 31. 22-42

GOD HATH SEEN MINE AFFLICTION

Jacob arrived in Haran a fugitive with nothing and left a wealthy man with family, servants and livestock. He does not hesitate to recognize that God was the source of his blessings, v. 42. Yet life in Haran during twenty years had not been easy.

In ten days Jacob and his large company reached the hills of Gilead. When Laban became aware that Jacob had left, he and his men made the trip to Gilead in seven days and pitched their tents facing Jacob's encampment. It was the encounter of two men who knew each other, but were never true friends. From Jacob's point of view, the long period of service to Laban were years of affliction and hard work. Laban had manipulated him repeatedly. Had God not intervened, their meeting in the hills of Gilead had all the potential to become a major disaster.

In spite of all he said, Laban seems obliged at last to make the theft of his idols the main issue, v. 30. Jacob was not aware of what had happened. He certainly did not know that Rachel was the culprit. Why steal the idols? If it was to rid her father's house of false deities, why did she not throw them into the first gully they passed? Did she respect them? Hardly, for, if she was telling the truth, to sit on them as she claimed would be the ultimate sacrilege, vv. 34, 35. Death was close for Rachel, v. 32.

Before Laban arrived in Gilead, God delivered to him a warning not to speak 'either good or bad', v. 24, to Jacob which may suggest he was to make no threats, no promises. Jacob was by no means faultless, yet God cares for His own. Abraham made mistakes and on one occasion God intervened informing Abimelech, the king of Gerar, in a dream not to dare touch Sarah, Gen. 20. 3. Through a vision God spoke to Ananias and sent him to help Saul of Tarsus when his life was totally turned upside down, Acts 9. 10. Later, when in missionary work, Paul found himself in a difficult situation, perhaps wondering how to proceed. The Lord spoke to him with clear instructions, Acts 18. 9, 10. As Peter was rescued miraculously from almost certain death, Acts 12. 1-12, he encourages all of us to cast our care on God for He does care for us, 1 Pet. 5. 7. In spite of everything, God definitely cared for Jacob and He cares for us.

March 7th

Genesis 31. 43-55

THE LORD WATCH BETWEEN ME AND THEE

After ten days of travel, Jacob camped in the rugged terrain of Gilead. Did he have a suspicion that Laban would come after him? Jacob knew it was not the ideal place for a violent clash between two armed bands. When the two men met, the encounter turned into a verbal confrontation, fuelled mostly by Laban. Starting with a bombastic attack against Jacob, he ended with a whimper, suggesting a covenant of peace be established between them. Laban had no alternative. God had spoken, v. 24.

Laban is definitely a pathetic figure about to fade from biblical history. Yet, in the present tension, he recognizes Jacob as an equal. He cannot manipulate him as he did repeatedly during twenty years. Struggling with a new situation may account for Laban's irrational claims, v. 43.

Laban wants a pact between them. Following ancient customs, Jacob raised a pillar and his men formed a mound of stones. More important is the verbal pact summarized in verses 48-52. Laban appears to call the God of Abraham and the god of Nahor, a possible reference to gods of the generations that preceded the patriarch, as witnesses. Scholars doubt that Nahor's god was Jehovah. After twenty years with Jacob, Laban appears unable to distinguish the true God from pagan deities.

Early the following morning, Laban kisses his grandchildren and his daughters, v. 55, and leaves. There is no record of a parting word for Jacob. Laban disappears. Jacob will continue.

Similar to the rugged hills of Gilead, we find ourselves in spiritually rough moments at times. A daughter marries and moves a thousand miles away. A son in the armed forces is sent to a very dangerous area. A very good friend is transferred to an office in a different country. Ironic that at such times the words spoken by Laban, of all people, come to mind. When he spoke to Jacob there was little warmth, for they were not friends. Yet we remember his words, 'The Lord watch between me and thee, when we are absent one from another', v. 49. It is a Galeed moment – a witness, a Mizpah moment – a lookout. We witness to a relationship that is special. We know that, like a tower, it will rise above the turmoil of change.

March 8th

Genesis 32. 1-23

A PRESENT FOR ESAU

Jacob is nervous, very nervous. He had probably thought often of the day he would meet Esau whom he had offended so deeply. Who knows how many nightmares he had about this coming encounter with his brother? This is sad, for twenty years before at Bethel God had promised to be with him wherever he went, Gen. 28. 15. Now the Lord had ordered Jacob to return to the land of his fathers, promising that he would be with him, Gen. 31. 3. Is there a lesson here for all of us? Do we take to heart the promises of God? God promised, and reconfirmed His promise to be with Jacob, yet we are looking at a man who is frightened out of his wits at the imminent encounter with Esau.

When the news arrives that Esau is on his way to meet Jacob with four hundred men, Jacob is terrified. He entertains the possibility of a massacre. He quickly divides all he has into two groups. If one group is lost, the other might survive. He is extremely apprehensive about meeting his brother, vv. 7-8.

No wonder Jacob prays to the God of his father and grandfather, vv. 9-12. He reminds God that he is on this trip in obedience to His orders, that he is not worthy of all he has received and that he is afraid of what his brother might do. What is missing in Jacob is a quiet, deep confidence in God's promises.

The carefully laid plans to send a gift to his brother indicates a deep need to appease ('propitiate') Esau. Jacob has a guilty conscience and seems almost sure he is going to reap the consequences of what he did to his twin brother twenty years ago. He will send on ahead well over five hundred animals from his flocks, most of them female, vv. 14, 15. He is seeking to mollify Esau with a very substantial gift! Jacob is not at peace with himself and with every passing hour his fear appears to grow.

Many of us learned as children the words of the psalmist. 'Yea, though I walk through the valley of the shadow of death, I will fear no evil: for thou art with me', 23. 4. Today's English Version reads, 'Even if I go through the deepest darkness, I will not be afraid, Lord, for you are with me'. In any deep darkness we Christians may encounter, God's presence with us should replace fear with confidence and even joy.

March 9th

Genesis 32. 24-32

NO MORE JACOB, BUT ISRAEL

When Laban and Jacob finally and permanently separated, Jacob was on his way home at last. Almost immediately angels met him. There was no verbal communication, but Jacob knew God was near, 32. 1-2. He may not have known just how close! At the river Jabbok, and in the middle of the night, Jacob had an experience he never forgot; it changed his life.

The experience was tangible, he wrestled with the 'man' for hours. Jacob was a very strong man, Gen. 29. 2, 10. For Jacob, it was a personal encounter with God and, amazingly, he did not die, v. 30. The incident raises so many questions that perhaps we, like Jacob, should stand in awe at the wonder of God's presence at Jabbok and accept that there are things we do not fully understand. Yet Jacob is beginning to understand, for it is usually one of lesser rank who asks a blessing from someone of higher rank. He will hold the 'man' until he blesses him, v. 26.

First, Jacob must tell the 'man' his name. H. L. ELLISON paraphrases his answer, 'Jacob, the smart fellow', for he had been outsmarting people all his life. Now he is uncertain of how to outsmart Esau. With a serious limp, Jacob may feel that his brother could easily bring his world to an end. Was Jacob surprised when the 'man' said, 'Your name shall no longer be called Jacob, but Israel, for you have striven with God and with men, and have prevailed', v. 28 ESV.

The name 'Israel' may carry the meaning, 'God strives', or 'He who strives with God'. Perhaps both ideas are involved in this name. God strives with His people because, as with Jacob, they strive against His guidance. Jacob was slow to learn! He would limp for the rest of his life, a reminder of his stubbornness. The new name suggests that the patriarch has matured. Could it be otherwise? He named the place Peniel – 'I have seen God face to face', v. 30. Would he be a perfect man? No. But he was maturing in his walk with God.

We are to 'walk worthy of the Lord', Col. 1. 10, to 'grow in grace, and in the knowledge of our Lord and Saviour Jesus Christ', 2 Pet. 3. 18. The name Israel indicates that Jacob was growing. Are we maturing in our walk with God?

March 10th

Genesis 33. 1-20

BEHOLD, ESAU CAME

Wedged between chapters recording cowardice, fear and distrust on the one hand and a sexual violation that led to a cold-blooded massacre on a large scale on the other hand, we find this literary oasis filled with respect, affection, generosity and peace! After the troubled history recorded in the previous chapters, we might think this a different book were it not for the fact that the leading personalities have the same names: Jacob, Esau, Leah, Rachel and Joseph. It is undoubtedly the same story.

Esau races to meet Jacob who can only limp. The suspense is almost unbearable. Will he kill his brother? Will he take all he has for himself? We must not minimize the fact that behind Esau are four hundred men! Remembering that we are not dealing with nations, but with families or tribes, this large group of men represent a sizable army! There is reason to be nervous!

Jacob has changed. Instead of hiding behind the women and children, he moves to the front. He does so, knowing that his brother is approaching with four hundred men! Jacob is not arrogant. With humility he bows seven times before the approaching Esau. His generosity is sincere, for he insists that Esau keep the gifts he offers him. The change can only be attributed to Jacob's encounter with God at Peniel the night before.

Esau is not the angry, embittered man of vengeance that had haunted Jacob's mind for years. Instead, with tears of joy and of reconciliation, he offers to accompany him on his journey or, at least, to give him some of his men to help Jacob along the way.

Had both men changed? Little from scripture suggests that Esau really changed. It does appear that Jacob, who believed God and yet acted so often as if God might not keep His promises, did change at Peniel. It was after Peniel that Jacob faced up to the serious issue of meeting his brother and he did so trusting in God's promises. Paul is not arrogant when he assures us he can do all things through Christ who strengthens him, Phil. 4. 13. Listing serious problems that he and many early Christians faced, and which so many still face today, he wrote, 'In all these things we are more than conquerors through him that loved us', Rom. 8. 37. This is trust in God!

Genesis 34. 1-31

DINAH THE DAUGHTER OF JACOB

We enter this chapter passing from tranquillity to turmoil; from surprising forgiveness to well planned vengeance; from an unexpected moment of happiness to a day of an exceptionally cruel bloodbath. We leave an atmosphere of light and enter a sphere of darkness. No wonder some just skip the chapter!

Jacob does not play the man in this tragedy. We would prefer not to think it was because Dinah was the daughter of Leah, the unloved wife. Does anyone act in an honest way in the story? While the phrase in English, '(Dinah) went out to see the daughters of the land', v. 1, sounds innocent enough, some scholars suggest that the Hebrew opens the door to possible impropriety on her part. However, absolutely nothing justifies Shechem's brutal act of violation against Dinah. His new feelings towards Dinah afterwards can hardly erase the fact that he publicly defiled her, v. 2. Shechem's father, Hamor, is also a man with selfish aims. He promotes a union between Jacob's family and his own, confidently asserting that, as a result, 'Shall not their cattle and their substance and every beast of theirs be ours?', v. 23. Dinah's shame is being used for ulterior motives!

In response to the tragedy, the sons of Jacob acted deceitfully, v. 13. All the male members of Hamor's extended family consented to be circumcized so that Dinah and Shechem could marry! On the third day of their acute discomfort Simeon and Levi, full brothers of Dinah, move to annihilate the males, beginning with Hamor and Shechem. Then, all the sons of Jacob act to appropriate for themselves the wealth of those who lay dead in the streets, v. 29.

In Paul's words, Jacob's sons were not acting as 'children of light', 1 Thess. 5. 5. They are at home in the darkness of deceit and slaughter. Jacob was right: his name would soon 'stink among the inhabitants of the land', v. 30. Yet God was working out His will in spite of the havoc. His people would not be assimilated into the pagan tribes. There are those who work in the cause of God, 2 Cor. 6. 1. Jacob's sons were not working with God. But God's work cannot be frustrated by the blunders of men. For this we truly thank God.

March 12th

Genesis 35. 1-8

ARISE, GO UP TO BETH-EL

Twenty years have passed since Jacob's encounter with God at Luz. It was such an awesome experience that Jacob thought he was standing at the gate of heaven. He named the place Beth-el, 'the house of God', Gen. 28. 17, 19. Now Jacob is told to return to Beth-el and, at God's command, to build an altar to God.

For twenty years Jacob has been growing, slowly to be sure, in his relationship with God. On his own he now orders his extended family to put away all their false gods. It is a sign that he understands at last that life with the God of Abraham and Isaac cannot be shared with the gods of the area tribes. Jacob is growing spiritually! The scriptures encourage all of us to grow.

The stench of Jacob's name had undoubtedly spread in the area between Shechem and Beth-el because of the massacre of the Shechemites. Gen. 34. 30. When God said to Jacob 'go up to Beth-el', v. 1, under the circumstances a very dangerous journey, Jacob obeyed and went; and no one dared touch him. He feared no evil. He was safe, for God was with him, Ps. 23. 4.

It is hardly surprising that Jacob changed Beth-el to El-beth-el, 'God of the house of God'. From little knowledge of God, Jacob in two decades experienced God's faithfulness, power and love. Now much more important than the place, is the One who never abandoned him, the God of the house of God.

Pilgrims and tourists converge on the great churches of Europe every year. They enter them with awe, startled by great Gothic architecture, Notre Dame, Paris, famous paintings by the great masters, the Sistine Chapel, Rome, and the tombs of outstanding persons, Westminster Abbey, London. Without detracting from the beauty and the history of such places, Jacob reminds us that more important than any place is God Himself.

In Thessalonica there were many religious shrines. Listening to Paul and his friends many 'turned to God from idols'. The first movement was to God and, as a result, the idols were left behind. Their first commitment now was 'to serve the living and true God', 1 Thess. 1. 9. Paul affirms, 'we trust in the living God', 1 Tim. 4. 10. He knew El-beth-el, the mighty 'God of the house of God'. Do we?

March 13th

Genesis 35. 9-15

TO THEE I GIVE THE LAND

If the contrast is with the Beth-el experience of twenty years ago, this is a different Jacob. He does not appear to be startled or afraid of God's presence. This time he is not running for his life from Esau. Instead, he is quiet, something quite unusual for Jacob! In the quietness, God again blesses him.

Jacob is back in his home country. For the second time God tells him his name is now Israel. The time has come to break with the past and display a new person. The announcement was first made at Peniel, Gen. 32. 28, yet the repetition is necessary and significant. Although the meaning of 'Israel' is the subject of much study, the thought that it may mean 'Let God strive or rule' is appealing. Up to this point Jacob has been ruling. The time has come in his life to let God rule. There are Christians who will identify with Jacob's experience. How close have any of us come to the example of the Lord Jesus when He prayed in Gethsemane, 'Not my will, but thine, be done', Luke 22. 42.

God's desire that Jacob's family increase abundantly is linked to the land promised to Abraham, Gen. 17. 1-8, a promise to be fulfilled in Jacob's descendents, v. 12. God is opening Jacob's mind to His purpose made known at the first Beth-el experience. Gen. 28. 13. Where Abraham was a stranger, Jacob's descendents will be at home. If he wondered how this would all come about, God identifies Himself as *El Shaddai*, v. 11, a term that appears in many English versions as 'I am God Almighty'. *El Shaddai*, the all powerful God, will fulfil His plans.

What a comfort for Christians to remember, in spite of what is happening in our world, *El Shaddai* is still in control. Paul writes of God's power 'according to the working of the might of his strength'. These words explode to a much higher level of meaning with the adjective, 'surpassing', Eph. 1. 19 JND. This awesome display of divine energy is seen in the resurrection of the Lord Jesus. Paul indicates that the intended destination of this power is toward us who believe. No one and nothing will ever be able to separate us from the love of God which is in Christ Jesus our Lord, Rom. 8. 38-39.

March 14th

Genesis 35. 16-29

THE PILLAR OF RACHEL'S GRAVE

At El-beth-el, Jacob is at his best in his relationship with God, but this is no guarantee that he is free from serious problems. Paul reminds us that trials common to the human race may also touch God's people, 1 Cor. 10. 13. Jacob is in for a rough time. We also know that our lives are not always easy.

To lose a spouse unexpectedly is devastating. Rachel was of childbearing age, not what we would call today a senior citizen. She had anticipated another son, Gen. 30. 24, not ever thinking that the birth of that child would end her life. Comforted by her midwife, she died knowing that she had borne another son. In this ordeal, Jacob is in the background, hardly surprising in a society where husbands were not usually present at childbirth, especially a very difficult birth. Jacob loved Rachel and raised a pillar over her grave that lasted well over four hundred years to the times of Moses, v. 20, and possibly much longer.

How often our sorrow is mixed with joy. As Rachel dies, she names her new son Benoni, meaning 'son of my sorrow', but Jacob called him Benjamin, meaning 'son of my right hand'. Jacob loved Rachel's sons, Joseph and Benjamin, hardly surprising in view of the way the other sons treated their father.

Immoral behaviour destroys relationships, something not unknown even in Christian circles today. Reuben did not violate Bilhah, Jacob's concubine. Their coming together appears to be consensual. It is definitely an act of flagrant disrespect for Jacob. By taking Jacob's concubine, Reuben sent a message to all concerned that he aspired to the leadership of the family.

The death of Isaac brought Esau and Jacob together in peace. They buried their father in the only property in Canaan bought by Abraham, a sign that Israel will eventually possess the land.

Jacob is quiet in all these situations. Could it possibly be a sign of weakness, or despondency? However, it is of interest to note that when the psalmist writes, 'Be still, and know that I am God', he identifies God as 'the God of Jacob', Ps. 46. 10-11. Is there a lesson for us here? Instead of analyzing the reasons why such things happen, it is better to be still in God's presence. He will be exalted in the events that overtake us in life.

March 15th

Genesis 36. 1-43

THE GENERATIONS OF ESAU

Very similar to Abraham and Lot, Gen. 13. 1-12, Esau and Jacob separated peaceably, vv. 6-8. They were both very wealthy in livestock, so they had no alternative but to separate. How different from the parting between them many years before when Jacob ran for his life from Esau. Now mature, they separate from each other quietly.

Jacob does not figure in the rest of this long chapter. Instead, and perhaps somewhat surprisingly, the author of this book gives a detailed genealogy of the descendents of Esau, also known as Edom, vv. 1, 8. Jacob and Esau may have parted in peace, but much later the Edomites were bitter enemies of Jacob's descendents. That this genealogy covers generations is a reminder that God has a record of all the races, tribes and nations of history. There will be, in God's presence, a day of reckoning for kings, dictators, presidents and their subjects. Although Obadiah's short prophecy confirms God's judgement against Edom's fierce antagonism towards Israel, there is a general principle here: nations have been judged, Exod. 15. 7, and nations will be judged, Ps. 2. 1-6. This is a sombre thought in today's world.

From this chapter springs also a strong message of salvation for the whole world represented by the genealogy of Esau. Amos writes about hope for the remnant of Esau and for all, whatever their race, culture or nationality might be, who call upon the name of the Lord, Amos 9. 11-12. This whole issue had a profound impact on the early church. It was not easy for the first followers of the Lord Jesus, who were Jews, to welcome Gentiles into the church. James answered the opposition, affirming from the Greek translation of the scriptures that salvation was available to 'the residue of men (Esau)' and to all who call on the name of the Lord, Acts 15. 17.

John writes of a day, when 'a great multitude ... of all nations, and kindreds, and people, and tongues' will stand in the immediate presence of God, Rev. 7. 9. There is no doubt this will happen, for 'the Father sent the Son to be the Saviour of the world', 1 John 4. 14. Why should we doubt that descendents of Esau will be there?

March 16th

Genesis 37. 1-24

A COAT OF MANY COLOURS

The way in which a man is introduced on the page of scripture will often give us an understanding of his future life and ministry for God. And so, at our first meeting, David is keeping the sheep; Elisha is ploughing with twelve yoke of oxen; and Saul of Tarsus is praying. Joseph, however, is wearing a coat of many colours. He was the son who was loved by his father and because he was so distinguished, his brethren hated him. Joseph wore the garment of a son but he also had the character of a son, for he was faithful to his father and brought the evil report of his brethren. This faithfulness would later mature into the ability to rule the world. Older saints should be encouraged to see that the dignity of sonship and potential for greatness can be found in a seventeen-year-old. All is not lost in our day!

The outstanding pictures of Christ as Son in the Old Testament are Isaac, Joseph and Solomon. Isaac portrays the One who, though heir of all things, out of love for His Father, has gone into death and has been raised again. Joseph is a picture of the Son who was loved by His Father, hated and rejected by His brethren in Israel, yet who will one day be recognized as their deliverer and as the Saviour of the world. Solomon gives us a glimpse of a Son who will establish the kingdom of glory and peace that was the desire of His Father's heart.

The key to understanding the life of Joseph is found in the words of Pharaoh to his servants, 'Can we find such a one as this, a man in whom the Spirit of God is?' Gen. 41. 38. Joseph is presented as a Spirit-controlled man and therefore, as it has often been observed, his life is recorded as blameless. Joseph's history is set in contrast to that of his father Jacob. In situations where Jacob would have planned and schemed, Joseph is marked by waiting on the direction of the Spirit and perfect trust in the will of God.

Joseph sets an example to all sons of God in the present dispensation, for the Spirit 'maketh intercession for the saints according to the will of God. And we know that all things work together for good to them that love God, to them who are the called according to his purpose', Rom. 8. 27, 28 RV.

March 17th

Genesis 37. 25-36

COME LET US SELL HIM

Joseph was sent by his father to visit his brethren and enquire of their wellbeing. It was a mission of love. But his brethren saw him afar off and plotted to kill him. The thought of his future supremacy and glory filled them with hatred. Another Father would send His Son on a similar mission to Israel and He would be met with the response, 'This is the heir; come, let us kill him', Matt. 21. 38.

Joseph's brethren were the heads of the tribes of Israel, yet they were planning to murder their brother! God in sovereign choice gave them their position, 'For the gifts and calling of God are without repentance', Rom. 11. 29. What a lesson for us to see that what we are in our position before God can be denied by our practice before men.

An accomplished warrior like Benaiah could face a lion in a pit on a snowy day, 1 Chr. 11. 22. For a time, Jeremiah, the seasoned prophet, could tolerate sinking in the mire, Jer. 38. 6. But Joseph was young and inexperienced, so God ensured that there was no water in the pit. He also arranged for Ishmaelites to pass by at the precise moment that Joseph's brethren were discussing his fate.

Joseph was sold by Israel into Gentile hands. Reuben, the characteristically unstable firstborn son, acted decisively that day and delivered Joseph from death. The price for Joseph was twenty pieces of silver. To his brethren, he was of no more value than a slave.

It is suggested that Judas Iscariot also sold the Lord for the price of a slave. But perhaps he made a profit when he sold Christ, as he placed no value on Him. Satan was at work in Judas. Wicked hands crucified the Son of God. But God was also working out His eternal purpose. All was done according to the 'determinate counsel and foreknowledge of God', Acts 2. 23.

Joseph had a long time to reflect on the actions of his brethren but an appreciation of God's purpose preserved him from bitterness. For he would later say, 'Now therefore be not grieved, nor angry with yourselves, that ye sold me hither: for God did send me before you to preserve life', Gen. 45. 5.

March 18th

Genesis 38. 1-30

A WIFE, WHOSE NAME WAS TAMAR

Judah is introduced in this chapter as estranged from his brethren and living amongst the Canaanites. This typifies the place of Israel in the world today. But the story that unfolds is more than typical. It is a factual account of a period in the life of Judah that reveals the wickedness in man's heart and the relentless attempts of Satan to overturn the purpose of God in Christ.

Judah's downward course resulted from his distance from his brethren. The heart cannot live in a vacuum. Very soon he replaced his brethren's company with the friendship of Hirah the Adullamite. This was followed by an attraction to a Canaanite woman. She lived in a world where everything appealed to the flesh. But he had come from a heritage of faith. Had he lived according to faith, he would not have taken a daughter of the Canaanites to wife, Gen. 24. 3.

Adam learned in the Garden of Eden of the Seed of the woman who would come into the world and bruise the serpent's head. Satan moved through Onan to prevent Tamar from becoming the mother of an heir to Judah. His sin was a repeated one. It was his deliberate intention that Tamar should remain childless. It was for this reason that God slew him.

God's original intention for man and woman is marriage. The marital relationship is not Jewish or Christian in character but is embedded in creation and remains unchanged by mankind's moral history. After the fall of man, every perversion of God's original thought was introduced into the world. Prostitution has been accepted since earliest times but Paul warned that the 'one body' relationship with a harlot is very different from the 'one flesh' relationship of marriage, 1 Cor. 6. 16.

Nevertheless, if sin abounded, grace abounded much more in Tamar's history. Centuries later, Matthew would record her name in the genealogy of 'Jesus Christ, the son of David, the son of Abraham', Matt. 1. 1, 3. Satan intervened to try and defile the royal lineage in order to prevent the birth of Christ. Judah was marked by immorality and deceit; but God's purpose cannot be overturned. His promises must come to pass. 'The sceptre shall not depart from Judah', Gen. 49. 10.

March 19th

Genesis 39. 1-23

HE LEFT HIS GARMENT, AND FLED

The Bible is not a randomly arranged collection of the writings of men. Therefore, we can see the intention of the Spirit of God to contrast the behaviour of Judah in the previous chapter with that of Joseph in Egypt. Immorality in the lives of Reuben the firstborn and Judah the ruler would later be identified in scripture as the reason the birthright was transferred to Joseph, 1 Chr. 5. 1, 2.

Having borne his brethren's hatred, he must face the temptations of Egypt. His circumstances changed dramatically in a short period of time. Although in a strange land and living as a slave in Potiphar's house, his relationship with his God remained unchanged. It seemed that God drew nearer to him in this experience, 'and his master saw that the Lord was with Joseph'. Morality is linked with God consciousness in these scenes. Paul taught that a man's view of God is expressed in his moral behaviour, Rom. 1. 21-28.

If his brethren saw his moral character as something to hate, Potiphar's wife saw it as something to corrupt. Solomon warned that, 'the adulteress will hunt for the precious life', Prov. 6. 26. Immediately conscious of how her proposition would be regarded by God, Joseph took the only course of action – he ran away!

It has often been pointed out that Paul advised Timothy to follow Joseph's example and 'flee . . . youthful lusts', 2 Tim. 2. 22. However, Timothy was considerably older than Joseph and it may be that Paul was warning older men that they are not immune to the temptations normally associated with youth. David was not a young man when he lusted after Bathsheba, and Solomon was old when his wives turned away his heart from the Lord his God.

The moral beauty of Joseph is seen in his willingness to endure the false accusations of a woman seeking to cover up her own sin. He lost his reputation but kept his character. 'For what glory is it, if, when ye be buffeted for your faults, ye shall take it patiently? but if, when ye do well, and suffer for it, ye take it patiently, this is acceptable with God', 1 Pet. 2. 20.

March 20th

Genesis 40. 1-23

THINK ON ME WHEN IT IS WELL WITH THEE

In scripture Joseph commences the noble lineage of those who have been imprisoned for righteousness' sake and whose captivity has been used by God for the blessing of others. Paul was not allowed to speak of what he saw in paradise but we are indebted to him for the ministry that came from prison.

It was in prison that the Egyptians were given a glimpse of the wisdom that Joseph would later use to rule and introduce blessing to their world. The chief butler and baker had offended their lord and were put in prison to await his decision on their future. Their crimes were not revealed to Joseph but their subsequent dreams revealed that, as guardians of the Pharaoh's food and drink, one of them had made him vulnerable to assassination by poisoning.

The dreams of the butler and baker were told to Joseph but he did not engage in psychoanalysis. It has been said that the difference between a coal miner and a psychiatrist is that the psychiatrist digs down deeper and comes up dirtier! Joseph looked outside of the men for the interpretation of the dreams – 'Do not interpretations belong to God?' We do well in our day to look to God to be the guide and interpreter of our lives.

The dreams contained similar stories but the essential difference was that the butler had given no opportunity for others to interfere with the wine. He held the cup in his hand as he pressed the grapes, then delivered the cup personally into Pharaoh's hand. The baker's dream revealed his carelessness for, by placing the baskets of bake-meats on his head, he exposed the food to the birds. If not personally guilty of seeking to poison his master, he had allowed an opportunity for others to do so and therefore he could not be trusted.

Joseph had no knowledge that in three days the Pharaoh would celebrate a birthday. Yet he confidently predicted that in three days the decision would be made that would bring the butler into favour and the baker into judgement. The butler's ingratitude would be used by God to arrange the meeting between Joseph and Pharaoh. Stephen would later say of this period in Joseph's life, 'but God was with him', Acts 7. 9.

March 21st
Genesis 41. 1-36

WHAT GOD IS ABOUT TO DO

In the world of fictional writing there are few, if any, characters that are taken from slavery and prison to become the ruler of the most powerful nation in the world within the course of one day!

Joseph's story, however, contains an element that fiction does not allow for – the sovereign purpose of God. The very first verse of the Bible should teach us that God owns heaven and earth. Man has decided that earth belongs to him and its future destiny is entirely in his control. But God has determined, 'That in the dispensation of the fulness of times he might gather together in one all things in Christ, both which are in heaven, and which are on earth; even in him', Eph. 1. 10.

It is interesting that Pharaoh did not contest Joseph's explanation of his dream, or even engage in further discussion with his wise men. In Egyptian mythology, when a child was born the Seven Hathors came to his bedside to announce his future fate. They were depicted in the shape of cows. Perhaps God appealed to Pharaoh in visual language that he fully understood – the fate of Egypt was already determined!

Men today spend endless hours in debate and discussion about the future of the earth. The heart of man is never satisfied but few recognize that we are living in 'years of great plenty' when the gospel of the grace of God is being declared throughout the world. Soon shall come the years of famine that 'shall consume the land'. 'And I looked, and behold, a pale horse: and his name that sat on him was Death, and Hell followed with him. And power was given unto them over the fourth part of the earth, to kill with sword, and with hunger, and with death, and with the beasts of the earth', Rev. 6. 8.

What God was about to do in Pharaoh's day, was govern Egypt by one who had been rejected by his brethren, was cast into prison, and forgotten by the world. What God is about to do in our day is govern the universe by the Man who was 'despised and rejected' and who was 'taken from prison and from judgement'. Like Joseph, who foreshadowed Him, when the Lord Jesus Christ comes to the throne 'the pleasure of the Lord shall prosper in his hand', Isa. 53. 10.

March 22nd
Genesis 41. 37-57

I HAVE SET THEE OVER ALL THE LAND OF EGYPT

Nathaniel looked forward to a day when Christ would be acknowledged as the Son of God and King of Israel. But the Lord assured him, 'thou shalt see greater things than these', John 1. 50. What could be greater than Israel restored to the head of the nations and ruled by her divinely appointed king? A man shall rule over the universe with His bride by His side! What will be true of Christ in a future day is foretold in the life of Joseph.

Joseph was first declared by Pharaoh to be a 'man in whom the Spirit of God is'. The world's history books tell of men who sought the prize of world dominion but none ever had this moral authority. The reign of Christ will be supremely that of the Spirit filled man. 'And the spirit of the Lord shall rest upon him, the spirit of wisdom and understanding, the spirit of counsel and might, the spirit of knowledge and of the fear of the Lord', Isa. 11. 2.

Joseph was taken from the lowest place of the prison to the highest of the throne. All men were commanded to 'bow the knee' to him. But Jesus has gone lower than Joseph, to 'even the death of the cross'. And the divine response to this self-humbling has been, 'wherefore God also hath highly exalted him, and given him a name which is above every name: that at the name of Jesus every knee should bow, of things in heaven, and things in earth, and things under the earth', Phil. 2. 9, 10.

Furthermore, the despised one became Zaphnath-paaneah, the Saviour of the world. Jacob would later remember his son as 'a fruitful bough, even a fruitful bough by a well; whose branches run over the wall', Gen. 49. 22. One day our Lord Jesus sat by a well and caused the men of Samaria to exclaim, 'this is indeed the Christ, the Saviour of the world', John 4. 42.

The administration of Joseph secured blessing for a world beset by seven years of famine. Those who acknowledged his authority found he had gathered 'corn as the sand of the sea'. And, by his side, Asenath his Gentile bride shared his glory. Even this scene will have its ultimate fulfilment in Christ. For it was the angel that held the seven last plagues in his hand who showed to John 'the bride, the Lamb's wife', Rev. 21. 9.

March 23rd

Genesis 42. 1-28

YE ARE SPIES

The book of Genesis reveals the beginning of all truths and principles that are to be worked out in the history of our world. In the formation of Babylon, under Nimrod, we are given a glimpse of Satan's world as it will be established by the Man of Sin in a future day. In the blessing of the Gentiles and the twelve tribes of Israel under Pharaoh, administered by Joseph, we see the future of our world as it will be established by God and Christ. It is interesting to note that, in Genesis, Pharaoh is a picture of God whereas, in Exodus, he is a picture of Satan.

Our Lord Jesus is presently in heaven but God intends to bless Him in the land where He was rejected. These two truths are brought out in the names of Joseph's sons. Manasseh means 'forgetting' and Ephraim means 'fruitful'. It is part of the great purpose of God to bless Christ in the land where He suffered. 'For God hath caused me to be fruitful in the land of my affliction', Gen. 41. 52.

Joseph's dealings with his brethren are complex and revealed to them a part of his nature they had not seen in Dothan. There, he had meekly accepted their hatred and false evaluation of him. Now, in the palace, 'Joseph saw his brethren, and he knew them, but he made himself strange unto them, and spake roughly unto them', Gen. 42. 7. We must not interpret Joseph's behaviour as that of a man seeking revenge for the past. Joseph's actions toward his brethren were a mixture of righteousness and love. The sons of Jacob could have no blessing until they acknowledged their sin against the man that God had purposed to be the Saviour of the world. Every step in his dealings with his brethren was calculated by Joseph to convict them of the seriousness of their sin and bring them to the confession of verse 21.

These events will see a greater fulfillment in Christ's future dealings with the nation of Israel. He was first introduced to them by John the Baptist – 'Behold the Lamb of God, which taketh away the sin of the world', John 1. 29. They have yet to know 'the wrath of the Lamb: for the great day of his wrath is come; and who shall be able to stand?' Rev. 6. 16, 17.

March 24th

Genesis 42. 29-38

BRING YOUR YOUNGEST BROTHER UNTO ME

Men do not generally appreciate that God is presently extending to the world 'the riches of his goodness and forbearance and longsuffering', Rom. 2. 4. It is because this day of opportunity is rejected that there will be 'the day of wrath and revelation of the righteous judgment of God', Rom. 2. 5.

God's dealings with Israel in that day of wrath are the subject of prophecy. For the nation, it will be a time of particular judgement, 'it is even the time of Jacob's trouble, but he shall be saved out of it', Jer. 30. 7. This is the great difference between God's dealings in wrath with the Gentile nations and Israel – Israel shall be saved! In the same way that Joseph loved his brethren despite all they had done to him, it will be seen that the Lord's wrath towards Israel will be tempered with love. 'For I am with thee, saith the Lord, to save thee: though I make a full end of all nations whither I have scattered thee, yet will I not make a full end of thee: but I will correct thee in measure, and will not leave thee altogether unpunished', Jer. 30. 11.

Joseph understood that Benjamin was crucial to his dealings with Jacob. Benjamin and Joseph were the children of Rachel. They represent two aspects of the person and life of Christ. Benjamin, the son of sorrow and the son of the right hand, represents Christ as the Man who suffered in this world and is now exalted in heaven. Joseph represents the Man who will be brought again into the world in glory and power. It was through a contemplation of Benjamin, that Jacob and his sons were led into an appreciation of Joseph. And God will lead Israel into days of sorrow, so that they will appreciate Christ in His days of sorrow, before they can enjoy the blessings of His presence and rule on earth. It is for this reason that Jacob in a future day will feel that 'all these things are against me'.

God will yet win over the minds and hearts of Israel and they will enter into the blessings of the new covenant as described in Jeremiah chapter 31. The days of Rachel weeping for her children will then be over. In that day, worshippers from 'the land of Benjamin' will come up to Jerusalem, 'bringing sacrifices of praise, unto the house of the Lord', Jer. 17. 26.

March 25th
Genesis 43. 1-15

I WILL BE SURETY FOR HIM

It is interesting to note that King Solomon wrote extensively on the subject of a surety in the book of Proverbs. The overwhelming conclusion that he reached was, 'He that is surety for a stranger shall smart for it: and he that hateth suretiship is sure', Prov. 11. 15. Solomon's difficulty lay in his understanding of human nature. The more he pondered the subject, the more he realized that the surety would always be left in a vulnerable position and would be the person who would suffer loss in the agreement.

It is very striking, therefore, to see that only one man in the Old Testament offered to be a surety. Judah takes the place of surety for Benjamin to save the tribes of Israel – 'that we may live, and not die, both we, and thou, and also our little ones'. In these verses there is recognition of the authority of Joseph and the unbending nature of his will. They understood that he would not change his mind about Benjamin coming to him and yet they could not bear to see the anguish this brought to Jacob. It is important to see that Jacob is called Israel in these verses. Jacob was his name as a man after the flesh; Israel is what he became in the purpose of God.

At Calvary, Israel understood that Christ was 'smitten of God and afflicted', that His sufferings were not only from the hand of men. Israel thought His sorrows had come because He was an imposter who had falsely claimed to be the Son of God and the King of Israel. This is the Benjamin character of Christ's sufferings. The day will come when Judah will appreciate these sufferings and confess that, 'he was wounded for our transgressions', Isa. 53. 5.

A greater than Judah has offered to be a surety. Jesus is the only man in the New Testament who takes this place. But He is 'the surety of a better testament', Heb. 7. 22. The reservations of Solomon do not apply to the new covenant, as it is a one party agreement. There is a Man in heaven who guarantees the terms of the covenant that apply to His people today. It is Jesus, the despised and rejected Man, who will introduce the house of Israel and Judah to all its blessings in a future day.

March 26th

Genesis 43. 16-34

THESE MEN SHALL DINE WITH ME

We live in days when men have done all they can to remove thoughts of God from their mind. It has often been noted that the spirit of the age will eventually reach believers. Far too many Christians have low thoughts about their God. Particularly, there appears to be a worrying trend of minimizing His sovereignty in their thinking. It will therefore come as a surprise to many that the inspired Psalmist, in Psalm 105 verse 16, would later record that it was God who caused the famine in the days of Joseph. God was turning dreams into reality. The same God is moving in our world to turn prophecy into history.

Immediately Joseph saw Benjamin, he recognized that his brethren had responded to his purpose for them. Although they still did not recognize him, they had been through experiences of heart that enabled him to welcome them into his house. The men who once envied him were now afraid when they entered Joseph's house. But it was an Egyptian who reminded them about the nature of the God of their fathers. The God of Abraham, Isaac and Jacob had provided 'treasure in your sacks'.

The dreamer had told them many years before that 'your sheaves stood round about, and made obeisance to my sheaf', Gen. 37. 7. A sovereign God working in the scenes of their lives now brings them to bow down their heads and make obeisance to Joseph without a spirit of envy or resentment.

The tears of Joseph are very touching. They were tears for 'Benjamin, his mother's son'. Does this not give us an insight into what the Lord's supper means to Christ? Can he forget the 'days of his flesh' and the sufferings that were His? What must it mean to Him when we gather to remember Him as the Son of sorrow who became the Son of the right hand?

And so, the brethren of Joseph were reunited with him and marvelled at his understanding of them. Israel has yet to marvel at the power of God to bring the scattered nation together again in fellowship with Christ. The wonderful grace of God will also ensure that, instead of being kept at a distance, 'the Lord shall be known to Egypt, and the Egyptians shall know the Lord in that day', Isa. 19. 21.

March 27th

Genesis 44. 1-17

HOW SHALL WE CLEAR OURSELVES?

From the earliest days of man's history in this world, he has instinctively tried to deal with sin by concealment. Adam and Eve, Achan, David, Ananias and Sapphira are just a few of those who have tried to hide their sin from God and men. The sons of Jacob were only following in their father's footsteps when they came to him with the invented story of Joseph's death. He had once been marked by scheming and deception, although perhaps not to the same degree. Joseph realized that his work would not be over until his brethren were willing to confess their sin.

Again, the test had to do with their attitude to Benjamin. Their hearts had been quite indifferent to the distress of Joseph. Once Benjamin's sack was opened and the silver cup found, would they leave him to his death? Would they return to Jacob with another lie about the fate of his youngest son in Egypt? The narrative again is stressing the connection between Benjamin and Joseph. Israel will only know Christ in glory and power when they are prepared to accept His sufferings. This was the lesson the disciples on the road to Emmaus had to learn, 'Ought not Christ to have suffered these things, and to enter into his glory?' Luke 24. 26.

The rent clothes and prostration of his brethren showed to Joseph that his work was nearly done. All that remained was for Judah to ask representatively, 'how shall we clear ourselves?'. As soon as they realized their sin was exposed before God, they sought its complete removal. How good for the believer today to know that 'the blood of Jesus Christ his Son cleanseth us from all sin' and 'if we confess our sins, he is faithful and just to forgive us our sins', 1 John 1. 7, 9.

Zechariah tells of a day when the Lord 'shall save the tents of Judah first'. Judah will lead the nation in its repentance and recognition of Christ as their true Messiah in 'the spirit of grace and of supplications'. 'And they shall look upon me whom they have pierced, and they shall mourn for him as one mourneth for his only son, and shall be in bitterness for him, as one that is in bitterness for his firstborn', Zech. 12. 7, 10.

March 28th

Genesis 44. 18-34

HOW SHALL I GO UP AND THE LAD NOT WITH ME

Judah appeared before Joseph as the representative of his brethren. He had been their leader in selling Joseph to the Midianites, now he would lead them in their repentance and recognition of Joseph's supremacy. His statement, 'for thou art even as Pharaoh' revealed a complete adjustment of his thinking.

Nathaniel too is seen to be a representative of the nation of Israel. He once asked, 'can there any good thing come out of Nazareth?' But, as an Israelite without guile, he changed his mind and exclaimed, 'Rabbi, thou art the Son of God; thou art the king of Israel', John 1. 46, 49.

Joseph learned for the first time, through Judah's confession, the deception of his brethren and the lie they had told Jacob. How often he must have thought of his father and how he would have taken the news of his slavery. Now he discovered the truth, 'Surely he is torn in pieces'.

His brethren had sinned against him and his father. Judah poured out his feelings to Joseph, 'it shall come to pass, when he seeth that the lad is not with us, that he will die: and thy servants shall bring down the gray hairs of thy servant our father with sorrow to the grave'. His feelings for Benjamin and Jacob showed that his heart had been adjusted. The sin that he had thought of so lightly in the past had become a burden to him.

Judah's personal interview with Joseph is a picture of the believer at the judgment seat of Christ. 'For we must all appear before the judgement seat of Christ; that every one may receive the things done in his body, according to that he hath done, whether it be good or bad', 2 Cor. 5. 10. It is often wrongly assumed that wrongs in our life will be put right at the judgement seat. Like Judah, we will discover that wrongs committed on earth will not be undone in heaven. Paul realized this, which is why he lived every day in anticipation of the judgement seat.

But if, like Judah, we cannot undo past mistakes, we will discover, as he did, that our God in His sovereign purpose intends to bless His people. For despite our past sins and regrets, we will be 'conformed to the image of his Son, that he might be the firstborn among many brethren', Rom. 8. 29.

March 29th
Genesis 45. 1-15

I AM JOSEPH; DOTH MY FATHER YET LIVE?

Joseph weeping for his brethren is a most touching scene in the word of God. Their hearts had been hardened to him but the years had not changed his love for them. All thought of the injustice of his suffering is removed by the restoration of his brethren to him. It surely foreshadows the day when Israel's Messiah 'shall see of the travail of his soul, and shall be satisfied', Isa. 53. 11.

Of course, Joseph had known that he would meet his brethren but what a shock for them to hear him say, 'I am Joseph your brother, whom ye sold into Egypt'. They were so shocked they could not speak to him. But he calmed their fear by explaining to them that his pathway in the world had been ordered by God to 'preserve life'.

What, then, will be the reaction of Israel when Christ reveals Himself to them? Peter was given a preview of that day when he told the men of Israel about 'Him, being delivered by the determinate counsel and foreknowledge of God, ye have taken, and by wicked hands have crucified and slain', Acts 2. 23. When he had finished preaching, they exclaimed 'Men and brethren what shall we do?' Acts 2. 37.

His brethren then learned how God had used the wisdom and power of Joseph to preserve the land and 'to preserve you a posterity in the earth, and to save your lives by a great deliverance'. They were, in fact, a divinely preserved remnant. Had they remained in Canaan, the further five years of famine would have entirely destroyed them.

In a future day the nation of Israel will find itself in the same position as Joseph's brethren. 'Esaias also crieth concerning Israel, Though the number of the children of Israel be as the sand of the sea, a remnant shall be saved: for he will finish the work, and cut it short in righteousness: because a short work will the Lord make upon the earth', Rom. 9. 27, 28.

In that day, Israel will acknowledge that all their blessings came to them from the Lord who had ascended on high. 'Blessed be the Lord, who daily loadeth us with benefits, even the God of our salvation. Selah', Ps. 68. 19.

March 30th

Genesis 45. 16-28

JOSEPH MY SON IS YET ALIVE

It is remarkable that Joseph did not reveal his ill-treatment at the hand of his brethren to Pharaoh or the Egyptians. Pharaoh and his servants took pleasure in seeing a family reunited. How different the scene would have been had they known the truth! In his dealings with his brethren, Joseph displayed the highest and most Christ-like of moral features.

The glory of Joseph in Egypt brought them into a place of favour with Pharaoh and his house. They were Joseph's brethren and blessed because of him with all the 'good of the land of Egypt'. This all has its answer for the believer today in, 'the God and Father of our Lord Jesus Christ, who hath blessed us with all spiritual blessings in heavenly places in Christ . . . wherein he hath made us accepted in the beloved', Eph. 1. 3, 6.

Although reunited with their brother, and laden with goods bestowed on them by the pleasure of Pharaoh, Joseph gave them a warning for their journey, 'See that ye fall not out by the way'. He knew them better than they knew themselves. And, sadly, has it not been our own history, that even when enjoying the blessings of God in our lives, strife seems to come so easily amongst brethren? Even after witnessing the transfiguration, the Lord had to ask his disciples, 'What was it that ye disputed among yourselves by the way?' Mark. 9. 33.

Jacob had once been told a lie about Joseph's death and had believed it. His sons returned to him telling the truth about Joseph being alive and exalted in Egypt and he did not believe them. It was only when he saw the wagons laden with good things that his spirit revived and he anticipated seeing Joseph. The gospel message tells of a man alive and glorified and the human heart immediately rejects the news. But Paul recognized that the hard and impenitent heart of man could be led to repentance by the 'goodness of God', Rom. 2. 4, 5.

Having believed the message that Joseph was alive and exalted, Jacob's great desire was to 'see him before I die'. Surely, this is the desire and hope of every believer today, 'We which are alive and remain unto the coming of the Lord . . . shall be caught up . . . to meet the Lord', 1 Thess. 4. 15, 17.

March 31st
Genesis 46. 1-34

FEAR NOT TO GO DOWN INTO EGYPT

The journey of Israel from Egypt to Canaan, recounted in the book of Exodus, is well known and its typical teaching understood. But before that could take place, Jacob and his family must journey into Egypt and live with Gentiles in the land of Goshen. Although seemingly taking them out of the land of promise, this journey was part of the divine purpose and covenant that was revealed to Abraham in chapter 15 verses 13-14. The journey to Goshen required Jacob to give up the land but he did so with the divine assurance, 'and I will surely bring thee up again', v. 4.

Jacob made the journey in the realization that Joseph was alive and exalted in a position of supreme authority. Therefore, the journey is a picture of Jews today who, by faith, have recognized the present position of Christ as raised from the dead and all things put under His feet. Paul was one who made the journey into Goshen to enjoy the present blessings of Jew and Gentile united to the risen Christ. He gave up the land of promise for a greater inheritance in Him. Those Jews who pre-trust in Christ, before the rest of the nation, are 'according to the purpose of him who worketh all things after the counsel of his own will', Eph. 1. 11.

A greater than Jacob made the same journey centuries later. God took His own Son from Israel down to Egypt and, when the threat to His life ended with the death of Herod, He brought Him back into the land again. The statement, 'out of Egypt have I called my son', applied by Matthew to Christ, originally referred to Israel. But God's evaluation of the nation was, 'Israel is an empty vine, he bringeth forth fruit unto himself', Hos. 10. 1. The Son of God retraced the journey of the nation and, at the end of His life, could confidently say, 'I am the true vine, and my Father is the husbandman', John 15. 1.

And so, seventy people left the land of covenant to live with Gentiles in Goshen. Together they looked upon the face and glory of Joseph. Paul reminds us that such a company exists today, 'Even so then at this present time also there is a remnant according to the election of grace', Rom. 11. 5.

April 1st

Genesis 47. 1-12

AND JACOB BLESSED PHARAOH

Here we have a most remarkable statement. Jacob, a herds-man, meets the most powerful potentate in the civilized world at that time, and we read that Jacob blessed him. We would have expected the reverse to be true, and that Pharaoh, being who he was and having all the power and wealth he possessed, would have blessed Jacob. But it was Jacob who blessed him. Jacob did not feel the least bit inferior standing before Pharaoh, because his God was the creator of the vast universe, who had directed his life for well nigh 130 years. Jacob himself had been greatly blessed by God, Gen. 28. 13-15, and he in turn had been a blessing to others during his lifetime. For example, we learn that Laban prospered, and was blessed, because of Jacob, Gen. 30. 27. Because of this, Jacob felt himself to be in a position to bless Pharaoh – to give him something that he did not already have.

As believers in the Lord Jesus Christ, though yet in our state of humiliation, Phil. 3. 20-21, we are the sons of God, and have been blessed 'with all spiritual blessings in heavenly places in Christ', Eph. 1. 3. We are also 'heirs of God, and joint-heirs with Christ', Rom. 8. 17. The Christian need never feel inferior in the presence of this world's greatest, because he has something much more valuable than the material wealth and status that they have in this world. The Christian can also offer 'eternal life' through Jesus Christ our Lord, the enjoyment of which will endure, not only for time, but for eternity.

Not only so, but the very presence of the people of God on the earth is a source of blessing to the world at large. The Lord Jesus said, 'Ye are the salt of the earth', Matt. 5. 13, and he also said, 'Ye are the light of the world', Matt. 5. 14. Salt and light are beneficial because of their very presence alone, because they do not act in any obvious way. Salt stays corruption, and light illu-minates. Scripture makes it abundantly clear that when the salt and the light are withdrawn, this world will become a terrible place during the Great Tribulation.

May the Lord enable us who are so blessed to be a source of blessing to others with whom we come in contact.

April 2nd

Genesis 47. 13-31

THOU HAST SAVED OUR LIVES

The context of today's reading introduces us to moments of crisis in the world of that day, due to a great famine. God had made known through Joseph that seven years of famine were coming, and as advisor to Pharaoh, he had prepared for the famine by storing grain in Egypt. His foresight not only provided for Egypt, but other nations also beat a path to Joseph's store-houses to find relief.

In the verses before us, the famine had taken its toll in Egypt, and the people had forfeited their land, their flocks and herds to Joseph. Now Joseph is asking for a fifth part of the increase of their fields for Pharaoh. The people might have rebelled against this added burden, but such was their confidence in Joseph that they responded by saying 'Thou hast saved our lives'. They were prepared to surrender all to him who had saved them. Whatever he asked, and the amount he asked for, they were willing to give.

Joseph is one of the most blessed types of the Lord Jesus in the Old Testament and in his provision, not only for his nation but for the world, we see a picture of the scope of the redemptive work of the Lord Jesus on the cross. The Lord did not die for one nation. His salvation extends to the whole world, 'that whosoever believeth in him should not perish, but have everlasting life', John 3. 16.

We learn also what is expected of us in response to the salvation that God has provided. The people gave all in response to the salvation that Joseph gave; so it should be with us. The apostle Paul, writing to the Romans, exhorted them, 'I beseech you therefore, brethren, by the mercies of God, that ye present your bodies a living sacrifice, holy, acceptable unto God, which is your reasonable service', Rom. 12. 1. Note that the impetus behind the yielding of our bodies lies in our appreciation of the 'mercies of God'. God does not want forced servitude from His people; He wants our service to emanate from a heart filled with appreciation for all that He has done for us at Calvary. He has indeed 'saved our lives' and our reasonable 'service' is to give ourselves unreservedly to Him.

April 3rd

Genesis 48. 1-22

I KNOW IT, MY SON, I KNOW IT

The verses under consideration bring before us a unique situation whereby the two sons of Joseph were adopted by Jacob as his own sons. Jacob said to Joseph, 'And now thy two sons, Ephraim and Manasseh . . . are mine; as Reuben and Simeon, they shall be mine', v. 5. One might wonder, why the comparison with Reuben and Simeon? Reuben and Simeon were the eldest sons of Jacob, so here the sons of Joseph were not only adopted into the family, but brought into the unique position of the firstborn. Again, it could also be that because Reuben and Simeon had disgraced his name, Gen. 49. 3-5, that Jacob is finding in the sons of Joseph those who would restore his name and his honour, 1 Chr. 5. 1

Now, as Jacob began to bless Joseph's sons, he put Ephraim, the younger, on his right hand, and Manasseh, the elder, on his left. Joseph was displeased at this breach of protocol and remonstrated with his father. But Jacob was not acting under human protocol, but under the sovereign direction of God and he maintained his posture, putting Ephraim in the place of firstborn with its attendant blessings, saying to Joseph, 'I know it, my son, I know it', v. 19.

We can readily see a picture of ourselves in this incident. Although not partakers of the blessings that Israel enjoyed, we have been brought into the favoured position of sons. The apostle Paul reminds us, 'Having predestinated us unto the adoption of children by Jesus Christ to himself, according to the good pleasure of his will', Eph. 1. 5, all the blessings associated with this position are ours. We have been 'blessed . . . with all spiritual blessings in heavenly places in Christ', Eph. 1. 3. We are 'heirs of God, and joint-heirs with Christ', Rom. 8. 17, and 'when he shall appear, we shall be like him; for we shall see him as he is', 1 John 3. 2.

> 'Behold, what love, what boundless love
> The Father hath bestowed
> On sinners lost, that we should be
> Now called the sons of God'.

[M. S. Sullivan]

112

April 4th
Genesis 49. 1-7

IN THE LAST DAYS

In the verses before us, Jacob is on his deathbed and he calls his sons, the progenitors of the nation of Israel, around him to review their past, and to predict their future.

Jacob begins by addressing Reuben, his firstborn son. His first words are complimentary, v. 3, and have to do with what Reuben was through his links with Jacob. But the second part of his message, v. 4, was condemnatory, relating to what he had become. The first part has to do with Reuben's **position**, the latter part had to do with his **condition**, and the two were poles apart. His sin had been particularly heinous. We read, 'Thou wentest up to thy father's bed; then defiledst thou it: he went up to my couch'.

The apostle Paul, writing to the Corinthians, begins by describing them as 'sanctified in Christ Jesus', 1 Cor. 1. 2, but we quickly discover that their condition did not correspond with their position. This is always a challenge to the Lord's people, to ensure that our position in Christ has its practical expression in our daily lives.

Having dealt with Reuben, Jacob grouped Simeon and Levi together, and all his words are condemnatory. Jacob said, 'Instruments of cruelty are in their habitations', v. 5. Jacob's righteous anger was provoked by the memory of their unconscionable behaviour towards the men of Shechem, murdering them in cold blood, Gen. 34. Jacob's prophecy was, 'I will divide them in Jacob, and scatter them in Israel'. In Deuteronomy chapter 33, when Moses blessed the tribes, Simeon was passed over. However, Levi, as a result of Exodus chapter 32, obtained the blessing of priesthood, and was thus 'scattered' in Israel.

We learn from these cases that the principle 'whatsoever a man soweth, that shall he also reap', Gal. 6. 7, is still valid in the lives of God's people today. The terms of grace do not cancel the government of God in our lives. We are also reminded of the solemn fact that 'we must all appear before the judgment seat of Christ; that every one may receive the things done in his body, according to that he hath done, whether it be good or bad', 2 Cor. 5. 10

April 5th

Genesis 49. 8-13

UNTIL SHILOH COME

In this passage, Jacob continues prophesying to his sons before he departs the scene and now he addresses Judah. Judah and Joseph were lauded by Jacob above their brethren. Jacob had nothing negative to say about either and in them we see Christ foreshadowed in a remarkable way. Jacob began by describing the glory that would surround Judah: (i) he would be the praise of his brethren, v. 8; (ii) he would be victorious over his enemies, v. 8; (iii) his brethren would bow down before him, v. 8; (iv) he would be as a lion conquering the prey, v. 9; (v) the sceptre would not depart from Judah, until Shiloh come, v. 10; (vi) unto him shall the gathering of the people be, v. 10.

It is clear that these statements must have their fulfilment, not in Judah personally, but in Him who would proceed from Judah in later times – the Christ of God. In the ultimate sense, Christ will be the praise of His brethren, Ps. 22. 23-27. His brethren will bow down before Him, Ps. 22. 29; Phil. 2. 10. He will finally triumph over every enemy, and wield the sceptre of universal sway, as the Lion of the tribe of Judah, Ps. 2. 6-9; Ps. 22. 28; Rev. 5. 5; Rev. 19. 11-16. Jacob then says, 'Unto him shall the gathering of the people be', v. 10. J. N. DARBY's translation puts it this way, 'To him will be the obedience of all peoples', and indeed this will be the ultimate triumph of the Crucified when the entire universe of God will acknowledge him as Lord to the glory of God the father, Phil. 2. 10-11; Rev. 5. 13-14. Before Jacob moves away from Judah, he makes this remarkable prophecy: 'The sceptre shall not depart from Judah, nor a lawgiver from between his feet, until Shiloh come', v. 10. This establishes the royal line in the tribe of Judah, from which the Lord Himself would proceed in due course, Matt. 1. 1-2; Luke 2. 4-5.

Shiloh means 'peace', or 'rest', and it is true that this poor world will never know true peace or rest, until Christ assumes the sceptre of universal rule and governs the nations with a rod of iron. It is Isaiah who tells us that 'the government shall be upon his shoulder' and that this One who will govern is 'The Prince of Peace', Isa. 9. 6.

April 6th

Genesis 49. 14-21

I HAVE WAITED FOR THY SALVATION , O LORD

In these verses, Jacob addresses Zebulun, Issachar, Dan, Asher and Naphtali. Zebulun and Issachar are spoken of in unflattering terms. Zebulun is seen to be in pursuit of material gain from his links with the world, v. 13. Issachar is compared with the ass, yet one who was lazy and content to be at ease, unwilling to engage in conflict with the enemy, and content to be 'a servant unto tribute', v. 15. Dan is spoken of as 'judge (of) his people', but this is followed by a description of him as 'a serpent by the way', v. 17. Dan had great potential, but he became 'a serpent by the way', in the satanic sense, when he led the people of God into idolatry, Judg. 18.

All the things identified with these men bring challenges to our hearts today. Could we, like Zebulun, pursue worldly contacts and gain? Or could we, like Isaachar, just lie down at ease and refuse to take up the battle? Or, like Dan, become tools of Satan to lead the people of God away from Him. None of us is exempt from such possibilities and we have to be constantly on our guard against them.

The turning point in the chapter is found in Jacob's brief prayer in verse 18, 'I have waited for thy salvation, O Lord'. Jacob saw no hope unless it came from God and, like the psalmist, we can say, 'I will lift up mine eyes unto the hills, from whence cometh mine help', Ps. 121. 1. It was only when this point was reached that Jacob began to see light ahead.

He now turns to Gad, Asher and Naphtali. Gad is seen as one who knows some of life's ups and downs, but although overcome at times, ultimately he is an overcomer. Asher is seen to be one who enjoys good food, and who also has food for others. We read, 'he shall yield royal dainties', v. 20. The apostle Paul writing to Timothy exhorts him to be dedicated to the pursuit of the word, then he adds, 'thou shalt both save thyself, and them that hear thee', 1 Tim. 4. 16. He would provide for others as well. Naphtali is described as 'a hind let loose: he giveth goodly words'. Here is a man of energy and intensity who enjoys liberty, and he is able to give 'goodly words'. May the Lord enable us in our day to be like these three men.

Genesis 49. 22-26

JOSEPH, A FRUITFUL BOUGH

By this time, Jacob had spoken to ten of his sons. Their past conduct had caused him to speak to some in rebuke, and to bestow upon others many desirable blessings. But his greatest accolades and best blessings are reserved for Joseph, his first-born of the beloved Rachel. There is no cloud from the past across the path of Joseph that would call for Jacob's rebuke. All is blessing on the head of Joseph. He truly was, as Jacob later said, 'separate from his brethren', Gen. 49. 26. What a picture of the Lord Jesus! The Lord Himself said, concerning the Father, 'I do always those things that please him', John 8. 29. There was never a moment in the life of the Lord Jesus when the Father did not find delight in Him. In this He was separate from the sons of men.

Jacob proceeded to say, 'Joseph is a fruitful bough, even a fruitful bough by a well; whose branches run over the wall', v. 22. The emphasis here is on his fruitfulness and the assurance that blessings from this would be extended to others. Here, again, we see the Lord Jesus as the 'true vine', John 15. 1, and His fruitfulness is evident, not only towards God, but also towards man. The statement made concerning Joseph anticipated the time when the blessings that Christ had yielded would extend far beyond the bounds of Israel, and embrace the Gentiles. We see a glimpse of this in John chapter 4, where the Lord introduces the fact that the time had come when importance would no longer be attached to physical places and their boundaries but the criteria for true worship would be 'in spirit and in truth', John 4. 24.

But now Jacob speaks concerning the sorrows that Joseph had endured, 'The archers have sorely grieved him, and shot at him, and hated him', v. 23. How true this was of the Lord. The fruitfulness of the Lord Jesus, and His consequent favour with the Father, brought out the venom and hatred of His brethren.

Finally, Jacob refers to Joseph's strength and victory over all enemies, v. 24. The blessing is heaped upon him, anticipating the ultimate triumph of our Lord over every foe.

April 8th

Genesis 49. 27-33

BURY ME WITH MY FATHERS

This meditation brings us to the scene of Jacob's departure. He finished blessing his sons then he gave them instructions about his burial. Although Egypt had played a part in the purposes of God, it was not the land of promise. Jacob did not belong in Egypt and he wished to be buried in the land that God had promised to Abraham, to Isaac and to himself. Canaan did not yet belong to the children of Israel. The only part of it they owned was the cave of Machpelah, which Abraham had bought as a burial ground from Ephron the Hittite, the place where Sarah, Abraham, Isaac, Rebekah and Leah were already buried. It could be said of them 'these all died in faith not having received the promises', Heb. 11. 13. Jacob wished to be buried there, beside men and women of faith.

The situation in our day somewhat parallels the conditions described above. God has placed us here, but we do not belong here. The Lord Jesus said, 'They are not of the world, even as I am not of the world', John 17. 16. We are 'strangers and pilgrims' here, 1 Pet. 2. 11. We also have received 'great and precious promises' yet to be fulfilled, and ultimately the only thing we have in this world is a burial ground. Millions of saints have died in faith, anticipating the day when the Lord will return to rob the tomb of its prey and transport us to glory; there to enjoy 'an inheritance incorruptible, and undefiled, and that fadeth not away, reserved in heaven for you', 1 Pet. 1. 4.

It is also worthy of note, that when Abraham asked for the cave of Machpelah to bury Sarah, he refused to accept it as a gift. He wanted it to be secure, and he insisted on paying the full price, and weighing out the silver before all the sons of Heth.

This is a precious thought when related to the saints today. The Lord Jesus has paid the price in full before the world of men and demons, and the dust of saints down through the ages is secure, awaiting the voice of the archangel and the trump of God which will awake them from the grave, and raise them incorruptible to join with those who are living, 'and so shall we ever be with the Lord. Wherefore comfort one another with these words', 1 Thess. 4. 17-18.

April 9th

Genesis 50. 1 -14

GO UP, AND BURY THY FATHER

Jacob had bound Joseph by an oath to bury him with his fathers in the cave of Machpelah. Since this would involve a considerable exodus from Egypt, Joseph thought it necessary to seek permission from Pharaoh. It is interesting to note that whereas previous chapters described the ready access that Joseph had to Pharaoh, here he approaches him through intermediaries. Is it possible that the disposition of Pharaoh towards Joseph was not as it once had been and that here we have the first hint of Pharaoh distancing himself from Joseph and his brethren? It is also true in our day; once the world had taken from us all that we can give, how readily it turns its back on us and popularity soon gives way to toleration and ultimately to hostility. So it was with the Lord, and so it will be with us.

But Pharaoh was entreated and he sent the intermediaries to Joseph saying, 'Go up, and bury thy father'. Joseph went with all his brethren, but left behind their flocks, herds and their families. Pharaoh saw to it that the funeral procession was escorted by the symbols of Egypt's might and power, 'chariots and horsemen . . . a very great company'. Isn't it wonderful to see how God can use the 'powers that be' to protect and to preserve the people of God in days of crisis, cf. Acts 23. 10-24.

Jacob's passing was a time of deep mourning. The Egyptians themselves mourned for seventy days, v. 3. Then, when the funeral procession reached the threshing floor of Atad, we read, 'there they mourned with a great and very sore lamentation: and he (Joseph) made a mourning for his father seven days', v. 10. The passing of men of God produces both corporate and personal mourning. Scripture does not deny us the right to mourn and indeed it would be a strange thing if we did not shed tears when loved ones depart. But our sorrow is different from the sorrow the world experiences. The apostle said, 'that ye sorrow not, even as others which have no hope', 1 Thess. 4. 13. This is the difference – we have hope. The apostle Paul wrote, 'now is Christ risen from the dead, and become the firstfruits of them that slept', 1 Cor. 15. 20, and we, the harvest, will follow shortly, 1 Cor. 15. 23.

April 10th

Genesis 50. 15-26

YE THOUGHT EVIL, GOD MEANT IT UNTO GOOD

As we read the story of Joseph and his brethren, we learn that they gave him cause for tears on many an occasion. The verses before us tell of yet another occasion when Joseph wept. Not this time because of what they had done to him, or even because of their response to some test that Joseph had applied, but now because of their failure to appreciate the completeness of his forgiveness. After Jacob had been buried, Joseph's brethren were of the mind that his beneficence towards them had only been because their father was alive and they feared that Joseph would now repay them for their cruelty towards him. When Joseph learned of their fears it broke his heart and when they prostrated themselves before him he said, 'Fear not', v. 19.

How it must also grieve the Lord when believers do not enjoy peace of mind and heart despite the completeness of the forgiveness that He has procured for them. When they keep going back to the past, asking God for forgiveness of their sins, forgetting that their sins were all dealt with judicially at the cross. God has done with the sin of the believer for all eternity. 'Therefore being justified by faith, we have peace with God through our Lord Jesus Christ', Rom. 5. 1.

But notice the basis upon which Joseph was able to be so beneficent and kind to those who had been the cause of all his grief and sorrow. He said to them: 'ye thought evil against me; but God meant it unto good', Gen. 50. 20. Joseph had an expansive view of the events that had transpired and was able to see that even the shameful cruelty of his brethren had been used to fulfil God's purposes for his life.

As believers, we can become bitter in the face of injustice if we lose sight of the sovereign purpose of God in our lives. But we will find the ability to be expansive in our forgiveness if we remember that 'all things work together for good to them that love God', Rom. 8. 28.

> 'His purposes will ripen fast,
> Unfolding every hour;
> The bud may have a bitter taste,
> But sweet will be the flower'. [WILLIAM COWPER]

April 11th
Exodus 1. 1-22

A NEW KING, WHICH KNEW NOT JOSEPH

By this time, Jacob, and Joseph, and the Pharaoh who had favoured them, had departed the scene, and another Pharaoh arose of whom it is recorded, he 'knew not Joseph', v. 8. It is most unlikely, given the impact that Joseph had on Egyptian history, that the new Pharaoh did not know about him historically, but rather that he consciously denied the greatness of Joseph in Egypt and wished to have nothing to do with his people. Pharaoh lived up to the worst expectations that Israel could ever have imagined and began a systematic attempt to eliminate them.

Pharaoh made a fatal mistake in this regard because he was entirely ignorant of the plans that God had for this people. These plans had been ratified under covenant with Abraham, Isaac and Jacob, and in taking this action against them he was effectively setting himself and his kingdom against God. When at last God began the process that would bring Israel out of Egypt in triumph, Pharaoh said to God's messengers, 'Who is the Lord, that I should obey his voice to let Israel go? I know not the Lord, neither will I let Israel go', Exod. 5. 2. The same man who did not know Joseph, did not know the Lord. Yet he was soon to find out who the Lord was, and would be broken and crushed by His power, as he was compelled to send Israel out.

In our lives there may be times when we find ourselves being favoured by this world's great ones; only later to find that the tide has turned and we are left vulnerable and oppressed. We should not be surprised at this. Think about our blessed Lord. There was a time when men would have taken Him and made Him King. They spread palms in His path, and cried, 'Hosanna: Blessed is the King of Israel that cometh in the name of the Lord', John 12. 13. But it was not long before there were those who cried, 'Away with him, away with him, crucify him', John 19. 15. Like Pharaoh, they were entirely ignorant of God's purposes being wrought even through their hostility. So, we take courage amidst the increasing hostility of this godless world, knowing that God's sovereign purposes cannot be thwarted and that soon ours will be the victory.

April 12th

Exodus 2. 1-10

BEHOLD, THE BABE WEPT

On the human level the tears of a baby may soften the hardest of hearts. However, we would never imagine that the tears of a baby would ever be used to save an entire nation. But such was the case when the cruel Pharaoh gave the edict that all the male children born to the Israelites should be cast into the Nile. Undoubtedly Pharaoh knew that his powerful dynasty could be threatened by equally powerful nations with their weaponry and armies, but he never dreamt that his power would begin to be broken by the cry of a child.

Pharaoh's daughter went down to the Nile to wash, and, under God's direction, she came upon the small ark of bulrushes that Moses' mother had made for him, to put him in the Nile. As soon as Pharaoh's daughter opened it the child began to cry and, we read, 'she had compassion on him', v. 6. That weak cry had more power that all the armies around, and before long the future deliverer of the children of Israel was being nurtured by his own mother for Pharaoh's household.

This is the story of our Bible, how that God delights to take the things that are weak and powerless to destroy the mighty. We see this exemplified at the cross. Here was a scene of apparent weakness and defeat, but Paul writing to the Corinthians tells them, 'For the preaching of the cross is to them that perish foolishness; but unto us which are saved it is the power of God', 1 Cor. 1. 18. Again, speaking of worldly wisdom, Paul wrote, 'But God hath chosen the foolish things of the world to confound the wise; and God hath chosen the weak things of the world to confound the things which are mighty; and base things of the world, and things which are despised, hath God chosen, yea, and things which are not, to bring to nought things that are: That no flesh should glory in his presence', 1 Cor. 1. 27-29. Of our Lord Jesus, the poet wrote,

> 'By weakness like defeat
> He won the meed and crown;
> Trod all our foes beneath His feet
> By being trodden down'.

[SAMUEL GANDY]

121

April 13th

Exodus 2. 11-25

WHO MADE THEE A JUDGE OVER US?

When Moses turned 40 years old, he saw the affliction of his people under Pharaoh and, thinking to make a start in reversing the situation, he slew an Egyptian who was abusing one of his brethren. He did this with a pure motive because, we are told, 'He supposed his brethren would have understood how that God by his hand would deliver them: but they understood not', Acts 7. 25. Moses misjudged his brethren's attitude towards him but, more seriously, he misjudged the mind of God as to how and when he would deliver Israel. Later, when he attempted to intervene in a dispute among his own brethren, they asked him the question, 'Who made thee a prince and a judge over us?', Exod. 2. 14.

The question his brethren asked was a legitimate one, because Moses had acted on his own authority and ahead of God's time. Although 'learned in all the wisdom of the Egyptians', Acts 7. 22, he had much to learn in the school of God before he would emerge as 'a prince and a judge' among His people. Moses had the right motive but the wrong method and the wrong timing.

So it is in our experience. Very often we see problems clearly, as did Moses, and act precipitously under our own authority and alienate our brethren. Moral authority to act in leadership among the people of God must be given by God and no other. Even a right motive is not a licence to proceed to correct a situation if God has not created the circumstances to do so, and given the authority to act in them.

The Lord Jesus is the supreme example of the principle we have in mind. He was always aware that the right thing must also be done at the right time if it was to be effective. A recurring phrase in the Gospel of John is, 'His hour had not yet come'. He would not act precipitously, even if pressured to do so by Satan in the wilderness, or by Mary at the wedding in Cana of Galilee. Nothing would provoke Him to act ahead of His Father's will. May God give us the wisdom to act in His time and in His way in every situation, and to wait upon the Lord to direct and control.

April 14th

Exodus 3. 1-10

OUT OF THE MIDST OF THE BUSH

These verses record the great moment of Moses' call and commission by God. Moses had made an abortive attempt to be a deliverer forty years earlier, Exod. 2. 11-12, but now God's time had come and Moses would be fitted for the task.

The manner in which God revealed Himself to Moses was most instructive to him, as it is to us. Moses turned aside to see a bush that burned yet it was not consumed, and it was from there that God spoke to him. Undoubtedly, the burning bush was symbolic of the trial through which the children of Israel were passing at that time, where Pharaoh was intent on their destruction. But, as with the bush, the fires of affliction had not consumed them. This miracle has been repeated countless times in the history of Israel. Many nations have tried to destroy them, but they cannot achieve their objective, the bush is not burned; God has great plans for them.

When God first spoke to Moses, He reminded him that He was the God of Abraham, Isaac and Jacob. How this must have thrilled the heart of Moses, because he knew about the unconditional promises that God had made to them regarding the future of His people. Now that their God had appeared to him, he was ready to take up His call. When God called to him from the bush Moses said without hesitation, 'Here am I', v. 4. God then told Moses that the affliction of His people had not gone unnoticed and that the time of deliverance had come; he was to be God's instrument in delivering them. God told Moses that He was going to 'bring them . . . out', v. 8, that He might bring them in, and we know that's exactly what He did.

There is much in this event to encourage the people of God today. We learn that God will never renege on His promises to us. God always keeps His word and, whatever fires of affliction may beset us, we hear Him tenderly say, 'Fear not: for I have redeemed thee . . . thou art mine . . . when thou walkest through the fire, thou shalt not be burned; neither shall the flame kindle upon thee', Isa. 43. 1-2. True it is, as Nebuchadnezzar confessed under similar circumstances, 'there is no other God that can deliver after this sort', Dan. 3. 29.

April 15th

Exodus 3. 11-22

I AM THAT I AM

When God commissioned Moses to be the deliverer of Israel, he was a reluctant candidate. One of the concerns he had was that just as the people had rejected him as a deliverer forty years before, they would do so now. Moses wanted to be able to tell them by what authority he was coming to them as a deliverer; he wanted a name. It was then that God revealed to him this, perhaps the greatest of all His names – I AM THAT I AM. God told Moses, 'Thus shalt thou say unto the children of Israel, I AM hath sent me unto you', Exod. 3. 14. Indeed, this was not a title given only for the immediate moment of crisis, but later God said to Moses, 'this is my name for ever, and this is my memorial unto all generations', Exod. 3. 15.

Here is a title that embraces every other title by which God has ever made Himself known to His people. Whatever His people needed Him to be, He would be. An author of a past century wrote so eloquently, 'Jehovah in taking this title was furnishing His people with a blank cheque, to be filled up to any amount. He calls Himself 'I AM,' and faith has but to write over against that ineffably precious name whatever we want', C. H. MACKINTOSH.

It is significant that in the New Testament this great 'I AM' title is claimed by the Lord Jesus in the Gospel of John. The conclusion is inescapable, that the Jesus of the New Testament is Jehovah of the Old Testament. Just as God promised His ancient people Israel that He would be to them whatever they needed, so also the Lord Jesus showed Himself to be the answer to every need. Using the 'I AM' prefix, the Lord added seven powerful metaphors – the Bread of Life; the Light of the World; the Door of the Sheep; the Good Shepherd, the Resurrection and the Life; the Way, the Truth and the Life; the True Vine. What sufficiency lies in the Lord Jesus! He is the Saviour of sinners, and Succourer of His saints.

> 'Jehovah, great I AM!
> By earth and heaven confessed,
> We bow and bless the sacred Name,
> For ever blessed'. *[THOMAS OLIVERS]*

April 16th

Exodus 4. 1-17

WHAT IS THAT IN THINE HAND?

While the Israelites were suffering under Egyptian bondage, unknown to them God had already initiated a plan whereby they would be rescued from slavery and led into a land of their very own. He had chosen an unlikely leader for the project. Named Moses, he had been born to an Israelitish family in Egypt, raised and educated as a member of the royal family but had fled from Egypt when he was discovered to have raised his hand against an Egyptian citizen and killed him. Pharoah sought his life. Now, happily married, he was busily employed minding his father-in-law's sheep in the wilderness. Ever fearful, he suffered from a lack of confidence. On the other hand, he had a deep interest in the Lord's people and knew the local terrain intimately, which was just as well as he would have to lead a whole nation out of Egypt, through the wilderness and into Canaan.

One day, while tending sheep near Horeb, the mountain of God, he noticed a bush fire. This was not unusual for, in the arid and combustible conditions, it often happened, but what was strange was that though the fire burned the bush was not consumed. On closer investigation Moses discovers that God is there and the ground is holy. God tells Moses of His rescue plan and recruits him to lead the operation. Moses has second thoughts, however, and protests his inability to do such a thing. At this point, God says, 'What is that in thine hand?', v. 2. Like Moses, God, of course, knew exactly what it was – an ordinary shepherd's rod. Instructed to cast it on the ground Moses was appalled when it turned into a vicious serpent. God tells him to catch it by the tail and suddenly it was a rod again! This lesson was to show Moses that God could and would use everything that was ordinary to Moses in extraordinary ways.

We need to be aware that God can take the common possessions, talents or circumstances we have and turn them into things he can use for His service. And, for Moses, this rod became famous. So, there is no excuse. Whatever you have, God can use, provided you offer it to him. Your smallest talent can become His biggest weapon. 'What is that in thine hand?'

April 17th

Exodus 4. 18-31

LET MY SON GO

This passage is about firstborn sons. Firstly, we have, by implication, Moses' son, Gershom, v. 20; then God's son, Israel, v. 23; followed by the firstborn son of Pharaoh; then those of the Egyptians. The firstborn son had a very special place of affection and honour with corresponding privileges and responsibilities. He carried with him the hopes and aspirations of his father for the future. To attack him was seen as an unacceptable challenge against all that his father and family held dear. Indeed, it was unforgivable and demanded a very strong response.

It appears that neither Moses nor his sons were circumcised and, for a man of God, that was a serious omission. On the journey to Egypt, therefore, this needed to be put right and the mysterious account of God 'trying to kill' him (either Moses or Gershom, but probably the latter) at the inn is the means of it being accomplished. Zipporah, Moses' wife, recognizes the threat to her husband and children and she responded with courage to rectify the fault. Moses owed much to the women in his life: his mother; his sister Miriam; the daughter of Pharaoh, an Egyptian; and his wife Zipporah, a Midianite. Many men who served God in the past (e.g., Timothy) and many today have cause to be thankful for the support of their womenfolk.

As Moses returns to Egypt he takes with him the rod of God and is under instruction to 'do all these wonders before Pharaoh'. God reveals to him the information that the king will be increasingly against the release of the people. There would be a heart-hardening process, the result of which would be sheer obstinacy to God's demands and his people would suffer horrible plagues due to his intransigence. Moses was told to say, 'Israel is my son, even my firstborn. And I say unto thee, Let my son go'. The nation is described as the firstborn indicating its place of blessing and privilege in the divine plan.

In anticipation of refusal, Moses is told to say, 'If thou refuse to let him go . . . I will slay thy son, even thy firstborn'. The brothers now meet the leaders of Israel and share their hopes for divine intervention. When they heard, they 'believed, bowed their heads and worshipped'. Let us join them!

April 18th

Exodus 5. 1-23

I WILL NOT GIVE YOU STRAW

This chapter highlights the suffering of the people of God together with the questions, complaints, failures and blame-culture which accompanied it. Moses and Aaron had visited Pharaoh alone, though God had said that elders should accompany Moses, 3. 18. They requested release to worship the God of the Hebrews. To Pharaoh this was intolerable and he commanded that the people should be made to pay for their impudence because he thought that they, as the Egyptians did, should see him as divine. Straw for brickmaking would no longer be provided, yet the daily tally would be the same. This was wholly impossible to achieve. Yet, the tyrannical dictator steadfastly maintained, 'I will not give you straw'.

Brutal aggression, the beating of the overseers, the harsh and repeated demands, the ill treatment, etc., remind us of a later generation of Jews who also found themselves in similar circumstances in the evil concentration camps of Europe during World War II. Pharoah's objective was to divide the people, as they fought for survival, were exhausted by hard labour and mentally threatened. There would be no time allowed to think of God, worship or escape. Simply to be alive would be a great achievement. If their ambition was worshipping God then working for Pharoah would soon extinguish that!

In evil circumstances many questions are asked and so here we have six: 'Who is the Lord?'; 'Why do you hinder the people's work?'; 'Why have you not fulfilled the task?'; 'Why dealest thou thus?'; 'Why has thou so evil intreated the people?'; 'Why is it thou hast sent me?'. Complaints are very evident too. Pharoah complains to Moses; the taskmasters to the officers; the officers to Pharoah; then the officers to Moses; finally, Moses complains to God. Blame is pinned on various people: Pharoah blames Moses; the taskmasters blame the officers; then, the officers the taskmasters; the officers then blame Moses; Moses blames God.

Grievous suffering and persecution are not easy to bear. Let us remember the suffering people of God and 'weep with them that weep'.

April 19th

Exodus 6. 1-13

I WILL REDEEM YOU

It must have seemed to Moses and the Israelites that the attempt to cut a deal with Pharaoh had gone tragically wrong. Obviously, Moses and Aaron had been outmanoeuvred by the king of Egypt and innocent people were now suffering the consequences of cruel bondage and anguish of spirit, v. 3. So, what is to happen now? Five times in the chapter God announces, 'I am the Lord' – a new revelation of Himself. Delegated control by Pharaoh will be seen to be ineffective as Jehovah Himself takes over. The Lord explains to Moses that the people will not escape but will be expelled! It is not that they will be brought back; they will not even be allowed back!

This is a chapter of communication between God, Moses and the people. At least twelve times it is mentioned, as God prepares to move on with the divine plan. He is concerned that Moses continues to be actively involved, even if currently no one will listen to him. God reaffirms His determination to bring the people out to the Promised Land by making reference to three steps He had already taken: 'I have established my covenant'; 'I have heard their groaning'; and, 'I have remembered my covenant', vv. 4, 5. This is followed by seven promises of divine action: 'I will bring you out'; 'I will rid you out of their bondage'; 'I will redeem you'; 'I will take you to me'; 'I will be to you a God'; 'I will bring you unto the land'; 'I will give it you', v. 7. These seven solemn undertakings are enveloped between the two statements, 'I am the Lord'. Among them, as we have seen, is the promise of redemption, 'I will redeem you', and how it will be accomplished in great judgement and power. The thought of redemption sometimes occurs in connection with land and, in Leviticus 25, it is regarding a near kinsman redeeming, for market price, a family member out of slavery.

God is the only near kinsman of Israel. He declares His willingness to pay the price to bring His son out of Egyptian slavery into freedom. The price will be suffering, the blood of a lamb shed as God passes through and passes over in what will become known as Passover evening. The redemption price for enslaved sinners today is still the same: the blood of the Lamb.

April 20th

Exodus 6. 14-30

HEADS OF THEIR FATHERS' HOUSES

The main body of today's reading is a genealogy, though it is not in the usual Old Testament form. It starts with the mention of the first three sons of Jacob and, when Levi is reached, his line is then pursued, while his younger brothers go unmentioned. This is possibly because the genealogy seeks to follow the priestly line of Levi and its primary purpose is to show that Moses and Aaron are not only in that priestly line but are also direct descendents of Levi, and so, of course, of Jacob and Abraham. Having said that, it also demonstrates that the family from which they came was really pretty ordinary. Look at the names. Not many of them are well known. But, ordinary men and women with access to God can change the world!

The people concerned are described as 'heads of father-houses'. The thought may be that fathers are responsible for all that happens within their family circles and should be appreciated for their position before the Lord. The genealogy also tells us the names of Moses' parents, Amram and Jochebed, she being either Amram's aunt or cousin, v. 20. The purpose of this genealogy interrupting the narrative at this point is shown in verses 26 and 27, 'these are that Aaron and Moses'. It is to identify them clearly to Israel as being fit for leadership responsibility. In verse 26, Aaron is mentioned first, as he was older than Moses (by three years), and in verse 27 Moses is first, because he is the chosen leader for this venture of faith. It is salutary to remember that now, as then, God can use very ordinary people from ordinary families in a most extraordinary way. May He be graciously disposed to use you and your family.

Verse 28 returns to the story left earlier at verse 12. God repeats, 'I am the Lord' in both verses 28 and 29. Divine power will be at work. Moses, however, is still reluctant. He says, 'I am of uncircumcised lips, and how shall Pharaoh hearken unto me?' In view of what had happened following the initial visit to the king, this may be understandable. However, it is a return to the old excuse, 'I am not eloquent'. Moses needed to learn that his weaknesses were God's strengths and what he was not able to achieve God could. Perhaps we should remember that today?

April 21st

Exodus 7. 1-13

I WILL HARDEN PHAROAH'S HEART

Let battle commence! This section reveals a re-invigorated Moses as he and Aaron make an official visit to the king of Egypt. Jehovah had said He would arrange that Moses would be 'a god' to Pharoah and that Aaron would be his prophet, indicating that, in all confrontations with Pharaoh, Moses would be in control. With God so obviously on Moses' side we might have imagined the result would be a softening of the monarch's heart but the opposite was true. His heart 'was hardened'. This hardening is spoken of in three different ways. On ten occasions the Lord did the hardening. On three occasions Pharoah did it himself. On five occasions there is the statement that 'his heart was hardened' without attribution to either God or Pharoah. Subsequently, the hearts of his servants were also hardened.

In verse 3, God promises to multiply His signs and wonders in Egypt and, in the following chapters, we note nine plagues leading to the ultimate and terrible tenth judgement of the death of the firstborn ones. The nine are in three sets of three:

1 water to blood	4 flies	7 hail
2 frogs	5 murrain	8 locusts
3 lice	6 boils	9 darkness

The first two in each set came with 'health warnings' while the last one of each set came unannounced. Signs 1-3 covered the whole land, affecting both Egyptians and Israelis, while 4-9 affected Egyptians only. This demonstrates God's power over nature and His ability to discriminate when He chooses so to do. The signs grew in intensity as they hit the gods of the river (1- 2), the land (3-6) and the sky (7-9) and Pharoah's heart hardened in proportion. All this was known to God and Moses in advance yet the plan must be pursued step by step so as to give sinners opportunity for repentance and for God to show mercy.

As they go into Pharaoh he demands a miracle – and he certainly gets one! Aaron casts down Moses' rod and it becomes a large and aggressive serpent. The magicians somehow seem to do the same but find theirs 'swallowed' by Aaron's just as the Egyptians would later be 'swallowed' by the Red Sea. The magicians were left rodless; a permanent reminder of God's power.

April 22nd

Exodus 7. 14-25

WATERS TURNED TO BLOOD

The River Nile is of huge importance to Egypt. It is nearly 2,000 miles long and is formed from The Blue Nile and The White Nile which themselves are each over 1,000 miles long. It enters the Mediterranean Sea on the north coast of Egypt and at that point is over 100 miles wide. The river provided everything for Egypt's prosperity: water for drinking, washing and irrigation; fish to eat; it was also the means of transportation. Economically, it was vital and dependence on it was total, so much so that the Egyptians worshipped it as a god. These signs, sent by God, are later described as plagues ('blows') against the gods of Egypt and this first is obviously against the river gods.

The claim of God for the release of His people is once again put to Pharaoh and yet again he flatly refuses. Aaron lifts his rod, stretches it out over the river, strikes the waters and they are turned to blood. Some would seek to explain that it was not blood but was merely blood-like. No doubt the Egyptians had theories as to why it was not real blood. The Bible says it was. We who believe in the power of God have no need to rationalize the miraculous. Blood was everywhere! It was in the river, streams, ponds, pools and even in wooden and stone containers. The blood quickly killed off all the fish and no doubt other aquatic creatures also and their decaying bodies, together with the sickly smell of blood, caused an unavoidable stench throughout the whole land.

Another Pharaoh's daughter, eighty years earlier, had gone to see what was in the river and there she discovered the baby Moses, helpless and vulnerable and depending on the mercy of God. Pharaoh had that morning gone to the river perhaps to bathe, rest and worship and had discovered there the now mighty Moses, the servant of Jehovah. Now Egypt would look to him for mercy! The magicians soon appear on the scene and while not able to reverse what had happened they again seem to replicate the miracle. But this must have been spurious; all the water had already been turned to blood. As the people panic and dig for water Pharaoh returns to his palatial comforts, hardens his heart and still refuses to let the people go.

131

April 23rd

Exodus 8. 1-19

FROGS AND LICE

It is said that frogs are a symbol of fertility and, for the Egyptians particularly, they played an important role in nature worship. Normally, these small Nile frogs, known as *dofta*, stayed in the river but, annually in the summer, could be seen sporting and sunning themselves on the exposed banks of the retreating waters. They could be fun to watch. However, some time after the end of the blood plague these harmless creatures were called out of the river after yet another refusal by Pharaoh of Moses' reasonable request to let the people go. But they were no longer fun! In their millions they evacuated the river and invaded the land entering unhindered into the homes of the people. They were to be found in rooms, beds and ovens. They even attached themselves to the people. They were everywhere! The magicians in their zeal could not stop the frogs and succeeded only in bringing even more out of the river, thus adding to the discomfort and irritation of the people.

Eventually, Pharaoh calls for Moses and begs that he intreat the Lord to take away the frogs and, if that happens, he promises to let the people go. Moses does so and, on the morrow, the frogs die. The Egyptians gather them up and pile them in heaps and, as the sun rises, they decay and stink. However, Pharaoh sees the respite as a window of opportunity to go back on his commitment and chooses to do so. He again hardens his heart and spurns the grace of God shown to him. So, unheralded, the dust of the earth is made into lice. These small stinging gnats soon cause havoc. The magicians cannot replicate this act as it is a work of creation which is the province of God alone. They warn Pharaoh that 'this is the finger of God'.

Alas, today there are many who continue to spurn His grace. They seem to treat grace as a sign of weakness and take up the refrain so clearly rejected by Paul, 'Shall we continue in sin that grace may abound?' God is indeed longsuffering but in every experience there comes a time when 'enough is enough' and God will bring judgement on those who tempt Him with promises of reform and undertakings to be obedient to His word. We must all take heed and not presume on God's mercy.

132

A GRIEVOUS SWARM OF FLIES

In spite of all these setbacks Pharaoh continues his life as normally as possible and unashamedly and publicly worships his gods on a daily basis. As he approaches the river to bathe, meditate and worship he is confronted by Moses and Aaron. They warn him of a further plague of flies unless he relents. Furthermore, these swarms of insects which would very probably be 'armed to the teeth' with stings, bites and infection will attack the Egyptians and 'corrupt' their land and homes, but they would be forbidden of God to enter the land of Goshen where the Israelites lived. Perhaps Pharaoh viewed this as a minor irritation compared with the earlier plagues so he does nothing. Maybe God is running out of ideas and His arsenal is becoming depleted. Maybe he could see this thing through after all!

So, the great army of an evil mixture of disease-carrying flies arrives. It is much worse than Pharaoh had imagined. Stings, bites, eggs laid everywhere. They enthusiastically devour the land. This is not just inconvenient – it is horrendous. In Goshen, however, all is peace and quiet as the swarms stop at the border, as though hitting a screen and do not enter. Clearly, the God of Israel is One who can control the uncontrollable, order the smallest of His creatures exactly what to do and where to go, and differentiate between the world and His own people. What a God He is!

Eventually, Pharaoh relents, at least partially. He is prepared to negotiate – to do what he thinks will be the minimum to satisfy God's demands yet to retain his own pride and position with his people. The Israelites can stop work for a few days to worship but they must not leave Egypt but sacrifice in the land. Moses explains that would be an abomination to the local people and cause ill feeling if not outbreaks of violence. So Pharaoh moves a little bit more. They can, at a push, go to the wilderness but 'not far away'. He asks Moses to put his offer to the Lord. Moses does so and in grace God accepts and the flies are removed instantly so that not even one remains.

But Pharaoh again hardens his heart and reneges. He continues in sin hoping that grace will abound. Beware!

MURRAIN AND BOILS

Today, we meditate on the scriptures which describe for us the fifth and sixth plagues in this series of strikes against Pharaoh and Egypt. Verses 1-7 cover the murrain of livestock and verses 8-12 the sore boils which afflicted the people. Once again, neither of these two plagues affected Goshen, the dwelling-place of God's people.

The murrain is supposed to be a kind of fever, maybe a Redwater fever, which attacks the animals' nervous systems making them irritable and dangerous, before leaving them exhausted and incapable of eating or drinking. Death quickly ensues. All the domestic animals are affected including 'cattle, horses, asses, camels, oxen and sheep', v. 3. Pharaoh is, in grace, offered another opportunity for repentance which, predictably, he spurns. A 'set time on the morrow' is determined for the blow to land. It does, and it is 'very grievous'. The result? All the animals of Egypt die, but not a single animal in Goshen is affected. Pharaoh determines to check out this phenomenon for himself and, discovering it to be so, he inexplicably and wickedly hardens his heart.

Whereupon, God instructs Moses to go to the lime kilns, take the residual fine black soot from the furnaces and, in the sight of Pharaoh, ceremoniously sprinkle it towards heaven. As he does so the soot is carried away on the wind and falls throughout Egypt and where it falls on man or beast it becomes nasty boils. It is clear that not all beasts were destroyed by the murrain. All beasts 'without distinction' were indeed killed but perhaps not all 'without exception'.

These boils are probably sore and itch, and soon they break open and become infected. But where are our 'friends' the magicians? Can they do the same, or similar? Verse 11 tells us that they cannot any longer stand before Moses. They too are covered in boils. They have had enough and retreat discomfited and demoralized.

Now we read in verse 12 that God hardens Pharaoh's heart. This may seem harsh but it would have happened anyhow. God only does to him what he was doing to himself.

April 26th

Exodus 9. 13-35

MIGHTY THUNDERINGS AND HAIL

We noted in yesterday's reading that the magicians were absent at the vital moment. So, apparently, was Aaron. This has come down to a straight battle between the two main protagonists, Moses and Pharaoh. We now arrive at the first of the last three plagues. Through Moses, God tells Pharaoh that it was He who had raised him up and set him on the throne of Egypt. And why? So that in him God's mighty power should be demonstrated and His name be revered throughout the whole world. Pharaoh may have thought the throne was his by legal descent, but not so, God had put Him there. And He controls those who rule today and puts them in place according to His own plans. Political position may seem to be achieved in a number of ways but in the end it is God who puts men in positions of leadership in the kingdoms of the world. God then asks Pharaoh why he is being obstructive, 'Why, in view of My goodness to you, are you building up in your heart and mind a great dam of opposition against My plans and My people?'

Moses is told to indicate that 'tomorrow, about this time' a very grievous hail will strike Egypt, but not Goshen. All remaining livestock should therefore be moved indoors to avoid destruction in the ferocity of the hail. Some Egyptian people had learned to fear God and did so; others did not and suffered the inevitable consequences of their carelessness. When the hail arrives it is accompanied by thunder and lightning with balls of fire running along the ground. While some animals could be protected, the crops growing in the fields could not, especially those almost ready to harvest, such as the flax and the barley. The 'wheat and the rie', however, are spared as they were not yet grown up. This plague was dangerous and frightening and its ferocity made Pharaoh, in a rare moment of realism, send again for Moses.

This disaster causes him to confess his sin (only modified by the phrase 'this time') and admit that he and his people are guilty and that God is righteous. He implores Moses that the hail, the thunder and lightning should be stopped. They do stop. Yet, callously, he and his servants harden their hearts yet again.

April 27th

Exodus 10. 1-11

HOW LONG WILT THOU REFUSE?

At the beginning of this chapter we are given three reasons why God will continue His signs in the land of Egypt: i) so that Pharaoh might see, understand and respond to them; ii) that the story of the signs and God's great power should be told to succeeding generations of the children of Israel; and iii) that it be demonstrated with clarity that He is the Lord. All three objectives have, of course, been more than fully met as the story of the plagues of Egypt and the divine deliverance of a nation from slavery continue to interest children and inspire adults over 4000 years later. God's purposes are always fulfilled.

The question, 'How long?' occurs twice in the passage. Firstly, it is asked by Moses, and secondly, by Pharaoh's advisors who can see that Egypt is being destroyed. Moses in his question shows us that what was keeping Pharaoh from compliance with the will of God was pride. He refuses to humble himself. Pride is a great wickedness which resists even the most obvious solutions to problems and, as in Pharaoh's case described here, finds problems to solutions.

Moses now describes in vivid detail the awful consequences of Pharaoh's continuing obstinacy. There will be a plague of locusts. The way this is put in verse 4 is indicative of the horror and fear this brings to the people and the devastation to the country. Says Moses, 'I will bring the locusts'. Verse 6 shows that this will be the greatest locust invasion that the world has ever or will ever see. Pharaoh's officials get the message. They have had more than enough already and they tell Pharaoh to bow to the inevitable and to let *all* the people go. They remind the king, 'knowest thou not yet that Egypt is destroyed?'

Everything that Egypt depended on for economic prosperity and now its survival had already gone or was about to go. The great river had been polluted, there was no longer a fishing industry, decaying dead bodies of animals filled the streets, agriculture was destroyed and, if the locusts come, the remaining fruit trees and crops which had survived the hail will be wiped out. Famine is imminent. Pharaoh's late offer that men only could go is rejected by Moses. That is not God's way!

April 28th

Exodus 10. 12-29

I WILL SEE THY FACE AGAIN NO MORE

In the remaining verses of this chapter we have described for us the plague of locusts as it happened and the further plague of darkness. As Moses stretches out his rod, an east wind springs up and blows all day and all night (giving Pharaoh further time to change his mind) and, in the morning, the locusts arrive. Locusts are described in Proverbs as 'having no king'; they are uncontrollable. Again, they are described as 'creeping things that go on all fours and have legs above their feet', that is, they are jumping insects. They breed and multiply more rapidly than any other insect and Joel says they can 'fly, run, leap, march and climb', but, worst of all, they 'swallow' all in their path. Joel also tells us they have teeth like lions – a powerful ability to destroy everything. Indeed, he speaks graphically of them in his prophecy in terms of a hostile invading army. 'A fire devoureth before them; and behind them a flame burneth; the land is as the garden of Eden before them; and behind them a desolate wilderness; yea, and nothing shall escape them'.

Eventually, Pharaoh is persuaded and in grace the Lord sends a strong west wind which blows away the locusts and dumps them dead in the Red Sea. But still Pharaoh will not let the people go! Now, the last of the nine plagues arrives without warning. It is 'thick darkness' – a darkness that can be felt. It is impossible to see anything. Everybody is alone in their own darkness. Not only is natural light gone but it appears artificial lights also fail. In our terms there was a complete power outage, and no sun moon or stars to relieve the darkness. The country comes to a complete standstill for three days, 'but all the children of Israel had light in their dwellings'.

Pharaoh sends for Moses and makes another offer. Women and children may go, but not the cattle or the herds. Moses bravely replies, 'Our cattle . . . shall go with us; there shall not an hoof be left behind'! At this, Pharaoh, whose country has been brought to its knees and whose people are humiliated, looses his temper and says, 'See my face no more; for in that day thou seest my face thou shalt die'. Moses replies, 'I will see thy face . . . no more'. The stage is set for the final denouement!

April 29th

Exodus 11. 1-10

YET WILL I BRING ONE PLAGUE MORE

This plague is the tenth and the last. It is significantly different to the previous series of nine as it is targeted to kill the most precious of Egypt's people. This is the end!

Indeed, the effect of this action, says God, will be that Pharaoh 'shall surely thrust you out hence altogether', v. 1. Moses now encourages all his people to borrow from their Egyptian neighbours jewels of gold and jewels of silver. God sees to it that the Egyptian people will look very favourably on this unusual request and, when the Israelites leave, they will come out with 'great spoil'. By now the common people of Egypt had come to the conclusion that Moses was a powerful leader of a significant people and they respond to the request with open-handed generosity. Egypt is stripped of gold and silver which later will be used in the making of vessels for the tabernacle.

The timing of the fatal blow is set for midnight. It will mean the death of 'all the firstborn in the land of Egypt . . . from the firstborn of Pharaoh . . . to the firstborn of the maidservant that is behind the mill; and all the firstborn of beasts'. The realization of what has happened will result in a great strangulated cry from a people devastated in life and now also by death. But the firstborn of the children of Israel will be safe because the Lord 'will put a difference' between the Egyptians and the Israelites. This seems to be an awful thing that God will do to Egypt. Could it not have been lessened somewhat? No! It reminds us of just how seriously God regards sin and what He is prepared to do in the defence of His people. And He will still take drastic action today, as He deems it necessary, for their protection.

The message of judgement is conveyed to Pharaoh but he remains unmoved. Moses tells him that all his servants and all the people of Egypt will bow down to Moses and urge him to go and take his people with him. But Pharaoh will not budge. Moses, the meekest man in all the earth, marches out of the palace 'in a great anger'. The Lord meets him and reassures him that he has not failed. Pharaoh will not move even for God, at least for the moment. But release will come! It will be death for the Egyptians and life through the blood for the Israelites.

April 30th
Exodus 12. 1-20

I WILL PASS THROUGH . . . I WILL PASS OVER

In the verses before us we have the announcement of the preparations to be made for leaving Egypt. They are most significant as they point forward to the Lamb of God, and the efficacy of His shed blood for our salvation.

Moses tells the people that a New Year is to begin now, six months ahead of time, and this will set the pattern for the Jewish religious year; it is a new beginning. On the tenth day of this month a one-year-old male lamb without blemish is to be selected. Kept under close observation for four days (lest any hidden fault becomes apparent) it will be killed on the evening of the fourteenth day. Its blood will be sprinkled on the door-posts and lintels of the houses so that it is visible from outside. Innocent blood was to be shed for Israel's redemption. This all speaks beautifully of Christ. He is perfect, yet was examined for any fault or weakness during the four days of His last visit to Jerusalem for the final Passover. Matthew 21 verses 1 to 17 is one day, verses 18 to 25. 46 is the second day and, at the beginning of chapter 26, He says there are another two days to Passover. Then, He was slain, shed His blood and became a substitute, wholly effective when His blood is applied.

Inside the house there will be great activity. The slain lamb is to be roasted whole and, when ready, eaten with bitter herbs and unleavened bread, speaking, perhaps, of the bitter sufferings of slavery and an eagerness to depart. The whole family will eat together and all should have their loins girt, shoes on their feet and staff in hand. All must be ready to leave in the morning, immediately the order is given.

The Lord's activities are described in two phrases: 'passing through'; 'passing over'. In 'passing through' all the firstborn in Egypt die. In 'passing over' all of Israel is saved. The 'passing through' is delegated to a destroying angel. The 'passing over' is done by the Lord Himself. He says, 'When *I* see the blood *I* will pass over you'. The wings of divine protection are more than sufficient for the claims of any destroyer. *This is the Lord's Passover* to be celebrated annually, until finally the Lamb is slain at Calvary, and the price of redemption is paid in full.

May 1st

Exodus 12. 21-39

A GREAT CRY IN EGYPT

Reconciling God's grace with His judgement is impossible, naturally speaking, but W. E. VINE writes, 'While the gospel reveals Him as infinitely merciful, His mercy is not characterized by a leniency toward sin. The Scriptures never reveal one attribute of God at the expense of another. The revelation of His wrath is essential to a right understanding of His ways in grace'.

It is important to remember therefore that there was a judicial aspect to the first Passover night. The Lord's initial message to Pharaoh was, 'Israel is my son, even my firstborn . . . if thou refuse to let him go, behold, I will slay thy son, even thy firstborn', Exod. 4. 22-23. Subsequent events revealed that Pharaoh did not heed the warning. Indeed, he hardened his heart long before the Lord hardened it, Exod. 9. 12. The Lord's long-suffering towards him ended with this tenth, and final, judgement. His judgements are never a first resort; they come in only when mankind's sin reaches its peak. In Egypt's case it fell at midnight; a time when they would have least expected it. None was precluded, and thus 'a great cry' was heard throughout the dark streets of Egypt, 'for there was not a house where there was not one dead', v. 30. Such will be the judgement that ultimately falls upon this godless world. Today, in grace, the Lord 'is longsuffering to us-ward, not willing that any should perish, but that all should come to repentance. But the day of the Lord will come as a thief in the night', 2 Pet. 3. 9-10.

However, the Lord's ways in grace were displayed in the fact that there was no 'great cry' from the children of Israel's 'sheltered' houses. They 'did as the Lord had commanded', v. 28. They took the hyssop, which spoke of humility and simple faith, cf. Lev. 14. 4, 6; Ps. 51. 7; 1 Kgs. 4. 33, and applied the blood to the lintel and the doorposts, v. 22. The Lord had promised, 'When I see the blood, I will pass over you', v. 13. His provision was the ground of their peace. Later on, when their children enquired as to its meaning, they were able to say, 'It is . . . the Lord's passover, who passed over the houses of the children of Israel in Egypt', vv. 26-27.

Have we, by faith, appropriated the value of Christ's blood?

140

May 2nd

Exodus 12. 40-51

THE ORDINANCE OF THE PASSOVER

It was on Passover night in an upper room in Jerusalem that the Lord Jesus introduced something new by taking bread and saying, 'This do in **remembrance** of me', Luke 22. 19. It has been the privilege and responsibility of believers ever since to obey His command on the first day of every week, Acts 20. 7. Similarly, the first Passover had **remembrance** at its heart.

A promise remembered, vv. 40-41. The Lord promised Abram that He would deliver his seed out of bondage, Gen. 15. 13-14. He remembered that promise and delivered them, v. 41. He was, indeed, faithful that promised.

A night to be remembered, v. 42. The children of Israel were moving on to a better land, but they were encouraged to look back to 'a night to be much observed unto the Lord', v. 42. It was not envisaged that any should neglect to 'keep it', v. 47. MATTHEW HENRY writes, 'a yoke heavier than that of Egypt was broken from off our necks, and a land better than that of Canaan set before us'. It is unthinkable therefore that Christians should neglect to remember the Lord Jesus as He requested.

The ordinance to be remembered, vv. 43-51. Firstly, all 'outsiders' were excluded, unless they were circumcised. A. W. PINK writes, 'A wall was erected to shut out enemies, but the door was open to receive friends'. By God's grace we 'are no more strangers and foreigners, but fellow-citizens with the saints, and of the household of God', Eph. 2. 19, and thus we are among those who are in a position to remember Him. Secondly, there was unity; the same law embraced both Jew and Gentile, v. 49. The bread at the Lord's Supper speaks of the unity of the local assembly, 'For we being many are one bread, and one body: for we are all partakers of that one bread', 1 Cor. 10. 17. This unity was further displayed in that the Passover lamb was to be eaten 'in one house . . . neither shall ye break a bone thereof', v. 46, which points us forward to the cross, John 19. 36. Do we display the same unity when we 'come together in the church . . . into one place', 1 Cor. 11. 18, 20?

The children of Israel did 'as the Lord commanded', v. 50. Do we have the desire to be obedient and to remember Him?

May 3rd
Exodus 13. 1-16

SANCTIFY UNTO ME ALL THE FIRSTBORN

C. A. COATES writes, 'No one is entitled to say, "All I want is to be sheltered from judgement by the blood of the Lamb". The same voice that said, "when I see the blood, I will pass over you," says, "Hallow unto me every firstborn." All that is sheltered by the blood is hallowed to God'. Paul reminded the believers at Corinth that 'your body is the temple of the Holy Ghost . . . ye are not your own . . . ye are bought with a price: therefore glorify God in your body, and in your spirit, which are God's', 1 Cor. 6. 19-20. A redeemed people belong to the Redeemer. Sadly, disobedience prevents us from walking a pathway of separation to God that glorifies Him. It was forty years before Israel reached the land and obeyed these ordinances!

It was fitting that 'the firstborn . . . among the children of Israel, both of man and of beast', v. 2, should be sanctified (dedicated) to the Lord, because each one of them was a living testimony to redemption through the death and shed blood of the lamb. They may have been in the position of the firstborn, but this would have counted for nothing if the blood had not sheltered them. C. H. MACKINTOSH writes, 'The grace of God alone had made them to differ, and had given them the place of living men in His presence'. The firstborn ass, an unclean animal, that was redeemed with a lamb or otherwise it died, v. 13, reminds us that 'we are all as an unclean thing', Isa. 64. 6, but we were redeemed 'with the precious blood of Christ, as of a lamb without blemish and without spot', 1 Pet. 1. 19. Such grace deserves a personal response of gratitude and dedication for 'that which the Lord did unto *me*', v. 8. It is vital that we pass on the challenge of sanctified living to succeeding generations, v. 8.

The presence of leaven, which speaks of evil, will prevent holy living. Thus, all the children of Israel were instructed that 'there shall no leavened bread be eaten . . . there shall no leavened bread be seen . . . in all thy quarters', vv. 3, 7. Even the very sight of leaven would have aroused their appetites. We must guard every area of our lives against the corrupting influences of the world. Like the children of Israel, we would do well to keep these precepts ever before us, v. 9.

Exodus 13. 17-22

THE LORD WENT BEFORE THEM

Moses reminded the children of Israel that 'with a strong hand hath the Lord brought thee out of Egypt', v. 9. However, this was only the beginning of a long and challenging journey. They were vulnerable when Pharaoh let them go and a great deal of uncharted territory lay before them. JOHN RITCHIE wrote, 'As sinners we need a Saviour, as captives we need a Deliverer, and as pilgrims we need a Guide'.

Firstly, 'God led them not through the way of the Philistines', v. 17. He knows the condition of His people at any given time and therefore He will always take them along a pathway He knows they can manage. There was much warfare ahead for the children of Israel, but they were not ready to face it so soon after their years of hard bondage. The obvious route away from Egypt was 'through the way of the land of the Philistines', v. 17, because it was the nearest and the shortest. However, He spared them from facing war, knowing that this would have discouraged them and led to their return to Egypt.

Secondly, 'God led the people about', v. 18. Naturally speaking, the direction He took them was incomprehensible. It was longer and there were formidable obstacles in the way: the wilderness and the Red Sea. However, the psalmist reminds us, 'As for God, his way is perfect', Ps. 18. 30.

Thirdly, God visited them, v. 19. Joseph had predicted this day by saying, 'God will surely visit you; and ye shall carry up my bones away hence with you'. It must have been a great encouragement to the people to see Moses taking 'the bones of Joseph with him', thus fulfilling this prophecy and testifying to the faithfulness of God.

Fourthly, 'the Lord went before them', v. 21. He went before them in a pillar of a cloud by day and a pillar of fire by night. It was the visible sign of His constant presence with them to guide and protect them in every circumstance of their wilderness journey. We may not have the cloud today, but we have the ministry of Christ, the indwelling Holy Spirit and the completed word of God to guide. Let us be conscious of, and dependent on, their guidance and protection throughout today.

May 5th

Exodus 14. 1-14

STAND STILL,
AND SEE THE SALVATION OF THE LORD

It is thrilling to enjoy the same sense of security that Paul experienced as he wrote to the saints in Rome, 'If God be for us, who can be against us? . . . Who shall separate us from the love of Christ? . . . we are more than conquerors through him that loved us', Rom. 8. 31, 35, 37. As God's redeemed people, we belong to Him and nothing can reverse this. Sadly, like the children of Israel, we oftentimes find our confidence wavering.

Satan moves swiftly to sow seeds of doubt when he loses possession of us, particularly when he senses our insecurity about the way that the Lord is leading us. Sometimes, of course, that pathway can be perplexing, v. 3. The children of Israel obeyed the Lord's guidance and yet found themselves in an impossible situation, where it seemed as if all was lost, v. 2. Surrounded by mountains, sea and desert, and with the Egyptians in pursuit, their confidence was shaken to the core. They took their eye off the Lord and focused on the enemy, which was a sure recipe for doubt and fear, v. 10. They reached such a low ebb that they turned upon their leader, and even expressed the desire to return to the ownership and service of Egypt.

If we fixed our gaze upon the Lord more, we would be saved from despair when the way becomes hard. The God who redeemed us will not let us out of His grasp, no matter what tactics the enemy might use. The children of Israel belonged to Him and He was not about to allow them to die in the wilderness. It is not surprising to discover how soon Pharaoh forgot the Lord's dealings with him in judgement, but it is sad to see how quickly His people forgot His deliverance of them. They were occupied with self, but His concern was with His own honour and to this end He hardened Pharaoh's heart, v. 4. Far from deserting them, His clear command to them was, 'Fear ye not, stand still, and see the salvation of the Lord . . . the Lord shall fight for you', vv. 13, 14. C. H. Mackintosh writes, 'It is only when we have learnt to "stand still" that we are able effectually to go forward . . . wait only upon God . . . there is no uncertainty when God makes a way for us'.

144

May 6th

Exodus 14. 15-31

INTO THE MIDST OF THE SEA ON DRY GROUND

It is evident that the crossing of the Red Sea was a major landmark in Israel's history. The Lord reminded His people of it through the prophet Isaiah, 'I have redeemed thee, I have called thee by thy name; thou art mine. When thou passest through the waters, I will be with thee', Isa. 43. 1-2. If only they had clung on to this promise they would have been spared so much heartache. However, Paul highlighted the sad reality when he wrote, 'All our fathers were under the cloud, and all passed through the sea; and were all baptized unto Moses in the cloud and in the sea . . . but with many of them God was not well pleased: for they were overthrown in the wilderness', 1 Cor. 10. 1, 2, 5.

It is hard to believe that the Israelites forgot their deliverance so quickly. This life-changing event had separated them from the oppression of Pharaoh and had linked them to Moses. He had commanded them to 'stand still', v. 13, but the time came when the Lord told them to 'go forward', v. 15. They witnessed the angel of God (a pre-incarnation appearance of Christ) moving behind them to protect them from the enemy, vv. 19-20. Miraculously, they saw the seemingly insurmountable barrier of the sea divided, v. 21, and 'by faith they passed through the Red sea as by dry land: which the Egyptians assaying to do were drowned', Heb. 11. 29. They ought to have moved on with confidence, but instead they displeased God.

However, lest we become complacent, Paul reminds us that, 'All these things happened unto them for ensamples: and they are written for our admonition', 1 Cor. 10. 11. They point us to the great landmark of the death and resurrection of the Lord Jesus. Just as Moses led the people into the midst of the sea, so the Lord Jesus took upon Himself flesh 'that through death he might destroy him that had the power of death, that is, the devil; and deliver them who through fear of death were all their lifetime subject to bondage', Heb. 2. 14-15. Our baptism bears witness to our deliverance through the death, burial and resurrection of Christ, and our commitment to walk in a way that brings pleasure to Him. Let us take care that we do not, like Israel, forget such a great landmark and displease the Lord in our walk.

May 7th

Exodus 15. 1-21

HE HATH TRIUMPHED GLORIOUSLY

Imagine you were encouraged to worship, but at the same time instructed not to sing! This first recorded song in the Bible allowed the children of Israel to express the deep feelings of their hearts. It provides an excellent example for us as we sing and 'make melody' in our hearts to the Lord, Eph. 5. 19.

The precentor of the song. Although all the people were involved, it was Moses who led them in their worship, v. 1. If he, as their spiritual leader, had not struck up the note of praise, it is unlikely that they would have done so.

The participants in the song. The opening statement, '*Then* sang Moses and the children of Israel this song', v. 1, confirms that it is only a redeemed people who can truly sing. There had been no song from them when they were in Egypt, only sighing and groans. However, they now stood upon redemption ground and therefore they had much to sing about. Although there was a corporate aspect to the song, it was intensely personal; hence the use of 'I', v. 1, and 'my', v. 2. The worship of a congregation will only reach its potential as each individual contributes and has a personal relationship with God.

The pre-eminent Person of the song. The first words set the tone, 'I will sing unto the Lord', v. 1. The Egyptians revealed their pride when they said, 'I will', v. 9; however, the children of Israel ascribed all the praise to the Lord. The focal point of their worship was, indeed, 'He', 'Him', 'Thy', 'Thou' and 'Thee'; there was a total absence of self-glorification. They ascribed their salvation to Him, 'for he hath triumphed gloriously', v. 1. They knew Him as a 'man of war' in relation to their enemies, v. 3, but they also appreciated that they were recipients of His mercy, v. 13. True worship stems from a desire to honour Him for who He is and what He has done.

The panorama of the song. It opens with, 'The horse and his rider hath he thrown into the sea', v. 1, and concludes with, 'The Lord shall reign for ever and ever', v. 18. C. H. MACKINTOSH writes, 'It begins with redemption and ends with the glory. It begins with the cross and ends with the kingdom'. How comprehensive is the scope of our worship?

May 8th

Exodus 15. 22-27

MARAH . . . THERE HE PROVED THEM

Many of the Lord's people will be passing through 'bitter waters' today. We can rejoice and sing when all is well with our lives, but it is all too easy for the song to be silenced when the way becomes hard. The Red Sea experience led to an uplifting song, v. 1, but the children of Israel's mood soon changed, even though they were where the Lord had sent them.

Firstly, 'they went out into the wilderness', v. 22. They would, no doubt, have preferred to be found in more hospitable surroundings. Indeed, they soon discovered that it was a water-less place. It is a vital, but often painful, lesson for believers to learn from the Lord the true nature of the world.

Secondly, 'they came to Marah (bitterness)', v. 23. They had experienced a God who was in control of the waters, vv. 8, 19, but it now seemed as if He had lost control. Their relief at finding Marah turned to dismay when they discovered that the waters were bitter. They had to learn, as we do, that the Lord does not always lead us 'beside the still waters', Ps. 23. 2. Neither does He promise to remove the bitter waters, but He makes them bearable and delivers us out of them, cf. 2 Tim. 3. 10-12.

Thirdly, 'the people murmured', v. 24. They murmured against Moses, instead of seeking wisdom from God, Jas. 1. 5. However, Moses cried to the Lord and He gave him the answer in the form of 'a tree, which when he had cast into the waters, the waters were made sweet', v. 25. The **closeness**, the **cutting down** and the **casting into** the waters of that tree speaks power-fully of Christ and His cross. He experienced the bitter waters of Calvary; therefore He is able to minister to the needs of His people in the midst of their trials. He has been, 'touched with the feeling of our infirmities', Heb. 4. 15. He, alone, can 'sweeten every bitter cup'. He says to us in the midst of the furnace of our trials, 'I am the Lord that healeth thee', v. 26.

Fourthly, 'they came to Elim (strength)', v. 27. Obedient believers, v. 26, come through times of testing the stronger for it. Suddenly, the experience of Marah seemed worth the suffering as the children of Israel camped by the 'twelve wells of water, and threescore and ten palm trees'.

Exodus 16. 1-13

BEHOLD, I WILL RAIN BREAD FROM HEAVEN

It is natural for us to want to remain at the comfortable points in our lives, when all appears to be well with our souls. There is little doubt that, given the choice, the children of Israel would have opted to remain encamped by the waters and palm trees of Elim. Nevertheless, the Lord led them into the wilderness of Sin, an unattractive place to the natural eye. It was situated 'between Elim and Sinai', v. 1; the law had not yet been given. It was a place where the grace of God was revealed.

God's grace is undeserved. The backdrop was dark. The 'whole congregation', not just a few, were murmuring about their lot and they turned upon both Moses and Aaron, v. 2. Moses charged them with murmuring against the Lord, vv. 7-8. They were so disgruntled that they would rather the Lord had slain them in Egypt than redeemed them, v. 3. They even argued that life had not been so bad in Egypt, v. 3. It is hard to comprehend that only a month had passed since their release from Egypt. Their ingratitude deserved judgement, but instead it gave an occasion for the Lord to display His grace. He promised them, 'I will rain bread from heaven for you', v. 4.

God's grace tests. We might be led to the conclusion that it is permissible to murmur against God, so that His grace might abound towards us. The Lord made it clear that the bread was given 'that I may prove them, whether they will walk in my law (that is, the commands concerning the bread), or no', v. 4. He took them up on their boasts. They lusted after the 'fleshpots' of Egypt: therefore He gave them 'flesh to eat'. They claimed to have eaten 'bread to the full'; therefore He gave them 'bread from heaven'. Every act of God's grace towards us tests the motives of our hearts and our willingness to obey.

God's grace points to Christ. The people ate flesh (the quails) in the evening, but they gave no satisfaction; however, in the morning they were 'filled with bread', v. 12. In that bread that came to them just where they were, they saw 'the glory of God', v. 7. In our following meditations we will discover that it speaks to us of Jesus as 'the bread from heaven' who can satisfy our spiritual needs, John 6. 35. Do we feed on Him, daily?

May 10th

Exodus 16. 14-22

MANNA

An amazing sight greeted the children of Israel each morning; real bread lay on the barren face of the wilderness. The Lord called it 'bread', but they called it 'manna' – 'What is it?' It was a mystery to them; they had not seen its like before, v. 15.

The bread given. Moses said, 'This is the bread which the Lord hath **given you** to eat', v. 15. What a contrast it was to the quails! They **came up** on this particular evening, and only once more in Israel's history; however, the bread **came down** each morning. It was unasked for, unheralded and given in grace for their sustenance. The quails lay on the face of the camp, but the gentle and refreshing dew accompanied the manna. The arrival of the quails would have been far from silent, whereas the giving of the bread was as silent as the fall of the dew. How beautifully this speaks to us of the Lord Jesus who said, 'My Father giveth you the true bread from heaven', John 6. 32.

> 'How silently, how silently,
> The wondrous gift is given!
> So God imparts to human hearts
> The blessings of His heaven'. *[PHILLIPS BROOKS]*

The bread's glory. There was nothing outwardly spectacular about the manna. It appeared as 'a small round thing', v. 14, and yet, as such, it was a picture of the eternal Son who stepped into time. He was, indeed, 'the glory of the Lord', v. 7.

The bread gathered. The manna was given in grace, but every man had a responsibility to gather a fresh supply each morning; it was the first work of the day, with the exception of the Sabbath. We must feed on Christ through His word at the outset of every day if we are to be kept from falling. The appetites of the people determined the amount that they gathered, just as our spiritual appetites determine our capacity to feed upon Christ. However, if they gathered more than they needed, they were not to hoard it, as it would not keep; therefore they shared it. This ought to stir in us a desire to pass on to others, in both a spiritual and a practical way, what we have gleaned from feeding on Christ, cf. 2 Cor. 8. 15. May others benefit today from our feeding on Christ, because He can meet every need.

May 11th

Exodus 16. 23-36

SIX DAYS YE SHALL GATHER IT

Moses penned the words, 'And God blessed the seventh day, and sanctified it: because that in it he had rested from all his work', Gen. 2. 3. Sadly, that rest was disturbed when sin came in. Moses did not therefore write of the seventh day again until the Lord rained 'bread from heaven'. Indeed, this is the first time that it is referred to as the 'Sabbath'. It was only that which spoke of Christ that could restore the broken rest.

The gift on the sixth day. The bread from heaven was a miracle of God's grace, but a further miracle was needed for the rest of the Sabbath to be regained. It came in the words of the Lord to Moses, 'the Lord . . . **giveth you** on the sixth day the bread of two days', v. 29. They could cook it if they wished, v. 23, but it was the Lord who ensured that it was preserved until the next day, v. 24. Thus, the people were able to rest on the seventh day, v. 30. Some of them took away from the enjoyment of the day and with impure motives went out to gather; however, 'they found none', v. 27. It was as well that their sin was committed in a time of grace and before the law came in!

The gift of the seventh day. The Sabbath was the Lord's gift for His people's enjoyment: 'the Lord hath **given you** the sabbath', v. 29. He described it as, 'the rest of the holy sabbath unto the Lord', v. 23. It was only One who was holy who could bring in that which was holy; therefore the manna was 'like coriander seed, white; and the taste of it was like wafers made with honey', v. 31, speaking of Christ's holiness and sweetness. We do not observe the day, because we have the substance. We have true and eternal rest through His work on the cross.

The gift of the pot of manna. The pot containing the manna was a constant reminder from the Lord to the children of Israel of His provision for them in the wilderness, v. 32. It was eventually placed within the Ark in the Holy Place of the Tabernacle and therefore it was hidden from the people's view. There are aspects of the life of Christ that are only seen by God; however, true believers today, who rise above difficult spiritual conditions, are promised a share with God in the appreciation of His Son, cf. Rev. 2. 17.

May 12th

Exodus 17. 1-7

SMITE THE ROCK

The smiting of a rock with a rod in a barren wilderness would be ascribed no importance by ungodly men. However, the words of Paul highlight why it is so significant to believers: 'that Rock was Christ', 1 Cor. 10. 4. This seemingly unimportant event is vibrant with meaning, because it speaks of Him. We stand back and marvel at the Lord's words, 'Smite the rock', v. 6.

The commandment of the Lord, v. 1. It is so easy for us, like Israel, to allow adverse circumstances to come between the Lord and us. They pitched in Rephidim, but found that 'there was no water for them to drink'. However, they did not grasp that it was the Lord who had commanded them to go there.

The chiding of the people, vv. 2-3. They ought to have learned by now that the Lord was in control of the waters. They had seen Him divide them and make them sweet. Nevertheless, they were slow to learn that He was able to deliver them out of, not from, the most testing of situations. Sadly, instead of trusting Him, they turned upon Moses and charged him with seeking to kill them. They were incensed enough to have stoned him. Their rejection of him was tantamount to rejecting the Lord.

The cry to the Lord, v. 4. Moses could have been vindictive, but he turned to the Lord; thus providing an example to all spiritual leaders as to how to respond when under attack.

The coming of the water, vv. 5-6. The people deserved judgement, but the Lord was gracious. Judgement fell, but not on them. The rod used in judgement against the Egyptians, Exod. 7. 20, smote (slew) the rock. It points to Christ who bore the stroke of God's judgement. Once the rock was smitten, water gushed out, speaking to us of the coming of the Holy Spirit. Paul wrote that they 'did all drink the same spiritual drink: for they drank of that spiritual Rock that followed them', 1 Cor. 10. 4. Wherever they went in the wilderness, Christ cared for them. May we be conscious of His daily presence with us through His Spirit as we pursue our pilgrim journey. Tragically, Moses had to name the spot Massah (temptation) and Meribah (strife), recalling the people's failure in causing strife by tempting the Lord. Let us resolve never to presume upon His grace.

May 13th

Exodus 17. 8-16

THEN CAME AMALEK

There is an air of inevitability about the opening of today's reading, 'Then came Amalek', v. 8. In spite of the murmuring of the children of Israel, the Lord had graciously caused water to gush out of the rock and an undeserving people had drunk freely. It was at this vulnerable time that Amalek struck.

The Amalekites, one of the bitterest of Israel's enemies, traced their origins back to Esau's children, Gen. 36. 12. They represent an ever-present enemy, v. 16, who has no fear of God and longs to see the extinction of His people, Deut. 25. 18. They speak of the power of the flesh (our fallen nature, inherited from Adam) in the life of every believer. Each one of us will be fighting this battle today. We can never lose our salvation in the midst of it, but we can lose our bright testimony for the Lord, Rom. 8. 13. C. H. MACKINTOSH writes, 'Pharaoh represents the hindrance to Israel's deliverance from Egypt: Amalek represents the hindrance to their walk through the wilderness'.

How can we be victorious in this battle? Firstly, develop a long memory. 'Remember what Amalek did unto thee', Deut. 25. 17. We must never forget the damage the flesh can do. **Secondly, be prepared to do battle against it.** Up to this point the Lord had done everything, but now the children of Israel had to act, 'Choose us out men, and go out, fight with Amalek', v. 9. We cannot change the flesh, but we can, with the help of the Holy Spirit, 'mortify the deeds of the body', Rom. 8. 13. **Thirdly, depend on the power that comes from above.** Success in the battle that was waged in the valley below depended on what took place in the hill above, vv. 9-12. We can face the battle against the flesh with confidence, knowing that we have One 'who is even at the right hand of God, who also maketh intercession for us', Rom. 8. 34. **Fourthly, persevere in prayer.** If there is harmony and support for each other, as there was with Moses, Aaron and Hur, we will discover the power of prayer to deliver us. **Fifthly, get to know God.** Proving God in the battle led the people to know Him better. Moses called his altar, 'Jehovah-nissi'; the Lord my Banner (a beacon in the storm). 'If God be for us, who can be against us?', Rom. 8. 31.

May 14th

Exodus 18. 1-27

WHY SITTEST THOU THYSELF ALONE?

Effective spiritual leadership is absolutely vital if the Lord's people are to flourish. It was while he was with Jethro that Moses had 'led the flock to the backside of the desert', Exod. 3. 1. He learned key lessons about shepherding that were to stand him in good stead. Shepherding the people of God is a demanding and often lonely work. We need to pray that godly leaders will be raised up among us. Important lessons about leadership can be gleaned from this encounter between Moses and Jethro.

Firstly, true leaders are exemplary in family life, vv. 1-7. It would have been a poor testimony if Moses had abandoned his family now that he was leader of two million people. Paul writes, 'For if a man know not how to rule his own house, how shall he take care of the church of God?', 1 Tim. 3. 5.

Secondly, true leaders recognize that they are under-shepherds. When Moses spoke to Jethro, he rehearsed 'all that the Lord had done . . . and how the Lord delivered them', v. 8. He gave praise to the Lord for all that he had achieved.

Thirdly, true leaders understand that leadership is a work among the people, not a position over them. Moses was available among the people 'from the morning unto the evening', v. 13. Jethro was genuinely concerned about his workload. Paul writes of elders, 'If a man desire the office of a bishop (overseer), he desireth a good work', 1 Tim. 3. 1.

Fourthly, true leaders 'feed' the Lord's people, cf. Acts 20. 28. When the people came to Moses, they found a leader whose one exercise was to 'make them know the statutes of God, and his laws', v. 16. He did not give them his opinion on matters; he simply imparted to them the word of God.

Fifthly, true leaders appreciate that they are not alone in the work. Although he was well-meaning, Jethro suggested to Moses that he was alone; therefore this led to the setting up of a system of leadership that was not of God, vv. 17-26. Moses was not alone: the Lord had raised him up and therefore would fit him for the task. Sadly, for a moment, he lost sight of this truth.

Let us value, honour, obey and pray for those who 'have the rule over you' and 'watch for your souls', Heb. 13. 17.

153

May 15th

Exodus 19. 1-8

A PECULIAR TREASURE

No servant of the Lord worked harder than Paul, but he confessed to the believers at Corinth, 'by the grace of God I am what I am . . . I laboured more abundantly than they all: yet not I, but the grace of God which was with me', 1 Cor. 15. 10. All that he was and all that he did could be traced to God's grace. It is good to remember the distance that grace has brought us. JOHN NEWTON expressed his appreciation in one of his hymns,

'Tis grace that brought me safe thus far,
And grace will lead me home'.

The distance the grace of God had brought His people is encapsulated in His words, 'Say to the house of Jacob, and tell the children of Israel', v. 3. Their links with Jacob had led them into Egypt, but by grace Jacob became Israel, 'prince with God'; therefore they bore the name, 'the children of Israel'.

The display of the grace of God was seen in what He had done to the Egyptians, but it was also captured in the graphic description of what He did for them, 'I bare you on eagles' wings, and brought you unto myself', v. 4. They had experienced the speed, strength and tenderness of His deliverance. All that had happened to them since that time had displayed His grace. They had been in the wilderness only for a short time, but had they been left to their own devices they would have perished. They had murmured, complained and lacked faith, whereas the Lord had guided, delivered and provided for them. It was grace that had brought them 'safe thus far'. His great desire was to make them 'a peculiar treasure (special jewel) unto me . . . a kingdom of priests, and an holy nation', vv. 5-6.

Their disregard for the grace of God proved to be a life-changing moment in Israel's history. Against the backdrop of Sinai the Lord tested them by promising the blessings, 'If ye will obey my voice indeed, and keep my covenant', v. 5. Foolishly, instead of casting themselves upon His grace, they boasted, 'All that the Lord hath spoken we will do', v. 8. At that point the law was brought in; that could not save them.

It is divine grace that has made us 'a chosen generation, a royal priesthood, an holy nation, a peculiar people', 1 Pet. 2. 9.

MOUNT SINAI

The children of Israel did not realize the consequences of their boast, 'All that the Lord hath spoken we will do', v. 8. The One who had borne them on eagles' wings was about to reveal Himself to them in thunders, lightnings, a thick cloud, the voice of a loud trumpet, smoke and fire, vv. 16, 18. How grateful Christians should be that we do not stand upon such ground. The New Testament highlights the contrast in two statements, 'For ye are not come unto . . . but ye are come unto', Heb. 12. 18, 22. Let us consider for a moment what the children of Israel came to on that highly significant third day.

Sanctify them, v. 10. They were unfit to appear in the presence of the Lord and therefore they had to sanctify (set apart) themselves and wash their clothes. It was something they had to do, but it did not remove their fear or allow them to enter into God's presence. It ought to have taught them that the cleansing was merely external, but it did not touch their consciences.

Set bounds, v. 12. The people were commanded to 'come up to the mount', v. 13, but they were instructed, 'go not up into the mount, or touch the border of it', v. 12. Any offender would be 'stoned, or shot through (with an arrow)', v. 13. Only Moses and Aaron, who point us to Christ, were called up to the top of the mount, vv. 20, 24. All the people could do was to stand 'at the nether part of the mount', v. 17. The Law could never remove that distance: only Christ can!

Sinai, vv. 16-20. An awesome sight greeted the people, encapsulated in the words, 'and the whole mount quaked greatly', v. 18. The effect was 'that all the people that was in the camp trembled', v. 16. It spoke of the holiness and righteousness of a God before whom the sinner cannot stand on the basis of keeping the law; He is, indeed, 'a consuming fire', Heb. 12. 29.

As believers, we should be thrilled that we have 'come unto mount Sion, and unto the city of the living God, the heavenly Jerusalem'. We have come spiritually and morally to a position that speaks of grace, rest, peace and worship, because we have first come to 'Jesus the mediator of the new covenant', Heb. 12. 22, 24. Israel will come to it in the future, but we enjoy it now!

May 17th

Exodus 20. 1-6

I AM THE LORD THY GOD

Exodus chapter 20 records a crucial point in the history of the children of Israel. Having returned from being with God on Mount Sinai, Moses gave the people the law he received from God. The law, often known as the ten commandments, deals firstly with their responsibilities Godward, vv. 3-11, then those towards their fellow men vv. 12-17. The Lord Jesus summarizes it beautifully by saying, 'Thou shalt love the Lord thy God with all thy heart, and . . . thy neighbour as thyself', Mark 12. 30-31. In the law, God has made known something of His own holy character. It was sin in the human heart that necessitated the law, as Paul indicated when writing to Timothy, 'the law is not made for a righteous man, but for the lawless and disobedient', 1 Tim. 1. 9. Prior to this, God had been dealing with the Israelites in grace. Now He gives them an instrument by which to regulate their conduct and render them accountable to Him, to whom they owe everything.

In these verses God makes Himself known as the great Deliverer of His people. He is omnipotent, eternal, and higher than any created being. The title 'Jehovah' embraces past, present and future. John learnt this on Patmos, 'I am . . . which is, and which was, and which is to come, the Almighty', Rev. 1. 8. He therefore expects His people's undivided loyalty and affection.

Egypt had many gods of man's making, but now the people are linked to the one true God who stands alone in solitary grandeur. 'I am the Lord: that is my name: and my glory will I not give to another, neither my praise to graven images', Isa. 42. 8.

God is holy and just, but His people then, and now, should be thankful that He is also rich in mercy, ready to bless those who love Him and keep His commandments. The law was given to Israel, but we, by grace, enjoy a more intimate relationship with God, through His Son our Lord Jesus Christ. However, we must bear in mind that God's holy character remains unchanged. Obedience and conformity to His will is the path to blessing and happiness. Living for self and the world will bring neither pleasure to Him, nor happiness to us. Paul wrote, 'We make it our aim to please him', 2 Cor. 5. 9 ESV.

May 18th
Exodus 20. 7-12

REMEMBER ... AND ... HONOUR

In reading these familiar verses we may be tempted to think that they were written for Israel and therefore have less relevance for us today than other parts of our Bible. However, apart from the requirement to keep the Sabbath, which is not mentioned in our New Testament, the principles enjoined in these verses are relevant to every child of God in this present age of grace. We are not under slavish bondage to the Mosaic law, yet the Holy Spirit enables us to uphold these principles which display the character of God in any age. 'The law of the Spirit of life in Christ Jesus hath made me free from the law of sin and death', Rom. 8. 2. His power enables us to live for God.

Observe in this section that there is a name to be revered, v. 7, a day to be remembered, v. 8, and a relationship to be respected, v. 12.

In this Godless world, the name of our God and of His Son is normally uttered only in mockery or blasphemy, but this must never leave us insensitive to divine holiness, 'holy and reverend is his name', Ps. 111. 9. James tells us that men 'blaspheme that worthy name by the which ye are called', Jas. 2. 7. The believer must separate himself from such profanity.

The Sabbath day was set apart by God as His day of rest following the finished work of creation, Gen. 2. 1-3. Its mention in Exodus chapter 20 indicates that God intended this day of rest for the good of his people. It is also proof that God completed the work of creation in six literal days, defined by the words 'evening and morning'. God has set aside another day observed by the early church, namely, the first day of the week. This is also based on a finished work – that of redemption, accomplished by the Lord Jesus at Calvary. The first day of the week celebrates His resurrection, and that greater, future rest which His people are to enjoy through Him, Heb. 4. 9.

In an age where family relationships have seriously deteriorated, there is a very real need to honour one's father and mother. This is 'the first commandment with promise', Eph. 6. 2. Young people who follow this precept will have no regrets but ample reward.

May 19th

Exodus 20. 13-17

THOU SHALT NOT . . .

In reading these words, our first reaction may well be that we could never stoop to those levels, and the very thought of such a possibility may be abhorrent to us. However, such is the evil and deceptive condition of the human heart that, apart from the grace of God and the enabling power of His Holy Spirit, nothing is beyond its capability. Furthermore, the Lord Jesus adds fresh light to these injunctions by teaching that, before God's all-seeing eye, the evil tendency of the heart in anger or lust is tantamount to committing the actual deed of murder or adultery, Matt. 5. 21-28; this is high ground indeed!

The last five commandments concern human relationships, and are closely related to each another. However, it is likely that our hearts are most susceptible to the one which says, 'Thou shalt not covet', v. 17, since the other sins spring from that. Writing to the Romans, Paul argues, 'I had not known lust, except the law had said, Thou shalt not covet', and that because of the law, 'sin . . . might become exceeding sinful', Rom. 7. 7, 13.

Only one man, our Lord Jesus Christ, has perfectly fulfilled the law in its every detail, saying 'I delight to do thy will, O my God: yea, thy law is within my heart', Ps. 40. 8. He met its every claim, and died that we might be delivered from its demands. Having died with Christ, we are no longer to live to sin, but unto Him who died for us and rose again, 2 Cor. 5. 15.

The believer's responsibility to the law is beautifully summed up by Paul, 'Owe no man any thing, but to love one another: for he that loveth another hath fulfilled the law. For this, Thou shalt not commit adultery, Thou shalt not kill, Thou shalt not steal, Thou shalt not bear false witness, Thou shalt not covet; and if there be any other commandment, it is briefly comprehended in this saying, namely, Thou shalt love thy neighbour as thyself', Rom. 13. 8-9.

May we renew our exercise today to live so that we may please God, and seek, by His grace, to be a blessing to all with whom we come in contact. May our daily walk and conduct reflect in some measure that of our Lord Jesus, the only One who magnified the law and made it honourable, Isa. 42. 21.

May 20th

Exodus 20. 18-26

SPEAK THOU WITH US, AND WE WILL HEAR

The people have heard God speak from Mount Sinai, and have seen the visible evidence of His presence as He makes known His law to them. The result is that they fear before the august majesty and holiness of God lest they die. 'When the people saw it, they trembled, and stood afar off', v. 18 JND.

Conscious of their sinful hearts, they appeal to Moses to stand between them and God, and God graciously concedes, 'Let not God speak with us, lest we die', v. 19. We find here one of the early illustrations of a mediator. Job was conscious of a similar need when he said in his distress, 'Neither is there any daysman betwixt us, that might lay his hand upon us both', Job 9. 33. Thankfully, our New Testament reveals just how fully this need has been met. 'There is . . . one mediator between God and men, the man Christ Jesus', 1 Tim. 2. 5. He is 'the mediator of a new covenant', Heb. 9. 15 RV. It is through Him alone that we are able to draw near to God, and He to us. As Moses the mediator enters 'the thick darkness where God was', v. 21, we are reminded of the darkness into which our mediator entered at Calvary, when, alone, He bore the judgement for our sin.

In this connection, we may also notice the provision of an altar as the place of blessing. 'An altar of earth thou shalt make unto me, and shall sacrifice thereon', v. 24. 'And if thou wilt make me an altar of stone, thou shalt not build it of hewn stone', v. 25. This is the altar in its simplest form, giving an opportunity for all to approach God in worship with their offering. Any attempt by man to improve or embellish the means of approach to God by his own effort is but to pollute and devalue what God has prescribed. Neither must there be steps to God's altar. Nothing that would speak of man's achievements or display anything of the flesh will find acceptance with Him.

Today, we may think of the perfect, once-for-all sacrifice by which we have been brought into blessing, and, as we do so, we echo the sentiments of Augustus Toplady's hymn, 'Nothing in my hand I bring, simply to Thy cross I cling; naked, come to Thee for dress; helpless, look to Thee for grace; foul, I to the fountain fly; wash me, Saviour, or I die'!

May 21st

Exodus 21. 1-11

I WILL NOT GO OUT FREE

Having given the ten commandments to Israel, God now sets out in chapters 21 to 23 a series of regulatory judgements covering all aspects of life. This is in order that those who administer justice in the land can do so in accordance with the mind of God, adhering to principles which He had decreed. The first of them concerned the welfare of bondservants, both of men, vv. 2-6, and women, vv. 7-11. It was never God's mind that His people should be in servitude, He had recently delivered them from Egypt's tyranny! There were circumstances, however, where men and women were sold as slaves and here God ensures that they are treated humanely and with compassion.

The servant, having served a master for six years, should be free to leave in the seventh year. If he came in by himself, he was to leave by himself; if he came in with a wife, his wife went out with him. If, however, his master gave him a wife, and children result from that marriage, then in the year of release he must go out alone, leaving his wife and children as his master's possession.

However, provision was made for a servant to remain in a lifetime bond of willing devoted service to his master, generated by love. If he 'shall plainly say, I love my master, my wife, and my children; I will not go out free', v. 5, then under the scrutiny of the judges, he was taken to the door of the house and his master would bore his ear as a token of his perpetual service.

Attention has often been drawn to our Lord Jesus as God's perfect bondservant. Motivated by love to His Father and to man He willingly stooped to fill that role, Phil. 2. 7. The idea is expressed in the words, 'Sacrifice and offering thou didst not desire; mine ears hast thou opened . . . Then said I, Lo, I come . . . I delight to do thy will, O my God', Ps. 40. 6-8. To do His Father's will and to finish His work was His meat, John 4. 34. Only when all was fulfilled, He said, 'It is finished; and having bowed his head, he delivered up his spirit', John 19. 30 JND.

As we think of His supreme example in service, we should ask ourselves, 'How devoted are we in our service for Him who is now our Lord and Master?', cf. John 13. 14.

May 22nd

Exodus 21. 12-27

IF ONE SMITE ANOTHER

We have in these verses a reminder of the sacredness of life in the eyes of God, and His protective care over those who may be unjustly victimized. Immediately we think of God's decree to Noah, 'Whoso sheddeth man's blood, by man shall his blood be shed: for in the image of God made he man', Gen. 9. 6. Disregard of this principle exposes the offender to just retribution.

Notice that God distinguishes between wilful killing and that resulting from accident or carelessness, that is manslaughter, v. 13. So far as the former is concerned, there is nothing in our New Testament to suggest that, subject to indisputable proof of guilt, the ancient principle of 'life for life' has been rescinded, cf. Matt. 5. 21; Rom. 13. 4; Jas. 2. 11-13. In the case of manslaughter, God's law has tempered justice with mercy and made provision for the slayer to find refuge. When Israel entered the land, God provided cities of refuge for such, Num. 35. 6-34. Abner provides an example of an opportunity gained by this provision, then lost by a careless act. Abner died at the hand of Joab outside the gate of Hebron, 2 Sam. 2 and 3.

Although the demands of the law were just and equitable, no more, no less, the Lord Jesus, in His 'sermon on the mount', taught that the Christian era makes even greater demands upon His followers, some of whom may have suffered unjustly at the hands of their fellow men, Matt. 5. 38-48. Our Lord Jesus was the supreme example, 1 Pet. 2. 21-23.

The fact is that we have greatly wronged God, yet by His grace we have been freely forgiven. Any wrongs done to us by others must be of a lesser nature and so, in view of God forgiving us, we should emulate that spirit in forgiving others. Such an attitude is demonstrated by the parable of a man who owed his lord ten thousand talents and was freely forgiven the debt. Then, as he went out free, he found a fellow servant who owed him a mere one hundred pence, but refused his plea for forgiveness, Matt. 18. 23-35.

Paul beautifully phrases the idea, 'be ye kind one to another, tenderhearted, forgiving one another, even as God for Christ's sake hath forgiven you', Eph. 4. 32.

May 23rd

Exodus 21. 28-36

ACCORDING TO THIS JUDGEMENT SHALL IT BE

The Israelites were on the whole a rural community and, as well as agriculture, keeping livestock played a large part in their life-style. The Lord God takes this into account and ensures that the principles of judgement protecting the sanctity of life are extended to cover this area. Degrees of punishment are applied in keeping with the degree of responsibility, or otherwise, of the parties whose stock has caused injury.

In the first instance, if an ox gores a person and death results, the ox must die, but the owner is acquitted, v. 28. If, however, from previous experience, the animal is known to be dangerous, then both ox and owner must be put to death, v. 29. Yet, provision is made, in certain cases, for the death sentence to be commuted on payment of a specified ransom, especially where a son or daughter is involved, vv. 30-31.

In the event of a bondservant, whether man or woman, being injured by an ox, the master of the servant shall be paid thirty shekels of silver and the ox shall be stoned, v. 32. The transaction reminds us of the sum for which Judas Iscariot delivered Jesus into the hands of the Jewish leaders – 'thirty pieces of silver', Matt. 26. 14-15. This paltry sum represented man's contemptuous estimate of God's precious Son who came as the perfect Servant and good Shepherd, cf. Zech. 11. 12-13.

God expected His people to act responsibly and with consideration to their fellow men and women. So He gives detailed instructions even regarding the digging of a pit and leaving it uncovered. An unsuspecting farm animal may fall into it and die. The owner of the pit must make restitution to the owners of the beast, 'and the dead beast shall be his', v. 34. The Lord Jesus alludes to the possibility of such accidents in His teaching regarding the Sabbath, Luke 14. 5. God also provided for difficulties occurring between beast and beast where one attacked the other, thereby causing death, vv. 35-36. These rules of government enabled matters to be dealt with in a way that would preserve a harmonious spirit within the community. His statutes and judgements are righteous, and are designed not to impose hardship, but rather to ensure the well-being of all.

ALL MANNER OF TRESPASS

It is clear that God expects His people to live and act in a responsible and considerate way in relation to their fellow men and women, and to ensure that no ill is done to one's neighbour, Rom. 13. 10, or to his property, whether it be beast, corn, or other goods. Failure in the duty of care must be punished and so laws are given here for the protection of property and chattels.

The emphasis here is on the principle of making restitution for damage incurred through actual theft or careless actions, cf. vv. 3, 5, 6 and 12. Note the repetition of the words 'restore', vv. 1, 4, and 'make good', vv. 11, 13, 14, 15. The thief who could not make restitution was to be sold as a slave, v. 3.

Leviticus chapter 6 verses 1-13 gives details of the trespass offering to be brought to the Lord where a trespass has been committed and, again, in addition to the offering, restitution must be made, 'He shall even restore it in the principle, and shall add the fifth part more thereto', Lev. 6. 5. David, when confronted by Nathan in the matter of Uriah's wife, using the parable of the ewe lamb, responded that the offender should die and 'restore the lamb fourfold', 2 Sam. 12. 5-6. Zacchaeus also applied this principle to his actions, Luke 19. 8. Applying divine principles of making good meant that the victim was better off after the event than had the trespass not taken place.

When Adam sinned against God in Eden the tragic consequences were immediately felt by both God and man. However, at the same time, God promised that a Redeemer would come to repair all the damage incurred by the fall and, in addition, to bring about something even better than had originally existed in man's relationship with God. The Lord Jesus is the antitype of the trespass offering, and we recall the psalmist's prophetic words concerning Him, 'then I restored that which I took not away', Ps. 69. 4.

We had offended God by our sin; we could do nothing to make restitution, but the Lord Jesus came as our substitute and, by His death, paid the price that sin incurred, thereby bringing us into fellowship and favour with God. This is a lovely aspect of the sacrificial work of our Lord Jesus Christ.

YE SHALL BE HOLY

People who are in relationship with God and are instructed by Him, as was Israel, must be different from those who do not enjoy such privileges. A righteous God will hold His people accountable to Himself for their conduct in this world. God is also holy and, in keeping with His own character, has called His people to holiness, v. 31. Here then, God instructs the people on some important matters which confirm this.

A man who has seduced a virgin who is not betrothed is to marry her, or, if her father's approval is refused, to provide for her future, v. 16-17. Then follows God's judgement upon certain obnoxious sins where, in order to preserve the purity of the land, the death sentence is to be applied. This includes any who practise the occult, a witch or sorceress, v. 18, or who engage in perverse sexual activities, v. 19, and who seek to displace the worship of God with idolatry, a practice often accompanied by gross immorality, v. 20. Alas that this world in which we live has sunk so low in moral behaviour that things once unthinkable are now accepted without question. It is important for the believer to view these things from God's standpoint, whose standards are unchangeable.

God also instructs the people to have proper regard for the defenceless. Strangers, fatherless, widows and the poor are to be treated with care and compassion, remembering that the Israelites themselves were strangers in Egypt prior to their deliverance. God is not indifferent to the needs of the oppressed; He says that when they 'cry at all unto me, I will surely hear their cry', v. 23. God's people were also to respect those who were judges and rulers amongst them. This reminds us that 'the powers that be are ordained of God', Rom. 13. 1.

The Israelites had always to ensure that God was given His portion. This was an essential element in the life of the people, v. 29-30, and they would be blessed by observing this.

We live in a world stained by sin, but the standards of God have not changed. Peter writes, 'As he which hath called you is holy, so be ye holy in all manner of conversation (conduct); because it is written, Be ye holy; for I am holy', 1 Pet. 1. 15-16.

May 26th
Exodus 23. 1-13

KEEP THEE FAR FROM A FALSE MATTER

God expects that His people behave differently from the men and women who know Him not. These continued injunctions relate to truthfulness, integrity and impartiality. As we think of God's will for His people in the wilderness in relation to their fellow men and women, we, as the Lord's people today, need to live before our fellow men so that they may see in us, in word and deed, those features that will enhance rather than hinder our testimony.

The Lord understands the tendency of the human heart, and warns here about raising a false report. Both ear and tongue are insignificant but important members of the human body and care is needed both in receiving and transmitting rumour, cf. Jas. 3. 2-5. Included here are some matters that are subject to the judicial process, and this should remind us that we live under the eye of 'the Judge of all the earth', Gen. 18. 25. Immeasurable damage can be done to innocent folk when reports are embellished to suit a particular viewpoint.

Even if a man is hostile, God's people must be prepared to help in the recovery of his straying ox or the relief of the burdened ass. God cares for all His creatures, but such acts of kindness may also win over some difficult person, Rom. 12. 20.

Bribery, although so common in our day, is nothing new. It is prohibited by God, as liable to interfere with the course of justice, v. 8. Both bribery and perjury, v. 2, were used by Israel's religious leaders at the trial of the Lord Jesus, and in their denial of His resurrection. It should never be used by believers to secure any advantage in dealing with men of the world.

Again, the people are reminded that they were strangers in Egypt. They should therefore understand the feelings and emotions of those who feel alienated, and they must not oppress them. The Lord has always had a special care for the poor and the stranger, and we need to follow His example.

God decreed that the land was to enjoy a Sabbath every seven years. One reason given here is so that the poor and the beasts of the field may eat from the land. How gracious is our God to meet man's need in such a variety of ways.

May 27th

Exodus 23. 14-19

THREE TIMES IN THE YEAR

In the previous verses God has emphasized the importance of the Sabbath for rest and refreshment, and warns His people to be careful to heed His word. The names of other gods, particularly those which they will find in Canaan, must not be even mentioned. As a redeemed people Israel belonged to the Lord, who had a right to their undivided love and loyalty.

Three times in the year their sons were to appear before the Lord in the place where He was pleased to set His Name and they were to bring some offering to Him. They must not appear before the Lord empty. These feasts, or appointments, span Israel's sacred year. The feast of unleavened bread was observed in the springtime and is closely linked to the Passover. Fifty days later the feast of Harvest, a thanksgiving for God's goodness and, at the end of the year, a gathering to celebrate the harvest and vintage, Exod. 34. 23-25; Lev. 23. 1-44; Deut. 16. 16.

The first of these gatherings would remind them, and us, of the great fact of redemption and the need to purge away the leaven of evil from their midst, 1 Cor. 5. 6-7. The second gathering anticipates the day of Pentecost and the coming of the Holy Spirit, Acts 2. 1. The third gathering anticipates the joyous time when restored Israel shall dwell safely in their own land under the reign of their Messiah, the Lord Jesus Christ, Mic. 4. 1-4. In response to their appearing before the Lord in the place of His choice, they will suffer no loss, for He promises to keep everything at home safe under His protection, Exod. 34. 24.

The sacrifice, v. 18, seems to refer directly to the Passover lamb. Nothing symbolizing evil can come into contact with that which speaks of the unblemished Christ. The fat of the offering, which is for the Lord, must also be offered on the same day.

Seething a kid in its mother's milk seems to have been a heathen practice, maybe connected with fertility rites, but it was abhorrent to God and He gives instructions accordingly. 'God will guard his people from the violation of any single instinct of nature. The milk of the mother was the food, the sustenance of the kid, and . . . must not be used to seethe it as food for others', *Typical Teachings of Exodus*, E. DENNETT.

May 28th

Exodus 23. 20-33

MINE ANGEL SHALL GO BEFORE THEE

What assurance and comfort is to be found in the promises of God to a people tested by the hostile conditions around them. I will 'send an Angel before thee, to keep thee in the way, and to bring thee into the place which I have prepared', v. 20. This divine messenger, with such immeasurable power, is no doubt the angel of His presence, namely the Lord Himself, Isa. 63. 9.

In spite of their rebellion and the vexing of His Holy Spirit, He would preserve them through the wilderness and bring them safely into the good land He had promised them. The certainty of the Lord's presence and power is a formidable asset. Obedience to His voice will bring blessing and prosperity. He will be for them and against their enemies, especially those nations in possession of the land, who are about to be evicted from it.

We too, have the promise of the Lord's presence and power each day of the pilgrimage, He hath said, 'I will never leave thee, nor forsake thee', Heb. 13. 5.

God chose Israel as His own peculiar people, Exod. 19. 5, and they were not to become entangled with the idolatry of Canaan. Jehovah is the one true God and there is none else beside Him. Their love and loyalty to Him is their pathway to victory.

Not only does He assure them of His continued presence, and their safe arrival, but He graciously reminds them of the extent of their inheritance. As He promised Abram in Genesis chapter 15, God has set the boundaries of the land, and that territory is theirs to possess. The sea of the Philistines is the Mediterranean, and the river mentioned here is the Euphrates. Such was the extent of Solomon's kingdom, 1 Kgs. 4. 21. He was but a type of our Lord Jesus Christ, the true King of Israel. Although presently troubled and harassed, a restored Israel will yet enjoy the place prepared for them and dwell in peace and safety under the reign of their Messiah, Ps. 72. 1-19.

The final verse in this section underlines the importance of separating themselves from all that would hinder and ensnare them. We too have before us, a rich inheritance of glory. May the precious promises of God preserve us from everything that would hinder or deflect us on our heavenly pilgrimage.

May 29th

Exodus 24. 1-8

ALL THE WORDS ... WE WILL DO

In chapter 19 the Israelites arrived at Sinai and there Moses was called to the Mount to meet with God. Chapters 20 to 23 record the giving of the law and ordinances in keeping with God's holy character.

In chapter 24, the time had come for Moses to make known God's words to the Israelites as the basis of the covenant relationship between God and them. So, together with Aaron, Nadab and Abihu and seventy elders, Moses was summoned into the mount to meet with God. Only Moses as mediator was permitted to draw near to God. The others worshiped God at a distance.

From being with God, Moses came and communicated God's law to the people, just as he received it, and the unified response of the people was, 'All the words which the Lord hath said will we do', v. 3. The words of the Lord were then written into a book which was called the Book of the Covenant.

Next morning Moses built an altar to God under the mount, and raised twelve pillars representing the twelve tribes. He arranged for sacrifices of burnt offerings and peace offerings to be made. Half the blood was sprinkled on the altar and the people solemnly re-affirmed their obedience to God's word. The rest of the blood was kept to be sprinkled on the people. The Epistle to the Hebrews alludes to the ratifying of this covenant and there we read that the book also was sprinkled, Heb. 9. 18-20. The Lord Jesus also spoke of the new covenant which was ratified by the greater sacrifice of His own blood, Luke 22. 20.

How little these people knew of the propensity of their evil hearts. To their cost, they soon discovered that they were unable to comply with the law to which they had so readily agreed and, in chapter 32, they are found worshipping a golden calf. Well wrote the prophet later, 'The heart is deceitful above all things, and desperately wicked: who can know it?' Jer. 17. 9.

In this age of grace, all believers are encouraged to draw near to God through the sacrifice of our Lord Jesus at the cross. As we consider this wonderful privilege, we should humbly seek each day, in the presence of the Lord, the grace which will enable us to 'walk worthy of the Lord', Col. 1. 10.

Exodus 24. 9-18

INTO THE MOUNT OF GOD

The blood was put upon God's altar and the people, so bringing
both parties together. Having ratified the covenant with blood,
Moses, and Aaron with the elders, returned to the mount. There,
above the cloud and devouring fire, v. 17, God was pleased to
reveal Himself to the company in a remarkable way. 'They saw
the God of Israel'! How much of God or in what form they saw
Him we are not told, but it is unlikely that the actual form or likeness of God was seen, Deut. 4. 15. Reference is made to His feet,
beneath which the sapphire pavement is spread like a footstool,
and the heavens are seen in their brightness and purity, cf. Ezek.
1. 26. The psalmist says of God, 'who hast set thy glory above the
heavens', Ps. 8. 1.

Now that the covenant is in place, the title 'the God of Israel'
seems most appropriate. They were assured by the fact that,
having seen God, they were not smitten by Him, but lived. Others who had seen God, such as Gideon, and Manoah and his
wife, felt similarly, Judg. 6. 23; 13. 20-23. Their eating at this time
seems connected with the covenant, cf. Gen. 31. 54.

Moses was again summoned into the mount to meet with
God, but this time he took Joshua, not Aaron with him, leaving
Aaron and Hur to look after affairs in the camp below. The glory
of God covered the mount, so Moses must wait until God spoke
on the seventh day. Once again alone, Moses was with God forty
days and forty nights. It was during this period that Moses was
given the law on tablets of stone, and was also given the instructions and plan for the tabernacle, clearly indicating God's desire
to dwell amongst His people.

The majesty and glory of God revealed here is truly awesome; but interwoven with those attributes of glory is His grace,
seen making provision for those whom He now owns as His
people to enjoy communion with Him.

We live in a different age with a fuller, more perfect revelation
of God through His Son our Lord Jesus, 'The only begotten Son,
which is in the bosom of the Father, he hath declared him', John
1. 18. Paul teaches us that we are privileged to see 'the glory of
God in the face of Jesus Christ', 2 Cor. 4. 6.

May 31st

Exodus 25. 1-9

BRING ME AN OFFERING

God had called Moses to Mount Sinai, and there, having given him the law on tablets of stone, He told him of His desire to have a sanctuary where He may dwell among His people. The fascinating details of that sanctuary are to be found in later meditations. Here, however, the wonder is that God, who cannot be contained by the heaven of heavens, should deign to dwell in a tent with men, and that he should allow men a part in the work of that sanctuary, cf. 1 Kgs. 8. 27.

Here God graciously makes two requests. Let them 'bring me an offering', v. 2, and 'let them make me a sanctuary', v. 8. In prescribing the required materials, God instructs Moses that all that is offered must come from willing hearts.

God deserves the best from a people who owe everything to Him. But where could this wealth be found in the wilderness? The most likely answer is that on the night of the Exodus, the Israelites were instructed to ask their neighbours for gold and silver, and God gave them favour with the Egyptians, Exod. 11. 2-3; 12. 35-36. The psalmist wrote, 'He brought them forth also with silver and gold', Ps. 105. 37.

All that they had was from God, so the offerings that God desired came from what He had given them in the first place. The principle is also seen in David's exercise regarding the building of the temple, 'All things come of thee, and of thine own have we given thee', 1 Chron. 29. 14. This appreciation was lost in Malachi's day, with the result that the people gave to God only what was unfit for men's use, Mal. 1. 8!

The need for exercised giving for the Lord's work is well documented in our New Testament. The Macedonian churches were a lovely example of that, 2 Cor. 8 and 9. Their giving was based on the fact that they 'first gave their own selves to the Lord'. It is the privilege of every believer who has known the grace of God to show gratitude by practical giving in this way.

Although Moses was to receive and administer the precious things that were brought, the offerings were made to the Lord, given by the willing-hearted, and then handled by wise-hearted men, Exod. 28. 3!

170

June 1st

Exodus 25. 10-16; 37. 1-5

THEY SHALL MAKE AN ARK

The order in which the furnishings of the tabernacle are given is both interesting and significant. We may suggest that if it had been left to Moses' initiative, the natural order may have been to start with the brazen altar and work through the court, to the holy place and into the inner sanctuary, reaching a pinnacle with the description of the ark, the very throne of God. Maybe Bezaleel would first have laid out the plans of the court, and set up the solid framework of the sanctuary. God's way is different. He begins in the inner sanctuary, the place of His presence, and moves out towards man in all his need. When the brazen altar is reached and the order of priesthood has been established, only then do we read of those things associated with man's approach to God, the laver and the golden altar.

The ark of the covenant of the Lord, as it is repeatedly referred to throughout the wilderness journey, was central and fundamental to Israel's national well-being. To us it is a beautiful type of the Lord Jesus; the wood of His humanity overlaid with the pure gold of His deity. Hidden within was the unbroken law, the manna with which He sustained His people and the blossoming rod of His priestly authority. To Israel, although they possibly never saw the ark until much later in their history as it was always covered on the journeys, it was the abiding symbol of the presence of God with them.

The 'crown of gold' not only displayed the glory and majesty of the God of Israel, but had a practical purpose in keeping the mercy seat in place. Hence, the hand of Uzzah in 2 Samuel chapter 6, though with the best of intentions, was seeking to add to a work for which God had already made full provision.

The staves, by which the sons of Kohath transported the ark, were left in place throughout the wilderness journey, a reminder that the 'rest for the people of God' had not yet been reached. Later, when the ark was brought into the temple in Solomon's days, the staves were drawn out but left in such a way that the ends were seen in the holy place, 1 Kgs. 8. 8, a constant reminder to the priestly family of the faithfulness of their covenant-keeping God in bringing them to the place of their rest.

171

June 2nd
Exodus 25. 17-22; 37. 6-9

A MERCY SEAT OF PURE GOLD

In Hebrews chapter 9, the apostle reminds his readers of the pattern of 'things in the heavens' as seen in the Tabernacle, the 'earthly sanctuary'. He draws their attention to the various articles of furniture, then, having reached the 'cherubim of glory shadowing the mercy seat' in verse 5, he restrains himself from developing the detail in order to continue his main theme. His phrase 'of which we cannot now speak particularly', leaves us wondering what gems of spiritual truth would have come from his pen to help us in our understanding of the Tabernacle.

The word translated 'mercy seat' implies a covering, and that aptly describes the purpose and function of this most important feature of the inner sanctuary. Made entirely of pure gold and adorned with cherubim beaten from the same piece, the mercy seat formed the lid of the ark, thus covering the unbroken law placed within. When sacrificial blood was sprinkled upon it on the Day of Atonement, a covering for Israel's sin was provided in the sight of God. This truth finds expression in the New Testament where, 'Christ Jesus: whom God hath set forth to be a propitiation through faith in his blood', Rom. 3. 24-25, is seen to be the One who has met the righteous claims of God against sin. Because of Calvary, a provision is now made whereby God remains just, and yet becomes 'the justifier of him which believeth in Jesus', v. 26.

The mercy seat was also the place of meeting between God and man. This could only be possible when the blood-sprinkled covering was between the tables of stone and sinful man. The men of Beth-shemesh discovered this to their cost when they removed the mercy seat and 'looked into the ark of the Lord', over fifty thousand died, 1 Sam. 6. 19! How good to know that our eternal safeguard will never be removed, 'He shall not fail', Isa. 42. 4; 'he is able . . . he ever liveth', Heb. 7. 25.

Cherubim would seem to be guardians of the holiness of God. As we see them gazing down upon the mercy seat, we are reminded of angelic beings on the resurrection morning, 'one at the head, and the other at the feet', John 20. 12, looking at the empty grave clothes, clear evidence of a work completed.

June 3rd

Exodus 25.23-30; 37. 10-15

THOU SHALT ALSO MAKE A TABLE

We now move from the inner sanctuary, the most holy place, into which the High Priest entered only on the Day of Atonement, to the holy place wherein the priests undertook daily responsibilities.

The first item of furniture brought to our attention is the table of shewbread. Positioned on the north side, to the right as one entered the holy place, it was made of the same material as the ark, wood overlaid with pure gold; thus, we would expect to find lovely features of the Lord Jesus in its construction and use.

This is the first mention of a table in scripture and the word implies a place where provision is made or spread out. So it was that every Sabbath, bread was placed upon the table as food for the priests. For Israel in the wilderness, manna was provided from heaven, and to this the Lord Jesus refers in John chapter 6 in application to Himself as the bread of God which 'giveth life unto the world', v. 33. For the priestly family, however, the shewbread was their food. It was placed fresh upon the table each week, fragrant with frankincense, presenting in type before God the perfections of Christ in both His person and work. The twelve loaves as representing redeemed Israel would also remind us that those who are His own are 'accepted in the beloved', Eph. 1. 6. Having been under the eye of God for His appreciation, the bread then became sustenance for the priests. Our blessed privilege as believer-priests is to 'feed upon' the One who ever delights the Father's heart. We notice also that the table was exactly the same height as the mercy seat. His ability to sustain His people is in equal measure as His power to save.

A double crowned border of 'a hand breadth' was an integral part of the construction. This would ensure the security of the bread and the vessels as they journeyed through the wilderness. Do we not hear the words of the Lord Jesus to His own, 'neither shall any man pluck them out of my hand . . . and no man is able to pluck them out of my Father's hand', John 10. 28-29. What a security there is in that 'hand breadth'!

June 4th

Exodus 25. 31-40; 37. 16-24

A CANDLESTICK OF PURE GOLD

It is difficult to imagine the wonderful scene which met the eye of the priest as he entered through the hangings of the door into the holy place of the Tabernacle. In front of him, the blue, purple, scarlet and fine linen of the vail with its in-worked cherubim. To each side, the boards, overlaid with gold and set in silver. Some five metres from the ground the ten curtains formed a ceiling of beautiful colour and craftsmanship above him. To his right was the shewbread table, before the vail the unique fragrance ascended from the incense altar, and all was illuminated by the shimmering light from the seven branched lampstand. Only the desert sand beneath his feet would remind him that this was an earthly sanctuary, all else were 'patterns of things in the heavens', Heb. 9. 23.

Note that 'lampstand' is preferable to 'candlestick'. The latter is self-consuming, whereas the lights of the lampstand were fed with oil continuously, Exod. 27. 20. No natural light was needed in that sanctuary. God is light! Just as in creation's day, light issued forth from God before the sun was brought into existence. So in the eternal day there will be 'no need of the sun', the glory of God will be the light of it.

The lampstand does not portray in type the Lord Jesus as the 'light of the world'. Remember, it was seen by none but the priestly family ministering in the sanctuary. The talent of pure gold, beaten into its beautiful symmetrical form speaks to us of the glory of deity seen in all its perfection in the Lord Jesus. The word 'beaten' comes from a root meaning harsh or even cruel. Do we perhaps appreciate in this something of the added glory brought to the Saviour through the sufferings of Calvary? Cf. John 12. 28.

Like Aaron's rod which budded, blossomed and bore almonds in one night, signifying the man with priestly authority, Num. 17. 8, so each stage of development is seen in the branches of the lampstand. The oil, like the Holy Spirit, maintains the light, revealing to us as believer-priests the intrinsic beauty and glory of the Lord Jesus in all the glittering splendour of the sanctuary, John 16. 13-15.

June 5th

Exodus 26. 1-6; 36. 8-13

CURTAINS OF FINE TWINED LINEN

After their primary mention in chapter 25, these lovely colours are now brought together with fine twined linen to make the curtains which formed the 'ceiling' of the Holy Place and of the Most Holy. The glories associated with the Lord Jesus as seen in these colours will be considered on a number of occasions as we view the Tabernacle. The blue would remind us of His heavenly character. Though truly man in incarnation, yet He was 'the Lord from heaven', 1 Cor. 15. 47. Purple is ever the colour associated with rule and authority. His glory as the Son of Man who 'must reign', 1 Cor. 15. 25, 'from sea to sea, and from the river unto the ends of the earth', Ps. 72. 8. The scarlet would bring to our minds the glory which accrues to Him on account of His sacrificial work, of which the Tabernacle service was a beautiful and expressive type. The fine twined linen in its spotless purity must proclaim the moral glories of the Saviour, the sinless perfection which marked Him out from all others.

This first of the four coverings is itself called the Tabernacle, and each of the ten curtains, joined together to make the one complete whole, was twenty-eight cubits by four cubits. In other words each was seven times longer than its width. The number four in scripture speaks of that which is universal, while seven is the number of perfection. Hence, even in the dimensions we see displayed the all-embracing excellence of the Lord Jesus in His Person and His work. When joined together, the one piece was forty cubits long. Forty is the number which brings out the full time of testing and trial. Surely we are reminded of One who was fully tested in wilderness conditions throughout His earthly pathway, of whom the Father could say, 'my beloved Son, in whom I am well pleased', Matt. 17. 5. All was held together by golden taches or hooks through loops of blue. All that God in Christ will accomplish is secured on the basis of divine righteousness (gold), and heavenly grace (blue).

Note too, when in place over the framework of the Tabernacle, the material each side was two cubits above the desert sand.

'Thy stainless life, Thy lovely walk, in every aspect true,
From the defilement all around no taint of evil drew.' *[WYLIE]*

Exodus 26. 7-14; 36. 14-19

A COVERING FOR THE TENT

Just as the first covering was called the Tabernacle, so the word used to describe the curtains of goat's hair is simply 'a tent'. A Tabernacle is essentially a dwelling place; a tent, however, is a temporary, mobile shelter, that which speaks of a pilgrim character. Garments of hair were associated with men of the prophetic office; those who brought the word of God to the people. This layer of covering would be hidden from view when the Tabernacle was in place, save only for the 'sixth curtain' which was doubled over the front and visible above the door of the Tabernacle, v. 9. We are reminded that in the Lord Jesus were 'hid all the treasures of wisdom and knowledge', Col. 2. 3. His constant meditation was in 'the law of the Lord', Ps. 1. 2. He was 'that Prophet' raised up, Deut. 18. 15. Just as a small part of the goat's hair tent was seen, so just a small proportion of the life lived by 'the Word made flesh' was openly seen by men.

Above the goat's hair tent was a covering of 'ram's skins dyed red'. This covering was not seen at all when the Tabernacle was erected. In Leviticus chapter 8, when the priesthood was consecrated for service, it was a ram that was taken for sacrifice. The complete and devoted consecration of the Lord Jesus could only be fully seen and appreciated by the Father. 'I delight to do thy will', He would say, Ps. 40. 6. The deep red dye would emphasize the faithfulness of His pathway, obedient, even though it led onward to death, and that, 'the death of the cross', Phil. 2. 8.

The outer covering was of 'badgers' skins'. There is some difference of opinion as to the exact animal from which these skins came. Suffice it to say that it would have been of durable, weatherproof material, covering and protecting the sanctuary. It may have lacked the colour and texture of the hidden layers, but speaks eloquently to us of the Lord Jesus in the eyes of those to whom He had 'no form nor comeliness . . . no beauty' to attract the faithless heart. How different He is in our affections. In the words of the hymnwriter, W. ROBERTSON,

All beauty may we ever see in God's beloved Son.
The chiefest of ten thousand He, the only lovely one.

June 7th

Exodus 26. 15-30; 36. 20-34

BOARDS FOR THE TABERNACLE

The items that we are considering today form the inside framework of the Tabernacle. In all there were forty-eight boards around the north, south and west sides of the structure. Each board was made of shittim wood, v. 15, and overlaid with gold, v. 29. At the base of each board were two tenons or peg-like joints fitting into sockets of silver, v. 19. Giving stability to these boards, there were five bars, v. 26, passing through rings, v. 29. The middle of these five bars reached from end to end, v. 28, whereas the other bars seemed to be half length.

We have met the shittim wood before in other parts of the Tabernacle and will meet it again. There is so much that relies upon the perfect, spotless humanity of Christ. Equally, the significance of the gold has been mentioned before as descriptive of deity. We concur with HENRY SOLTAU when he wrote, 'Each board of the tabernacle, each bar, each pillar, reiterates again and again these great verities, on which salvation depends, on which the whole basis of Christianity rests . . . the person of the Lord Jesus Christ, the Son of the Father, made of a woman, God and Man, one Christ'.

The base of each board resting upon sockets of silver reminds us of redemption. The payment of the atonement money provided the resources from which the Tabernacle was built. The details of this silver are given us in chapter 38 of Exodus, indicating that the majority, one hundred talents of silver, were used to make 'the sockets of the sanctuary, and the sockets of the vail', Exod. 38. 27. Similarly, all of our appreciation of the significance of the Tabernacle depends upon redemption. But we were not redeemed with 'corruptible things, as silver and gold . . . But with the precious blood of Christ, as of a lamb without blemish and without spot', 1 Pet. 1. 18-19.

Finally, the bars that passed through the rings on each board to provide stability for the structure and bind it together remind us that 'All the truth in Scripture concerning the Lord Jesus stands together, and to deny any of it weakens the total. His deity, humanity, work of redemption, and all else taught in the Word of God must be accepted completely', JOHN GRANT.

June 8th

Exodus 26. 31-37; 36. 35-38

THE VAIL AND THE DOOR

In our reading today we are considering that which formed the division 'between the holy place and the most holy', v. 33, and that which was the door of entry into the holy place. The order in which they are given indicates that we are proceeding outwards from the most holy place.

The vail provided a barrier between the holiest of all and the remainder of the tent of the Tabernacle. Only the high priest could pass through this vail and that was once annually on the Day of Atonement. As it shielded that which spoke of the presence of God from human view so it also provided a covering for the mercy seat and the ark of testimony when the children of Israel took their journey.

The vail was made of 'blue, and purple, and scarlet, and fine twined linen of cunning work', v. 31. The colours and the material are a reminder to us of the person of Christ. Fine linen speaks of righteousness, Rev. 19. 8, and it featured prominently in the Tabernacle as well as the garments of the High Priest and priests who were to serve within it. How important to know the righteousness of Christ, 'the fine linen displaying every form of bright and holy purity; righteousness in every aspect', HENRY SOLTAU. Of the colours used, blue is pre-eminent as the colour of 'the celestial canopy that surrounds the earth; the heavenly blue that encircles the glory of creation', DUNCAN MAXWELL. We may see this as the deity of Christ or the grace and love He manifested. Scarlet is said to be the colour belonging to earth and this colour seems to typify the perfect humanity of the Lord Jesus. Purple is created by a mingling of blue and red and owes its beauty to both. There is in Christ a perfect bringing together of deity and humanity, 'God . . . manifest in the flesh', 1 Tim. 3. 16.

As New Testament believers we rejoice in the truth that the barrier has been removed and we have access into the very presence of God, 'By a new and living way . . . through the veil, that is to say, his flesh', Heb. 10. 20. The death of Christ has given us boldness, assurance, to enter into the holiest. We do so in all the value of 'the blood of Jesus', Heb. 10. 19. Hallelujah!

June 9th

Exodus 27. 1-8; 38. 1-7

THE ALTAR SHALL BE FOURSQUARE

Of all the vessels of the Tabernacle this might be said to be the most important. Without it there could be no approach to God. As it dominated the people's view of priestly activity within the Tabernacle, so it was central to the religious life of the nation. As the sweet savour offerings, sin and trespass offerings, and offerings for cleansing and purifying were brought, the offerer would behold the slaying of the victim, the pouring out of the blood before and the flames arising from off the altar. It must have been an awesome sight and yet a constant reminder of human sinfulness and divine holiness as the sacrifices were unceasing, Heb. 10. 3.

We acknowledge how different all this is to the work of the Lord Jesus Christ and yet how much of the person and work of Christ we can see in this vessel. The two materials used in its construction were 'shittim wood', v. 1, which was to be overlaid 'with brass', v. 2. At the centre of the altar there was found a wood that was renowned as being 'resistant to disease and attack by pests', TOM RATCLIFFE. Such incorruptible wood is a suitable type of the perfect and holy humanity of the Lord. The brass which overlaid it provided 'the durability . . . and the power to sustain the fire', HENRY SOLTAU. It is difficult to imagine how this vessel could bear such constant and consistently high temperatures but in doing so there is a testimony to the One who bore the fullness of divine judgement upon sin without wavering.

One point of which the title of our meditation reminds us is that the altar was 'foursquare', v. 1. Much profit might be gleaned from a consideration of the numbers five and three that form its dimensions but what is also remarkable is that 'its dimensions are such that all the other vessels of the Sanctuary could be included within it, and . . . there seems to be a manifest connection between its size and that of the Ark', HENRY SOLTAU. What a testimony to the work of Christ! There can be no appreciation of or fellowship with God apart from the altar. There can be no priestly approach to God except by virtue of the death of the Lord Jesus.

June 10th

Exodus 27. 9-21; 38. 9-20

THE COURT OF THE TABERNACLE

In the construction of the court there are a number of essential components: linen hangings, vv. 9, 11, 12, 14-16, 18; pillars and their sockets, vv. 10-12, 14-17; hooks and their fillets of silver, vv. 10-11, 17; and pins of brass, v. 19. From the dimensions given, it is apparent that the gate of the court was situated on the east side, vv. 13-15.

The purpose of the court of the Tabernacle was to establish a clear distinction between the dwelling place of God and that of His people. Those that lived nearest to the court were the Levites or, on the side nearest the entrance, the priests. Similarly, the linen hangings shielded the activities that took place within from the casual observer. Only those who had brought their sacrifice to the gate would observe that which took place within the court and then only from a distance. What a reminder to the people of the holiness of God and the distance that exists between sinful man and a holy God! Only the offering of a sacrifice could bring them nigh. The fact that there was only one entrance also taught that there is only one approach to God and that by means of the sacrifice of Christ.

The pillars and their sockets, the hooks and fillets of silver, and the pins of brass were all necessary components to keep the hangings intact. They provided the stable framework that ensured that the hangings did not fall or droop. How important that all that displays the character and work of Christ should be constant and unchanging!

Finally, in these verses we have the details of the 'pure olive oil beaten' that would be the fuel to maintain the lamp burning 'from evening to morning', v. 21. Whilst the lamp and the constancy of the light may speak of Christ, the oil is usually seen as figurative of the Holy Spirit.

A consideration of these verses causes us to wonder at the contrast between our portion and that of God's earthly people. We are not kept at distance, barred from the presence of God by the hangings of the court. We have 'boldness to enter into the holiest by the blood of Jesus', Heb. 10. 19. We can 'draw near with a true heart', Heb. 10. 22. What a privilege!

June 11th

Exodus 28. 1-14; 39. 1-7

HOLY GARMENTS FOR AARON

To describe these garments as 'holy garments' was to indicate that they were set apart for the sole use of the High Priest in the performance of his role in the presence of God. Although the fact that they were holy was not because of the materials or construction specifically, they were more than the simple priestly garments afforded for priestly work.

They were holy because holiness characterizes the God into whose presence the High Priest was to enter in the Tabernacle, Lev. 11. 44-45; 19. 2; 20. 26; 21. 8; 1 Pet. 1. 16. It was essential that the priest was appropriately attired. He could not enter as he wanted but only as God wanted. The donning of 'holy garments' outwardly was designed to make the wearer conscious of the inward state of heart necessary for the God into whose presence he was about to enter. To do so foolishly was to court judgement and destruction.

In a similar way we cannot function as priests in the presence of God without being in a fit state of heart – having the righteousness of saints, but also having no unconfessed sin to break the fellowship and communion befitting priestly work.

They were set apart for a distinct use. When Aaron was adorned as the High Priest he was visibly set apart for all to see – his separation was real. Leviticus chapter 8 verse 5 tells us that 'Moses said unto the congregation, "This is the thing which the Lord commanded to be done"'. How important for us to be holy in an external sense as well as in an internal sense. Can others see by our manner of life, and, perhaps, even our dress and demeanour, that we are different?

It is remarkable that these garments should be intended for the family, 'Aaron, Nadab and Abihu, Eleazer and Ithamar, Aaron's sons', v. 1. Yet, two members of the family, Nadab and Abihu, would later rebel and perish. In the purposes of God Nadab and Abihu would have succeeded to the position of High Priest had it not been for that seed of rebellion in their heart. There is a testimony here to the fact that God's sovereignty does not override man's free will – God does not elect men to judgement and condemnation.

June 12th

Exodus 28. 15-30; 39. 8-21

THE BREASTPLATE OF JUDGEMENT

In our reading today, we see that upon the ephod was placed the breastplate. As verse 15 shows, it was made of the same material and by the same method of construction as the ephod.

Looking at the detail, verse 16 tells us it was square and doubled to form a kind of pouch or bag. Into the front of the breastplate were set twelve precious stones, in four rows of three. Each precious stone had its allotted place in the pattern or array of stones on the breastplate. From verse 21 we learn that these stones were engraved with the names of the children of Israel. Thus, as the High Priest went about his function in the presence of God he bore the names of the tribes before him. This indicates the representative nature of the priestly function. He was there on behalf of the people.

It is significant that the breastplate, as its name suggests, covered the chest or area in which the heart is prominent. It suggests to us that the names and tribes of Israel were to feature in the affections of the High Priest, 'And Aaron shall bear the names of the children of Israel . . . upon his heart', v. 29. It was not just that he bore their names as a burden upon his shoulders, although that was true, but that they also had a place in his heart. The fact that there was only one tribe on each stone also means that each tribe in its individuality was loved and each in their own way. Today, we rejoice in the truth stated by Paul, 'Nevertheless the foundation of God standeth sure, having this seal, The Lord knoweth them that are his', 2 Tim. 2. 19. However, the difference is that we are known, not as part of a tribe or by our genealogy, but individually.

It is interesting too to note that these stones were 'a memorial before the Lord continually', v. 29. There was a constant reminder. That constant reminder of each of the tribes was made possible because of their place on the breastplate over the heart of the High Priest. In a similar way our position and standing is in Christ – our names are graven in the Lamb's book of life because we are linked with Him.

What lessons these verses contain for our own priestly activity as saints of God and what tremendous pictures of Christ!

Exodus 28. 31-43; 39. 22-31

THE ROBE AND THE MITRE

The robe was to be all of blue, v. 31. The construction was remarkable in that it would appear to be one piece of cloth with 'an hole in the top of it', v. 32. This hole was to be reinforced with a binding of woven work. At the opposite end of the garment there was to be a golden bell and pomegranate attached in sequence around the hem, that, 'his sound shall be heard when he goeth in unto the holy place before the Lord, and when he cometh out, that he die not', v. 35.

The fact that the robe is underneath the ephod and the breastplate shows that we are getting closer to the actual body of the High Priest. Therefore, this garment begins to display, in a typical sense, something of the essential characteristics of our Great High Priest. It is blue in colour, and that typifies the heavenly character of the Son of God. It is woven throughout, as one piece, signifying this as an essential and eternal characteristic of Christ – He is unchanging.

In the bells upon the hem we have a reminder that much of the work of the High Priest was hidden from view inside the Tabernacle. To reassure the people, and let them know that he was still at work for them, they could listen for the sound of the bells. However, we can be assured that our Great High Priest is unfailing in His ministry, 'seeing he ever liveth to make intercession for them', Heb. 7. 25.

Verse 39 tells us that the mitre was made of fine linen and attached to it by blue lace was a golden plate engraved with the words, 'Holiness to the Lord', v. 36.

The use of fine linen for the coat signified the moral purity of the High Priest so a similar thought would be carried forward into the making of the mitre. How important to remember that our Great High Priest knew no sin, did no sin, and in Him is no sin. The fact that the mitre was upon the head and the golden plate affixed to it might also suggest to us the character of the thought life of the Lord. Even that which was hidden and known only to God, was marked by the same purity and spotlessness as the rest of His life.

How infinitely precious is the person and work of Christ!

June 14th

Exodus 29. 1-9

HALLOW THEM TO MINISTER

This chapter as a whole indicates the procedures that were necessary in the consecration of the priests for service in the presence of God. The garments that we have considered in chapter 28 are now used to adorn Aaron. They are seen in reverse order to that given in the previous chapter because this would be the order that they were applied rather than the order in which they would be seen. Three other factors are mentioned in these verses. Firstly, there were the items for sacrifice, 'one young bullock, and two rams without blemish . . . unleavened bread, and cakes unleavened tempered with oil, and wafers unleavened anointed with oil', vv. 1-2. Secondly, there was the washing of Aaron and his sons, v. 4. Thirdly, Aaron was to be anointed, v. 7. We shall consider the first of these factors in our meditation tomorrow.

The washing of Aaron, which took place at the door of the Tabernacle, is a reminder of the need for spiritual cleanliness. Before the garments could be put upon Aaron, it was necessary that any defilement should be removed. There is a two-fold importance to this activity. Only those who have been saved 'by the washing of regeneration', Tit. 3. 5, can be fit to enter the presence of God in priestly service. Equally, that condition needs to be maintained if we are to walk in the light of God's presence. Thus, sin needs to be confessed and removed on every occasion it occurs.

In the anointing of Aaron, there is that official setting apart for the service of God. This was individual – only Aaron was anointed, for only Aaron was called of God to perform the High Priestly function. It is to be noted that this anointing oil was to be used later to sprinkle the garments of Aaron and his sons, v. 21. The oil was symbolic of the Holy Spirit and its usage reminds us that priestly activity must be Spirit inspired and controlled, John 4. 24.

But this ritual also has a typical significance. Our Great High Priest needed no washing to remove defilement, Heb. 7. 26. Equally, only of the Lord was it said that He was, 'full of' and 'anointed with the Holy Ghost', Luke 4. 1; Acts 10. 38.

June 15th

Exodus 29. 10-37

AN OFFERING MADE BY FIRE

In the consecration of the priests there were three offerings: the sin offering, the burnt offering and the peace offering.

It is instructive that the first mention of a sin offering should occur not in the book of Leviticus but here in Exodus. All previous offerings were burnt offerings but now the Tabernacle is to be constructed so the sin offering is introduced. As there was no priest to function in the Tabernacle, here, the procedures stated in Leviticus are changed. The steps taken with this offering were that of identification, v. 10, application, v. 12, and incineration, vv. 13-14. Identification was necessary in order that sin might be confessed and the sacrifice of the bullock might be applied for the priest's sin. The application of the blood to the horns of the altar and the pouring out of the remainder at the foot of the altar testified to the value of the sacrifice made – a testimony which remained. Finally, the incineration of the bullock reminds us of divine wrath borne by the Saviour on account of our sin.

Following the sin offering the first of the rams was offered as a burnt offering. In this offering there were four stages: identifying, v. 15; sprinkling, v. 16; washing, v. 17; and burning, v. 18. Although the process of identifying appears the same, it has the idea more of appropriation – making the value of the sacrifice one's own. Here, there is the truth that I am accepted in all the value of the work of Christ. In the washing there is the reminder of the perfections found in Christ – inward as well as outward. That the whole ram was burnt upon the altar shows us that all the sacrifice ascended to God as 'a sweet savour', v. 18.

Similarly, the ram of consecration, vv. 19-28, is described as 'a sweet savour before the Lord', v. 25, instituted to consecrate the priest for service. For this reason the blood of the sacrifice is applied to the right ear, the thumb of the right hand and the great toe of the right foot. This indicates that every faculty both mental and physical is committed to the service of God. We note too that the hands of Aaron are filled in order that the offerings might be waved before the Lord. That which occupies them in service is that which speaks of Christ. What about us?

185

June 16th

Exodus 29. 38-46

DAY BY DAY CONTINUALLY

There are eleven occasions in the King James Version, where this little phrase 'day by day' occurs. In today's reading, the value and the import of the sacrifice are stressed. The specific command of the Lord was two young lambs, of the first year, day by day continually; one offered in the morning, the other at even. The result was to be a 'sweet savour', an offering made by fire unto the Lord. It was to be continual, through all their generations. It was to be offered at the tabernacle door, where the Lord Himself promised to meet the offerers, speak with them, and sanctify them.

Many of the 'day by day' phrases in scripture deal with our responsibilities as believers. But this one speaks of that which the Lord receives, the value and worth of the sacrifice. It would seem that Jehovah wanted to keep before Himself a daily reminder of another sacrifice, One yet to come. God knew the value of Calvary long before any of us ever learned it. Ever before Him was the death of the Lamb of God who would bear away the sin of the world. Christ said, 'I do always those things that please' My Father, John 8. 29. Nothing that He did ever pleased Jehovah more than His selfless sacrifice at Calvary.

Where would we be if the value of that death ever ceased to fully please the God of heaven? We would have no hope of His grace, no assurance of His mercy, no promise of His forgiveness, and no confidence of His salvation. In fact, everything we now enjoy would be stripped from us in an instant. Such is the everlasting value of the death of God's Lamb; far greater than simply pleasing us, the Saviour pleased God by His death on the cross. Day after day, the value of this sacrifice stands. The savour of this death pleases the God of heaven. The worth of this death answers the great question of sin. The blood from this Victim only had to flow once.

To Israel, the continual offering of these two little lambs guaranteed the presence of a loving God. Understanding a little of the Godward value of Calvary, and how eternally great is the satisfaction and pleasure brought to the Father by the Son, we bow our hearts in inexpressible gratitude.

June 17th

Exodus 30. 1-10; 37. 25-28

AN ALTAR TO BURN INCENSE UPON

The blueprint for the construction of the incense altar was given in chapter 30; the construction of it, according to the plan, is recorded in chapter 37. It was the first place to which the priests came as they began their approach to the Mercy Seat, and the sacred presence of the Lord above it. No priest was permitted to go past this point, except on the Day of Atonement. It was the responsibility of Aaron and his sons to keep an offering of perpetual incense burning on this altar.

This was one of two altars associated with the Tabernacle. Both were made of wood, but each was covered with a different metal. The brazen altar was placed just outside the building in the court, before the tabernacle entrance. It was a place of sacrifice, called 'the altar of burnt offering', 40. 29.

This altar in our study today, was covered with gold, and called 'the golden altar'. It was inside the holy place, and stood before the veil. Instead of a place of sacrifice, it represented a place of worship. The burning incense, day and night before Jehovah, is a beautiful picture of the intercessory and mediatory worth of our Great High Priest. Had this altar been outside the tent, it would have been connected with sacrifice. The fact that it was inside speaks of our exalted Lord Jesus in heaven's holy of holies, our Great High Priest before the throne of God. We read in Exodus chapter 30 that there was a 'crown of gold round about' this altar, and Christ, exalted to the highest, is 'crowned with glory and honour', Heb. 2. 9.

It had only one use, the burning of incense. The fire used on this altar had been taken from the brazen altar, where the sacrifices had been slain. The incense was burned upon the very fire that had first consumed the sacrifice, Lev. 16. 12-13. What a glorious truth is this! The work being done for us now in the glory by an exalted High Priest, is based upon His enduring the fires of the cross. Those He bled and died for, He now intercedes for.

'Great are the offices He bears,
And bright His character appears,
Exalted on the throne'

[Samuel Medley]

June 18th

Exodus 30. 11-16

HALF A SHEKEL

From every Israelite male over 20 years the Lord required this amount of money as 'atonement' money. It has been said that this was a strange requirement of the Lord, considering Israel was already a redeemed people. It was a census tax, used when the people were numbered for the Lord. God was numbering the people that He had redeemed for Himself, and in so doing was devising the very structure of parts of the Tabernacle itself.

The price was the same for each man. A half-shekel was ten gerahs; in scripture, ten denotes human responsibility. Each man paid the same; each was fully responsible for himself. The monies collected were for a specific use, Exod. 38. 25-28. The silver collected was to be melted down and used as the foundation sockets for the Tabernacle. A total of 603,550 men over 20 years of age donated and from this amount of pure silver the base sockets of the sanctuary and the veil were made.

The type of this offering and construction is a beautiful one. In countless ways, the Tabernacle itself is a series of pictures of the Lord Jesus Christ. So long as it was obediently set up it was a testimony by the God of heaven to His beloved Son, yet to come to earth to tabernacle among men. This money signified redemption, the very basis of God's dealings with mankind. The Israelites failed many times to truly value the fact that their lives had been redeemed. Sadly, Israel's repeated disobedience and failure caused the discontinuation of the Tabernacle's use but the blessed truth of redemption was ever before the Lord.

It has been estimated that, in today's terms, the monetary value of this silver alone would be over £3.6 million or $7 million US. But the redemption of which it testified was far more costly, far more precious. This silver tarnished, faded, and was finally lost forever. But our redemption is costly, priceless, permanent, and ever pleasing to the God of redemption. It will never fade away. Peter wrote in his first epistle, 'Knowing that you were ransomed from the futile ways inherited from your forefathers, not with perishable things such as silver or gold, but with the precious blood of Christ, like that of a lamb without blemish or spot', 1 Pet. 1. 18-19 ESV.

Exodus 30. 17-21; 38. 8

A LAVER OF BRASS

The laver of brass was critically important to the priesthood. It was situated between the 'tent of the congregation and the altar', 40. 30. Aaron and his sons were to wash their hands and feet at the laver. They were twice commanded to do this that they 'die not'. Might they have considered this an important task, one not to be neglected? Their very lives depended on it as another commandment to be observed 'throughout their generations'.

The truths of the altar were positional. The blood had to be shed, collected and sprinkled against the mercy seat, for the sins of the people and the priests themselves. No man would dare enter the holy place without blood. But the truths of the laver are conditional. The daily defilement of the dust of the camp had to be washed from their hands and feet.

In a far greater way it is the same with those of us cleansed by the precious blood of the Lord Jesus Christ. His blood 'cleanseth us from all sin'. Hallelujah! What a Saviour! That blood redeemed us from the slave market of sin, loosed us from the bondage of sin and delivered us from the penalty of sin. We are seen, in Christ, as being 'perfected forever' by His one great sacrifice for sin.

But what of the sin that affects us each day, that so easily 'besets' us? The world without, the flesh within and the 'dust of the camp' seem to cling to our hands, our feet, and even our hearts. The blessed truths of the New Testament assure us that once forgiven by the grace of God in salvation, we are always forgiven. But we must confess the sin that defiles us each day, and wash in the laver of God's grace. His promise still stands, 'If we confess our sins, he is faithful and just to forgive us our sins, and to cleanse us from all unrighteousness', 1 John 1. 9.

The Lord Jesus acted out this truth in the upper room. He had cleansed the hearts and souls of the eleven when they had decided to follow Him. But, as gracious host, He bowed before them to wash their feet. We can take great confidence in His words to the disciples, 'now are ye clean'. His blood has cleansed us from all sin. But day by day, we need the laver. We must keep short accounts with God.

Exodus 30. 22-33

AN OIL OF HOLY OINTMENT

In our reading today, God gives the exacting prescription for the compounding of the holy anointing oil. It was so precise that it was as if the Great Physician ordered it 'after the art of the apothecary', 30. 25. It was a unique and singular composition; they were not to make anything else like it, and were to consider it most holy. It had specific uses, and also had potential uses that were forbidden. It was to be made of myrrh, cinnamon, calamus, cassia, and olive oil. Throughout scripture, the spiritual significance of these ingredients is worthy of our consideration.

Myrrh speaks of love in the Song of Solomon, but, in its bitterness, it signified death as well. Cinnamon was a spice with a sweet but burning quality; the root words mean 'zealousness, a burning zeal'. Calamus is from a reed, whose root-word means 'upright'. It must be crushed to obtain the fragrance. Cassia is a spice taken from another root; the Hebrew word can mean to 'stoop', or 'bow down'. Combining these four fragrances, as only God could do, provides us with a picture that only the Lord Jesus could fulfil.

In the Lord Jesus there is one who loved as no other has ever loved and who proved it by passing through the bitterest of deaths. One whose holy zeal burned towards His Father's house, cleansing it of those who had polluted its meaning; One who was the epitome of righteousness and morality, yet who was crushed for iniquity that was not His own. One who stooped from the heights of heaven, and came among the dregs of a tainted world, bowing Himself to His Father's will, the abuse of His own creatures and the death of the cross.

These four were combined with olive oil, a picture of God's Holy Spirit. The oil enabled a perfect blending together of the fragrance of the spices. Thus, Christ, in every word and deed, did all in the power and under the control of the Holy Spirit. The Gospels record the occasions when Jesus was 'led by the Spirit', or moved 'in the power of the Spirit'. Finally, He 'offered himself without spot to God' by this same eternal Spirit, Heb. 9. 14.

June 21st

Exodus 30. 34-38; 37. 29

A PERFUME, PURE AND HOLY

Once again, the Lord writes another prescription, as if giving it to a master pharmacist. In the first, He gave orders for an ointment; in this, He prescribes a confection. This, as well, was to be considered most holy. It was to be so unique that, in today's language, we would say that the fragrance was patented. God clearly ordered that the specific smell of this perfume was never to be recreated or duplicated; if anyone attempted it, that soul would be 'cut off from his people'.

Stacte, a gum resin, very valuable, and hard to obtain, speaks of the extremity of death. This would teach us of the servant character of the Lord Jesus, who went to great lengths from the heights of heaven to the depths of Calvary, 'to minister, and to give his life a ransom for many', Mark 10. 45.

Onycha was from mussels, which came from the sea. The root word is 'nail, or claw' – the claw gave a sweet odour when burned. There are depths to the Saviour we will never uncover. But there were also depths to which He sank for us that we will never comprehend. He endured the 'waves and billows' of God's wrath against our sin, the 'waterfloods and the deep waters'.

Galbanum, a rubbery resin, taken from the roots of a flowering plant, was from trees that grew in the heights – there had to be upward effort to obtain this fragrance. Would this not remind us of His deity? The One who was 'verily God, yet become truly human, lower than angels, to die in our stead', H. d'A. CHAMPNEY. From what heights He came; to what depths He sank for us; to what heights He has now ascended!

The frankincense was from trees slashed open, weeping their fragrance through the night. In the darkness of the cross, the Saviour, opened by the thorns of the curse, the nails of the cross, the scourge of the whipping post, and finally the spear of the Roman, His precious blood came forth as a fountain for sin.

Tempered together, beaten small, pure, holy, all of these beautiful types thrill our hearts! But, today, let us also anticipate that the fragrance of the One of whom it speaks will fill all of heaven.

June 22nd
Exodus 31. 1-18

MAKE ALL THAT I HAVE COMMANDED THEE

For the first time in this discourse the Lord mentions to Moses the names and the qualifications of the specific craftsmen He had selected for the work of the Tabernacle. He was soon to give to Moses the instructions for the sabbath, and then end their time on Sinai by presenting to Israel's leader the tablets of stone. But He first mentions two men, Bezaleel and Aholiab.

Bezaleel's name means 'the protection of God', or 'in the shadow of God'. Aholiab's name means 'the tent of the Father'. Both of these names readily lead us to think of the value of the place that they were to build. These men were skilled, the Hebrew word for 'wisdom' found in verses 3 and 6. But what was most important about these two men was that their skills and wisdom were from the Lord Himself.

The Lord calls men and women to His work. He did then; He does now. As He calls them, He prepares them. They were wise in their thinking, as well as in their hearts, and their hands skilled to carry out the minutest details of divine orders in the construction of the Tabernacle. From the ark to the furniture, from the holy garments of the priests to the lampstand, all came from their capable and expert hands.

But twice in these verses we see the critical requirement for the success of these two men. Their success was not from their wisdom or skill, nor from their knowledge or workmanship. It was from their obedience to the Lord, their singular willingness to do exactly what He asked them to do. They were not to move out on their own or to change or re-think His plans. They were to obey, nothing more, but nothing less.

And so, we are to obey today. The gifts with which He may have gifted each of us are essentially of no use, unless used in total obedience to Him. Saul learned the tragic lesson of partial obedience, 1 Sam. 15. 22-23. The Lord Jesus says to us, 'If you love me, keep my commandments', John 14. 15. He also asks of His own, 'Why call ye me, Lord, Lord, and do not the things which I say?', Luke 6. 46. These men were brilliantly gifted, yet their obedience to His purposes and plans was what eventually made the Tabernacle 'according to the pattern'.

June 23rd

Exodus 32. 1-14

THESE BE THY GODS, O ISRAEL

In Israel's history this day has to be considered Aaron's worst. While Moses was on Sinai, receiving the law from God, Aaron misled the people in different ways. He first had them melt down the jewellery with which they had adorned themselves; most likely, that which they had plundered from Egypt as they fled captivity. He personally fashioned a golden calf, told Israel 'these be thy gods', and attributed their redemption from Egypt to a just-created pagan image. To make it worse, he built an altar of sacrifice, and proclaimed the next day a 'feast unto the Lord'. The people rose up early and began a day of pagan worship, perhaps even indulging in the naked orgies that the heathen practised as fertility rites to their man-made idols, v. 25.

It is little wonder that the Lord said to Moses 'they have turned aside quickly out of the way which I commanded them'. The Lord's wrath burned hot with fury against Israel, v. 11. Moses' righteous anger burned as well, v. 19, as he saw the wicked spectacle before him. As if to symbolize how grievously Israel had broken God's law, Moses shattered the tablets in anger on the ground at his feet.

How could they have gone so far, so fast? As we contemplate this question, let us ask another. Are we any different than they?

All that the Lord had really asked of Adam and Eve in the garden was their obedience. Obedience for our first parents assured them of the continued presence of, and fellowship with, the Lord Himself. As we might categorize sin and sins, theirs does not seem heinous. But God commands obedience; fully and completely. Saul discovered this lesson. His partial obedience, 1 Sam. 15, was equated, by Samuel, as being equal to 'witchcraft and idolatry'. In the Lord's sight his partial obedience was actually stubborn disobedience and it cost him the throne.

To this day, the Lord asks for our obedience. Aaron's influence, and the people's following of him, should affect us all deeply. May God help us to obey Him fully!

Exodus 32. 15-35

WHO IS ON THE LORD'S SIDE?

This section is a pivotal one in Israel's history. Perhaps their greatest decline, it set the stage for their protracted years of disobedience to God. Moses had been on the mount in Jehovah's presence, receiving the law, and the Lord had told him what had been transpiring in the camp. Incredible disobedience, disgrace and idolatry had occurred in Moses' absence.

Moses descended Sinai with the tablets of the law in his hands, God's own work, and God's own writing. As soon as he saw the calf, and the Lord's people dancing naked around it in pagan obeisance, his fury overwhelmed him, and he smashed the tablets of stone to pieces. The children of Israel drank the bitterness of their sin that day and learned a number of vital lessons on the subject of disobeying the Lord.

Aaron blamed the people, and said that they were 'set on mischief'. Yet the Lord plagued the people, because of the calf which, scripture records, 'Aaron made', v. 35. Three thousand died that day.

What exactly happened here? How did this almost unbelievable turn of events occur so quickly? We would do well to learn these lessons for Paul states these happened 'for ensamples' and are 'written for our admonition', 1 Cor. 10. 11. First of all, their spiritual leader was away, and they behaved differently than if he were present. Secondly, they had befriended the evil around them and adopted paganism for themselves. Thirdly, their hands were idle. They had apparently lost sight of the fact that they had been redeemed, purchased by blood. And, finally, they seemed to have totally lost sight of the promised land and acted in ways completely unbecoming their calling.

Moses stood in the camp's gate, and called out this searching question, 'Who is on the Lord's side? Let him come unto me'. How quickly they forgot! This cry for separation from evil and idolatry was only three months after their redemption from Egypt. It echoes Paul's lament to the Galatians, Gal. 1. 6.

The sons of Levi stepped forward when Moses called. May we be exercised about our separation from uncleanness and that it can be realized by our obedience as believer priests.

June 25th

Exodus 33. 1-11

YE ARE A STIFFNECKED PEOPLE

Israel's great corporate sin, in making the golden calf, had already wrought terrible judgement upon the camp. Three thousand Israelites had been slain and, apart from the pleading intercession of Moses, it might have been far greater. Now, they learned of further punishment for their idolatry and disobedience. Instead of the Lord Himself going with them to Canaan, He told them that it would be an angel. In fact, so greatly displeased was the Lord with this stiffnecked and stubborn people that were He to go with them, in their midst, so great was His displeasure with them, that He might consume them in the way. What sadness!

Israel mourned as they heard the Lord's further judgement against them. A long journey ahead of them, with many alien peoples opposing them, and they would not have the Lord in their midst. In these verses, He called them 'a stiffnecked people' twice over. It is said of Israel twice that they stripped themselves of their jewellery and ornaments, in self-humbling before a displeased God.

Then Moses, their faithful mediator, pitched a tent of meeting outside the camp where he would, once again, meet the Lord on behalf of the people. Those who sought the Lord from their hearts, including Joshua, the future leader of Israel, went out of the camp, to meet the Lord in this place. The cloudy pillar descended, and the Lord came near. Those watching from their tent doors bowed in worship at this sight. The Lord spoke to Moses 'face to face', as He would to a friend, and communed with him there.

What similarities and contrasts this scene paints for the Lord's people today. We have been called 'outside the camp' of Christendom to meet the Lord and gather to His blessed Name. Our Mediator is none other than our own and personal Saviour, the One who has come for us, lived for us, bled for us, died for us, rose again for us, and now lives again for us, in the power of an endless life. This God will never leave us. His presence will never be replaced by any angel. This Saviour will always be our gathering centre.

SHEW ME THY GLORY

Moses, the greatest Old Testament example of an intercessor, was hard at work. He was pleading his case to the Almighty, who had plagued Israel for the sin of the golden calf. No sooner had the people cried in unison, '**All** that the Lord hath spoken we will do', Exod. 19. 8, than they sinned terribly. Moses had descended Sinai, newly-given Law in his hand, to find them worshipping a golden idol. Grinding the idol to powder, mixing it with water, and making the people drink it, was not nearly retribution enough. The sons of Levi, separated unto the Lord, were commanded to raise the sword against their fellow-men, and three thousand died in a day.

And so, Moses pleaded for the people. He even asked the Lord to blot him from the book of life, willing to try to make a personal atonement for their terrible sin. In his prayer to the Lord for His continued presence among a sinning and stiff-necked people, Moses, to whom the Lord spoke face to face, asked the Lord to shew him His glory. The Lord told him that his request was denied – it could not be granted at that time. Instead, He graciously promised His goodness, and assured all Israel of His mercy and the continued story of the exodus demonstrates these over and over again.

Moses died without ever setting foot in the Promised Land. One might even think that his request to behold the glory of the Lord was also an unrealized longing. But this good and merciful God, one day many centuries later, answered Moses' request. Both Moses and the prophet Elijah were allowed by God to stand with the Lord Jesus on transfiguration's mount. Elijah represented all who would be raptured to Heaven without dying; Moses, all who had died in faith. And, as they spoke with the Lord Jesus 'of his decease, which he should accomplish at Jerusalem', Moses finally got to see God's glory!

Moses had already seen the glory of God in deliverance, in creation, in miracles, in preservation and protection, and in the meaning of the Tabernacle. Yet **none** of this was God's ultimate expression of His glory. That was to be seen in the death of His Son and the Lord allowed Moses a glimpse of this focal event.

June 27th

Exodus 34. 1-17

PARDON OUR INIQUITY AND OUR SIN

The great problem of man's sin permeates the entire Bible. From Eden's garden until there is sin no more in the New Jerusalem, Rev. 21. 27, the iniquity of mankind is one of the most frequently mentioned subjects in Scripture.

After Israel's great sin of idolatry, it was primarily the intercession of Moses that stopped the plague of God's wrath. In this section, the mediation of Moses is once again demonstrated and it is a beautiful type of our Saviour, the Lord Jesus Christ.

The Lord descended in the cloud, stood before this humble man and proclaimed His Name. God then listed a number of His wonderful attributes, still to be claimed by us, through grace, today: His mercy; His grace; His goodness; His truth; His patient longsuffering. And then He stated the twin truths of the Just and the Justifier; the One who will not indiscriminately clear the guilty, yet the only One who can forgive sins.

This revelation put Moses on his face on the ground, worshipping. He pleaded for the grace of God – still the only hope any of us have before Him – and for the Lord's presence with them as he confessed their disobedience. Then, he prayed 'pardon our iniquity and our sin, and take us for thine inheritance'.

Our Advocate before the Father humbled Himself to the earth, as well. He worshipped the God of heaven by His total obedience. He showed the grace of God with His every word, His every step. But, unlike Moses, who included himself in the sin of the people, our spotless Mediator came, sin apart, and placed Himself between a holy God and our incurable wickedness. From His cross He prayed for our pardon for our forgiveness. And, then, bowing His thorn-crowned head towards an earth cursed by our sin, He yielded up His spirit to God, having finished salvation's work. As a result of that death, we have now been taken by God for His everlasting inheritance.

What approach would we ever have to God, apart from our Mediator's grace? What hope would there be for the removal of our sin, apart from His forgiveness? What judgement has been lifted because of His mercy? With the hymnwriter we can say 'O what wonders love hath done!' J. KENT.

June 28th

Exodus 34. 18-35

THE SKIN OF HIS FACE SHONE

Three times over in this section, we read of Moses that 'the skin of his face shone'. This was the description of his face as he descended from Sinai the second time; at the first, his face was full of wrath and anger. When he came down at the first the sin of the people caused him to dash the tablets to pieces. Now, with the people humbled because of their sin and the Lord's judgement, Moses safely deposits the tablets into the ark.

So remarkable was his time spent over forty days and forty nights with the Lord that his countenance was changed. He was not immediately aware of the change, but the people were and they feared even drawing near him. Paul helps us understand why, 'the ministration of death, written and engraven in stones, was glorious, so that the children of Israel could not steadfastly behold the face of Moses for the glory of his countenance; which glory was to be done away', 2 Cor. 3. 7. Israel had been so convicted of the absolute holiness of the Lord, that when they saw the effect on Moses of his being in the Lord's presence, they shrank back from him.

The law, which condemned them, also became a 'veil over their hearts'. So blinded did Israel become to the real meaning the Lord wanted to teach them through the law that their hearts were veiled when Christ came. 2 Corinthians chapter 3 teaches that there will come a day when the veil will be lifted and they will see the Messiah for who He really is.

But what of us, in the day of grace? We are no less sinful or disobedient than Israel. But, by grace, the Lord has allowed us to behold the 'glory of God in the face of Jesus Christ'. We no longer fear His presence although He is no less holy than He was at Sinai. But, instead, we are invited to come near 'with boldness', Heb. 10. 19, and enter His presence by a new and living way accomplished for us at Calvary.

There is a practical lesson for us here. Moses' face clearly showed others that he had been with the Lord. In a similar way, the Sanhedrin knew, looking at Peter and John, that they 'had been with Jesus', Acts 4. 13. The more time we spend in His presence, the more others will be able to see Him in us.

June 29th

Exodus 35. 1-29

A WILLING OFFERING UNTO THE LORD

This section represents the first glimpses of God's plan for the Tabernacle. Perhaps no type or shadow in the Old Testament has more fulfilments in the Person and work of Christ than does the Tabernacle in the wilderness. As we read through this chapter we are immediately impressed by this profound truth: the building of the Tabernacle was to be a work of the heart. The following references will illustrate: 'whosoever is of a willing heart', v. 5; 'every one whose heart stirred him up', v. 21; 'as many as were willing hearted', v. 22; 'all the women that were wise-hearted . . . whose heart stirred them up', vv. 25-26; 'the children of Israel . . . every man and woman, whose heart made them willing', v. 29; and, finally, of Bezaleel and Aholiab, 'them hath he filled with wisdom of heart', vv. 30, 35.

This is a crucial lesson for us, in our personal lives, our homes and families and in our assembly responsibilities. As God never forces His will upon a sinner to repentance, He never forces His will upon a saint to obedience. It is a sad but true phenomenon that man will seek to negate the will of the Almighty on any occasion. How then did the tabernacle ever become a completed work from a divine plan? By the willing, obedient, and subjected hearts of the Lord's people who 'offered up' the gorgeous jewellery, materials and colours that would make each stand out individually, and sacrificed them for the good of the corporate whole. They gave to the Lord many of the things that might mean the most value to each of them; they understood that His plans and purposes were paramount. They may not have fully grasped what they were doing or why, but the Lord knew. After some of their recent and horrible disobediences, these acts of sacrifice must have touched His heart, as He planned this incredible multi-faceted display of His own dear Son.

Today, the Lord still tenderly stands amidst His own, and gently entreats, 'Why call ye me, Lord, Lord, and do not the things which I say?' Luke 6. 46. He will not force us to obey. But His work is best accomplished through the devoted and obedient hearts of His people. How 'willing' are our hearts?

June 30th

Exodus 35. 30-36. 7

BEZALEEL AND AHOLIAB

We have already met and considered a little about these two men. The Lord God was the architect of the tabernacle and these men were the skilled craftsmen who made it all happen. Little did they realize then, as they laboured tirelessly to follow every minute detail given them, that their efforts would produce the most exhaustive set of types of the Messiah that the law would provide. To this day, lectures, books, lessons and meetings on 'the Tabernacle' are still popular.

The Lord called them both by name. Their fathers and tribes of origin were mentioned. He filled them both with His Spirit for the work at hand. He provided them with understanding, knowledge and the skills of workmanship. He stirred their hearts to not only teach one another, but to teach others as well.

Chapter 36 begins with the words, 'Then wrought'. These men, above all else, were obedient. This is a great lesson for us today. Their considerable expertise would be of no value to the Lord at all had they not been willing-hearted and obedient. So much so, that they, and 'every wise-hearted man', commenced to do '**all** that the Lord had commanded'.

He has called us by grace. Each one of us, saved and redeemed, has practically and personally known what 'every good and perfect gift' means, for He has lavished us with countless blessings. He has filled us with His Spirit: not just a filling for a work, as these two men experienced, but an indwelling forever. The Spirit is able to 'teach us all things'. So, we must ask ourselves in His presence, how obedient have we been?

Jesus plaintively asked His disciples, 'And why call ye me, Lord, Lord, and do not the things which I say?', Luke 6. 46. So often we seek to demand obedience in others but forget about ourselves. Paul gets right to the heart of this matter when he says, 'And having in a readiness to revenge all disobedience, when your (own) obedience is fulfilled', 2 Cor. 10. 6.

What must we learn from these two men? That gift and skill mean nothing; personality is of no value; knowledge and wisdom count for nothing, unless it is all used for Him, with willing hearts and full obedience behind it all.

July 1st
Exodus 38. 21-31; 39. 32-43

THE SUM OF THE TABERNACLE

What a difference redemption makes! These Hebrews had earlier been building houses for Pharaoh, now they were building a house for Jehovah. But what a house this was! Not now the straw and stubble, bricks and mortar of the days of their slavery, but gold and silver, copper and shittim wood, with blue, purple and scarlet embroidery on fine twined linen. There were cloths of service, and priestly garments adorned with precious stones. There was so much furniture, and so many vessels and accessories, all made fragrant with sweet incense and anointing oils, and all to be protected with a covering of gorgeous curtains, badger skins, and rams' skins dyed red.

Inside the beautiful veil in the holy of holies the sacred ark was to be covered with a mercy seat of pure gold overshadowed by the cherubim of glory, Heb. 9. 5. Without the veil, in the holy place, a golden lampstand would shed its light across the sand to the table of gold for the shewbread, while between the lampstand and the table would stand the golden altar of incense from which eventually there would ascend a daily sweet savour to Jehovah. In the outer court, at the approach to the tent, there would be the great copper altar of burnt offering and the laver. God had given detailed instructions about everything, even concerning pins and hooks, pillars and cords, rings and sockets, and in response to the divine command willing hands and wise hearts had contributed all that was needed, and more. Men inspired of God and endued with wisdom and understanding had worked tirelessly. The people had freely given shekels of silver and talents of gold in their thousands. The women had laboured too, and soon the house would be filled with the glory of God. All this in the barrenness of a desolate wilderness!

And yet, this magnificent blending of wealth and beauty was all but a shadow, Heb. 8. 5; 10. 1. It pointed forward, a figure of something and Someone more excellent who was to come.

Believers today have an advantage. The Redeemer has come. He has made an end of sin and has gone up on high, a minister of the sanctuary, the true tabernacle in the heavens which the Lord pitched and not man, cf. Heb. 8. 2.

July 2nd

Exodus 40. 1-16

THOU SHALT SET UP THE TABERNACLE

At last the work was finished and that was a memorable day when the tabernacle would be set up. This first month of the year was an historical month, never to be forgotten, for it was on this same month that Jehovah had brought the Hebrews out from their bondage in Egypt, Exod. 12. 2; 13. 4. Now they had built Him a house, and in this first month of the year it would be set up so that He might dwell among them in His glory, Exod. 25. 8. As it had been prepared, so it must be set up, according to His directions, everything in its order.

The sacred ark must have precedence. It would be brought into the tent covered with the veil. Its place would always be behind the beautiful veil, to be seen by the high priest alone, once every year. Then they must bring the table, with the bread to be placed in order upon it. The lampstand with its lighted lamps would stand across from it in the holy place. Between these two and immediately before the veil would stand the golden altar of incense, and then table, lampstand and altar would be enclosed by the hanging of the door of the tent.

Outside was the outer court, surrounded by a fence of white linen suspended on pillars. Before the door of the tabernacle they must place the great altar of burnt offering, and between the door and this brazen or copper altar they must position the laver, at which the officiating priests would wash.

With everything in place all would now be sanctified, being anointed with the holy oil, Exod. 30. 22-25. The golden furniture, the many vessels, Aaron and his sons cleansed and in their priestly garments, all would be made fragrant, while from the golden incense altar there would ascend a sweet savour to God.

Soon, very soon, the tent would be filled with glory. It would all become, though these Hebrews would hardly know it, a delightful picture (though faint) of One who was to come. In Himself, and in His ministry, our Lord Jesus is the great Antitype of all this beauty and glory. His was a life impeccable, a death incomparable, and now in the heavens He is engaged for His people in a priestly ministry untransferable. Israel's tabernacle in the wilderness was temporary. Christ continues ever!

Exodus 40. 17-38

THE GLORY OF THE LORD

It is difficult, if not impossible, to adequately define glory. Every dictionary and lexicon, whether Hebrew, Greek or English, struggles for words to describe glory. 'Beauty; magnificence; majesty; renown; radiance; lustre; splendour; light; effulgence; honour'. All these words have been used in vain attempts to define the indefinable, but 'the glory of the Lord' will forever remain greater than human intellect!

Following that significant word of verse 33, 'so Moses finished the work', then the glory of the Lord filled the tabernacle. This phrase is repeated in verse 35 and such was the glory that Moses was not able to enter into the tent. So, having finished His work on earth, our Lord Jesus now fills the heavens with His glory and a consideration of the details of the tabernacle in the wilderness illustrates something of that glory. As a psalm declares, 'In His temple everything saith glory', Ps. 29. 9 ASV, or, as others prefer, 'every whit of it uttereth glory'.

The holy ark in the inner shrine, with its incorruptible wood encased in shining gold speaks of the glory of Christ as truly man and very God. This is inexplicable. We are not asked to explain or expound, or even understand. We can only bow in the wonder of it all, that the Man of Galilee was God incarnate.

Once He was, on earth in the days of His flesh, the light of the world, but now He is the light of the sanctuary, like the lampstand in the holy place. He is the glory of the heavens.

Just as the golden table displayed the shewbread, the food of the priests, so the people of God now feed on the glorified Christ, fellowshipping together in Him who is the bread of God.

The ministry of the altar of incense is fulfilled in Him too. He now fills all heaven with that same fragrance of holy manhood which delighted His Father during His earthly sojourn.

He has been to Golgotha as the great altar. He has finished His sacrificial work and is now engaged in a laver-like ministry for the cleansing of His people who still live in a defiling world.

Everything, every whit in this tabernacle, cries 'Glory'! As that house was filled with the glory of the Lord so today the heavenly sanctuary is filled with the glory of the risen Saviour.

Leviticus 1. 1-17; 6. 8-13

THE PRIEST SHALL BURN ALL ON THE ALTAR

The tabernacle having been set up and filled with glory, now commences the story of the offerings which Jehovah required of His redeemed people. The burnt-offering is the high ground of worship, and, as might be expected, this is where Jehovah begins. These are not the hands of sinners which bring this offering. These are not troubled hearts looking for forgiveness. They are the hands and hearts of worshippers desiring to give something to Jehovah. There will be detailed directions concerning five principal offerings in these early chapters of Leviticus and in each of the other four offerings there will be some portion for the priests or for the people. However, apart from the skin, 7. 8, the burnt-offering would be in its entirety for God, all to be burnt upon the great altar, to ascend in a sweet savour to Him.

How beautifully this foreshadowed the One who was to come, whose whole life in its every detail was fragrant for God. Four parts of the offering are specifically mentioned, the head, the fat, the inwards and the legs. It was the Lord Jesus Himself who said, 'Thou shalt love the Lord thy God with all thy heart, and with all thy soul, and with all thy strength, and with all thy mind', Luke 10. 27. This complete devotion to Jehovah answers exactly to the inwards, the fat, the legs, and the head of the burnt offering. One Man alone lived and loved like this.

The offerer, having brought his offering to the door of the tabernacle, would lean his hand upon its head, and, without a word being spoken, two things were happening. He was, though silently, being identified with his offering. By his action he was saying, 'This is mine', and all the acceptability of his offering was being transferred to him, perfectly covering him in his personal shortcomings and failings. Soon he would stand back and witness the smoke ascending from the altar to Jehovah as a sweet savour. It was worship!

Believers today have a great, an inestimable privilege. We bring to God our appreciation of Christ. We speak to the Father about the Son, expressing as best we can the perfections of that lovely Man whose whole life, from the manger to the cross, was just a cloud of fragrant human incense rising sweetly to heaven.

July 5th
Leviticus 2. 1-16; 6. 14-23
A MEAT-OFFERING . . . OF FINE FLOUR

A thoughtful believer, coming to a study of this offering for the first time, may well ask, is it 'meat-offering' as in our King James Version? Or is it 'meal-offering', as in some other versions, and as many preachers seem to prefer? This was indeed a meal-offering in that substantially the offering was of fine flour. It was a meat-offering, however, in that it was a gift or oblation, which is the meaning of the Hebrew word *minchah*, STRONG 4503. 'Meat' does not mean 'flesh', but 'food', as in John 4. 32, 34. The meat-offering was a bloodless oblation, a gift of food for the altar, which later became the food of the priests, Lev. 2. 3. It is not in any sense an offering for sin, but is a delightful foreshadowing of Christ in His perfect humanity, living down here as a Man pure and fragrant for God.

Four ingredients are mentioned for the offering in its various forms. Two other substances are mentioned which at no time and in no way are to be included in the meat-offering.

First, fine flour, of smooth, even consistency, with no harsh lumps or coarseness. Such was His life who could at all times present Himself to God with every pleasing moral virtue in perfect blend and balance, and who is now the food of His people.

Second, oil, which either mingled with the flour, or anointed the baked cakes, or saturated the pieces. Our Lord's was a life and ministry of unbroken communion and fellowship with the gracious Holy Spirit, of whom the oil is so often a symbol.

Third, frankincense, white and pure, rich and rare, sweet and fragrant. It was one of the ingredients of the holy incense of the tabernacle, Exod. 30. 34, and surely speaks of that lovely life of Christ which ever ascended as a holy perfume to God.

Fourth, salt must always be included. This great preservative would be to the spiritual mind a constant reminder of a Saviour who did not sin because He would not sin because He could not sin. He was holy; He was impeccable; He had no ability to sin.

Leaven, that corrupting element, always, without exception, used symbolically of evil, must be excluded from the offering.

Honey too must be excluded; it has a sweetness which can be spoiled by circumstances, but not so the sweetness of Christ.

July 6th

Leviticus 3. 1-17; 7. 11-38

A SACRIFICE OF PEACE-OFFERING

In some ways the peace-offering is very similar to the burnt-offering, but there is one important difference. Whereas the burnt-offering was all burnt upon the altar, all, in its entirety, for God, the peace-offering was an offering to be shared by many. This is, in fact, the significance of the word 'peace' which is not the usual Hebrew *shalom* but a cognate word *shelem* meaning a fellowship or alliance. Of course, it typifies the same devotion of the Saviour, obedient unto death, who said, 'Therefore doth my Father love me, because I lay down my life', John 10. 17.

Like the burnt-offering, the peace-offering was essentially a sweet savour offering and the man who offered it was a worshipper. He was not a sinner looking for peace but one already in the enjoyment of peace desiring to give something to God. He may be offering in thanksgiving for some blessing enjoyed, Lev. 7. 12. He may be making a vow to the Lord, Lev. 7. 16, or he may simply be presenting a voluntary offering of worship, Lev. 7. 16. It may be asked, if this was the reason for bringing an offering, why did such a man, with such a desire, not bring a burnt-offering? The answer is that it was just because he wanted others to share in his enjoyment.

This being so there must first be a portion for God and so the inwards and the fat, or suet, which covered them was put upon the altar. This would burn in a sweet savour which ascended to Jehovah, speaking of those tender inner sensibilities of Christ which were so precious to God, while the blood of the offering was sprinkled round about upon the altar.

The priests then had their portion and fed upon the shoulder and the breast of the offering, typical of a priesthood today feeding on the strength of Christ and on His love, Lev. 7. 32-34.

The remainder of the offering was carried home by the offerer who prepared with it a special meal to be eaten in fellowship with his family and friends.

What a communion was this then! Jehovah, the priestly family, the offerer, his family, and his friends, together enjoying the sacrifice of the peace offering. So it is today, God and His people, and Christ Himself, all sharing in the fruits of Calvary.

July 7th
Leviticus 4. 1-35; 6. 24-30

IF A SOUL SHALL SIN THROUGH IGNORANCE

It is a sad reflection of the state of the human heart that a man may sin and not be aware of it. To sin, and know that one has sinned, is evil enough, but to sin and not know it reveals that depravity which is common to all. But, whether in ignorance or in wilfulness, sin is sin and requires an offering for acceptance before God. These early chapters of Leviticus expound the variety of ways in which a man may sin, but thankfully they also explain Jehovah's way of forgiveness. As soon as a sin committed in ignorance comes to light then forgiveness is necessary, and is possible. In Leviticus chapter 4 there is another thing, the universality of sin. None, it seems, is immune to its poison.

The chapter opens by envisaging the sin of the priest. How serious is this! One with all the privileges, enlightenment and responsibilities of priesthood actually sinning! He must bring a bullock, the highest grade of sin-offering. He must lean his hand upon its head so that he is identified with the victim whose life will be given for his. He is then responsible for slaying the bullock and will watch as the inwards and fat are **burned** upon the altar and the blood is sprinkled round about, after which the whole carcase will be carried outside the camp and **consumed** by fire upon the wood in a clean place.

But note this! The word for the burning of the sin-offering is not the same as the word used for the burning of the burnt-offering in Leviticus chapter 1. There it was a fire which produced a sweet savour for God. Here it is a burning as of refuse, a consuming out of sight of something abhorrent to Jehovah.

Though the details may be different, and the required victims different also, yet when the whole congregation sins, or when a ruler sins, or when it may be one of the common people, one thing is always needed, a suitable victim must be found and blood must be shed. The shedding of blood is the giving up of a life. It is the death of a substitute in the place of the guilty man. So do we say of the Saviour as we see Him die at Golgotha,

'In rich abounding grace He took my guilty place,
With all its deep disgrace,
And died for me'.

July 8th

Leviticus 5. 1-19; 6. 1-7; 7. 1-10

HE SHALL BRING HIS TRESPASS-OFFERING

Although there are essential differences between the sin-offering and the trespass-offering, yet there are basic similarities too. Sin is sin, whether committed ignorantly or wilfully, and always needs forgiveness. Ignorance, however, can never be pleaded for the sins envisaged in the above readings. Lying, cheating, defrauding, stealing, are all sins of the will. There is no excuse and they demand punishment either in the perpetrator of them or in an acceptable substitute. Jehovah had ordained a way of forgiveness but there was a four-fold requirement.

First, there must be a full confession. 'He shall confess that he hath sinned in that thing', Lev. 5. 5. The guilty man must freely and frankly and without reserve acknowledge his sin.

Second, there must be an offering. It may be a ram, a lamb, or two birds, and yet, in great grace even under law Jehovah would remember the meagre resources of some of the people and in cases of extreme penury would accept the tenth part of an ephah of fine flour. This, of course, would soon be saturated by the blood upon the altar where it would be offered.

Third, there must be suitable restitution. The value of that which had been misappropriated from the victim of the crime, must be restored in full if forgiveness was to be enjoyed.

Fourth, it was required that a fifth part of that value was also to be added and given to the one who had suffered, as compensation for the hurt and distress which had been caused.

All of this was a foreshadowing of God's great plan for the forgiveness of sinful men and women by the death of Christ. The sinless Saviour has voluntarily become a substitute and surety for the guilty. The sinner desirous of making his way back to an offended God must begin by making a full confession of his sinful state, sinful by nature and by practice. God Himself has provided the offering in the Person of His Son who has, in deep suffering, restored that which He took not away, Ps. 69. 4. He has not only made restitution for sins which He did not commit but He has also added a revenue of grace, a fifth part, as it were, so that now it may be said, most reverently, that God has more glory than ever, even though man has sinned.

July 9th

Leviticus 8. 1-21

AARON AND HIS SONS

It was a memorable day in Israel when the priestly family was consecrated in the sight of the whole congregation. Many of the details had already been given, Exodus 28-29, but now, with multitudes watching, the priesthood was to be formally inaugurated. Aaron and his sons were to be consecrated in a solemn ceremony. There would be washings and anointings and offerings of various kinds, and the priests would be suitably attired in the priestly robes which had already been prepared. Note that 'all the congregation', v. 3, was to be gathered to observe. Does this teach us that all the saints should be interested in priestly exercise?

First, Aaron and his sons would be washed with water, but if Aaron is washed this does not at all imply that our Great High Priest needed such cleansing. Aaron was washed to make him typically what Christ was intrinsically, clean. His sons were washed too, meaning that eventually there was a whole priesthood acceptably clean for their priestly ministry.

Aaron was then dressed in his high priestly garments. Linen coat and robe of blue, ephod and breastplate, girdle and mitre and the holy crown were all put upon him by Moses. These were holy garments for glory and for beauty, Exod. 28. 2. They signified the holiness, the glory, and the beauty of Him who was to come.

With the holy anointing oil, prepared as was prescribed in Exodus 30 verses 22-25, Aaron was made fragrant, as was the tabernacle with its furniture and vessels, the scene of his future ministry. It was then that his sons were attired in their priestly garments and all was solemnly consecrated by the offering of a bullock and a ram, a sin-offering and a burnt-offering.

Believers today have in the glory a Great High Priest who ministers daily for them. Heaven is fragrant with His ministry which is based upon the value of one great offering at Golgotha which has superseded and eclipsed all that have ever gone before. If that was a memorable day when Aaron and his sons were consecrated for Israel, what a day was that when our Lord Jesus ascended from Olivet to engage in His heavenly ministry!

Leviticus 8. 22-36

THE RAM OF CONSECRATION

The consecration of the priestly family was now almost complete but there were two matters yet to have attention. At the commencement of the ceremony Moses had been instructed to bring a bullock, two rams, and a basket of unleavened bread. The bullock had been slain as a sin-offering and one of the rams as a burnt-offering, but the second ram and the basket of unleavened bread still remained.

This second ram is called 'the ram of consecration' and it is neither a sin-offering nor a burnt-offering. It has been described in its uniqueness as a restricted peace-offering, unique in that it was to be shared by Moses and the priests only.

When the ram was slain Moses took of the blood and anointed Aaron's right ear, the thumb of his right hand, and the great toe of his right foot, and he did the same for Aaron's sons. Ears which would hear the divine commands, hands which would handle the sacred vessels, and feet which would stand in the holy sanctuary, were all thereby consecrated by blood.

The fat and the inwards of the ram, the inner excellencies, were then put into the hands of Aaron together with cakes and wafers from the basket. All was waved before the Lord so that His eye would be upon that which was to be offered and so all would be burnt on the altar as a sweet savour.

Then there followed another anointing of Aaron and his sons, and so sanctified, this privileged priestly family enjoyed the boiled flesh of the offering, eating it with the unleavened bread which remained in the basket.

In all of this observe how Jehovah must have His portion first. This was most important. But notice too, that the sanctified priests fed on that which had already satisfied God and the altar. Our Saviour called Himself 'the bread of God', John 6. 33. This does not simply mean the bread which God has provided, but the bread upon which God Himself feeds. Then, He who has satisfied God becomes the food of His people.

This priestly ministry was costly! There was blood and fire, fragrant oil and the provision of bread, all having its grand fulfilment in Him who has satisfied both God and His people.

Leviticus 9. 1-24

GO UNTO THE ALTAR AND OFFER

How significantly does this chapter begin, 'And it came to pass on the eighth day'! This is, of course, the first day of the week which is so precious to believers of the present day, who ever remember and cherish it as being the day when their Lord rose triumphantly from among the dead. On the seventh day He rested in the grave; on the eighth day He rose from the dead.

It was not until the eighth day that Aaron and his sons were permitted to enter the sanctuary or engage in priestly ministry for the congregation. But now, cleansed, sanctified and consecrated they were to enter on their ministry with the promise that the glory of the Lord would appear to them.

They were now to go to the altar and offer. There would be, on this day, burnt-offerings, sin-offerings, peace-offerings and a meat-offering. The details were many and varied. There would be calves and a lamb, a bullock and a ram, pieces to be burned on the altar and flesh to be burned outside the camp. The details are of value only as we see them as prefiguring that great sacrifice which was to come at Calvary.

Our Lord Jesus is the grand fulfilment of every burnt-offering. His was a life lived entirely for God and eventually laid down in devotion at the cross. It was all, in life and in death, a sweet savour to God.

His death was a sin-offering too. 'He hath made him to be sin for us', 2 Cor. 5. 21. He who knew no sin has died laden with the sins of others and has made forgiveness of sins a glorious possibility for all who will believe.

Then, He was a peace-offering. God and His people share together in the greatness of the sacrifice of Christ. His death has made available a holy fellowship between God and men.

Of course, there was the fulfilment of the meat-offering too in that virtuous life which was lived in perfect sinlessness and then offered in death upon the tree.

On this 'eighth day', with a Saviour risen from the dead and exalted in the heavens, it is the privilege of believers to 'go unto the altar' and as sanctified worshippers present to God their appreciation of Him whom they have come to know and love.

July 12th
Leviticus 10. 1-7

STRANGE FIRE

How indescribably sad is this, that immediately after the solemn ceremonies of the inauguration, the consecration, the anointing and sanctification of the priesthood, there should be such disobedience on the part of two priests, and such judgement from God.

Aaron had four sons, Nadab and Abihu, Eleazar and Ithamar. They were highly privileged young men with a father who was high priest and an uncle like Moses. But privilege is not necessarily a safeguard against carelessness or disobedience and in this case Nadab and Abihu, whether individually or in unison, whether carelessly or disobediently, decided to take their censers and burn incense in their own way. There was always fire on the altar, a fire from the Lord. It was a fire which must never be put out nor allowed to go out, Lev. 6. 12-13. It was the fire upon which the burnt-offerings were burned and which accepted for God those chosen parts of the other offerings, and the priests and people alike had so recently watched that fire consuming the offering, Lev. 9. 24. How often the offerings were called 'the offerings of the Lord made by fire'.

Why then should these young men offer incense with 'strange fire', fire which did not come from the altar? It brought an immediate 'fire from the Lord', as if a solemn and awful reminder of the altar fire which they had chosen to ignore. God's work must always be done in God's way. Otherwise, though human reasoning may think it to be acceptable, He may blow upon it and judge those who have taken their own way.

It says much for the character of Aaron that he submissively accepted the judgement upon his sons. He watched his cousins carrying the two young men out from before the sanctuary and out of the camp and with what must have been a broken heart he 'held his peace'. As in the case of Ananias and Saphira in the earliest days of church testimony there had been a sad lapse in behaviour and a fearful judgement from the Lord, Acts 5. 1-11.

The lesson surely must be that if there are divine directions concerning the work of the Lord we must obey. A second solemn lesson is that even privileged priests can sin.

July 13th

Leviticus 10. 8-20

HOLY AND UNHOLY

This section of the chapter opens with a solemn directive given by Jehovah to Aaron the high priest, personally. It is a prohibition against the drinking of wine or strong drink by the priests who engaged in the ministry of the tabernacle. Many think, perhaps with some justification, that, coming immediately after the catastrophe which claimed the lives of Aaron's two sons, they may well have been inebriated at the time of their disobedience and that this might have been the reason for their behaviour. 'Wine is a mocker, strong drink is raging', wrote another, many years later, Prov. 20. 1. It dulls the senses and robs the indulgent person of the capability of distinguishing between the holy and the unholy, whether persons or things.

Such distinction is essential and it was necessary that the priests of the Lord, and His people everywhere, should have a clear understanding to be able to discern at all times between the clean and the unclean. 'Holiness becometh thine house', wrote the psalmist, Ps. 93. 5. It has ever been the mind of God that His people should be a holy people. 'Ye shall be unto me a kingdom of priests, and an holy nation', Exod. 19. 6, and as it was in the Old Testament, so it is in the New, 'Ye are a chosen generation, a royal priesthood, an holy nation', 1 Pet. 2. 9.

The word 'holy', Hebrew *qodesh*, 6944 in STRONG's *Concordance*, means, 'sacred; sanctified; consecrated; hallowed'. That which is holy is dedicated to Jehovah, separated for Him who is 'Holy, holy, holy', Isa. 6. 3. He is 'the Holy One', Isa. 40. 25, 'whose name is Holy', Isa. 57. 15. It was so necessary then, that His priests should be able, with a clear mind, to distinguish between the holy and the unholy, and still it is so.

The concluding verses of this chapter record a sad failure on the part of Aaron and his remaining sons to eat the sin-offering. Aaron acknowledged that the flesh of the sin-offering ought to have been eaten by the priests but gave as the reason why this had not been done, the calamity which had just befallen his two eldest sons. That judgement on the priesthood was so solemn a warning that they might properly feel that they did not have the holiness which was required for eating the general sin-offering.

July 14th

Leviticus 11. 1-47

THESE . . . YE SHALL EAT

This chapter records and explains the details of the dietary and sanitary laws which Jehovah imposed upon His redeemed people. There were several reasons for such laws, among them, and perhaps chiefly as some think, the health and hygiene of more than two million pilgrims in a wilderness environment. There were laws touching the eating, or abstinence from, beasts, birds, fish, and reptiles. Some of these creatures appear to be almost obviously unclean, from which a person would instinctively revolt. Others may at first sight appear quite acceptable but are forbidden by these laws. Refraining from unclean flesh would be a safeguard for the health and well-being of the people.

There was, however, another important reason for these laws. If they were observed as a rule of life they would preserve the uniqueness and national identity of this covenant people in their relationship to Jehovah. Those who would abide by them would be protected from any integration with the heathen nations around, whose diet was unrestricted and uncontrolled by any such regulations. Note how Daniel and his companions were blessed by their adherence to God's laws, Dan. 1. 3-20.

Yet another purpose in these laws was that the people might, like the priests in the previous chapter, learn to be sensitive, to distinguish between the clean and the unclean, whether practical, moral, or ceremonial. There were practices which were acceptable among the heathen which must not be tolerated among the people of God. Learning to obey Him even in matters of diet would attune the individual to doing only what would be pleasing to Him. As MATTHEW HENRY has written, 'God would thus teach his people to distinguish themselves from other people, not only in their religious worship, but in the common actions of life . . . that thus, by having a diet peculiar to themselves, they might be kept from familiar conversation with their idolatrous neighbours'. How true this is!

It would hardly be possible, nor expected of us, that we should press a typical significance upon every detail here, but the responsibility to discern between the holy and the unholy, the clean and the unclean, devolves upon every believer today.

July 15th

Leviticus 12. 1-8

THE DAYS OF HER PURIFYING

This brief chapter deals with the uncleanness of a new mother in Israel and while this might primarily have been a ceremonial uncleanness, yet there were hygienic and health implications too. The regulations applied, with some differences, whether the new-born child was male or female.

If the child born was a son then there was to be an initial period of uncleanness of seven days after which the boy would be circumcised. This was to be followed by thirty-three days more. If the child was a daughter then that initial period would be fourteen days, followed by another period of sixty-six days. So then, the new mother of a son would be ceremonially unclean for forty days but the mother of a daughter for eighty days, exactly double the length of time. Why this extension of the unclean period should apply in the case of a female child is obscure. Few if any commentators venture an explanation.

Eventually, with both mothers the days of purification according to the law would be completed. Each would then be required to bring two offerings. She should bring a lamb for a burnt-offering and a bird for a sin-offering, either a young pigeon or a turtledove. Note how God must have His portion first, the burnt-offering was all for Him as has been observed in Leviticus chapter 1. But He is not unmindful of the need of His people and so a sin-offering will meet that need also.

However, a problem is anticipated. In certain cases, for certain reasons, a new mother may not be able to bring a lamb for a burnt-offering. It is good to notice that again and again, even under law, God is gracious! He recognizes the possibility of such difficulty or penury and introduces a law for the poor. If the young mother cannot bring a lamb then He will accept two turtledoves or two young pigeons, one for a burnt-offering and the other for a sin-offering, so that the demands of God and the needs of the offerer are still fully met.

Most will remember that when Mary, the virgin mother, brought forth her first-born Son in Bethlehem, she availed herself of the law for the poor and offered two birds. Well does the apostle say of her Son, 'Ye know . . . his poverty', 2. Cor. 8. 9.

215

July 16th

Leviticus 13. 1-59

THE PLAGUE OF LEPROSY

Leprosy is presented in the scriptures not so much as a disease needing to be cured, but a defilement needing to be cleansed; in that respect it is a fitting picture of sin. Today's passage is concerned with leprosy amongst God's people and these directions were given to enable the priest to recognize this plague in persons, vv. 2-46, and in garments, vv. 47-59. Making a practical application, the first aspect is typical of sin in the believer, the inward workings of his fallen nature, while the second is suggestive of sin about him, in his ways and associations.

Leprosy could develop from very small beginnings, a bright spot or white hair, some manifestation hitherto not seen, vv. 4-8. Similarly, in us sin can manifest itself in ways we had least expected or previously known. The plague might be in a man but dormant, later to become active again, 'an old leprosy', vv. 9-11, a reminder that we must take care lest sins that marked us in pre-conversion days re-appear later in our life. Leprosy might develop in a boil that had been healed, vv. 18-23, in like manner issues that took place in the past and were thought to have been dealt with can sometimes be allowed to flare up again and cause yet further sin. Leprosy could develop on a burnt place in the skin, vv. 24-28, figurative perhaps of the potential for anger or wrath to become a source of sin. Verses 29-37 deal with leprosy in the head; this might be visible or concealed in the hair or beard, suggestive maybe of sinful thoughts and sinful speech. Finally, it could occur in a 'bald head', vv. 40-44. The bald head would itself be indicative of decline and decay, and as the years advance and, with it, infirmities develop, old age can become an occasion for failure and sin.

All who, upon careful examination, had leprosy were pronounced 'unclean', unless it covered 'all the skin', then the person was declared to be 'clean', v. 12-13, his leprosy was no longer active, his condition was evident, typical of open confession, which is always the way to being clean before God, Ps. 32. 5. As we consider, and seek to practically apply to sin, the various ways in which leprosy might be manifest, are there any such sins in our life that we need to confess today? Be clean!

July 17th

Leviticus 14. 1-57

THE DAY OF HIS CLEANSING

Leprosy not only rendered a person unclean before God but also condemned him to dwell apart from the congregation of Israel, Lev. 13. 45-46. Thus the law concerning the cleansing of a leper had in view his return to the camp and a return to his privileges before God. The first is dealt with in verses 1 to 8; the second in verses 9 to 32.

The first phase began outside the camp where the priest, having established the leper was healed, initiated the service for his cleansing. The two birds to be taken for the leper are typical of Christ both in His death and resurrection, Rom. 4. 25. Both birds were to be 'clean' a reminder to us that Christ 'knew no sin', 2 Cor. 5. 21. One bird was killed and its blood wrung out into an earthen vessel over running water with which the leper was then sprinkled and pronounced clean. The blood reminds us that the basis of all cleansing is the death of Christ. The water can be viewed as figurative of the word of God applied in the power of the Holy Spirit to the conscience, bringing us back to Calvary and the confession of our sins, 1 John 1. 7-9. The living bird was then released but since it had been dipped in the blood it bore evidence of the death that had taken place, John 20. 27. Next, the healed leper was to wash himself, having been identified in type with Christ in His death and resurrection he must personally cleanse himself from all defilement, v. 8; cf. 2 Cor. 7. 1.

The second phase of his cleansing took place on the eighth day and concerned his presentation before the Lord and restoration to service before Him, v. 11. He brought a trespass offering and its blood was placed upon him. He brought oil which was also sprinkled on him, indicative of the fact that his life henceforth was to be yielded to God, vv. 10-18. Then he offered a sin offering and a burnt offering, thereby acknowledging the basis of his cleansing and acceptance before God, vv. 19-20. The leper put out in chapter 13 is now restored to both the congregation and the sanctuary, cf. 1 Cor. 5. 13; 2 Cor. 2. 6-9. That God desired this is seen in the gracious provision for a poor leper to fulfil this law, vv. 21-32. He still desires such restoration, Gal. 6. 1.

July 18th

Leviticus 15. 1-33

UNCLEANNESS

As with the leper, those unclean by reason of an 'issue' were to be put outside the camp, Num. 5. 2. But whereas in the leper we have a picture of the inward workings of man's fallen nature, in this chapter the teaching concerns its outward working.

Verses 2-18 deal with uncleanness in men; a running issue, that which is abnormal, verses 2-15 and the emission of seed, that which is natural, verses 16-18. Verses 19-30 describe uncleanness in women; that which is natural in verses 19-24 and what is unnatural in verses 25-30. Summarizing the lessons to be gleaned from this passage, the late C. H. MACKINTOSH commented, 'every movement of nature . . . even things which seem as far as man is concerned unavoidable weakness . . . required cleansing'.

In this chapter we learn that, sin having come in, everything that proceeds from the 'flesh', that is, man's fallen nature, is defiling, Mark 7. 19-23, an uncleanness that can so easily be communicated to others. It might be such a simple thing as a word spoken in haste or a momentary display of anger, yet sufficient to produce defiling thoughts within, or a sinful retort from another. Then, as to ourselves, we can daily hear and see things that so easily find a ready response in our fallen nature even though we never intend or desire they should. Alongside the recognition of what is defiling, there is equal emphasis in this chapter upon the means of cleansing. Broadly speaking, those with a 'running issue' were to wash their clothes and bathe seven days and on the eighth day bring a sin offering and a burnt offering, while those defiled by contact with uncleanness were to just wash and bathe and were unclean until the evening. Typically, these details remind us of the cleansing power of the sacrificial work of Christ, for the expiation of sin, and the cleansing power of the word of God, for purification, Rev. 1. 5; Eph. 5. 26. The chapter concludes with the reason for these commandments, God was dwelling in their midst, His presence required their purity, to reject His word and despise His holiness would expose them to judgement, v. 31. God still says to His people, 'touch not the unclean thing', 2 Cor. 6. 17.

July 19th

Leviticus 16. 1-19

MAKE AN ATONEMENT

The Hebrew word for 'atonement' is used sixteen times in this chapter in connection with a day that was central to the whole Levitical economy. The tabernacle was cleansed from the defilement incurred through the service of the people, vv. 16-19, and the people also themselves were cleansed, vv. 21, 30.

The chapter opens by recalling the sin of Nadab and Abihu. This was a reminder of the holiness of God, that it is no light matter to draw near to Him, and the reason why atonement was necessary if God was to continue to dwell in their midst and the people were to be fit for His presence.

First, we should consider *who* was active that day, just one man, Aaron, type of the Lord Jesus who alone could make purification for sins, vv. 3-29; Heb. 1. 3. Then, we must notice *when* he would draw near 'not at all times' but limited to one day of the year and of course each year, vv. 2, 29. Next, the *way* he was to draw near is carefully described, vv. 3-5. He was to wash, put on his 'holy garments' and bring an offering for himself, that suitably cleansed and clothed he might be 'ceremonially what Christ was personally', A. LECKIE. Finally, he brought an offering for the people. We must also look at the *work* of Aaron on that day. He entered 'within the veil', into the Holiest of all, on three occasions. The first and second entrance were in connection with the atonement for himself and his house. He went in first with incense, type of the fragrance of the Person of Christ and, secondly, with the blood of the bullock for a sin offering, type of the work of Christ, vv. 12-14. He then came out to deal with the people's sin, type of Him who 'appeared to put away sin by the sacrifice of himself', Heb. 9. 26. He then entered, for the third time, within the veil with the blood of the sin offering for the people, picture of Him who, in virtue of His work upon the cross, has entered into heaven as the representative of His people, Heb. 9. 24. Aaron entered in with the blood of animals, but Christ has entered with His own blood, Heb. 9. 12. Aaron then came out to make atonement for the altar and deal with the scapegoat, vv. 18-22. But we know when Christ appears it will be 'without sin unto salvation', Heb. 9. 28.

July 20th

Leviticus 16. 20-34

A LAND NOT INHABITED

On the Day of Atonement two goats were brought as a sin offering for the people, v. 5. Although but one offering, two goats were necessary in order to portray the significance of that day.

One goat was slain and its blood sprinkled 'within the veil', 'upon . . . and before the mercy seat', v. 15. Here, we see the *God-ward aspect* of Aaron's ministry, the blood satisfying God's demands in respect of sin, maintaining His glory, and enabling Him to continue to dwell in the midst of the people. In the second goat, the scapegoat, we see the *man-ward aspect* to the ministry, the removal of the people's sins. Aaron only dealt with the scapegoat after the blood of the slain goat had been sprinkled within the sanctuary, the order indicating that there can be no forgiveness for men until God's claims have been met, v. 20. Aaron was to confess over the live goat all the perverseness, rebellion and failure of the people that the scapegoat might bear their sins into 'a land not inhabited', vv. 21, 22. These directions find a parallel in the experience of the Lord Jesus as the One upon whom 'the Lord hath laid . . . the iniquity of us all', Isa. 53. 4-6. The scapegoat was sent out 'by the hand of a fit man', one both able and standing ready, a reminder not only of the moral fitness of Christ to suffer for sin but also of His willingness, John 10. 17. Sent into 'a land not inhabited', it became a graphic illustration of what Christ experienced for us on the cross, Ps. 22. 2. In the wilderness, apart from men, the sins the scapegoat bore would never be recalled again and, as to ourselves, we rejoice to be able to say with the psalmist, 'As far as the east is from the west, so far hath he removed our transgressions from us', Ps. 103. 12. In verse 26, 'he that let go the goat' returned and was to wash his clothes and bathe his flesh, picture of Him who arose from the dead and, in resurrection, was as holy after Calvary as He had been before, even though in the intervening period He 'was made sin', 2 Cor. 5. 21.

Despite the detailed service, there were limitations to the Day of Atonement, reflected in its annual repetition, vv. 29-34; Heb. 10. 1-4. Thank God there is no such deficiency with the work of Christ, Heb. 10. 14.

July 21st

Leviticus 17. 1-16

THE LIFE OF THE FLESH IS IN THE BLOOD

As the people of the Lord, the children of Israel were to be holy and that was to be reflected in their conduct respecting 'their sacrifices' and 'any manner of blood'.

The Lord had appointed one place where all animals, whether for food or sacrifice, were to be slain, vv. 3-9. Any domestic animals killed for food were not to be slain 'in the camp' or 'out of the camp' but had to be brought to the tabernacle and offered as a sacrifice to the Lord vv. 3-4. Two reasons are given. First, that they might present the animal to God as a 'peace offering' from which He would receive the blood and the fat and of which they could then partake in fellowship with Him, vv. 5-6. Involved in this there was a practical acknowledgement that the life they took belonged to God and the food was a provision from Him. In this way, it became an expression of their gratitude for it. The second reason is found in verse 7, where offering to the Lord would help to prevent the people making sacrifices to 'devils' in 'the open fields'. These practices were apparently common among them, something they had brought with them from Egypt. Likewise, we are to appreciate our dependence upon the Lord and eat our food with a thankful heart in fellowship with Him, 1 Tim. 4. 4, 5.

The remainder of the chapter concerns a prohibition against the eating of blood, vv. 10-16. The reason, given in verse 11, is that in the shedding of blood the life is taken. The sentence upon man is 'the soul that sinneth it shall die' but God in grace appointed the taking of the life of another in place of the sinner. The shedding of blood under divine judgement was the means to make 'an atonement for the soul', Ezek. 18. 4; Heb. 9. 22. The children of Israel, as well as strangers among them, were to appreciate the expiatory value of the blood. Their recognition that 'the life of the flesh is in the blood' was also to be demonstrated in their conduct when hunting game and their treatment of animals from which the blood had not flowed forth, vv. 13-16. Surely, these instructive precepts remind us of One who 'laid down his life for us' and through whose 'precious blood' we have redemption, 1 John 3. 16; 1 Pet. 1. 18-19.

July 22nd

Leviticus 18. 1-30

DEFILE NOT YE YOURSELVES

Three times in this chapter we read the words 'I am the Lord', a reminder of His glory, vv. 5, 6, 21. Three times we read 'I am the Lord your God', a revelation of His grace, vv. 2, 4, 30. Because He is Lord it follows that any relationship to Him will bring responsibility before Him.

The first five verses describe two basic requirements for the conduct of all who know God. First, their separation from the deeds of the nations and, secondly, their submission to the decrees of God's word.

Having laid down those basic principles, verses 6 to 18 give specific instructions regarding *unlawful marriages*, with blood relations, mother and stepmother, vv. 7-8; sister, half-sister and grand-daughter, vv. 9-11; aunts and the wife of a paternal uncle, vv. 12-14; daughter-in-law and sister-in-law, vv. 15-16; step-daughter and step-grandchildren, v. 17, and, finally, marrying two sisters simultaneously, v. 18. J. N. DARBY succinctly summarizes this section thus, 'We are not to confound the intimacies of marriage with . . . natural relationships'. In verses 19 to 23, the precepts are more general in character and focus on *unlawful associations*, sexually, v. 19; then in connection with adultery, v. 20; idolatry, v. 21; homosexuality, v. 22; and bestiality, v. 23. The terrible catalogue of evils embraced within these verses reveals the depth to which men can go in their pursuit of evil, the more so in that the nations were guilty of actually committing such deeds, 'in all these the nations are defiled', v. 24; Rom. 1. 21-32. While these evils appal us we should not forget the potential for evil that there is in our own hearts and that, sadly, it is not unknown for a believer to be guilty of conduct that, even in a morally lax society, is 'not so much as named among the Gentiles', 1 Cor. 5. 1.

The 'nations' were defiled, the 'land' was defiled, but the people of God were to be different, vv. 24-25. It is still the same today and so we are exhorted in the New Testament, 'Love not the world', 'Be not conformed to this world' and to keep ourselves 'unspotted from the world', 1 John 2. 15; Rom. 12. 2; Jas. 1. 27. Let us take care not to 'defile ourselves'.

July 23rd

Leviticus 19. 1-37

YE SHALL KEEP MY STATUTES

To keep God's word is to be kept from sin, a combination that is reflected in our reading today. The call to 'be holy' in verse 2 is accompanied by the commands to 'keep' and 'observe' the statutes of the Lord, vv. 19, 37. In each verse it is a translation of the same Hebrew word which has the idea, first, to take care of, secondly, to pay diligent attention to and, thirdly, to guard and preserve. Additional to these, there is the command to 'do them', to perform and accomplish them, in verse 37.

The various commands recorded here concern the people's behaviour towards God and towards men. The fact that the two aspects are interwoven throughout the chapter would suggest that they are both equally important and remind us that every facet of our lives is to be regulated by the word of God – spiritual life, family life, civil and social life. To the commands there was a positive and negative side, things to be done and things not to be done. These were requirements of the Law but the two sides are equally evident in the teaching of grace, Titus 2. 12.

Limiting ourselves to some of the commands that concern conduct towards men, we observe that parents are to be respected throughout their lives, v. 3. The needs of the poor and the stranger were to be considered and no advantage was to be taken of a man's disability, whether deaf or blind, vv. 9-10, 14. They were to respect the elderly and love the stranger, and in all of their dealings they were to act in a righteous manner, vv. 32, 34-36. Particularly notable in this chapter is the fact that here, for the first time in scripture, the command is given to 'love thy neighbour as thyself', v. 18; the importance of which the Lord Himself drew attention to, Mark 12. 31. A man who determined to fulfil that command would not seek to cheat or rob his neighbour nor withhold from him, even for one night, what rightfully belonged to him, v. 13. He would never display any spirit of partiality in matters of judgement, nor attempt to malign him or endanger his life or wellbeing, vv. 15-16. Neither would he harbour any hatred or grudge towards him but instead speak of any issue he had against him, v. 17-18. These are very practical issues. May these statutes challenge us today.

July 24th

Leviticus 20. 1-27

SANCTIFY YOURSELVES AND BE YE HOLY

As with the preceding two chapters, the present passage continues the theme of holiness. But, whereas the earlier chapters focus upon the precepts to be obeyed, this chapter describes the punishments for disobedience. In chapter 18 the teaching is given in light of what the nations were, defiled before God, 18. 24, in chapter 19 in light of what God is as essentially holy, 19. 2. In today's passage the teaching is given against the background of what the people were as set apart to God, v. 24.

Verses 1 to 6 primarily concern spiritual matters and have an echo of the first table of the Law, transgressing those commands regarding the worship and service of God. Two subjects are taken up: *sacrificing children to Molech* and *seeking after familiar spirits*. Such conduct involved a breach of their covenant relationship with God, defilement of His sanctuary, present in their midst, and profaning His holy name; that name by which they were called vv. 5, 3; Jer. 3. 14. Verses 9 to 21 relate to moral issues and reflect the second table of the Law, those commands concerning conduct towards our fellow men. Again two basic themes are taken up *cursing parents* and *corrupting practices*. Every transgression was to be punished whether by 'stoning', 'death', 'burning' after death, being 'cut off' whether by God or men, 'bearing iniquity' without any means of acceptance through sacrifice and finally 'childlessness'. These solemn matters reflect the holy character of God and His abhorrence of sin. God has not changed and even in a day of grace He cannot be indifferent to sin amongst His people, Heb. 12. 29.

These warnings were given that the children of Israel might sanctify themselves and be holy unto God, vv. 7, 26. In redeeming the people from Egypt God had separated them from the nations that they might be His. Now, as the people of God, they were responsible to set themselves apart from all sinful practices and keep His statutes, vv. 22-26. Like Israel, as to our standing, we have been set apart by God to be His, 'a peculiar people', and are to 'cleanse ourselves from all filthiness . . . perfecting holiness in the fear of God', 1 Pet. 2. 9; 2 Cor. 7. 1. It is our personal responsibility to do this.

July 25th

Leviticus 21. 1-24

THE PRIESTS SHALL BE HOLY

Priesthood in Israel was limited to one tribe and one family, Exod. 28. 1. But even with the right genealogy a man could be disqualified from officiating as a priest through defilement or personal defects.

Verses 1 to 15 concern defilements. With regard to the sons of Aaron, defilement could come through *contact with the dead*, vv. 1-5. An exception was permitted in regard to a close relative, but even then in their mourning they were not to follow the customs of the heathen v. 5; Lev. 19. 27-28; Deut. 14. 1. The priests were to be restrained in their grief and, even in the midst of sadness, display a spirit of holiness, cf. 1 Thess. 4. 13. Defilement would also come from *contracting a marriage* with an immoral, idolatrous or divorced woman, v. 7. Equally there was to be no *compromising with evil* even though a family member might be involved, v. 9. As 'a chief man among his people' and one set apart by God to minister in the sanctuary, he was to be holy, vv. 4, 6, 8. God is no less concerned with a 'holy priesthood' today, 1 Pet. 2. 5. Verses 10 to 15 relate to the high priest and the restrictions for him were even more stringent. In connection with his *ministry* nothing must be countenanced that would prevent or hinder him from acting as the anointed representative of the people before God, Exod. 28. 38. Even when a close relative died, he was not to forsake his service in the sanctuary, vv. 11, 12. In *marriage* he was restricted to a virgin and one of his own people, that his offspring be not profaned, vv. 13-15. A comparison of the requirements for the priests with those for the high priest suggests that the nearer a man is to God, the greater the standard demanded of him, cf. Jas. 3. 1.

Verses 16 to 24 concern personal defects. A priest with a blemish could not officiate at the brazen altar or minister at the golden altar, vv. 17, 23. Amongst the twelve blemishes mentioned there is defective vision, 'blind' and 'a blemish in the eye', vv. 18, 20; 2 Pet. 1. 9; impaired walk, 'lame' and 'brokenfooted', vv. 18, 19; 1 Cor. 3. 3; and stunted growth, 'dwarf', v. 20; Heb. 5. 12. Are there defilements or defects in our lives, affecting our ability to function as holy priests before God?

Leviticus 22. 1-32

THEY SHALL NOT PROFANE THE HOLY THINGS

It is possible for men entrusted with holy responsibilities to abuse and misuse their privileges, with the result that God's name and service is brought into disrepute, cf. Rom. 2. 17-24. In Leviticus chapter 21 the directions related to the priests personal holiness and fitness for service whereas in this present chapter the focus is upon their handling of holy things.

In verses 1-16 the subject concerns *the priests partaking of holy things*, those gifts and sacrifices brought by the people that were not offered upon the altar but appointed to the priests for their daily maintenance, Num. 18. 11-19. Verses 3 to 9 are an expansion of the statement in verse 2, concerning their separation 'from the holy things of the children of Israel'. No 'unclean' priest was to touch or eat of them. Further, only those who belonged to the priestly family, either by purchase or birth and who were directly linked to them, were to partake of this provision, vv. 10-16. To disobey these commands would not only profane the name of the Lord and His word but also cause the holy things themselves to be demeaned in the sight of the people, vv. 2, 9, 15. We must never forget that holy things require holy people, something that David appreciated even though not himself of the priestly line, Ps. 26. 6. In a similar vein, in connection with the Lord's Supper, Paul says, 'let a man examine himself, and so let him eat', 1 Cor. 11. 28.

The remaining verses of the chapter concern *the people's presentation of holy things* for sacrifice. Apart from the exception in verse 23, to be acceptable to God every animal offered for sacrifice must be 'without blemish', vv. 18-25. Even though foreigners might be unaware of this requirement, should such wish to offer to God nothing less was to be accepted by the priest, v. 25. The directions at the end of the chapter reveal that God is interested in: what we offer, v. 27; the way we offer, v. 28; the spirit in which we offer, v. 29, and the manner in which the offerings are appropriated by His people, v. 30. God still looks for 'acceptable' sacrifices and 'acceptable' service, 1 Pet. 2. 5; Heb. 12. 28. In the way we handle and partake of 'holy things', is His holy name profaned or is it hallowed, v. 32?

July 27th

Leviticus 23. 1-8

HOLY CONVOCATIONS

'Gather my saints together unto me', Ps. 50. 5. Such is the desire of God for His people. Leviticus chapter 23 describes the seven annual 'feasts of the Lord', those divinely appointed occasions for the gathering together of the people that God might meet with them, v. 4. The feasts are also designated as 'holy convocations', a reminder of their sacred character and of the holiness that should mark the gathering together of the saints, vv. 2, 3, 4. The feast of unleavened bread is also spoken of as being 'unto the Lord', a time when the people were gathered together to worship and to serve Him, v. 6. Sadly, when the Lord Jesus was here, these sanctified occasions had degenerated into nothing more than feasts 'of the Jews', an empty formality, void of anything for the pleasure of God, John 2. 13. In the New Testament, instruction is given for the gatherings of God's people today. Some eight times in 1 Corinthians, Paul directly refers to those holy occasions when the saints are 'together', yet even here disorder was evident, 1 Cor. 11. 20-22. Do we value and sanctify those times as we should?

An interesting feature of the first eight verses of this chapter is that they commence with a weekly observance, the Sabbath, vv. 1-3. Then, we seem to have a re-commencement of the chapter in verse 4 before specific details of the seven feasts are given. This order is full of typical significance. The Sabbath day is a reminder of God's rest at the accomplishment of creation, a rest disturbed by the entrance of sin, Gen. 2. 1-3; Gen. 3. The seven feasts that follow describe, typically, the activity of God to restore conditions in which He can again rest. Fundamental to this is the sacrifice of Christ, and the absence of sin, typified in the feasts of Passover and of Unleavened Bread, 1 Cor. 5. 6-8.

The 'feasts of the Lord' were a tangible expression of national unity, and that unity was essential if the sacred character of each feast was to be maintained, Deut. 16. 16. For the same reason, it is important in the gatherings of God's people today that we 'speak the same thing' and have 'the same mind', 1 Cor. 1. 10. When we gather is there unity or discord? Which of these two is our conduct and attitude most likely to promote?

July 28th

Leviticus 23. 9-22

A SHEAF OF THE FIRSTFRUITS

Following the feasts of Passover and Unleavened Bread, the next in Israel's annual calendar were the Feast of Firstfruits and the Feast of Weeks, the two being separated by a period of fifty days. Both feasts concerned 'firstfruits', the former 'a sheaf of the firstfruits', the firstfruits of the barley harvest, the latter 'the bread of the firstfruits', the firstfruits of the wheat harvest, vv. 10, 17, 20. As 'firstfruits' both were an earnest of a coming harvest, and waving them before the Lord was a practical acknowledgment that it was He who gave the increase and an expression of the people's faith that these were indeed the pledge of a harvest yet to be gathered. Likewise, we must remember that any bounty or provision we enjoy is ultimately to be traced to the Lord, to whom we should be careful to give thanks. Before the people partook of the harvest, the Lord's command had to be obeyed; He must have the first portion, v. 14. Are we diligent to do that, to see that His claims are met, that He is given His rightful place and portion in all that we have and do?

Both feasts have a prophetic significance. The 'sheaf of the firstfruits' is a beautiful type of the risen Lord, while the 'bread of the firstfruits' is figurative of the commencement of the church on the Day of Pentecost, that is, the fiftieth day after the resurrection of Christ, 1 Cor. 15. 23; Acts 2. 1.

The 'sheaf of the firstfruits' was waved before the Lord 'the morrow after the Sabbath', the very day that Christ arose, v. 11; Mark. 16. 1, 2, 9. Intimately linked to the waving of the sheaf was the acceptance of the people, 'to be accepted for you', and in like manner the believer today is 'accepted in the beloved', the risen and exalted Christ, v. 11; Eph. 1. 6, 20-22. Just as the sheaf was the pledge of a harvest to follow, so the resurrection of the Lord Jesus is the guarantee of the coming resurrection of the saints who 'sleep', v. 10; 1 Cor. 15. 20. All the offerings presented that day were 'sweet savour' offerings, there was no sin offering, and the resurrection of the Lord Jesus powerfully demonstrated that sin had been dealt with, the sacrifice had been accepted and God had been satisfied, vv. 12-13; Rom. 4. 25. Are our hearts satisfied with Him, Ps. 73. 25?

July 29th

Leviticus 23. 23-25

BLOWING OF TRUMPETS

There were no appointed Feasts of the Lord between the third and the seventh months of the year, a period in which the people would be gathering in the harvest. The Lord appreciated how busy those months would be and therefore graciously spared His people from added responsibilities. Three feasts remained in their religious calendar. These all took place in the seventh month and foreshadowed events that are yet to be fulfilled, prophetically, relative to the nation of Israel.

On the first of the month there was 'a memorial of blowing of trumpets', the word 'memorial' indicating that this was a feast of remembrance. In respect of the people, after the months of labouring in the fields, it served as a reminder to them of their responsibilities before God and a summons to seek after Him, cf. Num. 10. 2-3. In respect of the Lord the blowing of trumpets in the Old Testament is frequently linked to the people being remembered before Him, that He might shew favour to them, Num. 10. 9-10. In the anticipation of future events the Feast of Trumpets looks on to the time when, after their present dispersion amongst the nations, a period in which nationally there has been no temple nor priesthood and so no divine festive gathering, God will once more turn to Israel as a nation to gather them to Himself and fulfil His purpose respecting them, Hos. 3. 4; Isa. 27. 13; Matt. 24. 30-31; Zech. 14. 4. On the part of the people the unfolding events will awaken them to the imminence of the Lord's return and, with that, a conviction of their sin and an urgency to seek after the Lord, Isa. 58. 1; Joel 2. 1, 12-13. Other features associated with the 'blowing of trumpets' add further details to the prophetic picture. No 'servile work' was to be done, picturing the fact that the re-gathering of the nation will be a work of divine grace independent of human effort or merit, Jer. 30. 3. They were to 'offer an offering', a reminder that the basis for the coming restoration of the nation is the merits of the work of Christ, Num. 29. 1-6.

These verses should impress upon us not only that God will accomplish all He has promised concerning His people, Israel, but also the lesson that He always keeps His word, Isa. 46. 10.

July 30th

Leviticus 23. 26-32

A DAY OF ATONEMENT

The service of this day is described in Leviticus chapter 16. But whereas there the emphasis is upon the presentation of sacrifices for sin, in today's passage the focus is upon the people's sorrow for sin. In the prophetic sequence of events it typifies the day when a repentant remnant of the nation of Israel will enter into the good and blessing of the work of Christ upon the cross.

It was a day when the people were to afflict their souls, a day for self-judgement, when they were to reflect upon their failure and sins and humble themselves before God, vv. 27, 29, 32. Three times it is stressed that no work was to be done, vv. 28, 30, 31. A breach of either of these commandments would issue in judgement, vv. 29-30. Here are two essential steps before the blessing of the forgiveness of sins can be experienced in the soul. First, there must be repentance of sin and, secondly, the recognition that the work is entirely of God, that atonement is something that is beyond our own ability to accomplish.

Returning to the prophetic picture, in the past the brethren of Joseph were humbled before him, as they realized the very one they had rejected and sold was now exalted to the throne of Egypt, Gen. 45. 1-3. So, in the future, at the manifestation of the Lord in glory, the Jewish remnant will look upon Him whom 'they have pierced, and they shall mourn for him, as one mourneth for his only son, and shall be in bitterness for him', the One whom they had rejected and crucified, Zech. 12. 10-14. Then, in repentance, they will take up the language of the prophet and confess 'he was wounded for our transgressions . . . bruised for our iniquities . . . and the Lord hath laid on him the iniquity of us all', Isa. 53. 5-6. As a consequence of this personal appropriation of the work of Christ their sins will be forgiven and 'all Israel shall be saved', Rom. 11. 26.

The joy of complete forgiveness that Israel will experience in that day is something that every believer in Christ enjoys today. The writer to the Hebrews reminds us that on each Day of Atonement there was a 'remembrance again made of sins', but, for the believer today, appreciating the value of Christ's sacrifice, the call is to remember Him, Heb. 10. 3; Luke 22. 19.

July 31st

Leviticus 23. 33-44

YE SHALL DWELL IN BOOTHS

The Feast of Tabernacles, typically, looks forward to the millennial reign of Christ, 'the regeneration, when the Son of man shall sit in the throne of his glory', Matt. 19. 28, and to the fulfilment of God's purpose regarding the nation of Israel and the kingdoms of this world. As such, it formed a fitting conclusion to the seven Feasts of the Lord. When the seven days of this feast were past, they were immediately followed by an 'eighth day', the latter bringing the annual cycle of feasts to a conclusion and foreshadowing the eternal day, the 'day of God', 2 Pet. 3. 12; 1 Cor. 15. 28.

The Feast of Tabernacles began with a day of *rest*, 'ye shall do no servile work', verse 35, and, with the people dwelling in booths for the entire seven days, there is a portrayal of conditions of peace and tranquillity such as will prevail on earth in the millennial day, Isa. 32. 17-18; Mic. 4. 4. Equally, it was a time of *remembrance*, the people were to dwell 'in booths', an intended reminder to them of how the Lord 'brought them out from the land of Egypt', vv. 42-43. The word for 'booths' is in Hebrew *sukah* and comes from the same root word as the name 'Succoth', the first location where the children of Israel stopped on their journey from Egypt, Exod. 12. 37. As they kept these seven days the children of Israel were to remember that once they had been a pilgrim people, entirely dependent upon the Lord for their existence and continuance, and so recall how He had loved and taken care of them. Even in millennial days they will not forget the wilderness experiences and God's wondrous works towards them, Ps. 105. 2, 5, 38-43. The seven days were equally a period of *rejoicing*, 'ye shall rejoice before the Lord your God', v. 40, and so it will be in that coming day, Isa. 12. Here are a people at rest, remembering the grace of the Lord towards them and rejoicing before Him, delightful features that attend submission to the authority and rule of Christ.

Although these verses point to future days can we anticipate that even today, in every company and every heart where Christ is pre-eminent, these same spiritual features will be evident? Are they found with us?

August 1st

Leviticus 24. 1-9

PURE AND HOLY

Consistency is of the utmost importance and, in our passage, measures had to be in place to ensure that the light of the sanctuary would burn 'continually', and that the table of shewbread would be ordered 'continually'.

As to the first, the people were under orders to provide pure olive oil. Nothing inferior was suitable for the 'pure candlestick', just as nothing less than cakes of 'fine' flour were suitable for the 'pure table'. God demands the best, and the purest and the finest. Doubtless, the lampstand illustrates the Lord Jesus, and its six branches the believers who are united to Him. While He was in the world, He was its light, John 9. 5, but the responsibility for shining now rests with us, Matt. 5. 16. Effective witness, whether by 'good works' or presenting the word, Phil. 2. 14-16, demands the constant flow of the oil of the Spirit. He is the power for Christian living, Rom. 8. 3-4: He is the power for Christian service, 1 Cor. 2. 4, 'Bring . . . pure oil'. The light must shine continually: how sad to read, 'ere the lamp of God went out', 1 Sam. 3. 3. It is equally tragic to quench the Spirit, resulting in darkness where the light of testimony should be burning brightly.

The twelve cakes on the pure table again portray the Lord Jesus, 'the bread of God', John 6. 33. They were renewed every Sabbath, and the eye of God feasted upon them for a whole week. They then became food for the priests. This depicts the fact that the one who satisfied God has become nourishment for His priestly people. Just as the shewbread was 'before the Lord', v. 6, so the Lord Jesus grew up 'before him', Isa. 53. 2, to His great delight. We have not seen the Saviour, and yet we feast upon Him as we view Him in the scriptures. The priest had to eat the bread in the holy place, away from the distractions of secular life. Similarly, to feast upon Christ needs the discipline of seclusion, when the mundane is set aside for the higher spiritual exercise of being occupied with Him. While only the priests ate the loaves, the fact that there were twelve indicates, symbolically, that there was a loaf for each tribe, illustrating that there is sufficient in Christ to satisfy all, Ps. 103. 5; 107. 9.

August 2nd
Leviticus 24. 10-23

BRING FORTH HIM THAT HATH CURSED

The offender here was the product of an unequal yoke, one of the 'mixed multitude' who accompanied the people of Israel in their exodus from Egypt. He illustrates those whose profession of faith is not genuine. This man was a cause of strife, just as Judas was a source of discontent among the disciples, John 12. 4-6. Mere professors create many a problem among God's people! Yet no child of an unequal yoke should be discouraged by this incident. A man in similar circumstances was a key figure in building the temple, 2 Chr. 2. 14. An upbringing that is less than ideal does not debar anyone from serving God!

In the scuffle, this man 'blasphemed . . . and cursed'. He knew the demands of the law yet he chose to disobey, again, a feature of those who are not genuine believers. To 'keep his commandments', is evidence that 'we know him', 1 John 2. 3.

Under arrest, he was brought to Moses. Forty years previously, Moses had shown that he knew how to deal with fighters! Exod. 2. 12. But the lessons of history had been learned, and this time there was no hasty action until the 'mind of the Lord' had been revealed. His strategy was similar in the case of the man who gathered sticks on the Sabbath day, Num. 15. 34. Sadly, Joshua did not exercise the same patience. In two disastrous incidents, he acted without consulting the Lord, Josh. 7. 2-5; 9. 14. We must learn from our previous mistakes.

The witnesses to this man's sin had to declare themselves publicly, v. 14, and only then was he stoned to death, for justice had to be seen to be done. God's verdict on the matter incorporated instructions about impartiality in judgement, vv. 16, 22. Clearly, this man's background did not condemn him, but his actions did, and the sentence would have been the same irrespective of who was guilty. Again, the lesson is important: matters have to be dealt with in an even-handed way no matter who is involved. Eli was harsh with Hannah, and yet lenient with his sons, but neither prejudice nor partiality should feature in our dealings with each other, 1 Tim. 5. 21.

The rest of God's decree is a restatement of former instructions regarding sentencing the guilty in Israel's courts.

A SABBATH OF REST, A JUBILE

One of the 'discoveries' of the agrarian revolution was that the rotation of crops was to be preferred to the custom of allowing fields to lie fallow, but really, human ingenuity can never substitute for a divinely ordered plan. There were instructions here for the land to 'keep a sabbath' every seven years, v. 2, and benefits were promised if this was observed, vv. 6-7. God guaranteed a surplus on the sixth year to cover the period when there was no cultivation, vv. 20-22, but the faith of the people of Israel never rose to accepting His promise. For 490 years they disregarded His command and a seventy-year captivity was the result, one year for every land-sabbath ignored, 2 Chr. 36. 20-21. 'God is not mocked', Gal. 6. 7. Refusal to obey Him, and reluctance to accept His promises rob us of His favour.

Every fiftieth year was to be the year of jubilee, when slaves were liberated, and property reverted to its former owners. The blowing of a trumpet on the day of atonement inaugurated this year of release, picturing the fact that on the basis of the death of Christ, there is the proclamation of 'deliverance to the captives' during 'the acceptable year of the Lord', Luke 4. 18-19. In Him 'we have redemption through his blood', Eph. 1. 7; in Him 'we have obtained an inheritance', v. 11. In a spiritual sense, the work of the cross has affected our persons and our property.

The value of land was determined by the proximity of the year of jubilee, v. 16. When a bargain was struck, no exploitation was tolerated, for it was all settled in the fear of God, v. 17. We will never be guilty of financial irregularities or injustices if the fear of God governs our business dealings.

Naturally, nobody would pay a big price for property shortly to be repossessed by its previous occupants. The practical lesson is this, material things diminish in value the nearer we are to the Lord's coming. Why become preoccupied with things that are destined for the flames, 2 Pet. 3. 10-11, when there is so much to do for Him? The tangible benefits of Lot's new legal career were consumed in the destruction of Sodom: he had overestimated the value of material things! Avoid his mistake.

August 4th
Leviticus 25. 25-46

IF THY BROTHER BE WAXEN POOR

'Make poverty history' was the popular slogan of 2005. It is a noble ambition, but as long as the world remains it will never be a reality. The Lord Jesus said, 'The poor always ye have with you', John 12. 8. Poverty will exist right into the kingdom age, but then the exploitation of the poor *will* be history, Isa. 11. 4.

This passage gave guidance to Israel for the care of a man who had fallen on hard times. Altered circumstances can mean that someone who has been able to help others today, can, in turn, need help himself in the future, 2 Cor. 8. 13-15. A kinsman could redeem mortgaged property and restore it to its owner, the price being determined by the number of years until the next jubilee. An upturn of fortunes could permit the debtor himself to repossess his land, but whatever way, the poor man was never to be dependent on handouts. Alleviating his need involved him in the effort of working his land, for 'if any (will) not work, neither should he eat', 2 Thess. 3. 10.

Different regulations covered the sale of a house in a walled city, vv. 29-30. The security of that environment inflated the price of housing; no one would think of buying an expensive dwelling if the property could revert to the vendor for nothing at the year of jubilee. God was protecting the interests of all; He is no respecter of persons.

If a Levite sold his house, he could redeem it at any time, but his fields in the suburbs were never to be sold, vv. 32-34. They were perpetual pasturelands for these families, a last line of defence against poverty when the support which ought to have been received was lacking, Neh. 13. 10. Barnabas sold his field and distributed the proceeds, an evidence of his kindly disposition, but also an indication that he had finished with the Levitical system and would live in dependence upon God, Acts 4. 36-37.

The brother who had become poor could be helped in other ways. He could be granted an interest-free loan, vv. 35-38. He could be hired as an employee, but never enslaved, vv. 39-46. He was to be treated with kindness and tolerance, v. 43, and never be oppressed. 'Remember the poor', Gal. 2. 10. 'Be ye kind one to another', Eph. 4. 32.

August 5th

Leviticus 25. 47-55

THE PRICE OF HIS REDEMPTION

'A decent provision for the poor is the true test of civilization', said Samuel Johnson. Our chapter continues to focus on the needs of the poor. A situation is anticipated in which a poor Israelite could be enslaved to a wealthy immigrant neighbour. No doubt the alien had prospered by hard graft as many do, but observe that he was to be subject to the laws of his adopted land as were the indigenous people. His slave could be redeemed or would go out free in the year of jubilee.

A potential redeemer for the slave is described as 'one of his brethren', v. 48, or 'any that is nigh of kin', v. 49, or 'himself', v. 49. As in a normal situation, the kinsman-redeemer principle comes into play, as illustrated beautifully in the little book of Ruth. With regard to 'the redemption of (the) soul', a treasure-trove of wealth could never effect it, Ps. 49. 6-8, and yet there is the need for a kinsman-redeemer in that sphere too. The eternal Son of God was eligible. He is God 'manifest in the flesh,' 1 Tim. 3. 16. He was sent 'in the likeness of sinful flesh', Rom. 8. 3. Just as His people are sharers in flesh and blood, He 'took part of the same', Heb. 2. 14. In His manhood He identified with us and thus is qualified to be our Redeemer.

The price of the slave's redemption was determined by the proximity of the year of jubilee. By contrast, the redemption of the soul 'is precious', requiring nothing less than the death of the Redeemer. To redeem from the curse of the law, He became 'a curse for us', Gal. 3. 13. To redeem us from all iniquity, He 'gave himself for us', Titus 2. 14. To redeem from a vain manner of life, His 'precious blood' was shed, 1 Pet. 1. 18-19. Peter was inspired to write that this redemption was not by 'silver and gold', a great relief to him, for he had none! Acts 3. 6. We bless God for 'the redemption that is in Christ Jesus', Rom. 3. 24, and rejoice that our 'redeemer liveth', Job 19. 25.

Our chapter concludes with a reminder that in the ultimate, God's people are *His* servants. Being 'bought with a price', 1 Cor. 6. 20, demands consecrated living and devoted service.

'Love so amazing, so divine,
Demands my heart, my life, my all!' *[ISAAC WATTS]*

August 6th

Leviticus 26. 1-26

IF YE WALK IN MY STATUTES; IF YE WILL NOT

The general welfare of the people of Israel hinged on their obedience to God's commands, and today's passage emphasizes the rewards for obedience and the consequences of rebellion. Verses 1-2 deal with three areas of responsibility. They must acknowledge the uniqueness of God's person; He has to be unrivalled. They must observe God's days, His sabbaths. They must respect God's house, His dwelling-place among them.

Walking in these statutes would secure a number of blessings. Gentle rain from God would ensure their prosperity, vv. 3-5. Preservation from God would ensure their security, vv. 6-10. The presence of God among them would ensure their liberty, vv. 11-13.

By contrast, wilful rebellion would invite a grim catalogue of disaster. Physical and mental disorders would ensue. Enemy activity would succeed. Economic calamity would result, vv. 14-17. If there were still no repentance the punishment would be sevenfold. The soil would be unproductive no matter the effort expended. Infections would increase. Wild animals would overrun the land, a danger to herds and humans, vv. 18-22. If they remained intransigent, there would be further invasions with inevitable epidemics, famines and rationing, vv. 23-26.

One would have imagined that these stern warnings would maintain a high level of obedience. Surely they would walk in His statutes! History tells another story. The period of the Judges was a constant cycle of rebellion, retribution, repentance, and restoration. The monarchy period was no better resulting in ten tribes being transported to Assyria, and the other two to Babylon. The threats of Leviticus 26 fell on deaf ears!

Believers are encouraged to learn from these failures, Rom. 15. 4; 1 Cor. 10. 11. Obedience ensures the enjoyment of divine favour, John 15. 10, and has to be in place to expect answers to prayer, 1 John 3. 22. Obedience evidences the reality of our conversion, 1 John 2. 3, and proves our love for Christ, John 14. 15. 'Whatsoever he saith unto you, do it', John 2. 5. 'To obey is better than sacrifice', 1 Sam. 15. 22. 'If ye be willing and obedient, ye shall eat the good of the land', Isa. 1. 19.

August 7th

Leviticus 26. 27-46

IF THEY SHALL CONFESS, I WILL REMEMBER

Israel's persistent rejection of God and His ways would result in the horrors of cannibalism, vv. 27-29. This became a reality during the siege of Samaria, 2 Kgs. 6. 29, and in the siege of Jerusalem, Jer. 19. 9; Lam. 4. 10; Ezek. 5. 10. The threats of this chapter were not empty words! They went on to include the prospect of exile, an exile that would leave them constantly on edge, forever glancing over their shoulders when really there was nothing to fear, vv. 30-39.

At verse 40, the tone of the chapter changes and a note of hope is struck. Recovery becomes a possibility, but it must start with confession on the part of the people, and the humbling of their proud hearts, vv. 40-41. 'If my people, which are called by my name, shall humble themselves, and pray, and seek my face, and turn from their wicked ways; then will I hear', 2 Chr. 7. 14.

Repentance would have a two-fold effect. It permitted God to allow His covenant with the patriarchs to come into play in respect of both the land and the people. The land would enjoy its sabbaths, restoring its productiveness, and the people in their exile would never be completely destroyed, vv. 42-45. God's promises to the people of Israel still hold good, ensuring that even though the nation is presently sidelined, its future is assured. Their present blindness is 'in part'; a few Jews are being saved in this gospel age. That blindness is temporary, it is 'until the fulness of the Gentiles be come in'. Thus, their rejection is neither total nor permanent, Rom. 11. 25. New Testament revelation confirms the teaching of today's passage. In God's programme, there is still a future for Israel.

There are lessons in the passage for believers. It is often perceived that the tone of the New Testament is less threatening than that of the Old, but a reading of the letters to the churches in Revelation leaves us with the distinct feeling that failure, departure and sin on the part of believers incur divine displeasure and serious censure. Inevitable consequences can be averted only by repentance, Rev. 2. 5, 16, 22; 3. 3, 19. On a personal level, confession of sin brings forgiveness and cleansing, 1 John 1. 9. Keep short accounts with God!

August 8th

Leviticus 27. 1-34

ALL THAT ANY MAN GIVETH SHALL BE HOLY

This final chapter of Leviticus anticipates men and women making a special vow to the Lord. These were voluntary commitments, but, by making the vow, they placed themselves under obligation. 'When thou vowest a vow unto God, defer not to pay it', Eccles. 5. 4. Men, women and children could be devoted to God. From childhood to old age there was the need for willing people for the service of His sanctuary. If for any reason they were surplus to requirements, or were unable to fulfil their obligation, a tariff was levied according to age and gender, vv. 1-9. Doubtless, this was used for the upkeep of the sanctuary, and the maintenance of the priesthood, Num. 18. 14.

Animals could be made available for the Lord's work, vv. 9-13, as could a person's home, vv. 14-15. A field with its produce could be His. If necessary, any of these could be redeemed, but in the case of the field a complicated calculation was necessary to determine the price, taking the proximity of the year of jubilee and other factors into account, vv. 16-25.

There had to be no pretence of giving to God what was already His by law, the firstling, the devoted thing, and the tithe, vv. 26-33. This chapter has to do with going the second mile; it is devotion and appreciation going beyond duty.

There were those in the Bible who gladly subscribed to the teaching of our chapter. Amasiah 'willingly offered himself unto the Lord', 2 Chr. 17. 16. Hannah pledged her child to the Lord, 1 Sam. 1. 11. An unnamed disciple donated his colt to the Lord, Mark 11. 3. Matthew used his home for the Lord, Mark 2. 15. Barnabas gave his field to the Lord, Acts 4. 36-37.

Apply the lessons in a practical way. Start with yourself, 'present your bodies a living sacrifice', Rom. 12. 1. Make spiritual rather than secular things the priority for your children. Is the modern equivalent of the colt available to God, your means of transport? Use your home for God, a centre of witness, as was Matthew's. Some have property such as a field that could be used one way or another. J. S. SMALL wrote,

'Nought that I have my own I call, I hold it for the Giver:
My heart, my strength, my life, my all, are His, and His for ever!'

August 9th

Numbers 1. 1-54

ALL THAT ARE ABLE TO GO FORTH TO WAR

The early chapters of Numbers deal with various groups among the people of Israel. This chapter majors on the *Warriors*. Subsequent sections deal with the *Workers*, the Levites who had responsibility for the tabernacle, with a small passage devoted to the *Worshippers*, the priests, the sons of Aaron, 3. 1-4.

Stress is laid on the fact that the warriors must be at least twenty years old. A certain level of maturity was necessary even for warfare. God does not expect people in their spiritual infancy to be in the forefront of conflict, as seen in that He did not take newly redeemed people by the way of the Philistines 'lest . . . the people repent when they see war', Exod. 13. 17.

Those enlisted as warriors, had to declare their pedigree, v. 18. Similarly, the man encouraged to be 'a good soldier of Jesus Christ', 2 Tim. 2. 3, was a man whose faith was unfeigned, 1. 5. He had a spiritual pedigree that qualified him to fight the Lord's battles. Unconverted people have no right to be involved in defending God's interests in the battlefield of this world. The first requisite for either work or warfare is the new birth.

With the exception of Levi, every tribe had to supply warriors. In the same way, every believer, whatever his background, has a part to play in the great conflict between right and wrong. The members of our bodies must be yielded as instruments (weapons) of righteousness unto God, Rom. 6. 12-14. In the Ephesian epistle, Paul addressed various segments of the assembly, wives and husbands, children and fathers, servants and masters, but every group is included in the subsequent teaching to take the whole armour of God, 6. 13. We all need to withstand in the evil day: we are all warriors!

The Levites were not conscripted since they had specific tasks in connection with the tabernacle. They encamped around it, shielding it from inquisitive eyes, vv. 47-54. Their location meant that they were on hand for their labours when the pillar of cloud moved. In Nehemiah's day, many were building 'over against his house', e.g., Neh. 3. 28. Like the Levites, they laboured just where they were living. We all have a responsibility to our own neighbourhood. 'Go home . . . and tell', Mark. 5. 19.

Numbers 2. 1-34

EVERY MAN SHALL PITCH BY HIS OWN STANDARD

God had a specific location for each of His people as they encamped around the tabernacle. They had no liberty to choose their own position, each tribe having a designated place. Believers today should be equally sensitive to God's will for their whereabouts in His great purpose for their lives.

Every tribe was positioned in relation to the tabernacle, either east, south, west, or north. The tabernacle was central. Similarly, the house of God should be central in the interests of God's people today, everything else subservient to their main concern in life, the welfare of God's assembly. Abram pitched his tent in proximity to Bethel, the house of God, Gen. 12. 8.

The order of the camp was impressive; there was nothing haphazard about the arrangement, for 'God is not the author of confusion,' 1 Cor. 14. 33. From his vantage point, Balaam acknowledged, 'How goodly are thy tents, O Jacob', Num. 24. 5. They were laid out like valleys, gardens or trees, v. 6. The surprising thing was the unimposing structure at the centre, with its covering of badger skin, a picture of Him in whom they saw 'no beauty that we should desire him', Isa. 53. 2. Israel came out of Egypt in an orderly way, 'harnessed', Exod. 13. 18, that is, in ranks. The Lord Jesus fed the crowd in an orderly way, Mark 6. 39-40. In assembly functions, 'Let all things be done decently and in order', 1 Cor. 14. 40.

The fact that the people were stationed 'far off' from the tabernacle, v. 2, is a pictorial reminder that the holiness of God demands befitting reverence on the part of His people, illustrated again in the two thousand cubits between the ark and the people at the crossing of the Jordan, Josh. 3. 4.

On the march, two ranks preceded the tabernacle with two to the rear, v. 17: the tabernacle was central. In the onward march of life, make the Lord Jesus the focal point of your interest.

In the groupings of the tribes, Simeon was wedged between Reuben and Gad, vv. 10-16. It is to their credit that the tribe of Simeon was not influenced by the others to remain on the east of Jordan, Num. 32. Be determined to resist pressure to be on the spiritual fringe.

August 11th

Numbers 3. 1-39

BRING THE TRIBE OF LEVI NEAR

The early verses give details of the priestly family. Sadly, two of Aaron's sons came under the judgement of God before their ministry really began. It is a sobering lesson that when unauthorized human initiatives intrude into the things of God, they incur His sore displeasure.

The Levites were divinely delegated to be Aaron's assistants, they were to 'minister unto him', v. 6. Some resented their subordinate role, Lev. 16. 10, but to do *any* task for God is a great honour; they were highly favoured to be responsible for the tabernacle and its furnishings. Before they functioned, they had to be brought 'near', v. 6, for God's service demands the intimacy of close fellowship with Him. Their dedication was to be total, 'wholly' given to Aaron, v. 9, for shallow, feigned commitment is distasteful to the Lord, Jer. 3. 10.

When the tribe was numbered, the census was to include the males from a month and upward, v. 15. Obviously, infants and children would never be involved in the strenuous task of removing the tabernacle, but the point is this, potential was being taken into account. It is important that potential be fully realised. The potential of 'blossom', S. of S. 2. 15 RV, could be ruined by the activity of 'little foxes'. Let every believer fulfil his full potential in the service of God.

There were three sections to the tribe of Levi, the families of Gershon, Kohath, and Merari. These three had different locations around the tabernacle and different tasks in relation to it. The Gershonites, vv. 21-26, encamped on the west and had responsibility for such as the coverings. The Kohathites, vv. 27-32, were stationed to the south, and took charge of the vessels. The Merarites, vv. 33-39, were located to the north and were accountable for the main structure. Moses and the priests were positioned outside the gate at the east end, v. 38. The New Testament equivalent of all this is that God positions believers in the body, 'as it hath pleased him', 1 Cor. 12. 18, every one with his own gift and responsibility, v. 28, 'to *every* man his work', Mark 13. 34. 'Take heed to the ministry which thou hast received in the Lord, that thou fulfil it', Col. 4. 17.

THE LEVITES SHALL BE MINE

When the people of Israel left Egypt, God laid claim to the firstborn among them, 'Sanctify unto me all the firstborn', Exod. 13. 2. These firstborn sons had been in danger from the destroyer, but were sheltered by the blood of the lamb. Now liberated, they were to be special for God. It has been said rightly, 'What God redeems, God claims'. The New Testament equivalent is this, 'Ye are not your own . . . ye are bought with a price', 1 Cor. 6. 19–20. The blood of the cross demands complete consecration.

It appears that Israel's firstborn sons did not rise to their responsibility, and so the Levites were taken 'instead of all the firstborn', v. 41. God's plans can never be thwarted by human failure, but the solemn lesson is, if *we* do not fulfil His purposes, someone else will. In Malachi's day, the people of Israel robbed God, but 'from the rising of the sun even unto the going down of the same', His name would be great among the Gentiles, Mal. 1. 11. The priest and the Levite refused to help the wounded man, but the Samaritan did, Luke 10. 30-35. A substitute will always be found, but if we are uncooperative, we deny ourselves the privilege of being His servants, and the recompense that such service brings.

The Levites had been quick to respond to the call, 'Who is on the Lord's side? let him come unto me', Exod. 32. 26. Possibly this made them suitable candidates to replace the firstborn as assistants to the priests and custodians of the tabernacle. When a tally was made of the firstborn and the Levites, there was a shortfall of 273. God did not overlook this, and for every firstborn for whom there was no substituting Levite, five shekels 'redemption money' had to be paid, and this was given to Aaron and his sons. The priests were to be compensated for the deficiency in the number of helpers. Two lessons can be learned. Firstly, God takes *every* individual into account, and all are precious to Him. Secondly, He is always absolutely equitable in His dealings, hence the recompense to Aaron. Let us be available to Him as were the Levites, His possession, in a positive practical way.

August 13th

Numbers 4. 1-15

THE SERVICE OF THE SONS OF KOHATH

This new chapter gives precise details of the functions of the Levites in relation to the tabernacle on its wilderness journeys. There are numerous references to the fact that they all laboured in the work from age thirty to fifty. The best years of their adult lives were being used for God. Are yours? A degree of maturity was required before they commenced their labours. (Possibly the mention of age twenty-five, 8. 24, suggests a five-year 'apprenticeship'). Similarly, in the assembly, an elder must not be a 'novice', 1 Tim. 3. 6, and a deacon must 'be proved', v. 10. Retirement at fifty did not place them on the scrap heap, but was an indication that God took into account the ageing process which left them less fit for the heavy task of transporting the tabernacle. Advancing years necessitate the shedding of certain responsibilities. As an ageing man, David struggled with a task that had caused him no problem as a youth, 2 Sam. 21. 15!

Moving camp, the priests were first to take responsibility. They would cover the holy vessels, vv. 5-14, in preparation for the Kohathites to carry them to the next location. The precise details of the operation holds lessons, not least, that great reverence must attend the handling of holy things, v. 15. The slaughter of the men of Beth-shemesh, 1 Sam. 6. 19, and the death of Uzzah, 2 Sam. 6. 6-7, give warning that curiosity and carelessness in these things invite the judgement of a holy God.

I shall not comment on the coverings, save to say that uniquely, the outer covering of the ark was a cloth of blue, v. 6. The ark illustrates the Lord Jesus, and blue is the colour of the heavens, so as the ark was carried through the wilderness there was a pictorial foreshadowing of a blessed Man who exhibited heavenly features, demonstrating that as the 'second man', He is 'the Lord from heaven', 1 Cor. 15. 47.

With all the vessels, except the laver, suitably covered, the Kohathites then moved in. Superintended by Eleazar, v. 16, they shouldered their burden, v. 15, and began the march. No wagons were provided for their task, Num. 7. 9. It was heavy work, as is the matter of carrying the responsibility of testimony today. Be willing to shoulder the burden.

August 14th

Numbers 4. 16-28

THE SONS OF GERSHON

The priests had a great responsibility for the welfare of the Kohathites, vv. 17-20. They had to ensure that every vessel of the tabernacle was adequately covered for transportation before the Levites arrived, v. 20. An inquisitive peep would result in death. They then assigned the Kohathites their tasks, v. 19, the word 'burden' again giving emphasis to the onerous nature of their service. Like the priests, we have a responsibility for our brother's welfare. Carelessness on our part could have a negative impact upon him. Like the Levites, we have a duty to be guided in our service by those who are 'over (us) in the Lord', and to perform any arduous task that we are assigned. 'Every man shall bear his own burden', Gal. 6. 5.

Eleazar had responsibility to supervize the Kohathites, v. 16, but Ithamar had charge of the Gershonites, v. 28, and the Merarites, v. 33. God never overburdens one man. A number of overseers should superintend a New Testament assembly, and a number of deacons should serve it, Phil. 1. 1.

With the exception of the veil, which was used to cover the ark, the Gershonites were accountable for the fabric and cords of the tabernacle, and to facilitate their work, two wagons were gifted to them, 7. 7. How considerate God is! He 'knoweth our frame; he remembereth that we are dust', Ps. 103. 14.

The curtains and coverings all speak of Christ, the one who 'tabernacled among us', John 1. 14 RV margin. The linen items remind us of His righteousness, Rev. 19. 8, for He 'loved righteousness, and hated iniquity', Heb. 1. 9. The curtains of goats' hair point to Him who was 'comely in going', Prov. 30. 29-31, every surefooted step in compliance with the will of God. The covering of rams' skins dyed red reflects His consecration, Exod. 29. 22, His commitment to the Father's will unto death, John 18. 11. The outer covering of durable but unattractive badgers' skins previews man's assessment of Him, 'there is no beauty that we should desire him', Isa. 53. 2.

How honoured were the Gershonites, to be responsible for that which spoke of Christ! How blessed are we, who reflect something of Him in *our* wilderness journey!

August 15th

Numbers 4. 29-49

THE SONS OF MERARI

The word 'service' is used extensively throughout this chapter, but on five occasions it translates a word with a military connotation, as in verse 30, for example. At verse 3, the word is translated 'host'. The inference is that although the Levites were not conscripted to military service, there was an element of spiritual warfare involved in their work for God. This is always the case. At Ephesus, Paul found that when a 'great door and effectual' was opened to him, there were 'many adversaries', 1 Cor. 16. 9. In Nehemiah's time 'the builders, every one had his sword girded by his side', Neh. 4. 18. Work and warfare go together: be prepared for spiritual conflict in the service of God.

The Merarites had responsibility for the main structure of the tabernacle, the boards and related items. Overlaid with gold, their weight was considerable, but again, the Levites had the benefit of four wagons to aid their transportation, Num. 7. 8. We can always rely on divine assistance when handling burdens of any kind: 'he shall sustain thee', Ps. 55. 22.

As well as the weighty boards, these men had charge of smaller items such as pins, v. 32. The use of the word 'reckon' in the verse indicates that an inventory was kept of every article, and that they were accountable for every last item: each pin was crucial. God's word stresses the importance of things that appear to be insignificant. There are 'members of the body, which seem to be more feeble' but are 'necessary', 1 Cor. 12. 22. There are commandments that are 'least' yet demand obedience, Matt. 5. 19. People who are unfaithful 'in that which is least', will never have responsibility for 'true riches', Luke 16. 10-11. Take care of the pins! Your service might feel like the equivalent of looking after pins. There is no glamour, and it is largely unnoticed. Remember, there will be some surprises at the day of review! Joab's armour bearer was commended, whereas there were no honours for his master, 2 Sam. 23. 37.

The latter part of the chapter gives the details of the number of Levites in the 30-50 age range, a very adequate number for the task in hand. It was labour intensive work, but God saw to it that there were sufficient resources, and He always will.

WITHOUT THE CAMP

Three different categories of people had to be expelled from the camp of Israel, vv. 1-4. Doubtless, there were very sensible and practical reasons for this, but it is delightful to see that when the Lord Jesus was here, He drew very near to such individuals. He touched a leper; a woman with an issue touched Him; He touched a young man's coffin, and a dead girl's hand; He remained uncontaminated. How superior grace is to law!

Ceremonial uncleanness necessitated the removal of these people. Their presence defiled the camp, v. 3, for uncleanness is contagious, Hag. 2. 13. God's presence among them demanded purity. The practical lessons seem obvious. The holiness of the assembly must be maintained. On occasions, it needs the heart-rending action of excommunication to preserve that holiness, but it has to be carried out, for tolerated sin defiles the assembly, 1 Cor. 5. 6. Also, the presence of the living Christ among His gathered people, Matt. 18. 20, requires suitable moral behaviour. His complaint against Thyatira was 'thou sufferest that woman Jezebel', Rev. 2. 20. Putting up with sin is distasteful to Him. Here, the people of Israel were quick to comply with Moses' command, v. 4, in contrast to the assembly at Corinth which gloried in its tolerance, 1 Cor. 5. 1-2.

Just as 'male and female' had to be put 'without the camp', v. 3, so 'a man or woman' could commit a trespass, v. 6. Defilement and guilt are not confined to any particular gender. More positively, it was open to both 'man and woman' to nobly separate themselves as Nazarites, 6. 2. The trespass, v. 6, is said to be 'against the Lord', but subsequent verses show that the wrongdoer had taken advantage of his fellow man. The fact is that *all* sin is against the Lord, for *He* gave the commandments; to violate any is rebellion against Him. Hence the prodigal's confession, 'I have sinned against heaven', Luke 15. 21. Here the offender must confess, make restitution plus a fifth, and offer a trespass offering. Should the offended party be deceased, a kinsman would benefit. In the absence of such, the beneficiary was the priest, a part of his upkeep in God's service, vv. 9-10, but restitution had to be made, Luke 19. 8.

BITTER WATER

As you have read the passage today you may have been asking yourself, 'What have we got here?'. This record seems to be unique in scripture and we have no account of this law being applied in any particular case. So we can conclude that here is a 'one and only' description of something relating to a principle that comes from the heart of God and He desires we understand and apply it personally.

It is a 'trial of jealousy' to be conducted as and when a husband seems to have cause to be concerned over the fidelity of his wife. Questions arise such as, 'Has she been unfaithful to me?'; 'Are her affections towards me what they should be as a wife?'. The matter becomes such a destroying force within the man that he has to resort to this 'trial of jealousy' to prove without doubt that the feelings of desertion and unfaithfulness he has harboured and that disturb him are not true!

The wife seems to be the one under the searchlight in the passage but the reverse is surely as applicable – the man could be just as much under suspicion by his wife. Is our God partisan in His ways in this seeming bias then? By no means! The principle underlying this action is the important element, *not* the sex of the individuals. The case must be seen as being beyond the natural and applying to the spiritual. It pinpoints for us a much higher relationship, and one in which our God is to be seen as the jealous husband. As He can never default in fidelity *it has to be* His spouse that is under suspicion.

Jehovah saw Israel as His wife and often spoke to that nation in the terms of this relationship. Hosea chapter 2 is an appeal based upon the comparison of Israel to an 'unfaithful' wife. In our New Testament, the simile of the church as being the Bride of Christ is not strange to us and is one that reminds us of our place in His affections and He in ours.

The nub of this trial was in the taking of the 'bitter water'. The results of this revealed to all as to whether the wife had been faithful or not. Taking the water can be compared to us having our devotion to the Lord exposed as we read His word. We need to pray often, 'Search me, O God', Ps. 139. 23.

August 18th

Numbers 6. 1-12

DAYS OF SEPARATION

Starting from chapter 5 of this book, we have several measures provided by the Lord for His people in order that they might be, in a practical way, the 'separated' people He required them to be. Here is yet another. The distinction of this one is that it is optional and offered to them as that which was available to the devout to demonstrate their 'devotedness'.

It was 'when', that is, 'at a moment in life when it was appropriate and fulfilling', and it was 'either' so that no one was excluded, any adult could 'vow a vow of separation'. What a channel of joyous opportunity this would provide for the godly soul! What a privilege to be able to express publicly and without compulsion your personal response to the grace of God in your life. In many ways the taking of this vow relates perfectly to our 'reasonable service' as set out in Romans, in the presentation of our bodies as a living sacrifice, holy, acceptable unto God, 12. 1. Such devotion delights God's heart.

For the Israelite it involved a sacred commitment to three external requirements. Nothing from the vine to be taken, no razor upon the head, and no contact with a dead body, however close the relationship with the deceased might be. Not actually over-demanding but very challenging to normal appetites and conduct. You knew you were under a Nazarite vow and so did everyone else. These external things reflected a willingness to live by another code of conduct, to be free for devotion to the Lord. No empty profession was allowed, defilement meant the shaving of the head and you started over again!

We too must examine our conduct, appetites, and activities to see how well we demonstrate our devotion to Christ day by day. We hear Him say yet again, 'Lovest thou me?' We don't need externals, such as here, to display our devotion; people should be able to read it in our eyes!

Few are spoken of in scripture as having been Nazarites. How lacking we are when it comes to being freely devoted to our God. But some rose to it: Samuel; Samson; and dare we exclude such as Hannah, Deborah or Mary, the Lord's mother? God knows His Nazarites for sure.

249

August 19th

Numbers 6. 13-21

WHEN THE DAYS ARE FULFILLED

Just as taking up and keeping the vow was a very serious commitment so was the fulfilment of it when the set period came to an end. You could not just say, 'That's it, I've done my bit now', and walk away. It was as demanding to **lay down** as it was to set in motion. The reason could well be that God has in view the time when there would be no need for a Nazarite vow and He anticipates it here by the requirements set for the conclusion of a Nazarite vow.

So what did God require? Well, firstly, He required appearance before the tabernacle door. Secondly, He required offerings; a burnt, sin, and peace offering, with their attendant meat and drink offerings. Thirdly, the priest should perform a wave-offering displaying the fact of a fulfilment before the Lord and, finally, all additional vows undertaken must be fulfilled exactly as promised. Then, and only then, would the Nazarite be free from his vow and walk away from it.

It all speaks of a sense of culmination, arrival, and release with a deep appreciation of things as God would like to have them. The New Testament clearly anticipates this time in God's calendar. Hear Paul building up to it as he declares, 'And when all things shall be subdued unto him, then shall the Son also . . . that God may be all in all', 1 Cor. 15. 28. Again, he is now, seemingly, on his tiptoes, 'For this corruptible must put on incorruption, and this mortal must put on immortality. Then shall be brought to pass the saying . . . Death is swallowed up in victory', vv. 53-54. The Lord Himself, the true Nazarite, anticipated it on the very night He was betrayed saying, 'I will not drink henceforth of this fruit of the vine, until that day when I drink it new with you in my Father's kingdom', Matt. 26. 29.

Clearly, this can only be when God at last brings in all that He has accomplished as set out in the offerings as fulfilled in the death and resurrection of the Lord Jesus. It is going to be the Day of God and it will be His long awaited Sabbath rest. No more sin or tears, dying or partings, we shall be 'going in and coming out' in the perfection of devotion and service in His presence forever! What a day that will be!

Numbers 6. 22-27

ON THIS WISE YE SHALL BLESS

Why this special blessing now? What is it that has moved God at this point to instruct the nation's high priest to pronounce His unique and gracious mercies upon His people?

It would seem to be an unreserved linking of the Lord and His people. Three times, it is the Lord: 'the Lord bless'; 'the Lord make'; and 'the Lord lift up'. His Name is upon His people, and His blessing is their portion. It can only mean one thing – He finds them in a condition and at a place that He can, without question, enrich them with all that He is!

In what condition and at what place have they arrived? It seems to have to do with order. Having dealt with so much that has arranged their lives and linked them to Him, He now sees them as a people He can bless. The warriors are in active stance, the workers are aware of the responsibilities of their service, the whole assembly is purified from defilement and the means provided for their separation and unwavering devotion. He has been preparing them for such a place and having got them there, He is free to pronounce His blessing.

So with what will He bless them? It is an outpouring of His unreserved love. There is active and positive promise of the divine presence, preservation and favour. He will be a fortress to ensure their peace; His watchfulness will empower their progress. Their being called by His name assures them of His blessing. Majestically grand, this blessing has become the recognized wording to express the utmost of desires for perpetual providence.

What more could anyone want? The sad fact is that they were never practically in a state that could bring the promised good. Constantly sidetracked into seeking their own prosperity, they cast away their spiritual revelations, embraced the idols of the nations and so despised His Name and calling that they lost the blessing. But God's desire to bless always has His end in view. Their failure did not negate His promise to bless. A remnant shall be saved and the city will be called 'Jehovah Shammah' – the Lord is there, Ezek. 48. 35! Shall we not ever wonder at the grace of God to them and to us?

August 21st

Numbers 7. 1-89

THE PRINCES OFFERED THEIR OFFERING

This is a long and yet a short chapter. It is repetitious and thus to us possibly 'boring'. To many minds such a listing could have been said in a dozen lines and every aspect of the event sufficiently covered.

However, because the record is divine we accept that there must be spiritual principle here and our minds need to be drawn to finding it and paying full attention to it when we do.

It was the day that Moses had fully set up the tabernacle and anointed all its instruments and vessels for service. Then, the princes came with their offering. It was a sensitive and spiritual gesture, for the tabernacle became the centre of the nation's spiritual life. The princes recognized the immense importance of the moment.

Firstly, they brought carts and oxen. A thoughtful consideration that was practical and supportive of the Levites as they were to carry the burden of the service of moving the tabernacle. It is so good when those on the frontline of God's service are encouraged from the evidence of concern for them by those not so engaged. Let us today encourage and strengthen the hands of those that work in the assembly outreach activities week after week and those commended to wider service at home or abroad.

Then, they came again on the day of the anointing and dedication of the brazen altar. This altar was fundamental to their worship and approach to God. So we note, firstly, that they brought that which would supply the altar's demands. It all spoke of Christ and surely thrilled the heart of God. We must remember that Christ-centred worship and service are the only exercises worth bringing to God's altar!

Then, note, that they all brought the same things and they each had their day to bring them so that it took twelve days to offer. Why all the repeated detail? This is none other than an expression of divine appreciation. To some it may be boring, but to God it was infinitely precious and He will have it put down in every detail!

His day of approval and appreciation is yet to come and every act of ours, even a cup of cold water, will be rewarded.

August 22nd

Numbers 8. 1-26

BRING THE LEVITES BEFORE THE LORD

Yesterday, we noted the inspiring moment when the princes offered their offering. It was at the anointing of the altar. Today, we see that the consecration of the Levites is set beside the instructions concerning the seven-branched lampstand and the instructions as to how it should be placed to allow it to shine on all that was in the sanctuary. These items are clearly linked in the mind of God and are not just haphazard records.

If we have learnt that offerings have to do with the altar, then here we learn that the service of God, for which the Levites were separated, has to do with the light of God's sanctuary. The principle seems to be that all service acceptable to God must be done to gain His approval. It must be able to be scrutinized in the light of His presence. It is no wonder, then, that we read concerning His judgement seat that the test of the quality of our service is His fire, for, 'the fire shall try every man's work of what sort it is', 1 Cor. 3. 13.

This passage reveals to us where God begins so that He can have service that is acceptable to Him. As with these Levites He removes past uncleanness and cuts away all that is of natural growth. We see the 'water and washing' and 'razors and shaving' at work. It is a cleansing that marks a 'new' beginning for these men and their ministry. So it is with us, for we cannot even begin to say we serve God unless we have had a 'new birth' and a 'washing of regeneration', Titus 3. 5. Nothing less will do. This new state of things, and the repudiation of the past, is witnessed to by our willingness to be baptized and to declare our new standing with God in Christ.

Were these Levites ready when they were washed and clothed, then? No, for they must first be linked with their sin and burnt offerings. May we never forget that the possibility of exercising service for God is only ever on account of what the Lord Jesus did for us at the cross. His atoning work and unique acceptability with God has made it possible for us to serve God.

Finally, these men were 'presented to the Lord' and in this way singularly set apart for His service. This privilege is ours too as we serve today, a 'holy priesthood', 1 Pet. 2. 5!

August 23rd

Numbers 9. 1-14

KEEP THE PASSOVER

The Lord now reminds Moses about the Passover feast and indicates how important a matter this is to both Him and them! It is the first anniversary of this historic event in national life and embedded in it were the essential reminders of at least two vital spiritual truths of which they needed to be continually aware.

Firstly, it re-enacted for them the fact of their redemption – they had been bought with a price from slavery in Egypt. They were a blood-bought people. Secondly, this feast was a uniting bond for them, establishing their oneness. The event had made them a nation and this was why every Israelite was solemnly required to participate, none was exempt.

The wording strongly emphasizes that it was to be conducted exactly as it had been originally, and on the pre-scribed date, without fail. Their future history was to reveal how rarely in fact this was to be the case. Scriptural records are scarce as to when they actually kept this sacred appointment. Joshua did in the land as soon as they got there, but 2 Kings chapter 23 verse 22 records that king Josiah's Passover celebration was the first since the days of the Judges! Hezekiah's revival brought Judah to it and so did Ezra in the days of the remnants' return, but after that in our Lord's day it was just called 'a feast of the Jews' and was reduced to form with no substance. How easily spiritual things slip into oblivion and men forget what great things God has done for them.

For us, as New Testament believers, the Lord clearly insti-tuted the weekly remembrance supper of the 'Breaking of Bread' for exactly the same reasons and to fulfil the same essentials. Every time we 'break bread' we take the loaf and drink the cup to declare His death and our oneness in Christ. It speaks of redemption and unity, and will do so until He comes, 1 Cor. 10. 17; 11. 26.

Someone enquired about defilement that prevented them taking part. A divine provision met the need. For us it is, 'But let a man examine himself, and so let him eat'. Nothing should be allowed to hinder us being at this unique occasion each week.

August 24th

Numbers 9. 15-23

ONE PILLAR OF CLOUD

The cloud over the tabernacle would have been visible from all over the camp whether it was day or night. The cloud marked the centre of the Israelites' world in the wilderness.

It had a very practical purpose in being so visible, for God intended that their lives would be directed by its movement. If it lifted upward then they packed up the camp and as it moved off they would follow in its path. If it remained over the tabernacle then they stayed in their tents. To be constantly looking up towards the cloud would become as natural as breathing. It would control and direct the whole of their lives.

What, then, is the significance of the cloud? Seeing that they were in a wilderness and everywhere seemed very much the same in whichever direction they looked, they would have been glad to know that they could trust the guidance and discipline the cloud provided. They were dependent on it to give them direction in a place where there may have been no other paths or markers to guide them on the way. It was a consoling cloud!

So the cloud called for dependence and provided direction and in following it rather than their own intuition or some wilderness specialist who professed to 'know his way around', they declared their wholehearted commitment and trust in the Lord to lead them and in His will as being best for them. They said in effect, 'Wherever He leads us we will go'.

Sadly, our lives have been usurped by so many other 'clouds' and 'guiding lights' that we have lost this sense of simple dependence on the Lord to show us the way day by day. It has been the course of a chosen career, the requirements, as we have seen it, of housing and education dictated by how we feel and what we want, which have taken over from the cloud of dependence upon the Lord to direct our ways. Pillars mark the pathway of our progress through life but are they His pillars, as for example with Jacob, cf. Gen. 28. 18?

But we are also in a wilderness and need to sense again our dependence for direction from the Lord to take us through. We must learn to move in the light of His word and at the gentle urgings of His Spirit within. Not to do so is spiritual suicide.

August 25th

Numbers 10. 1-10

TWO TRUMPETS OF SILVER

These trumpets follow on very suitably from the pillar of cloud. They are not just an addition to the cloud but an extension of its service, allowing a much more specific and varied understanding of the will of the Lord as He wanted it communicated to His people.

These instruments were to be made of silver, which always has to do with redemption, 1 Pet. 1. 18, and there were two of them which speaks of clear and confirmed testimony, Matt 18. 16. It indicates for us how near the Lord wants to be to His people and how He required them to know His will with such certainty that they could respond to Him immediately.

A wide variation of circumstances is provided for their use. It could be a coming together for solemn assembly, festive rejoicing or to bring worship offerings and, at times, even to prepare for battle and confront their enemies. The very nature of their circumstances demanded an overall directing voice to which they could respond with confidence, and the trumpets provided just that for them.

So they became a watching and listening people, God's instructive word giving their lives meaning and purpose. It is no surprise to us that when we come to the New Testament and read Paul's words concerning teaching believers that he draws upon the trumpet to illustrate his point. He says that musical instruments must have distinction in sounds else, 'how shall it be known what is piped or harped?' 1 Cor. 14. 7. If the trumpet gives an uncertain sound, who shall prepare for battle?

In a day when much of the doctrinal teaching in Christian circles comes from two thousand years of men's meddling in God's word, we do well to make sure that we, if teachers, teach clearly what scripture says and nothing else, and, if hearers, that we compare what we hear to what the word of God says! What a thrill it is as we come together for teaching that every heart hears the clear note of God's silver trumpets and all can say, 'Amen Lord!' Finally, don't forget to listen out today and every day for the 'last trump', will you? He is coming back to take us home and that may be today, 1 Cor. 15. 52!

August 26th

Numbers 10. 11-36

THREE DAYS' JOURNEY

As we view the nation on the move there is a wonderful sense of dignity and order about them. Each has his place in the procession and each has an unfurled banner at the head. What the Lord is doing here is to parade His people so that they display to whom they belong and the moral beauty and power of that relationship. That sense of purpose, progress and well-being is displayed to an outside world.

This is the nightmare of King Balak who, through the eyes and visions of the false prophet Baalam, saw the order and destiny of Israel whom God had blessed and no one could therefore curse, Num. 24. 2-6.

We should be reminded as to how much like this, and more, God now sees a company of those that believe on His Son as they meet together. Small or large, there should always be order and dignity that can only be the fruit of God's work in us, S. of S. 4. 7. Now, should there be constant division, disharmony and a lack of joy and power then there must be something fundamentally wrong for a company professing the presence and person of the Lord Jesus in the midst! This is surely to our shame.

Three days they marched as a people in ordered and pleasing form, truly 'terrible as an army with banners,' S. of S. 6. 4, bound for their promised home, led by God Himself. In scripture the third day is always the day of fulfilment or completion. On it Abraham saw Moriah, John saw Jesus and said, 'Behold the lamb', John 1. 29, and on the third day Christ rose from the dead! So, spiritually, on this their first journey out from Sinai, the Lord anticipates their arrival. This journey was three days, but in reality they never arrived at the ultimate destination beyond for, on account of their unbelief, the Lord kept them out of the land.

Our portion ends with the refusal of Hobab, Moses brother-in-law, to go with them to 'share the good things that the Lord will do for us'. Was it a lack of faith on Moses' part that he felt the need of Hobab's eyes for the journey, v. 31? What need did they have of human eyes when the ark and the cloud went before them? Come, let us walk today as the 'sons' we are!

August 27th

Numbers 11. 1-15

WHO SHALL GIVE US FLESH TO EAT?

So far we have enjoyed the thrilling scene of this people and their preparations as the Lord brought them slowly nearer to the fulfilment of His promise to give them a land. Now we read, 'And . . . the people complained'. We cannot help but be stunned by such a thing at this stage yet our Bibles are littered with examples of God *providing* and men *despising*. It is time we learned that we have a built-in capability to ruin what God is doing and to destroy the good He would have us to enjoy. The people of God often come to grief here!

Firstly, we are aware that the judgement of God as a result of their complaining was swift and dreadful. This is how much He hates it when we indulge in such behaviour. They are instantly taught that their 'complaining' leads to 'weeping' and they have to call the place 'Taberah', that is, 'the place of burning' to mark it for them.

Secondly, we note that some will still insist on this course and it is in the identifying of the subject of their objection that we discover the main root cause of all complaint. There are those that 'lust after', 'desire intensely', the things they left in Egypt. For them the new life had lost its attraction and in their hearts they had never really left Egypt behind. This is the real cause of the problem.

As believers we too can walk this pathway of failure, never fully entering into the blessedness of the new life in Christ but always allowing ourselves one foot in the world out of which God saved us. To be such a believer never allows you to know the full deliverance God intended and planned for you, cf. Eph. 5. 1-21.

Two clear consequences follow this desire of theirs for flesh. God's provision in the manna bread was despised; it spoke of Christ and only He can satisfy the heart. The old nature is still in us, still wants the old things; it is a lifetime's battle. The second result was the despair of Moses concerning his place in the service of God. To keep standing in front of an unwilling people and encouraging them to stick with God became too much for him to bear. Can we say we know the feeling?

258

TOMORROW YE SHALL EAT FLESH

'And the Lord said unto Moses'. How comforting to read this today. When all seems lost and to be falling apart, when a spiritual servant bares his innermost feelings of despair and sees no future for him, *it is then that the Lord speaks*. Praise Him, for all is not lost nor as dark as it may seem to be for He is still in control. At times like these it is so vital for us to wait patiently, listen and follow! We must grasp that these times of testing, part of the true wilderness experience, make us ultimately the people that God can use. *Don't run away from such situations – work them out with Him; He knows what He is doing.*

In His wisdom the Lord deals with the failing servant first and then the situation with the people. It is an issue concerning leadership for His people and with the Lord this is always of great significance. Never cease praying for the leadership God has raised up in the assembly. At any one time you will probably never know just what burdens they currently bear or what issues of importance they are having to handle.

The immediate provision met the need of Moses and shows how infinitely gracious our God is to us. His mind surely was that with God alone beside him Moses would have been more than adequate for the work, but nonetheless He will give him seventy elders, endued with the same Spirit, and thus allow His servant the respite he needs. Even the Lord sat wearied on the wall of Sychar's well and it is no disgrace to be similarly emptied in the service of God, John 4. 6. He knows our frame that we are but dust!

Now, new leadership always needs divine approval and public recognition and acceptance. Leadership organized in a corner is futile and often brings great distress to the people of God. It needs to be done with due preparation and solemnity as here and always in public view, no matter what problems you feel may ensue.

Dealing with Israel's complaint follows swiftly. The provision was overwhelming but it came with severe penalties. All they had in the end were 'graves of craving'. If we crave anything let's make it the things that will last for ever!

August 29th

Numbers 12. 1-16

HATH HE NOT SPOKEN ALSO BY US?

It would seem that 'complaining' is not limited to 'the people', as now we have members of Moses' family providing bitterness and dissent in what is a vicious personal attack. Complaints of this nature, that is personal attacks upon individuals in leadership, undermine confidence, destroy lives and break down fellowship.

It is difficult, if not nearly impossible for us, to identify motives for an individual's actions. Yet it would seem to be jealousy regarding Moses' status as God's spokesman that moved Miriam and Aaron to commence this public campaign to undermine his position and authority. Moses has just shared his responsibilities with seventy others and it may be that Miriam and Aaron were not included, but it was the worst of actions, blatant, ill-advised and ill-timed.

It is at this very juncture that we learn a startling fact about Moses that has really become his epitaph, for scripture records him to be 'very meek, above all the men . . . upon the face of the earth', v. 3. Meekness is strength veiled in gentleness. It is that vitality of character that can accept such critics yet is not ruffled or diverted by them.

Leadership is always under attack but if there are legitimate issues to be dealt with then deal with them privately and only with those that need to know. To seek to gain change or challenge decisions any other way is carnal and offensive.

Divine intervention is immediate and swift, for the tabernacle, the cloud, the voice, are all indicative of how vital the issue is with God. Both Miriam and Aaron are responsible for this action but Miriam seems to incur the divine wrath. She is made a leper and reprieved only on account of Moses' intercession and then banished from the camp for seven days.

Much of the narrative is God's justification of Moses' position and service. Elders have no such visible defence against attacks upon their person or service, but God will evaluate these things, and meanwhile elders and their fellow saints have a responsibility to equally respect, trust and esteem each other as better than themselves.

SPY OUT THE LAND

From the reading today you would understand that the sending of spies into the land was God's idea and intention. In fact, a reading of Deuteronomy chapter 1 verses 20-23 shows that it came firstly from the people. Does this really surprise us? As far as God was concerned He had already given a very satisfactory description of the land and guaranteed with solemn promises for centuries to give it to them? The spies were the people's idea and that is why the results of their going were so horrendously bad. The request reveals the state of heart of a people who were not willing to move forward solely on the basis of faith in the word of their God.

God often acts according to the level of faith offered, but it never results in the best that He had in mind for us, cf. 1 Sam. 8. 22. Let us walk by faith, simply and submissively, if we are going to walk with God at all. Has He clearly asked us to trust Him in a matter? Then let us leave it with Him and believe He knows best.

It took forty days for the search to be accomplished and when the spies returned well loaded, not only with the evidence of a fruitful and good land but with intelligence of the cities and the people that lived there, what had they really accomplished? It proved beyond doubt that what God had said was accurate and true. The land was as He had described and not a word of His could be doubted or disputed. It was a land that, 'surely . . . floweth with milk and honey', v. 27.

The challenge of today's reading is that of our willingness to accept God's word at its face value and not to travel the road of Thomas who said, 'Except I shall see', John 20. 25. The simple word of scripture is what God expects to be enough for His own. In a day when it is evident that believers are willing to set aside what they have held for years to be scriptural in order to take things into their own hands and walk in the light of their own wisdom, let us take heed to the warnings of our passage today. As DANIEL WHITTLE wrote,

> 'It is His word, God's precious word,
>   it stands forever true'.

August 31st

Numbers 13. 26-33

WE BE NOT ABLE TO GO UP

The reading today will show us the true nature of 'faith in God'. There is a sharp difference between the report and interpretation of the two spies as against that of the ten. They shared the same experience, saw the same sights, heard the same conversations but they produced opposing and contradictory testimony for the people of God upon which to move forward.

The first report is a combined and unanimous one, factual and without emotional overtones. It is the following advice that is so contrary for the two said, 'We are well able to overcome it', while the larger group declared, 'We be not able to go up'. How come they expressed totally opposite opinions?

They both saw the good of the land and both accepted that there were difficulties to be overcome. The divergence of opinion focuses on the difficulties that the land presented. They knew that the inhabitants were not going to roll over and submit to them readily. So, were the problems insuperable?

The ten provided an 'evil report' that begins with, 'Nevertheless', v. 28, and here begins a whole catalogue of issues that very swiftly blossom into an exaggerated and impossible barrier to progress, vv. 32-33. That is how unbelief works; it looks at the problems and focuses on them seeking to measure its own strength and ability to deal with them and concludes it cannot win. However, the two viewed the difficulties only in the light of the ability of God who was sufficient for them all. This led them to a faith that overcomes and a life on the victory side!

Unbelief is the 'grasshopper mentality' that sidelines God and frustrates His working. Faith invests in the ability of God to go before, intervene and fulfil promises. It is not ignorant, indifferent or reckless, but alive to the dangers and demands of the road it treads, yet will none the less trust God all the way. We have the many 'witnesses' of Hebrews 12 to this quality of living that 'go' calls for, and that bears out the value of such a course. Let us do a work for Him in our day that proves He is the same faithful God He always was and will be for us too. In the words of Caleb, 'Let us go up at once and posses it'.

September 1st

Numbers 14. 1-25

REBEL NOT YE AGAINST THE LORD

Two tests and their results are before us in this solemn and instructive passage.

Firstly, the people were tested. They had been brought to the border of the promised land and the twelve spies had returned with their reports. Sadly, at this critical moment in their history, the people failed. The writer to the Hebrews tells us that their failure was due to *unbelief*, 'they could not enter in because of unbelief', Heb. 3. 19.

Notice that they could not stand still – they must retreat, even if it meant going back to Egypt, v. 4! Nor can we stand still in our spiritual progress. If, for whatever reason, we refuse to advance, then we will certainly go back. To consider returning to Egypt, the scene of their recent slavery, seems incredible. Their plan effectively sought to reverse the purposes of God in redemption. He had redeemed them from bondage by the blood of the lamb! And yet, perhaps we too have been guilty of returning to things that once enslaved us in unconverted days, things from which we have been redeemed.

Secondly, Moses, too, was tested. Failure in others becomes a test to spiritual believers, Gal. 6. 1-2. God proposes that the nation be discarded and that another nation be created from Moses himself, vv. 11-12. Moses reveals his high spiritual state as he reasons with God in intercessory prayer for the people. He pleads the glory and character of God. He reminds God that His name would be dishonoured in the eyes of the heathen. He reasons from the faithfulness of God's character. The world would say that he missed a wonderful opportunity for personal advancement, but Moses was more concerned for the glory of God.

Although God pardoned the people He dealt with them in a governmental way. The rebels would perish in the wilderness and none of them would see the land. Acts of rebellion may be forgiven, but sometimes the consequences of our actions live with us for the rest of our lives.

As we ponder these principles may we be willing to submit to the word of God with renewed faith in His promises. Let us go forward into Canaan, not back to Egypt.

GO NOT UP FOR THE LORD IS NOT AMONG YOU

We are introduced to three disparate groups in our reading today; together they present a dispensational picture of the nation of Israel.

1. The rebellious generation. They would never enter the land. For forty years – a year for each day of their search, they would wander until death claimed them all, vv. 29, 34. They would become a lost generation. Their fate foreshadows the dreadful judgement facing Israel in the Tribulation period.

2. The children. In His grace, God undertakes to bring a new generation into the land, v. 31. The old generation is numbered in chapter 1 of the book; the new generation is numbered in chapter 26. At the Lord's appearing, a nation will be 'born at once', Isa. 66. 8. 'A seed shall serve him; it shall be accounted to the Lord for a generation', Ps. 22. 30. Every Israelite in that day will be a believer.

3. Joshua and Caleb. Their faithfulness would be rewarded by preservation through the wilderness and entry to the land, v. 30. Perhaps they picture the godly remnant who will be preserved through the Tribulation period and enter the Millennial Kingdom. These two men stood as a living testimony to the faithfulness and power of God.

In a remarkable change of heart, the people attempted to enter the land after all, v. 40. They were specifically told that the Lord was not among them, v. 42. The ark, the visible symbol of God's presence, remained in the camp, v. 44. There is a terrible irony here: they were afraid to enter *with* God, but not afraid to enter *without* God! In the present day the nation is acting in presumption without God and cannot count on His blessing.

There are important practical lessons for us. How much we need His presence! Anything attempted without Him is sure to fail. As the Lord Himself instructed His disciples, 'without me ye can do nothing', John 15. 5. The nations who discomfited them, Amelek and Canaan, represent respectively the flesh and the devil. We cannot stand alone against such foes!

As we 'go up' today, may we have the assurance of the Lord's presence with us.

September 3rd
Numbers 15. 1-31

WHEN YE BE COME INTO THE LAND

It is encouraging to note that God's plans cannot be thwarted by the failure of His people. It is *'when'* ye come into the land, v. 2, not *'if'*. There may seem to be a delay, but nothing can prevent God fulfilling His promises. In light of their entry into the land, three important issues are raised.

Firstly, instructions are given regarding offerings that should accompany the 'main' offerings, vv. 2-16. These were to be the meal-offering and the drink-offering. The land was to be a land of corn and wine, and these commodities speak of the bounty of God's provision. With each offering they acknowledged that every good gift came from above. Typically, the meal-offering speaks of life and the drink-offering speaks of death. Every offering had to be accompanied by that which spoke of our Lord's perfect life and the joy brought to God when He 'poured out his soul unto death', Isa. 53. 12.

Secondly, the issue raised is regarding the heave-offerings of their first dough, vv. 17-21. The meal-offering consisted of flour mingled with oil; this heave-offering consists of flour mingled with water. Dough is flour prepared for the oven. It is 'work in progress', pointing us forward to the baked product. Does this suggest to us that our Lord's perfect life always had in view the oven of Calvary?

Thirdly, the last section deals with provision made for sins of ignorance and the solemn judgement on sins of presumption, vv. 22-31. Notice that sinning is not expected – not *when* ye sin, but *if*, cf. 1 John 2. 1. Even established in the land, surrounded by the bounty of God, enjoying His blessings, there was the possibility of sin. Surroundings cannot change the wayward heart of man. The wilderness conditions were not responsible for their sin. We too are surrounded by the bounty of God's provision and blessed with every spiritual blessing. Yet, we too are prone to err. How good to remember that provision has been made in the sin offering. Whilst the distinction between sins of ignorance and sins of presumption seems to be an Old Testament concept under the dispensation of law, presumptuous sin is never expected in a believer in any age.

Numbers 15. 32-41

REMEMBER, DO AND BE HOLY

A man is stoned to death for violating the Sabbath, vv. 32-36; the Israelites are instructed to wear a blue fringe on their robes, vv. 37-41. At first glance the two incidents seem unrelated. Why does the Spirit of God bring them together?

The first incident is directly linked with yesterday's reading: the man sinned presumptuously, and could therefore only expect judgement. To our minds his crime may seem insignificant. We must remember that observing the Sabbath was designed by God as a major test of obedience for the nation of Israel, and kindling a fire was specifically forbidden, Exod. 35. 3. The man's sin was outright rebellion, but there is a deeper significance in this act. Fire speaks of the judgment of God. The Sabbath rest pointed forward to the rest God found in the finished work of Christ. As He lay in the tomb the judgement was over and there could be no fire kindled on the Sabbath day.

Following on from this solemn incident, God instructs the people regarding the ribband of blue. This symbolic emblem was to be a reminder to the people of the commandments of God and stimulate them to obedience and holy living.

Being blue, it reminded them that their laws had come directly from heaven. Moses went up into the mountain to receive the law, Exod. 19. 20; angels, heavenly beings, were involved in its administration, Gal. 3. 19. As part of their garments, it reminded them that the commandments of God were designed to be part of their character. Being on the fringe or hem of the garment, they were being taught that these heavenly laws reached down to their feet, affecting their walk.

And so the incidents are linked. A proper regard for the will of heaven will guard against presumptuous sin and also prevent us from inadvertently acting in a way that dishonours the Lord.

We cannot read of the hem of the robe without thinking of our Lord and those who touched the blue of His robe, Matt. 9. 20. He was entirely in accord with the mind of heaven and could therefore meet the need of earth. He indeed remembered the commandments and did them, and displayed a holiness not seen in the world before or since.

September 5th

Numbers 16. 1-35

SEEK YE THE PRIESTHOOD ALSO?

This incident occurred some twenty years after chapter 15, around the mid-point of the years of wilderness wandering.

It is instructive to see the source of this rebellion against the Lord. The instigators were from the tribes of Levi and Reuben.

God had called the tribe of Levi to tabernacle service, Num. 3. 6-9. From that tribe He had selected the family of Aaron to approach Him as priests. Korah was a Levite. Although his initial complaint was directed at the position which Moses and Aaron held, Moses correctly identified the problem – the Levite wanted to be the priest. In this Korah was rebelling against the sovreignty of God.

Dathan and Abiram came from the tribe of Reuben. It seems their desire was not so much for priesthood as for pre-eminence. Their father, Reuben, had lost that position through immorality, Gen. 49. 3-4. The blessings of the firstborn had been transferred away from the tribe. Now Reuben's descendents try to restore their position and thwart the governmental purposes of God.

We must appreciate too that God still acts sovreignly and governmentally. He has a purpose for each saint. We would do well to seek that out by the help of the Spirit of God and fulfil God's desires for our lives. To try to fill a role not allotted to us can have far-reaching consequences. God can act in government here too. Our own failures can have practical consequences that will affect the rest of our lives. Instead of rebelling against God we ought to seek grace to accept His governmental dealings with us in a spirit of submission.

Instead of submitting to Moses' rebuke, Korah gathers all the congregation against him, v. 19. Such behaviour will not be tolerated, and immediately the glory of God appears. The innocent Israelites must separate themselves from these 'wicked men', underlining the principle of separation from known evil. The earth then opens 'her mouth' to swallow up the rebels.

There is a gracious footnote to this solemn incident. Eleven psalms are entitled 'for the sons of Korah'. These sons had evidently been spared the judgement of God and were witnesses to His grace. In wrath, God had remembered mercy.

September 6th

Numbers 16. 36-50

BETWEEN THE DEAD AND THE LIVING

Two types of censer feature in this passage – the censers of false priesthood and the censer of the true priest.

The censer was used in tabernacle service to cause the incense to ascend before God. Incense speaks of the glories of Christ that delight the heart of God, Exod. 30. 34-38.

Censers in the hands of unbelieving rebels can only bring judgement. In our previous reading we noted that Korah and his company had been told to bring their censers before the Lord, vv. 16-17. It would seem that as they were attempting to offer incense they were consumed by fire from God. The brass censers, however, were preserved and these were beaten into plates to form a covering for the altar of incense, vv. 36-38. They guarded the incense altar from false priesthood.

In our dispensation all believers have the great privilege of drawing near to God as priests. We offer incense as we pray and worship. But worship can only be acceptable to God if it comes from those who are from the priestly family. In a sense the altar of incense is still guarded.

On the following day, the people murmured, blaming Moses and Aaron for the deaths of the rebels, v. 41. When God then judged the people, Moses recognized that the plague could only be stayed by the action of the censer. In the hands of a true priest, the censer is the means of salvation. Aaron stood between the dead and the living, v. 48. His action halted death.

This no doubt symbolizes the priestly ministry of our Lord Jesus, but there is a practical lesson for us too. Often today there can be a plague among the people. There was a plague of worldly wisdom at Corinth, 1 Cor. 1. 20; there was a plague of legalism in Galatia, Gal. 5. 1; there was a plague of Gnostic philosophy at Colosse, Col. 2. 8. In each case Paul acts as a priestly man. He confronts the plague by wielding the censer. A ministry of the glories of Christ will always result in the plague being stayed.

May we wield the censer today, whether in the sanctuary in prayer and worship, or in the congregation as we stand between the dead and the living.

THE ROD OF AARON BUDDED

It is interesting to note that a rod is taken for each tribe. The rod symbolizes authority. The question at stake was this: who had the authority or the right to minister before God as priest?

This dramatic test pictures for us the unique right of our Lord Jesus to be our Priest. The rods were laid up before the Lord. On the morrow only Aaron's rod blossomed. Significantly, it 'brought forth buds, and bloomed blossoms, and yielded almonds', v. 8. In the picture, 'dead' wood is brought back to life; and the full expression of life is here – the bud, the flower and the fruit. In the Middle Eastern spring, the first signs of life were seen in the buds of the almond tree. This is, indeed, a lovely picture of the resurrection of our Lord Jesus.

Although the Saviour was a priestly Man on earth and offered the ultimate sacrifice at Calvary, He was not officially a Priest until He was raised from the dead and glorified, Heb. 8. 4. His sphere of service is on the other side of death, indeed it is in heaven, not on earth. His resurrection is a vital factor in His ministry. 'He is able also to save them to the uttermost that come unto God by him, seeing he ever liveth to make intercession for them', Heb. 7. 25.

The three stages of life displayed are suggestive. The *bud* represents perhaps the first dawning to our souls that He is alive. The *blossom* leads us to appreciate the beauty and grace of that resurrection life. The *fruit* perhaps indicates an awareness of the results of His resurrection and the implications for each believer. We have the *bud* in the Gospel records of the resurrection, the *blossom* in the Acts and the full *fruit* expounded in the Epistles.

Aaron's rod was not returned to him, it was placed in the ark, along with the tables of the law and the golden pot of manna, Heb. 9. 4. These three items speak to us of the high-priestly ministry of the Lord Jesus.

The people were again taught that their only access to God was through Aaron. We can only approach God through our Lord Jesus. Let us draw near confidently, 'having an high priest over the house of God', Heb. 10. 21.

September 8th

Numbers 18. 1-32

THE CHARGE OF THE TABERNACLE

It is important to distinguish between the priest and the Levite. The priest approached God and carried out the ritual of the tabernacle: the Levite served in the practical matters pertaining to the tabernacle. Not every Levite was a priest, but every priest was a Levite.

In our dispensation every believer is both a priest and a Levite, 1 Pet. 2. 5. We have the wonderful privilege of approaching God in worship as well as engaging in the service of the tabernacle. The functions of the priest and Levite are now united in a spiritual sense in the New Testament believer.

Notice that the Levites were to be 'joined' to the priest, v. 2. They were to act together. We need to learn the lesson that worship and service cannot be separated. But although they are joined, it is clear that the Levite was subordinate to the priest. He was 'given' to the priest as a gift, v. 6, and the service of the Levite would be under the direction of the priest. The priestly man knew what to do in God's house. Service must spring from communion with God. Worship precedes service. The Father is looking for worshippers first, John 4. 23.

Perhaps this is one reason why our service may seem ineffective at times. Could it be that our service does not flow from our worship? We must not go into God's presence with our ideas for service: rather we should come from His presence with His ideas for service.

The remainder of the chapter deals with God's provision for both priest and Levite, vv. 8-32. Neither would have an inheritance in the land. Their function took priority over everything else. They must be free to serve the Lord without distraction. But although they had no inheritance, the priest and Levite had something better. The tithe or tenth of each offering was to be the portion of priest and Levite, v. 21. The tenth represents what is best and what was for God in the offering. God in effect is sharing His portion with the priest and Levite. As we understand priesthood and Levite service aright we will find that we are privileged to share in the very portion of God – adequate compensation for the lack of inheritance here!

September 9th

Numbers 19. 1-10

BRING THEE A RED HEIFER

As the Israelites wandered through the wilderness they could not avoid death. A whole generation would be wasted and their carcases would fall by the way. Contact with death defiled the people and there was constant need for cleansing. God's answer was the red heifer.

Our attention is drawn to the **animal**, vv. 1-3, the **anguish**, vv. 4-7, and the **ashes**, vv. 8-10.

The **animal** was unique, and, of course, it speaks of our Lord Jesus. It was red – the Hebrew word comes from the root *adam*, reminding us of the true manhood of the last Adam. It was 'without spot', lit., perfect, complete, and had no blemish. Nothing good was absent and nothing bad was present. It had never been under yoke. Truly our Lord Jesus is the only Man who had never known the bondage of sin's yoke. He was never dominated.

The ritual regarding its death pictures for us the **anguish** of Calvary, vv. 4-7. The blood is sprinkled towards the tabernacle. Approach to God must be on the basis of sacrifice. The body of the heifer is then incinerated entirely. Two words signify to burn in the Hebrew language; one means 'to cause to ascend as incense'; the other indicates 'to consume entirely'. The latter word is used here. This surely points to the intensity of divine wrath experienced by our Lord Jesus at the hand of God. Into the burning are cast cedar wood, hyssop and scarlet, symbols of His dignity, lowliness and glory. Such an One bore the judgement. This sacrifice was unique in that no part of it was placed on the altar.

The **ashes** are evidence of judgement borne, and these are preserved for future use, vv. 8-10. They will be mixed with the water of separation and applied when the need arises for defilement to be removed. The death of Christ not only meets my need judicially but His death and judgement-bearing is the basis on which I find cleansing from defilement.

We too are passing through a defiling world, but, by one sacrifice, provision has been made for our entire wilderness journey.

ASHES AND RUNNING WATER

In Leviticus chapter 6 verse 10 we read of 'the ashes of the burnt offering'. These speak of the intensity of the pleasure God found in the Lord Jesus. By contrast, the ashes of the red heifer speak of the intensity of wrath experienced on account of sin.

The ashes were kept in store for future needs, v. 9. Each time defilement occurred they would be employed in ritualistic cleansing in a striking way.

The ashes were mixed with running (or living) water and sprinkled on the unclean person, vv. 17-19. If the ashes speak of the sin-bearing of Christ, then running water speaks of the Holy Spirit applying the truth of these sufferings.

It is instructive that two sprinklings were needed – on the third day and on the seventh day, v. 19. There could be no cleansing without both applications.

This suggests to us two distinct ministries of the Holy Spirit with regard to the sufferings of Christ. First, there is a ministry of *conviction*, when the full horror of sin is brought home to the believer. It is only in the sufferings of Christ that we get a true appreciation of the dreadful character of sin. But then there is another ministry, that of *confirmation*. The Holy Spirit not only impresses upon us the terrible cost of sin to Christ, but also the fact that justice has been fully satisfied.

Scripture is full of examples of this double ministry. When David sinned, Nathan's first visit answers to the sprinkling on the third day. When the true character of sin was exposed to David and repentance had taken place, Nathan brought the message of assurance that forgiveness was granted – the sprinkling on the seventh day.

The Corinthians were unaware of the seriousness of sin in the assembly until Paul wrote his first letter – the first sprinkling. After godly sorrow had produced repentance, he wrote his second letter to assure forgiveness – the second sprinkling.

Perhaps we need the ashes and the running water today. The Holy Spirit would seek to apply these precious truths in order that defilement might be removed and communion restored.

September 11th

Numbers 20. 1-13

SPEAK YE UNTO THE ROCK

This solemn scene of failure had far-reaching consequences for both Moses and Aaron. Both would be denied access to the promised land as a result of their actions, v. 12. God is no respecter of persons in the matter of sin, and, in fact, the greater the privilege, the greater the responsibility. Failure of leaders is more serious than failure of those not in positions of authority.

Thirty-eight years earlier the people had faced a similar situation in Exodus chapter 17. Then, as now, they were in the wilderness of Sin. Then, as now, they thirsted and chode with Moses. Then, as now, the answer to their need lay in the Rock.

But there is a world of difference between the two incidents. In Exodus chapter 17, Moses was told to *smite* the rock; here he is told to *speak* to the rock. In Exodus chapter 17 the normal word for rock is used; here it is a different word meaning 'elevated rock'.

The typical teaching is clear; 'that Rock was Christ', Paul reminds the Corinthians, 1 Cor. 10. 4. Once smitten and elevated, the rock is a wonderful picture of His sufferings and ascension, securing the outpouring of blessing for His people. He will never be smitten again, and therein lies the seriousness of Moses' action.

Moses was sorely tried and as a result 'he spake unadvisedly with his lips', Ps. 106. 33. He called the people rebels; He failed to sanctify the Lord by simple obedience; He smote the rock in anger twice. It is solemn to think of this supremely meek man giving vent to an angry outburst. We should not, however, judge Moses harshly. How true it is that we too often fail on our strongest points.

The once-for-all sufferings of our blessed Lord are over. We sometimes sing, 'Never more shall God, Jehovah, smite the Shepherd with the sword', R. C. CHAPMAN. From His elevated position at God's right hand our Lord Jesus has an abundant supply to meet our needs.

Thirsty soul, 'Speak to the Rock'. Just as the waters gushed out for the nation of Israel, so His fullness is there today for the asking.

THOU SHALT NOT PASS

Have you come across a 'no entry' sign recently?

The enforced detour around the land of Edom must have been a sore burden to the weary Israelites. Perhaps they did not expect such a flat refusal. After all, was Edom not related to Israel? Edom was Esau, Jacob's brother, Gen. 36. 1, and Moses addresses the king of Edom in this way. But even an appeal to natural relationship falls on deaf ears, v. 18. Not only was this attitude unnatural, it was unreasonable. Moses offered to pay for all they consumed en route, v. 19. In natural terms it would have been a tremendous boost for Edom's economy! Why was Edom so implacably opposed to Israel? For the answer to this question we must go back to Genesis.

Esau and Jacob represented two types of humanity. Esau represented what was natural. He was a 'man of the field'. He valued earthly things and held spiritual things with a light hand. Jacob, for all his faults, was a spiritual man. His methods left much to be desired, but he truly valued God's inheritance. He was, of course, the second man who would displace the first, Gen. 25. 23.

It is clear that Edom knew of Israel's bondage and suffering in Egypt, vv. 14-16. Is it possible that they had secretly rejoiced and, perhaps, felt that now the inheritance would be theirs instead? Thus, faced with a re-born nation seeking to fulfil the purpose of God, Edom is determined to impede the progress of Israel.

This teaches us the lesson that the natural man can have no sympathy with the purpose of God, because it clearly teaches his own judgement and demise.

We should compare this section with chapter 21 verses 21-25. In the latter passage a similar situation arose. The response, however, was different. Here, God told them simply to by-pass the area; in chapter 21, God told them to fight.

Similar situations may require different solutions. We need to be cast on God for wisdom every hour – regardless of how familiar situations may feel. Applying the same remedy may not be the will of God.

September 13th

Numbers 20. 23-29

AARON SHALL DIE THERE

What a poignant scene is before us today!

Think of what it meant to *Aaron*. How solemn to take that last journey up Mount Hor, knowing that he would never descend. His death was a direct result of the governmental dealings of God. It is good to remember, however, that God called him home from a mountain. Despite the ups and downs of Aaron's life, he finished on the mountaintop.

Many saints have been conscious that the time of their departure was at hand, 2 Tim. 4. 6. As a result, they looked at all around them in a different light. How this should solemnize us and motivate us today.

Think of what it meant to *Moses*. Aaron was his older brother. They had been through much together. No doubt there had been tears and smiles, mutual fellowship and support. All that would now end. Moses would strip his brother of his priestly clothes, v. 26. The clothes would be taken from a living man, not from a corpse. No one would die with the priestly garments on, reminding us of the fact that our Lord's high priestly ministry cannot be touched by death. Moses had once dressed Aaron in these clothes, now he must strip them off. Our Lord Jesus will never be stripped of the dignity of His priestly office! 'Their priesthood ran through several hands, for mortal was their race; Thy never-changing priesthood stands eternal as Thy days', ISAAC WATTS.

Think of what it meant to *Eleazar*. He would both lose and gain. He lost a father – he gained an office. The garments are all that Aaron had to bequeath. He had no inheritance or property. Yet, what a rich legacy! Who can conceive the emotions of Eleazar as he feels the weight of the priestly garments rest on him! Both privilege and responsibility rest on his shoulders. And he was of such a stature that no alteration was needed.

If the Lord does not come each one of us must pass this way. May we end our journey on the mountaintop. May we have something of lasting value to bequeath to the next generation. Or, if we are 'Eleazers', let us rise to the challenge of new responsibilities.

MAKE THEE A FIERY SERPENT

The serpent is, at first sight, a strange picture of the death of Christ. Indeed, had we not the Lord's own authority for viewing it as such we might hesitate to do so, cf. John 3. 14.

The serpent is mainly used in scripture as a picture of evil, often personified in Satan himself. The Bible begins with the activity of the serpent in the Garden of Eden and closes describing the doom of 'that old serpent', Rev. 20. 2.

The key to this wonderful type is found in Paul's statement, 'For he hath made him to be sin for us', 2 Cor. 5. 21.

Brass symbolizes judgement. Therefore, the brazen serpent typifies God's righteous judgement poured out against sin in its most essential form. What an amazing description of the death of our blessed Lord! Although never a sinner, he was made sin – dealt with as God would deal with the principle of sin. This is indeed holy ground. The reverent and believing heart simply bows in gratitude and wonder.

The look is such a simple and clear picture of faith. To some it may have seemed illogical and unreasonable, but faith is simple reliance on God's word. It was not the intensity or sincerity of their look that counted – it was what they looked at! Similarly, in salvation the quality and measure of faith is not important, rather the vital matter is the object of faith, our Lord Jesus Himself.

This incident occurred towards the end of the wilderness journey. It is a solemn reminder that the 'new' generation was really no better than the 'old'. The root principle of evil was present in them too, despite their experiences of the provision and kindness of God. We do well to remember that in every redeemed heart there is an unchanged and undiminished capacity for evil, Rom. 7. 18.

The serpent of brass re-appears in scripture around 800 years later. Sadly, in their idolatry, Israel burnt incense to it. King Hezekiah had to destroy it when he restored true worship to the nation, 2 Kgs. 18. 4. The natural heart prefers a visible object of veneration to faith in the unseen. We too need to be on our guard in this respect today.

September 15th

Numbers 21. 10-35

THEN ISRAEL SANG

Three quotations are cited in this interesting passage – prose, praise and proverb.

Firstly, reference is made to *prose* contained in a 'book of the wars of the Lord', vv. 14-15. This relates to events in the borderland of Arnon, lying between the lands of Moab and the Amorites. The exploits that followed were recorded in a non-inspired and, therefore, unpreserved book.

Secondly, there is *praise* in song, vv. 16-18. Before they face the enemy, God graciously instructs Moses to gather the people together and enjoy His provision. The water was made available not by smiting a rock or even speaking to a rock, but by *digging*, v. 18. This reminds us that exercise is required to benefit from God's provision. In our experience there may be springs lying latent and untested – provision not enjoyed through lack of digging. The spring reminds us of the Lord's gracious ministry in John's gospel. In chapter 4 He speaks of a well of water springing up into everlasting life. Only in the joy and power of the Holy Spirit can warfare be effective. As they enjoyed God's provision, the joy of the Lord was their strength.

Finally, there is a *proverb* recounting the victories won by the Lord in this area, vv. 27-30. A proverb is not merely an historical account – it has a moral and instructive purpose. By heeding proverbs men act wisely. So this proverb, relating to the power of God, ought to have produced fear and submission in the hearts of the people of the land.

The battles recounted mainly concerned two kings, Sihon, king of the Amorites, and Og, king of Bashan, vv. 21, 33. It is interesting to note that in the walled city of Jericho, Rahab had heard of these victories. In her case it had the desired effect, 'our hearts did melt . . . the Lord your God, he is God in heaven above, and in earth beneath', Josh. 2. 11. She also linked the wonders at the Red Sea with the defeat of these two kings – as does the Spirit of God in verse 14 of this chapter. The lesson is clear, the power of God is in no way diminished, despite the passing of time and despite the failure of His people in the wilderness. May we know something of that power today!

THOU SHALT NOT CURSE THE PEOPLE

Such was the consternation when news was received of the victories of Israel over the king of the Amorities and over Bashan, that the king of Moab was terrified. In fact, his fear made him physically ill, v. 3. This was quite needless, for though they did not know it, God had specifically told Israel to leave Moab alone, Deut. 2. 9. The king evidently felt there was only one way to overcome Israel without facing them in battle, and that was to set a curse upon them. He was prepared to pay whatever it cost for the most famous diviner of the day, the prophet Balaam, to come and curse the Israelites.

On first reading the story of Balaam, he is a bit of an enigma. Is he a prophet of the Lord gone bad? After all, he does call Jehovah 'my God' in verse 18. He is more probably a pagan diviner who believed he could manipulate the God of the Israelites and so curse them by their own deity. Balaam insists to the princes sent from the Moabite king that he will consult this Jehovah God and do according to what He says, v. 8. God forbids him from cursing Israel. Balaam, initially, refuses to do so, but upon being visited by yet more important princes from Moab, his ego becomes inflated. He affirms, yet again, that he will consult Jehovah once more, but stresses, 'I cannot go beyond the word of the Lord', v. 18. This time, God gives him permission to go with the men, provided Balaam speaks the words God gives him and no more. Balaam saddles his ass and sallies forth.

The king of Moab had flattered Balaam, 'I wot that he whom thou blessest is blessed, and he whom thou cursest is cursed', he had said, v. 6. This may have been true in the past, as it would appear that no more successful diviner and prophet could be found in his day. As recovered prophetic writings from the sixth century show, he was famous many centuries after his death. Yet the ultimate power to bless and curse is in the hand of God, not man. God had said to his people, 'I will bless them that bless thee and curse him that curseth thee', Gen. 12. 3. God will not permit anyone to curse the people He has blessed. Balaam is going to have to be put in his place.

HAVE I NOW ANY POWER TO SAY ANYTHING?

Balaam's response to the second deputation of messengers from Balak is that he must yet consult with Jehovah, the God of the Israelites. This does not necessarily mean Balaam worshipped Jehovah; he is intending to communicate, through divination, with the 'god' of the people he is hired to curse, ostensibly to determine his will. This was part of Balaam's elaborate and impressive ritual. Again, the God of the Israelites approaches Balaam and allows him to go with the messengers, on condition that he speaks only what God permits. Balaam sets off to meet the Moabite king, yet God knows that, despite being told twice he must not curse the people, that is just what Balaam intends doing. The love of money was to prove his downfall.

Therefore, God intervenes in a remarkable way to show Balaam he has been blinded by his lust. Balaam's donkey sees the Angel of the Lord (God Himself in visible form) three times and, reacting in fear, is beaten by Balaam, who has failed to see anything supernatural once, let alone three times. Imagine Balaam's surprise when the donkey verbally rebukes the famous diviner for his failure to discern the presence of the Angel. An ass speaks to an ass! The Angel of the Lord rebukes Balaam for his lack of spiritual discernment and humbles him by pointing out to him it was the discernment of the animal that had saved Balaam from God's judgement. Balaam offers to return home, but is instructed by God to go on his way, though not in pursuit of his own agenda.

Balak, having only communicated with Balaam through messengers, reassures him of his power to make the magician wealthy, as though Balaam's seeming reluctance to come arose from his doubts that Balak would reward him handsomely. In reply, Balaam warns Balak that he can only speak what God permits, regardless of the wealth on offer, v. 38. Great though his fame and powers may have been, there is One greater than he, who could even discern the thoughts and intents of his heart, Heb. 4. 12. Because of Balaam's intention to curse, God had warned him of the consequences. The drawn sword in the way would remind Balaam whose wrath he faced.

September 18th

Numbers 23. 1-12

THOU HAST BLESSED THEM ALTOGETHER

And so the stage is set. Balak, Balaam and the great and good of the Moabites are gathered on a high point overlooking the tents of the Israelites. Balaam begins his pagan ritual of divination and his working of the arts of magic. Seven altars are set, seven bullocks and seven rams sacrificed, and all sorts of routines are employed, each one part of Balaam's impressive act, no doubt involving the entrails of the sacrificed animals. Balak, being the one who has called for the curse, is instructed to take his place by the offering he has brought, and once more Balaam follows the procedure of contacting the 'god' of the Israelites. How gracious of God, the one true God, to meet with Balaam, despite such abhorrent practices! The story of Balaam shows us that God is able to use anything and anyone to fulfil His purposes. He can meet and make an inarticulate donkey speak words of warning and He can meet and make a reluctant pagan magician speak words of blessing. There is no limit to God's grace and power.

Balaam returns to stand before the Moabite princes. But instead of the anticipated words of cursing, in his first oracle he pronounces a blessing upon the Israelites and refuses to curse those 'whom God hath not cursed', v. 8. Balak is appalled. Believing Balaam's words have supernatural power, he says, 'Do you know what you have just done? You have blessed where you should have cursed! This is the exact opposite of what I had sought from you'.

In speaking of Israel, Balaam stresses their unique position among the nations of the earth. They are a people unlike any other, set apart in terms of their relationship with God, and in terms of their irrevocable blessing from Him. No one can over-ride God's will. Pagan prophet though he may be, he is powerless to pronounce imprecations upon them. 'O that I could die the death of the righteous!' he says; 'O that I could have a part in their final end!' Balak, you can pay what you wish, and demand what you want. I am powerless to do anything other than to bless what God has blessed. God uses the words of the magician to confirm His blessing on His people.

September 19th

Numbers 23. 13-30

GOD IS NOT A MAN THAT HE SHOULD LIE

Balak is appalled at the blessing Balaam has just pronounced upon Israel. He insists that a curse must be pronounced and seven more altars are set in a different place, seven more bullocks and seven more rams sacrificed, and the whole rigmarole is re-enacted, even down to Balaam's renewed rites in contacting the 'god' of Israel. Again, God graciously meets with Balaam, despite all the pagan rituals, and once more confirms to him exactly what he is to say. Once more Balaam steps forth and Balak anticipates the cursing he has called for. Imagine his chagrin when he finds that, in the place of cursing, a new and even greater blessing is pronounced upon Israel. In this second oracle, Balaam stresses that no enchantment or sorcery can prevail against Israel, and no divination will work against them. No one can persuade their God to curse them. Nothing they do can make their God turn away from them. Rather, there is something regal and powerful about them. Jehovah, their God, is with them and there is a shout of a king amongst them. It is God who brought them out of Egypt and God will keep His promises to them. He, after all, 'is not a man that he should lie; neither the son of man that he should repent', v. 19; 1 Sam. 15. 29.

If we are amazed at the grace of God in condescending even to meet with a pagan prophet, how much more gracious of God to reveal such a key attribute of Himself to him. The one, true God, unlike 'gods' who are the imaginings of sinful human beings, can neither lie, nor fail to keep His word. 'Hath he said and shall he not do it?' His character is immutable, Mal. 3. 6, and so are His promises, Heb. 6. 18. He 'does not change like shifting shadows', Jas. 1. 17 NIV. It is simply inconceivable that God would fail to do what He has promised, for to fail in such a way would either be weak, and a sovereign God is never that, or to be fickle, and a perfect God cannot be that. In the same way as God confirmed His promises to His earthly people, the Jews, so He confirms His promises to His spiritual people, the church, for 'the gifts and calling of God are without repentance', Rom. 11. 29. No, Balak, God will not now curse a people He has promised to bless. He cannot.

September 20th

Numbers 24. 1-9

HOW GOODLY ARE THY TENTS, O JACOB

'What are you doing?' asks Balak. 'If you can't curse them, then don't, please don't, bless them!' Balaam replies, again, that he can do only what God tells him to do. Balak decides it is worth one more try. If Balaam can find it in him to curse the people of God, even once, then the exercise will be worth it. So, yet again, in a third place, seven altars are raised, seven bulls and seven rams sacrificed. But Balaam knows, now, that God is not going to change his mind, though Balak hopes he may yet. Balaam does not seek God this time. He has no need to. On the two previous occasions God put words into his mouth which he then spoke, Num. 23. 5, 16. This time, he enters into that ecstatic state when the Spirit of the Lord comes upon him and he speaks the third oracle. As later with Saul, 1 Sam. 19. 24, the Spirit of God came upon him in such a way that he was thrown to the ground, vv. 4, 16. If words Balaam has used until now give the gist of what God has told him to say, in this oracle we see how God really sees His earthly people. 'How goodly are thy tents, O Jacob', are the very words of God Himself.

This oracle, or saying, shows Israel in a double light. First of all, he is revealed in his beauty, vv. 4-7, and then in his strength, vv. 8- 9. There is a sense in which this is Israel as God sees him now; there is also a sense in which this is Israel as he will be seen, in Messianic days. He is, in verses 4-7, in domestic peace, spreading forth beside refreshing and productive waters. Yet he is also seen with latent strength, vv. 8-9. In domestic peace it is Jehovah who has planted him; in latent strength it is God Himself who is bringing him out of Egypt. Israel is as she is because 'God is in the midst of her; she shall not be moved', Ps. 46. 5. All is finally summed up when God Himself, through the pagan prophet, re-iterates His words to Abraham, 'Blessed is he that blesseth thee, and cursed is he that curseth thee', v. 9; cf. Gen. 12. 3.

The seer finally sees. How uplifting it is to think that this is how God sees, and how God will bless, what to all intents and purposes is still a sinful, rebellious people, cf. ch. 25. Thus, we too, seen in Christ, are seen perfect in Him.

Numbers 24. 10-25

A SCEPTRE SHALL RISE OUT OF ISRAEL

Balak is naturally furious with Balaam. Reminding ourselves of the common belief in the extraordinary powers of Balaam, this is appalling to Balak, who believed that all that Balaam said would take place. Ranting and raving, hitting his hands together, he all but threatens Balaam's safety, ordering him home and refusing to give him any of the huge reward he had previously offered, v. 11. Balaam's answer is clear: no matter what the financial inducement, no matter from whom the instructions came, he could not go beyond the will of Jehovah Himself. But then, to add insult to injury, he gives Balak a final word of prophecy for Israel. In Balaam's fourth oracle he foretells what Israel will eventually do to Balak's own people!

This fourth oracle begins with neither pomp, nor sacrificial preparation, nor high drama. There is no need for pagan rituals and ceremony now. Instead, with great dramatic phrases indicating that Balaam the seer sees clearly at last, he hears the very words of God Himself, knows the Most High and falls before the Almighty. Balaam announces the coming Messiah! The Great Deliverer of Israel will come as a star out of Israel. He will rule as a sceptre and crush the enemies of the people of God, whether they be the nations of the day, Moab, Edom, Amalek, and Kenite, or whether they be any nation, v. 24. All this will take place in a future day, says Balaam. 'Not now . . . not nigh'. In that day yet to come, all Israel's enemies will be subdued. Yet this final subjection will be accomplished not by Israel, despite the power seen in a previous vision; it will be accomplished by One who shall come out of that nation.

What an astounding revelation to give through a pagan prophet! God's ways are surely not our ways. There could hardly have been a more unworthy vehicle for such a magnificent prophecy of the coming Messiah than Balaam, who is condemned in no uncertain terms, 2 Pet. 2. 15; Jude 11. Yet, God's words were God's words, and He can use any and all in His service. The thought should humble us when we are used by God, and yet also cause us to exalt Him in His greatness.

PHINEAS TOOK A JAVELIN IN HIS HAND

The sad truth of this chapter is that the disaster which no power outside Israel could wreak and which no external curse could bring upon them, was brought upon them by themselves. What the men of Moab, Balak through Balaam, could not do, a woman of Moab succeeded in doing, namely to bring down God's plague upon His people. How careful we must be that the enemies of God's people should not triumph through our weaknesses.

But this is not just another incident in a long list of disobedience and intransigence which the Israelites showed as they passed from Egypt to Canaan; this takes us right back to the pagan excesses of the worship of the golden calf at the foot of Mount Sinai. Their grumbles, murmuring and disbelief are as nothing compared to this, when 'Israel joined himself unto Baal-peor', and engaged in the moral excesses of heathen worship. Balaam was behind this plan to weaken and betray from within, 31. 16. Despite the superior power God had shown in forbidding him to curse His people, Balaam went under cover and seduced the Israelites into the worship of false gods, into the rejection of the one true God, and into public shame.

Two instances of holy anger are brought before us. First of all, God Himself instructs Moses to execute the leaders of the cult worship and to display their bodies openly as an example of God's fierce anger. As this took place, Zimri, a prince of Israel, seems to have approached the door of the tabernacle flagrantly engaging in lewd acts with Cozbi, a Moabite princess. It may have been his intention merely to flaunt his rebellion before Moses and the others, or he may have intended entering the tabernacle itself, to defile it with pagan worship and debauchery. Phineas, grandson of Aaron, grasped a spear in his hand and ran through both bodies in an act of holy anger.

Phineas' zeal was commended by God. Through his act of 'atonement' the plague that decimated the nation ceased, v. 11. God also promised that the priesthood would descend forever through Phineas and his children. God is pleased when His people are zealous for Him. Are we?

September 23rd

Numbers 26. 1-65

UNTO THESE THE LAND SHALL BE DIVIDED

The book of Numbers can be divided very easily into two main sections. The first section, from Chapter 1 to Chapter 25, deals with the first generation of the Israelites who came out of Egypt. In this section we read of the census of the people, their early march towards Canaan and their subsequent failures and judgements. The second section of Numbers, from Chapter 26 to Chapter 36, deals with the second generation, those born in the wilderness, and again begins with a census of the people, the preparation for their march into Canaan and the hope that they will not repeat the failures of the first generation that fell in the desert. The first section, detailing the experiences of the first generation, forms the major part of the book because the way in which the second generation succeeds or fails is recorded elsewhere, in the book of Joshua, and is not the subject of the book of Numbers. Thus, the last great gasp of the first generation in Chapter 25, which is alluded to as 'the plague' in the first verse of Chapter 26, points to the final judgement of God upon it.

As with the first census some thirty-eight years before, the men over twenty years old are numbered for military purposes. Though God had promised to give the land to His people, there was still work to be done and military campaigns to be fought. Moses, Joshua and Caleb were the only ones left of the first generation, vv. 63-65; Aaron had gone, Miriam had gone and Moses will soon be gone. All the others, even Eleazar, were sons whose fathers had fallen in the wilderness. How different it could have been!

The total number is given in verse 51. There is a major difference now with the first census, however. Where then it had been for military purposes only, now it is also for residential purposes. In numbering the people here, God would see to it that the inheritance of land would be apportioned fairly yet graciously. It would be fair in that the larger tribes would get a larger inheritance, vv. 52-53; it would be gracious in that the final placing of the tribes would be granted by lot, vv. 55-56. The whole disposing of the lot is in the plan of God, of course, Prov. 16. 33. He knows the right place for His people.

September 24th

Numbers 27. 1-11

THOU SHALT SURELY GIVE THEM A POSSESSION

The faith and courage of a band of women, the daughters of Zelophehad, is remarkable. Faced with the fact that the laws of inheritance among the Israelites were to be based on the male line, sons inheriting from their fathers, and the fact that possession of land was vital to identity amongst the people of God, these five daughters had a problem; they had no brother to carry on the line and name of their father and to give them a possession of land in Canaan. It would appear that these were remarkable women. Lacking a male to champion their cause, they were not afraid to stand in the presence of Moses and the people, though women were not permitted to have much say in public life in those days. They make a public plea for an exemption to be made for them. The reason being that their father Zelophehad, though he had paid the penalty for his personal lack of faith and had accordingly died in the wilderness, had done so merely as one of the unbelieving mass of people, and not for any particular sin of rebellion on his part. How harsh it would be, they argued, if surviving members of rebels like Korah were justly deprived of an inheritance, but their family, which had never been associated with rebellion, was unjustly deprived.

Moses did the right thing; he did not make any decision on his own, but sought the mind of the Lord on it. And God was pleased with the faith and courage of these women. He not only gave them land as the inheritance of their father, he also gave them the right to pass that land on to their heirs, v. 7. And God went further than that. He made it a law amongst the people of God, that, from here on, if a man died without sons his property would pass to his daughters. If he died childless, the property would pass on to the nearest relative. Land was to be kept within the family as much as possible, 1 Kgs. 21. 3.

So the faith of five women resulted in a great benefit to all the people of God and it has surely been a comfort to many to see the faith of these women who believed, after years of wandering in the wilderness, that the time had come when God was about to fulfil His promises. With faith and courage, any one of us can claim God's grace and mercy too.

September 25th

Numbers 27. 12-23

SET A MAN OVER THE CONGREGATION

If the first part of Chapter 27 shows us God's mercy to the daughters of Zelophehad and His reward for their faith, the last part of the chapter shows His judgement on Moses for his lack of obedience to God. On the one hand we see God's goodness; on the other we see His severity. Moses is told that, though others will see their inheritance in the land, he himself will not.

It is said that when Queen Mary died she told her people they would find the word 'Calais' engraved on her heart, for she had lost that city for her people. Calais was a great grief to her. To Moses, Meribah was surely a great grief, a life-long regret, almost as though it could be found engraved upon his heart. 'Ye rebelled against my commandment', in the company of Aaron, God reminds him. Aaron has already gone; it will soon be Moses' time. Yet God allows Moses to see the promised land from a distance. Moses tells us that he had pleaded with God to be allowed to enter the land to see it, but that God had been angry with him for his request, Deut. 3. 23-27. He would be allowed only to see it from a distance.

Moses had always been a great and selfless leader, and it grieved him to think that the people of God could be without a shepherd. He therefore pleads with God to set someone in his place, someone who would lead the people so that they were not as sheep without a shepherd. It is fitting to see that, in his last days, Moses is more interested in the future of the people than his own future. He longs to see God appoint his successor. And God does so; He instructs Moses to lay his hand upon Joshua, a man in whom was the Spirit of God, and to bring him before Eleazar the priest so that formal recognition was given by all that this was Moses' replacement. Moses does as God asks him, investing Joshua with some of his own honour and dignity, with neither jealousy nor resentment. There comes a time when all leaders amongst the people of God need to move on, to pass on responsibility to the next generation. True shepherds of God's people should never be self-promoting, neither should they be resentful of those who step into their shoes. God's people need generous-hearted shepherds.

September 26th

Numbers 28. 1-10

MY OFFERING, MY BREAD, MY SACRIFICES

The circumstances of the Israelites were about to change dramatically; they were to enter a new land, be led by a new man, and enjoy a new inheritance. Yet, certain things were not to change but were to remain the same; the sacrifices God had instructed the first generation to give Him were to be re-iterated to the second generation. To Moses is given the responsibility of reminding the people of these things before they entered the promised land.

Every day of their lives, every Sabbath and every new month, was to be marked by ritual and sacrifice. The worship which they had offered during the wilderness years was to be offered in the promised land. God had to be given His place in their lives and in their society wherever they were, as 'was ordained in mount Sinai', v. 6. And it was His place, for He reminds them that they are to offer 'my offering . . . my bread . . . my sacrifices' which were to be 'a sweet savour unto me'. The sacrifices of the old covenant were according to God's laws, not Moses'. They were a sweet savour unto the Lord, not unto Moses and the people.

Each day of the year, in perpetuity, a continual burnt offering of perfect lambs was to be given to the Lord, one lamb every morning and a lamb every evening. With each lamb was to be offered a portion of fine flour with a portion of beaten oil as a meal offering, and a portion of strong drink as a drink offering was to be poured out in the holy place. In addition to the daily sacrifice, every Sabbath day was to be marked by the offering of a further two lambs with attendant meal offerings and drink offerings. Each new moon was to be marked by even more burnt offerings unto the Lord.

The quantity and frequency of sacrifices were designed to show the Israelites that God could only be approached on the basis of blood-sacrifice. Man works to a calendar – and each new day, new week, new month, was to begin with God. Each sacrifice pointed, in one way or other, to the Lord Jesus who would eventually come to fulfil and render needless the ceremonial law by the sacrifice of Himself.

AFTER THIS MANNER YE SHALL OFFER

If the daily sacrifices and the weekly Sabbath sacrifices were to be continually offered, even in the promised land itself, so were the monthly sacrifices. At the beginning of every month, sometimes known as in the new moon, Isa. 1. 14, two bulls, one ram, seven lambs, accompanied by meal and drink offerings, were offered up to the Lord, as well as a goat for a sin offering. Thus, the beginning and ending of every day, the conclusion of every week and the beginning of every new month were marked by special sacrifices to God. The calendar, and the passing of time, was centred around worship to God.

In addition to all this, the people were to mark certain festivals in the year with extra sacrifices. The Passover feast, which was celebrated in the spring of the year (the first month) on the fourteenth day of the month, reminded the Israelites of their deliverance from Egypt under the sheltering blood of the sacrifice. Part of this Passover celebration entailed the 'feast' of unleavened bread, when special sacrifices were to be offered every day of the week and unleavened bread was to be eaten for the whole week. The special offerings of the festal week were again in addition to the continual burnt offering offered every day. During this week the people were to do no work. It is probable that the word 'holiday' in English comes from this week of special 'holy days'.

Fifty days after the Passover came the feast of First-fruits, the harvest feast, sometimes known as the feast of Weeks, Lev. 23. 15-22. This feast was known to Greek believers in New Testament times as Pentecost. Again, all special offerings at this one-day feast were made in addition to the daily sacrifice and in addition to the wave offering appointed, Lev. 23. 18. God was careful to make sure that even the agricultural year with its seasons was to be marked out by special offerings to God. He was to be the centre of their lives at all times. The feast of Passover has always had a special significance to believers in that we know that Christ is our Passover, 1 Cor. 5. 7. The feast of First-fruits speaks of the gathering in of the first spiritual fruits at the beginning of the church, Acts 2.

September 28th

Numbers 29. 1-40

BESIDE THE CONTINUAL BURNT OFFERING

The details of the offerings given to us in these chapters in Numbers emphasize the role of the priests, rather than the participation of the people, in each case. The feast of Trumpets came in the seventh month of the year, which was a particularly busy month for the priests! On the feast of Trumpets the ram's horn was blown, and a bull, a ram, seven lambs with meal offerings and accompanying drink offerings were offered to the Lord, along with a goat for a sin offering; all of this was in addition to the daily and the monthly offerings, v. 6. Then, on the tenth day of the month, came the Day of Atonement, the only day of the year when the High Priest entered into the Holy of Holies to sprinkle the blood of the sacrifice upon the mercy seat. Again, the record in Numbers is of the detail of the sacrifices from the priestly point of view. This was a feast that was marked by fasting and self-denial, rather than by feasting and celebration. It was the most sacred day of the year to the Israelites.

The Day of Atonement was followed, on the fifteenth day of the seventh month, by the feast of Tabernacles. Each day of this week-long feast was marked by its own formidable quantities of sacrifices, beginning with thirteen on the first day of the week and the significant number of seven on the last. All was concluded on the eighth day which was a special Sabbath day of worship. This feast is known in the New Testament as the feast of Booths, for it was characterized by the construction of temporary shelters in which the Israelites were to live for a week. The feast of Tabernacles celebrated the final ingathering of the harvest and was marked by great rejoicing at God's goodness.

In all these special feasts, the offerings were to be of animals 'without blemish'. Each one was to be a perfect sacrifice, and each pointed to *the* Perfect Sacrifice, the Lord Jesus Christ, who was a Lamb without blemish and without spot. The vast shedding of blood which was a direct result of all these offerings would, no doubt, turn the heart of the stoutest man or woman today, but reminds us of the central significance of the blood of Christ to which each sacrifice pointed, Heb. 9. 14.

September 29th

Numbers 30. 1-16

A VOW UNTO THE LORD

It may seem strange that, on the eve of marching into the promised land, when God considers it important to re-iterate that even there the pattern of sacrifices must be maintained, we should find instructions on vows to God. Yet, if we are to imagine an excited people anticipating entry into a land of which many of them have dreamed for so many years, we can well imagine some would make promises to God of what they would do once they got there. God here reminds them of two important aspects with regard to the making of these promises, or vows. The first is that none should do so rashly, for what is vowed God hears and notes. The second is that He expects all vows to be fulfilled.

Instructions about vows are given to the heads of the tribes, no doubt because they had a part to play in the conduct of family and social life. Attention is given to women making vows in verses 3-16. Much time is given to the vows women make because, in a society which was as man-led and man-centred as that of the Israelites, situations may well have arisen where a woman vowed to do something for God that the men in her circle, either fathers, husbands or others, may try to prevent her from fulfilling. In the case of an unmarried woman still living at home, she is subject to her father who can over-rule her vow. Obedience to a father is of greater importance than a self-imposed vow. In the case of a woman who makes a vow before she is married, her new husband can confirm or disallow it as soon as he hears of it and not later. Obedience to a husband is paramount. The vows of widows were to remain binding. A married woman has to gain her husband's consent at its commencement. Elkanah seems to have made no objection to the fulfillment of Hannah's vow, for instance, 1 Sam. 1-2.

The important thing to note here is that women, though prevented from participating in and leading public worship, were nonetheless spiritually-minded enough to vow to do certain things to please the Lord. God heard what they said as much as He heard what the men said. He always does. But He graciously overlooks failure that is due to the influence of others.

September 30th

Numbers 31. 1-24

GO AGAINST THE MIDIANITES

The military campaign against Midian that is detailed here is the last battle that Moses will fight for God's people. After this last commission, he is to die as God had said. Battles to win the promised land will, after this, be led by Joshua, but Moses has the responsibility and privilege of punishing Midian. With subtlety they had so successfully seduced the Israelites into terrible idolatry and debauchery and had brought down the severe anger of God upon His own people. Five kings of Midian are killed in the ensuing battle and so, also, is Balaam, son of Beor, who at last gets his just desserts.

Although we can understand the revenge of the people of God upon the Midianites in battle, there are aspects of the carnage which trouble our modern minds. All the fighting men were killed, their villages burnt down, and their livestock taken as booty. The women and children, however, are initially spared and taken captive. Of this we approve. Moses' anger at the mercy shown to these seemingly innocent people sits less-comfortably with us. We are horrified, however, to read of his command that all the male children and all the women who were sexually mature were to be killed in cold blood. Only the young girls who had not yet matured sexually (and these would doubtless have been very young indeed as women married at an early age in those days) were to be spared and taken as the spoils of war. After this terrible slaughter, the people were to purify themselves. Upon what moral grounds could such a slaughter be justified?

It has to be remembered that it was through engaging in the licentious worship of Baal that the people of God had reached their nadir since leaving Egypt, and that it was the women of Midian that had enticed them to it, Num. 25. Any Midianite woman of sexual maturity would have been involved in this idolatrous worship and would have brought with her the practices and beliefs of her people. In order, therefore, to preserve the people of God from further compromise, the possibility had to be removed. Severe though God's justice is, He will stop at nothing to preserve the purity of His people. Where do we stop?

October 1st
Numbers 31. 25-54

DIVIDE THE PREY INTO TWO PARTS

The destruction of Midian was not for territorial gain, but instead had a moral and spiritual dimension. For this reason, prominence is given to Eleazar and Phineas, the priestly men, whereas Joshua, the military leader, is not mentioned.

Midian had been allies of Moab in seducing the Israelites, and enticing them to follow 'the way of Balaam'. Now judgement had been visited upon them by God; five kings, all the males, together with Balaam and many of the women had been put to death. To many, in this 'enlightened' age, such action may seem barbaric and cruel. Yet it serves to emphasize the holiness of God, and the moral purity He desires for His people of every age. Midian speaks to us of those subtle worldly attractions which would rob us of the enjoyment of our inheritance; cf. Judg. 6. 3-5. How easy it is to allow ourselves to become ensnared by these things!

But now Midian was defeated. The initial reluctance to fulfil God's absolute demands had been addressed; not one man of the armies of Israel had been lost in the battle, v. 49, and vast quantities of 'the spoils of war' which lay outside the camp would now be divided. What spiritual lessons can we learn then from these verses?

Notice, first, the kindness and generosity of our God. Any spiritual victory that we are enabled by His grace to achieve will involve some cost. But our God is a God of compensation, and, in the words of A. J. FLINT, 'He giveth and giveth and giveth again'. In this chapter Israel had proved that too.

Now came the task of dividing the spoil. Half is given to 'them who went out to battle', the other half to 'the congregation'. A portion is then levied for the benefit of the priests and Levites. The soldiers are permitted to keep a larger share of the goods, since theirs was the greater conflict, but all the people benefit from the victory. As the people of God, we are not all called to undertake the same work, but we are all involved in the same battle! How encouraging to note in verses 48-54 that the soldiers willingly return a thank offering to God for their preservation, and this is kept in the sanctuary 'for a memorial'.

October 2nd
Numbers 32. 1-19

OUR INHERITANCE IS FALLEN TO US ON THIS SIDE

The Lord Jesus taught that 'a man's life consisteth not in the abundance of the things which he possesseth', Luke 12. 15. There are times, however, when we, just like the tribes of Reuben and Gad, allow our 'possessions' to determine the decisions we make which affect our lives, and the lives of others.

The crossing of Jordan to enter the land of promise was to be a significant and symbolic act for the whole nation. Yet now, on the very borders of the land, the unity of the people of God is put in jeopardy. Reuben and Gad decide that they know best how to look after their possessions, 'a very great multitude of cattle'. Their decision will in time influence others, as they are later joined by half the tribe of Manasseh, causing a further division among the people of God. If we are blessed with unity in the assembly, we must be vigilant in maintaining that harmony in a manner that is consistent with the word of God.

The decision of these tribes to forgo the opportunity to enter the land of promise brings a swift reproof from Moses. He interpreted their determined choice as a means of escaping the coming conflict and a decision which would weaken the resolve of others. Above all it indicated a lack of appreciation for the inheritance promised to Abraham and his descendants.

The actions of Reuben and Gad are not without parallel in our own day. There are still some of the Lord's people who consider their own interests to be paramount, their own comfort and well-being to be more important than the progress of the testimony. A loving God has prepared an inheritance for His people to be possessed and enjoyed here and now, 1 Cor. 2. 9. In order to enter into the good of this, we must experience practically what the crossing of the Jordan speaks of in type, i.e., to reckon ourselves 'dead indeed unto sin, but alive unto God through Jesus Christ our Lord', Rom. 6. 11. We are quickened 'together with Christ . . . raised up together and (seated) together in heavenly places in Christ Jesus', Eph. 2. 5-6, and with our affections set 'on things above, not on things on the earth', Col. 3. 2.

The response of the two tribes was the offer of a compromise. We will consider its value in tomorrow's reading.

October 3rd

Numbers 32. 20-42

WE WILL PASS OVER ARMED BEFORE THE LORD

On first reading, the offer of Reuben and Gad seems a perfectly reasonable and even gracious proposal. However, on closer examination other features come to light. The record of scripture will show that Reuben is invariably motivated by self-interest, both the man and the tribe. A consideration of the occasions from Genesis to Judges when Reuben is mentioned will bear this out; our reading today is no exception.

The seemingly magnanimous gesture to 'pass over armed before the Lord' is at best a compromise, and compromise is a word which does not sit comfortably with the word of God!

The warning of Moses does nothing to alter their resolve, the two tribes had already laid plans to safeguard their possessions, and provide secure homes for their families, v. 16. Instead of bowing to the will of God for their blessing, they had made up their minds that the east bank of Jordan was to be their inheritance, and they expected Moses and the Lord to fall in with their plans!

Yet, decisions we make invariably affect others. Lot discovered this when he selfishly 'chose *him* (for himself) all the plain of Jordan', Gen 13. 11, to the detriment and loss of his family. Now Reuben and Gad were to leave their families, and go over the Jordan to assist in the possession of the land. Their wives and children would never enjoy the intended inheritance. They would be denied an appreciation of the land flowing with milk and honey, with its wells, vineyards and olive trees. Instead they would dwell in 'fenced cities' in a hostile environment, v. 17, in a land that was good for cattle, v. 4! How careful we need to be as husbands and as parents in the decisions we make which have an impact on our families, and even on our testimony in the neighbourhood.

The Lord was very gracious in allowing Reuben, Gad and later half the tribe of Manasseh to occupy their chosen inheritance. He even provided cities of refuge for them, Num. 35. But finally, having turned from God to idols, these three tribes were the first to be taken captive by the Assyrians, who first 'took away their cattle', 1 Chr. 5. 21, then themselves, v. 26.

October 4th

Numbers 33. 1-49

THESE ARE THEIR JOURNEYS

Chapter 33 is one of those sections of the word of God which we are tempted to hurry by with only a passing interest when we reach it in our daily reading! Yet we will be the poorer in our appreciation of scripture, and of the character of our God, if we treat any part of the inspired word in this way.

Not only do we accept that, 'All scripture is given by inspiration of God, and is profitable', 2 Tim 3. 16, but we note further that the details of today's chapter are specifically attributed to 'the commandment of the Lord', v. 2.

The journey from Egypt to Sinai took just two months, and is recorded in Exodus chapters 13-19. Israel remained at Sinai almost a whole year while the law was given and the tabernacle was constructed. No further movement is recorded until Numbers chapter 10, when 'the cloud was taken up . . . and . . . Israel took their journeys', vv. 11-12.

From Sinai to Kadesh involved a number of movements, as seen in verses 16-36 of our chapter, yet only nine encampments are recorded during the forty years of wandering that followed, vv. 37-49. The history of those years is found in Numbers chapters 20-31.

Why then is Moses instructed to keep this detailed log of the journey? Remember, it was the Lord who led them by an angel, Exod. 23. 20 and fed them angels' food, Ps. 78. 25. For forty years neither clothes nor shoes wore out! Deut. 29. 5. Each place recorded is a memorial to the gracious keeping and leading power of our God; in spite of their waywardness, their murmuring and their sin.

It would be a challenging exercise for each one of us to think back to the time when He redeemed us 'out of Egypt', and to record the various staging posts on our journey through life. To acknowledge His faithfulness, His love, His mercy and His grace toward us. We would have to confess that at times we have been every bit as stubborn and self-willed as Israel. We have been unprofitable servants, not worthy of the least of His mercies. Yet at the end of the journey we will look back and say with gratitude, 'Jesus led me all the way', F. J. CROSBY.

October 5th

Numbers 33. 50-56

DRIVE OUT ... DESTROY ... DISPOSSESS ... DIVIDE

When the children of Israel took possession of the land of Canaan, a two-fold purpose was accomplished in the great plan of God. The Canaanite nations were removed, and Israel became custodians of the land of promise.

The tribal occupants of the land were devoid of any moral restraint, they were idolatrous and corrupt, ripe for judgement. Yet God had shown remarkable longsuffering in the face of persistent provocation, waiting until the cup of iniquity was full, cf. Gen. 15. 16. Now divine patience was exhausted and Israel would be the instrument of retribution in the hand of God to remove the offending nations.

As a result of this, the great promises made to Abraham and his descendents concerning the land would begin to unfold with unerring accuracy, foreshadowing a future occupation of the land for the chosen nation, which is equally certain.

The absolute terms in which the Lord instructs Israel to deal with the nations in the land is a measure of His abhorrence of their manner of life and behaviour. In Leviticus chapter 18, a detailed record is given of the sins for which these nations were brought into judgement. It is sobering to consider that those very same sins are rampant in our society today. How long will heaven remain silent? How long will a holy God withhold judgement?

In verse 52, there are three specific targets for destruction; their pictures, their molten images and their high places. We are reminded of the summary given by the apostle John of 'all that is in the world', 1 John 2. 16. Things which appeal to the lust of the flesh, the eyes and the pride of life.

The land once possessed would be divided for an inheritance in such a way that all would benefit on an equitable basis, v. 54. But the final two verses of our reading contain a solemn warning which the nation must heed. Equally so, if we as believers fail to deal with the persistent temptations and allurements of the world, we will not enjoy the vast spiritual inheritance which is ours. May we by His grace possess our possessions and enter into the good of all that is ours through the Lord Jesus Christ.

October 6th

Numbers 34. 1-29

THIS SHALL BE YOUR LAND

The small plot of land whose borders are defined in our reading today, has been from earliest times to the present day the most disputed territory on earth. Countless thousands have died seeking to possess it or defend it. The armies of empires have fought and perished within its boundaries. Yet, the final arbiter of ownership remains the word of God to the descendents of Abraham, **'this shall be your land'**, Num. 34. 12.

The area of land about to be possessed would be the homeland of the tribes descended from the sons of Jacob. However, the original promise to Abraham was 'from the river of Egypt unto the great river, the river Euphrates', Gen. 15. 18. This is land presently occupied by Lebanon, Syria and maybe Iraq and Iran as well, but which will one day be acknowledged as Israel's land, since the promises of God cannot fail. In the great millennial day, the land between the Mediterranean and the Jordan will be allocated to the tribes of Israel, including the two-and-a-half tribes who originally settled on the east of Jordan, with Levi having a portion and Joseph a double portion, Ezek. 48. 1-29. Although this will be their portion territorially, the kingdom, of which Jerusalem will be the centre, will extend administratively 'from sea to sea, and from the river unto the ends of the earth', Ps. 72. 8.

This must have been a very poignant moment for Moses. Having led the people for forty years through the wilderness, with all its attendant difficulties and discouragements, he knew that he would not go over Jordan to enjoy the land he was outlining to the children of Israel. Nevertheless, he remained faithful and duly appointed the princes of each tribe to divide the land, under the watchful eyes of Eleazar and Joshua. There would of course be several years of conflict before the land could be apportioned. They had to possess the land, make it their own, even though God had given it to them. The instruction to Joshua was, 'Every place that the sole of your foot shall tread upon, that have I given unto you', Josh. 1. 3. We too, like Israel, can be guilty of failure in appreciating 'the things which God hath prepared for them that love him', 1 Cor. 2. 9.

October 7th

Numbers 35. 1-15

SIX CITIES SHALL YE HAVE FOR REFUGE

The tribe of Levi may have wondered why they appeared to be overlooked in the preparations of the previous chapter! They had, of course, been given the important task of transporting the tabernacle through the wilderness, but now it would find a more permanent resting place in the land, and their sphere of service would develop accordingly. Maybe they remembered that many years before, Jacob had prophesied that their tribe would be divided and scattered in Israel, Gen. 49. 7. At the time it seemed a prophecy of judgement, as a result of their anger and self-will, but following their solitary stand against the idolatry of the people in Exodus chapter 32, the prophecy would be fulfilled in blessing! Such is the mercy and grace of our God.

Instead of one fixed area of land, the Levites would be given forty-eight cities, spread throughout the land, on both sides of the Jordan, in order that their spiritual duties and responsibilities in assisting the priests would be readily accessible to the entire nation. Among these cities, six were marked out, and called 'cities of refuge'. These would be places of safety for any responsible for causing the death of another, without malicious intent.

In addition to their obvious practical purpose for the children of Israel, we cannot fail to see that God had in mind a far greater place of refuge, when His own beloved Son would provide a place of safety through the work of the cross. For the Israelite, and for the stranger, v. 15, these cities were both accessible and available to all. There was no cost involved for the one who sought sanctuary, just a realization of a need to 'flee from the wrath to come'. Once inside there was safety, although his case was still the subject of investigation, a public enquiry being held to determine the merits or otherwise of his actions, v. 24.

For the believer in the Lord Jesus, the sanctuary of our salvation is far more secure. We rest assured that our eternal security is not subject to the arbitrary assessment of others! Our position is unassailable, 'There is therefore now no condemnation to them which are in Christ Jesus', Rom. 8. 1.

October 8th

Numbers 35. 16-34

THE REVENGER OF BLOOD

Throughout the word of God, murder carries only one penalty. Man was made in the image of God, and the giving and sustaining of life is God's prerogative alone. Those who would take the life of another intrude upon divine sovereignty and their own life becomes forfeit, 'the murderer shall surely be put to death', v. 16ff. From the time that Noah stood upon the newly cleansed earth and the decree was given in Genesis chapter 9 verse 6, no subsequent edict has ever been given to change or dilute that law. It is only laws framed by man which have presumed to abolish the law of God!

In our reading today a clear distinction is made between the act of premeditated murder, and a death caused by accident. In both cases the one who had caused the death was in danger from 'the revenger of blood', one near of kin to the victim. In the case of murder, to him was given the judicial right to carry out the sentence of death upon the murderer though it was not to be an act of revenge carried out in the heat of anger. The word 'revenger' is the Hebrew word *gaal*, used in other contexts for a redeemer. Here, however, the connection is that a price must be paid for the life taken, and 'the revenger of blood' had that responsibility as God's representative for justice, cf. Rom. 13. 4.

For the one who had taken a life by accident, the only means of escape was to a city of refuge (never far away). Once safely there he must remain within its walls until the death of the high priest, at which time he could return to his house. We thought yesterday of the lovely picture of salvation seen in these cities of refuge, and of course our Great High Priest lives in the power of an endless life, we are totally secure!

There was no provision for a ransom (a satisfaction) to be paid, allowing a murderer to live, v. 31. The greatest monetary price would be insufficient to compensate for one life, only the life of another could meet that demand, cf. Ps. 49. 7-8. Yet a great price *was* paid in order that *we* might live! For we who were guilty, deserving only death, there was One, 'the man Christ Jesus; who gave himself a ransom for all', 1 Tim. 2. 5-6. The greatest price ever paid to meet the greatest debt ever owed.

October 9th

Numbers 36. 1-13

EVERY ONE SHALL KEEP . . . THE INHERITANCE

The reading before us today has its background in chapter 27, and concerns five formidable ladies, the daughters of Zelophehad.

Zelophehad died in the wilderness leaving five daughters but no sons to carry on the family name. For most fathers in that day and society such a situation would have been a disappointment. But Zelophehad would have had every reason to be proud of his daughters because they had a true appreciation of the inheritance which God had provided. They had initiative and ambition to rise above their circumstances, not for selfish reasons, but with a genuine spiritual motive. They had no intention of allowing the family inheritance to lose its identity; they would take steps to make it their own, in spite of the prevailing custom, and the Lord honoured them for their exercise.

How often it is the women of scripture who show real desires for the things of God. We think of Achsah, Ruth, Hannah, the Mary's of the New Testament and others, all whose names are recorded with distinction on the pages of scripture.

The land which God gave to the children of Israel was not just provided in an arbitrary fashion as a convenient location, it was far more than that. Within its borders the greatest events in history would take place. To the heart of God it was unique, 'the pleasant land', Ps. 106. 24. His eye searched out Bethlehem, Nazareth and Calvary long before the moment came when He sent forth His Son. We can well understand why it is that meticulous detail is given for its possession and enjoyment.

We see in today's chapter that the inheritance of each tribe and family was to be jealously guarded, and not fragmented by succeeding generations. Instruction was given that 'the land shall not be sold for ever', Lev. 25. 23. This was in the mind of Naboth when he refused to sell his vineyard to king Ahab in 1 Kings chapter 21. 'The Lord forbid it me, that I should give the inheritance of my fathers unto thee', v. 3. His faithful stand cost him his life, but God fully vindicated Naboth and destroyed Ahab, as indeed He will ultimately overthrow all who seek to rob Israel of their inheritance.

October 10th

Deuteronomy 1. 1-18

ON THIS SIDE JORDAN

Israel now stood upon the very border of their promised inheritance. Before them was not just a new land but a new life, and they would cross the Jordan with a new leader. Before they do, however, Moses will make sure that they are well prepared for what lay ahead. In this important book he reminds them of all God's dealings with them from the time they left Egypt. Then he makes them aware of the conditions of blessing in the land, and finally, with prophetic insight, he tells them of the future.

The book of Deuteronomy is a charter for progress, a guide along the pathway to blessing, not just for the children of Israel but, by application, for all the people of God in every age.

Seven times in the opening chapters we find the expression 'on this side Jordan'. It represents the years of wandering, the wilderness experience. But now they were about to leave the wilderness to enter a land 'flowing with milk and honey'. They would exchange the manna for 'the old corn of the land'; no longer would they wander, but move with purpose. Yet from the moment they crossed the river there would be adversaries, and they needed to know that the Lord was with them every step of the way.

It is good to stop from time to time in the busy pathway of life, and just bring to mind the constant faithfulness of our God. Moses now begins to recall God's dealings with them from the time they left Horeb, where the law was given. First, he reminds them that although forty years had passed, God had not forgotten the great purpose for which He redeemed them. The land promised to Abraham was there to be possessed, vv. 7-8.

Moses then calls to mind the great responsibility he felt in leading such a vast multitude. On seeing the magnitude of the work, Moses' father-in-law observed, 'Thou wilt surely wear away', Exod. 18. 18. And as Moses himself later confessed, 'I am not able to bear all this people alone, because it is too heavy for me', Num. 11. 14. The Lord, as always, was mindful of His servant's need, reminding us that 'God is faithful, who will not suffer you to be tempted above that ye are able; but will . . . make a way . . . that ye may be able to bear it', 1 Cor. 10. 13.

October 11th
Deuteronomy 1. 19-46

YE WOULD NOT GO UP, BUT REBELLED

In recalling the details of the wilderness journeys, Moses is faithful in reminding the people not just of the high points, but of the low points as well. As we look back over our lives from time to time, we do well to consider the failures, which, we confess, for many of us outnumber the victories. Not that we wish to dwell upon past sins, but we can learn lessons from them which, in the goodness of God, will help us to avoid repetition. We must remember that the experiences of the children of Israel were 'ensamples . . . written for our admonition', 1 Cor. 10. 11.

The refusal to 'go up' and occupy the land following the report of the spies, had far-reaching and severe consequences. Not least for all those who perished in the wilderness during the forty years of wandering that followed! There are occasions when, as a result of sin among the people of God, a whole generation must pass before there can be any real progress in the testimony. Mercifully, these cases are few, but we need to be aware of the possibility.

The twelve spies were the first to enter the land and see its fruitfulness and abundance. However, instead of looking at the potential, as did Caleb and Joshua, the ten looked only at the problems; high walls and tall people! What more could God have done to convince Israel that He would bring them safely into the land? He had promised to fight for them, v. 30; He had carried them, 'as a man doth bare his son', v. 31; He went in the way before them by cloud and by fire, v. 33, and still He had to say, 'Ye did not believe the Lord your God', v. 32.

We read of their experience, and we say, 'How foolish they were', yet can we honestly say that we are never guilty of similar behaviour? We speak of the goodness and grace of our God; we sing words which express His love and His keeping power. Then when we are called to put His promises to the test, we are just like Israel and see only the obstacles in the pathway.

O that we might spend less time on 'this side Jordan', wandering in a wilderness of our own making! May we take time to view the inheritance afresh, then go up, enter in and enjoy the abundant provision found there for us in the Lord Jesus.

October 12th
Deuteronomy 2. 1-25

RISE YE UP, TAKE YOUR JOURNEY

There is so much contained in those three little words which open our reading today, 'Then we turned'. Moses was recalling that devastating moment of realization, that, because of their unbelief, they could not enter the land of promise. Forty years of wilderness wanderings lay before them, and the generation which left Egypt from twenty years old and upward, with the exception of Joshua and Caleb, would never enjoy the inheritance; they would die in the wilderness.

Unbelief is the ultimate sin! It was unbelief that put Adam and Eve out of Eden. Unbelief kept a wicked world out of the ark. It not only kept Israel out of Canaan for forty years, but sent them into captivity for a further seventy years. Unbelief put the Lord Jesus Christ on the cross, and unbelief will close heaven's gate to millions upon millions!

The antithesis of unbelief is faith; simple, child-like faith in God and His word. We know that 'without faith it is impossible to please him', Heb 11. 6; yet so often we are just like Israel in our failure to put this into practice in our everyday lives.

The years of wandering are passed over in the first fifteen verses. It is reassuring to note that Moses does not linger over their weaknesses and shortcomings, but soon directs their attention to the positive aspects of the journey. In verse 18 their faces are turned once more toward the land of promise.

Three nations are brought into contact with Israel in these verses; Edom, Moab and Ammon. In acknowledgement of their ancestral links with Abraham and Jacob, God had provided them each a land 'for a possession'. We are reminded that when Paul spoke to the Athenians he told them of the God who has not only made all men, but has 'determined . . . the bounds of their habitation', Acts. 17. 26. We can be assured that all nations are subject to His will for their territory and possessions.

In verse 24, the journey, which will ultimately bring them into the land, begins in earnest. From this point on it is a pathway of victory. Lessons have been learned often through hardship. They are now a fighting force ready to engage the enemy. The word of command is given, 'Rise ye up, take your journey'.

October 13th

Deuteronomy 2. 26-37

SIHON WOULD NOT LET US PASS

We are reminded in Proverbs chapter 21 that 'the king's heart is in the hand of the Lord', and in order to accomplish His purposes 'he turneth it whithersoever he will', v. 1. This applies to all rule and authority, since 'the powers that be' are subject to Him, and all will ultimately be seen to be 'under his feet', 1 Cor. 15. 27.

'The God of the whole earth' did not feature in the mind of Sihon, king of Heshbon; nevertheless, the God whom Sihon ignored had plans for him! Sihon was an Amorite, a people who occupied the mountainous region to the east of Jordan, but also had influence in Canaan. They were immoral and idolatrous, yet the longsuffering of God had borne with them over succeeding generations, withholding judgement even from the days of Abraham, because 'the iniquity of the Amorites is not yet full', Gen. 15. 16.

Now, however, the cup was full and overflowing, divine patience was exhausted, and Israel would be the instrument of retribution against the unrepentant Amorites.

The defeat of Sihon, and later of Og, king of Bashan, in chapter 3, served a number of purposes in the over-ruling plan of God. For these nations it was without doubt the righteous judgement of God against their sin. For Israel, the victories assured them that if they simply obeyed the voice of God then no nation would be able to stand against them. Furthermore, the news of the defeat of the Amorites soon reached Jericho, causing fear and faint hearts as they awaited the approach of Israel's army, v. 25; cf. Josh. 2. 9-11.

One final opportunity is given to Sihon, vv. 26-29, but in reality the die was cast, like Esau 'he found no place of repentance', and judgement fell. We notice that victory was assured even before a blow was struck, God's word through Moses was, 'I have given', vv. 24, 31. Yet, the people still had to go forward and engage the enemy. How true that is for us also. Our Saviour is Victor over sin, death and Satan, as such He supplies all the necessary resources to withstand the attacks of our spiritual foes, and victory is secured through our Lord Jesus Christ.

October 14th
Deuteronomy 3. 1-17
WE UTTERLY DESTROYED THEM

Og, king of Bashan, was a big player in every sense! He was the last 'of the remnant of giants', v. 11, a race who possibly owed their existence to demonic activity in days gone by, and who now barred the progress of the children of Israel. The Lord Jesus felt the presence of 'strong bulls of Bashan' opposing Him at Calvary, Ps. 22. 12; Satan will use every means and seize every opportunity to resist the purposes of God.

Og's physical presence and reputation made him great and famous, Ps. 136. 17-20, and his defeat sent shock waves throughout Canaan. Forty years before, the spies sent out from Kadesh had returned with a report of giants and great walled cities. As a result, Israel had wept with fear and murmured against Moses. Yet after all those fruitless years of wandering, the adversaries and the difficulties had not diminished! The difference now was that the people were prepared to trust in the Lord. The promise of victory was once more given, and with the conquest over Sihon still fresh in their minds, triumph was assured.

How often we try to avoid or circumvent the difficulties of life; behaving as though our own initiative and our own abilities are our only resources! Israel learned that problems don't just disappear, sooner or later we must face them and the only way to overcome is in the strength of 'him that is able to do exceeding abundantly above all that we ask or think', Eph. 3. 20. To learn the truth of Philippians chapter 4, verses 6-7, to be not anxious but asking!

The land taken from the Amorite kings became the inheritance of the two-and-a-half tribes who remained on the east side of Jordan. The destruction of these nations ensured that Israel in the land had no hostile neighbours on her immediate eastern border though later, on account of their sin, God would bring nations to oppress them, to draw them back to Himself.

A man of Manasseh called Jair is singled out for particular mention. Undaunted by the adversaries he made the inheritance his own, and stamped his name upon his possessions as an enduring memorial, cf. Phil. 4. 13.

October 15th
Deuteronomy 3. 18-29

I PRAY THEE, LET ME GO OVER

Once more in these verses Moses reminds the two-and-a-half tribes of their responsibilities toward the rest of the people. They had promised to 'pass over armed before . . . the children of Israel', v. 18, but in reality their heart was not in their actions. It must have brought great sadness to Moses when they said 'bring us not over Jordan', Num. 32. 5. Opportunity to enter and enjoy the inheritance was theirs for the taking, and they spurned it. Moses, on the other hand, pleaded with the Lord, 'I pray thee, let me go over and see the good land', v. 25, yet in the plan of God he was not permitted.

The two-and-a-half tribes remind us of so many believers today who are just content to be saved yet have no real desire to possess and enjoy all the good things 'which God hath prepared for them that love him', 1 Cor. 2. 9. Just like these tribes, their possessions determine their priorities. So many of the Lord's people reach Romans chapter 5, and stop at verse 1. They know themselves to be 'justified by faith', and to 'have peace with God', and their ambitions go no further. Verse 2 is like the crossing of the Jordan, 'we have access by faith' into a vast panorama of blessings made known in the verses which follow. The apostle uses phrases like 'and not only so', and, 'much more then', to introduce us to the immeasurable extent of our inheritance. The responsibility of 'entering in', however, is ours; Moses did not compel the two-and-a-half tribes to pass over Jordan. Equally so, we cannot force others to progress in Christian things. We seek to encourage, to teach and to show by example, but in the final analysis it is the willingness of the individual believer which determines his spiritual progress.

Moses, in spirit, was already in the land, he spoke of it in glowing terms. Yet, in the purposes of God as representing the law, he could not bring them in, such is the truth of Galatians. It must be our heavenly Joshua, the Lord Jesus, who brings His people into blessing, and that is Ephesian truth. But God was gracious to Moses, and at a much later day, on the mount of transfiguration he was privileged to stand in the land which his undimmed eyes had seen from Pisgah's height.

October 16th
Deuteronomy 4. 1-20

TAKE HEED TO THYSELF, AND KEEP THY SOUL

There are many enemies of the soul, which if they gain a foot-hold the believer's life will end in spiritual shipwreck. How necessary today, as it was in the days when Moses first enjoined the people of Israel, to 'take heed diligently' for the soul, v. 9!

But how do we do this? In the reading for today we have a number of guidelines:

1) Listen attentively to God's word and act upon it, v. 1. This is a continuous process throughout the lifetime of the believer. To listen but not act will lead to backsliding, but those who both listen and act upon the word will not be distracted and therefore will prosper spiritually.

2) Do not add to the word of God, v. 2 – this is legalism, which was that of which the Pharisees were later guilty. Equally, do not take away from the word, v. 2, as the Saddu-cees would do later. In the present era much damage has resulted from both legalism or ritualism and liberalism or rationalism. The constant exercise of each believer, and the assembly corporately, is to ensure that we adhere only to what the word says and not to alter our doctrine and practice, how-ever much it may seem the right thing to do.

3) The keeping of the word of God will bring with it further spiritual wisdom and understanding, v. 6. The believer will not be given fresh strength and wisdom for each new day unless, first of all, the word of the Lord given for previous days has been acted upon. The only way to grow as a believer is a pathway of obedience to the Lord in all things.

4) Moses also reminds them of all the blessings of the Lord in former days taking them back to their deliverance from Egypt and that they were now the people of His inheritance, v. 20. We do well, as believers today, to constantly revisit Calvary and remember what He has done for us.

In conclusion, a large part of the reading for today is taken up with a warning regarding idolatry, v. 15. Is there anything that is higher in our hearts affections than the Lord? To give Him the pre-eminent place is the primary means of guarding our souls.

October 17th

Deuteronomy 4. 21-38

I MUST DIE IN THIS LAND

Moses begins by emphasizing that these are to be his last words to God's people, for he will not be accompanying them over Jordan, but will die in this land, v. 21. It is well to be attentive to the last words of this godly man as they contain much wisdom gained from a lifetime of walking with the Lord.

He tells them to take heed, v. 23 – this should be the constant exercise of the believer – to watch, to be on guard lest the enemy trips us up. The special temptation of the people of that day was to fall into idolatry, v. 25. Today, the principle still applies in that we need to ensure that nothing takes the first place which should be His in our hearts. He predicts that their descendants will backslide, v. 25, but nothing will escape the notice of heaven. v. 26. 'Neither is there any creature that is not manifest in his sight: but all things are naked and opened unto the eyes of him with whom we have to do', Heb. 4. 13.

Moses tells them that unfaithfulness will lead to judgement, v. 27, and idolatry, v. 28, but that if in sincerity they seek the Lord He will always be found of them, v. 29. How merciful God was to them for even after many failures He was still willing to receive them back and start again, vv. 30-31.

He then reminds them of the great things God has done for them, v. 32. **God's voice** was heard, vv. 33, 36 – this can be the privilege of every sincere and believing reader of the scriptures in the present day, as they meditate upon His word. **God's choice** of them as His people, vv. 34, 37, reminds us of His sovereign electing grace in the case of each individual believer, 'According as he hath chosen us in him before the foundation of the world', Eph. 1. 4. **God's power**, as seen in their deliverance from Egypt, v. 37, reminds us of His power in the saving of souls today. 'And what is the exceeding greatness of his power to us-ward who believe, according to the working of his mighty power', Eph. 1. 19.

All this should be enough to have garrisoned their hearts and to have preserved them from the dangers ahead. Moses having a true shepherd heart and realizing these dangers reminds them of all God's goodness towards them, vv. 33-38.

October 18th

Deuteronomy 4. 39-49

THE LORD, HE IS GOD, THERE IS NONE ELSE

Moses reminds the people that Jehovah, the covenant-keeping God, is the only true God and the One to whom every living person will give account for their lives.

Today, many live either in ignorance or denial of God's existence which means, in their own minds, that they do not have to be accountable. This is the reason for much evil in the world, for once the conscience becomes marred what restraint is left? If there is no God, no heaven to gain or hell to shun, then why bother with morality? This may not be the way people think consciously but, if God is denied His rightful place in peoples's lives, there is bound to be a distortion of moral and spiritual values.

In the context of moral relativism right is considered wrong and vice versa, and common sense is discarded. Those who are believers will see evidence of such a decline in this present evil world. Godless governments in many nations do not support laws that are in accordance with the Bible and, added to this, introduce laws, often to appease vociferous minority interests which are directly at variance with God's law. Moses says, 'Thou shalt keep His commandments', v. 40. If they were prepared to listen then they would have been rewarded with long life upon the earth, v. 40. The believer today may not be rewarded with length of life and prosperity, as were many Old Testament saints, but a reward is certain for those who faithfully and loyally continue in obedience to His revealed word, v. 40. 'Knowing that of the Lord ye shall receive the reward of the inheritance: for ye serve the Lord Christ', Col. 3. 24.

The three cities of refuge on the east side of Jordan are set apart to shelter any who accidentally and without premeditation take another's life, v. 41. The justice of God is always fair, in contrast to the laws and justice of men. The responsible leaders of any country would do well to ensure that laws they introduce conform as closely to the Bible as possible. If this were the case there would be much less injustice and unhappiness.

There is only One to whom men **have** to give account, Heb. 4. 13. Therefore, as believers, may it be true that we live lives pleasing to Him.

October 19th

Deuteronomy 5. 1-10

LEARN, KEEP, AND DO

The message Moses communicated to Israel on this day was primarily positive – **learn** – **keep** – **do**. There is an obvious progression and advancement in this, which we would do well to heed today. From first learning the scriptures, the Lord would have us progress to keep and do what is enjoined in them.

Firstly, though, they needed to put themselves in a position where they were able to hear the word of God; how could they learn if they absented themselves from the meeting which Moses had called? They needed to be there to hear. It is a sad witness to the state of a local church when only a minority turn up for the teaching meeting. How can we keep His word if we do not know it? But to learn His word is more than just attendance at the meeting. It also involves application and energy in study, not as an intellectual exercise but in order that the word of God may be put into practice in our lives. If we are to avoid what someone has called 'spiritual indigestion', where there is no real spiritual progress, we must put into practice what He has told us. In that way fresh truth from God will be revealed each day and our spiritual lives will develop.

God talked to them face to face, v. 4, an indication of God's nearness to them. This reminds us of the far closer relationship a believer today has with the Lord, for we have the abiding presence of the Holy Spirit. That divine Person dwelling within us illuminates the pages of scripture and gives us the enabling power to obey – what grace! Moses constantly reminds them of the deliverance they had by the hand of the Lord, v. 6, and their release from the slavery of an evil master. Likewise, we need to often revisit Calvary, reminding ourselves of the great deliverance wrought for us by our blessed Lord Jesus. We bow in thankfulness that we have been redeemed, and released from the slave market of sin and our former master Satan. 'Thou shalt have none other gods before me', v. 7. The child of God must ever keep God on the throne of his or her heart.

'The dearest idol I have known, Whate'er that idol be,
Help me to tear it from Thy throne, and worship only Thee'.

[WILLIAM COWPER]

October 20th

Deuteronomy 5. 11-15

REMEMBER THAT THOU WAST A SERVANT

In this second giving of the law and in connection with the seventh day of rest, Moses reminds them from where they have come, slavery in Egypt.

This will serve to remind them that Pharaoh gave them no rest from the grinding labour of their servitude. In Exodus chapter 5 verses 1-14, they had asked for three days to sacrifice to the Lord, but he refused and instead of giving them respite, he increased the workload by withdrawing the supply of straw, but still expected the same output of bricks.

All this reminds us of the hardness and cruelty of the arch taskmaster of men, for Satan will mete out cruel treatment indeed to those who are enslaved to and by him. Having tempted and distracted them with the sinful pleasures of this world he will then leave them high and dry in regard to the eternal security of their souls. There will be no rest for such who follow him for he will drive on from one pleasure to another until the capacity to enjoy is no longer there.

How many lives have been shipwrecked by him, who knows neither love nor mercy. How necessary to flee from his clutches into the arms of a waiting and merciful Saviour who waits for the profligates to return, even as the father of the prodigal son, Luke 15. 20.

But why is the divine pattern six days and then a day of rest? The answer may lie in the fact that God as Creator knows what is best for His creatures. 'For he knoweth our frame; he remembereth that we are dust', Ps. 103. 14. Several attempts have been made to alter this pattern, notably during the French revolution, when a ten-day week was instigated and also in Russia from 1929 to 1940. These experiments had to be abandoned due to unrest among the population and an increase in ill health. It is always best to adhere to God's word.

Can you remember the time when God delivered you from the servitude of Satan and brought you into the lightness of His service? Jesus said, 'Come unto me, all ye that labour and are heavy laden, and I will give you rest. . . . my yoke is easy, and my burden is light', Matt. 11. 28, 30.

October 21st

Deuteronomy 5. 16-22

TWO TABLES OF STONE

After the Lord spoke from Sinai to the people, Moses was called up into the mount to receive the first two tables of stone containing the ten commandments, Exod. 24. 12. During his time on the mountain the Lord showed him the pattern of the tabernacle and instituted the priesthood. This took forty days which caused the people to become impatient and, before Moses arrived back with the tables containing the law, they had already broken it on a number of counts. So, Moses, in his anger, threw down the first tables and they were smashed. Now, as he recounts to them what the Lord had written on those first tables, remarkably he does not mention their failure. This indicates the grace of God towards them in restoration.

Today's reading contains the last six commandments, possibly contained on the second tablet, which are to do with relationships toward others. In these we have:

1) **Sanctity in respect of family life**, v. 16 – if God's law is thrown out, one of the first results is a breakdown in family life; a feature of the last days is that children will be disobedient to parents, 2 Tim. 3. 2.

2) The **sanctity of life itself**, v. 17 – life is precious. God gave it and no individual should ever take it, even if provoked.

3) The **sanctity of the body**, v. 18 – we live in a society obsessed with sex and where all kinds of illicit relationships are practised. God will judge all who are involved, Heb. 13. 4.

4) The **sanctity of another man's property**, v. 19 – to steal what belongs to another is always wrong.

5) The **sanctity of the truth**, v. 20 – to give false witness against another man is the most serious of sins, for such a sin led to the crucifixion of the Son of God.

6) The **sanctity of God's provision**, v. 21 – dissatisfaction with where God has placed us and what He has given us materially is the root of covetousness. It is directly equivalent to idolatry, Col. 3. 5, that is, the placing of another object or god where the Lord should be in the life. Many people's lives today are filled with anything but the Lord and His interests, 'Lovers of pleasures more (*rather*) than lovers of God', 2 Tim. 3. 4.

October 22nd

Deuteronomy 5. 23-33

HEAR ALL THAT THE LORD OUR GOD SHALL SAY

The words for our thought today were those of the children of Israel to Moses, they told him to go to the Lord, hear what He had to say, communicate it back to them and they promised that they would not only listen but do whatever the Lord said. The Lord commends them for this, v. 28. True faith will always follow through into works, 'Yea, a man may say, Thou hast faith, and I have works: shew me thy faith without thy works, and I will shew thee my faith by my works', Jas. 2. 18.

The word of the Lord was accompanied by a revelation of His glory and greatness, v. 24, and this should have been an encouragement to them. However, it seems that they were overcome with fear because of the consuming fire of God's presence. We as believers have had a far greater revelation of God's glory and grace made known so fully at Calvary. As a result, we should heed the words of the writer to the Hebrews, 'let us have grace, whereby we may serve God acceptably with reverence and godly fear: for our God is a consuming fire', Heb. 12. 28.

Moses was to be the one who would hear the word of the Lord and then pass it on. This ministry he did with great faithfulness missing out nothing of the message. In the church there are those whose responsibility it is to pass on the word of God. Let those so gifted remember the exhortation here, 'Speak thou unto us *all* that the Lord our God shall speak', v. 27. Of necessity, this will involve the brother concerned, as it did Moses, spending time in the presence of the Lord, and then coming forth with a word from the Lord and faithfully delivering it to the saints.

The desire of the Lord for His people is encapsulated in verse 29, 'O that there were such an heart in them, that they would fear me, and keep all my commandments always'. It proved to be an impossible standard for Israel generally, but there were those in the Old Testament who did please the Lord, Enoch being a prime example.

How much more we, therefore, who have the abiding presence of the indwelling Spirit of God!

October 23rd

Deuteronomy 6. 1-11

THESE WORDS SHALL BE IN THINE HEART

How can we walk in such a way as to please God? The answer must first of all involve us in being familiar with what God expects of us in His word and then we will need to take that truth to heart. In this connection, David says to the Lord, 'Thy word have I hid in mine heart, that I might not sin against thee', Ps. 119. 11. To make God's word part of us, to take it to our hearts, is the first and vital step towards living it out.

The Bible says that the unregenerate **heart** of man is 'deceitful above all things, and desperately wicked', Jer. 17. 9, poor material indeed for understanding and receiving God's word. Only by the regenerating power of the Holy Spirit as a person truly repents towards God and exercises faith in Christ, Acts 20. 21, is he made fit to receive spiritual truth.

The exhortation to bind the word of God as a sign on the hand and as a frontlet between the eyes, v. 8, later became an empty ritual, as practised by the Pharisees, 'But all their works they do for to be seen of men: they make broad their phylacteries', Matt. 23. 5. A phylactery was a small parchment worn in a box between the eyes, and containing a scripture text. Outwardly, they did what was the right thing, but it was not accompanied with inward change and reality as a result of obedience to God's commandments. With their lips they honoured God, but their **hearts** were far from Him, Mark 7. 6.

If we are to hang texts on the walls of our homes, v. 9, we will need to ensure that we are faithful to those texts. Hypocrisy in the home will be transparent to those who live with us and will be a stumbling block to them.

Bible reading in context of the family is of vital importance, v. 7. The truths of the Bible are to be communicated first thing in the morning and last thing at night, v. 7b – a big responsibility for parents, with so much in the world to distract.

In summary, heart condition is of vital importance. The word says, 'Keep thy heart with all diligence; for out of it are the issues of life', Prov. 4. 23. How better can we keep it than by meditating on God's word, Ps. 1. 2? The things that occupy our hearts build our characters, Prov. 23. 7.

October 24th

Deuteronomy 6. 12-25

FEAR THE LORD AND SERVE HIM

The fear of the Lord, as it relates to God's people here, is reverential fear – fear of grieving or offending Him. Later, the psalmist writes, 'The fear of the Lord is the beginning of wisdom', Ps. 111. 10. True reverence for God is respect for His law, His will, His government and Himself, which leads us to do right. 'This fear is not that of a slave; it is not mere dread; it is not terror. It is consistent with love, and springs from it. It is consistent with calmness of mind, and promotes it. So the Lord is to be venerated by His people. This is the very foundation of wisdom', ALBERT BARNES. Only when we are in the good of this fear can we serve Him.

Moses warns them not to tempt the Lord as had happened at Massah, v. 16. There they complained about the Lord's provision for them. So serious was their unbelief that they were almost ready to stone Moses and said in provocation, 'Is the Lord among us or not?', Exod. 17. 7. Rather, they were to be ready to teach their sons about the Lord's deliverance of them from the bondage of Egypt, v. 21. We can never start too early to teach our children of the mighty deliverance from sin's slavery, accomplished at Calvary, that they might come into the good of God's salvation. Tell them also of the Lord's great power and glory, v. 22, long before Satan fills their minds with the evil God-substituting false doctrine of evolution and to remind them of the final destination, in our case heaven, prepared by the Lord according to His promises, v. 23.

The context of these exhortations was that the Israelites were at the point of quitting a nomadic life for a settled abode in the midst of other nations; they were exchanging a condition of relative poverty for comparative material wealth with their own houses and vineyards. Therefore, there were before them the dangers of becoming worldly, and forgetting God, v. 12, and also of tolerating the evil practices of those nations around them, v. 14.

The lessons for us in all this are obvious. 'Only fear the Lord, and serve him in truth with all your heart: for consider how great things he hath done for you', 1 Sam. 12. 24.

316

October 25th
Deuteronomy 7. 1-11

BECAUSE THE LORD LOVED YOU

The great subject for today is the sovereign electing grace of the Lord, vv. 6-8. This is not just the choice of God for the nation but for each individual believer within it. The great motivation behind His choice is His deep love for them, a love that would go to any lengths to redeem them – ultimately involving the gift of His beloved Son.

There are two parallel lines of truth running through scripture, which are, seemingly, irreconcilable to our finite minds but nevertheless to be held to and believed in equally and fully. These are the sovereign electing choice of God of an individual and over and against this, human responsibility, that is, that God holds every individual accountable to respond to His offer of salvation through Christ.

In the reading for today His sovereign choice is emphasized, v. 6. Why did He choose Israel? It was not because of His fore-knowledge, as to how they would respond otherwise His choice would be dependent on their eventual response. But rather, and as it is simply put here, He chose them because He loved them, v. 8. On the other hand, God holds men accountable if they refuse His offer of mercy; indeed His wrath is upon all those who will not repent and trust Him by faith, 'he that believeth not is condemned already, because he hath not believed in the name of the only begotten Son of God', John 3. 18.

Some might question this and say, 'how can God condemn when He is the one who chooses?' But the apostle Paul asks, 'Shall the thing formed say to him that formed it, Why hast thou made me thus?', Rom. 9. 20. We must accept these truths in faith. We rest, as Paul did, on 'the depth of the riches both of the wisdom and knowledge of God! how unsearchable are his judgments, and his ways past finding out!', Rom. 11. 33.

The suggestion has been made that salvation is like a door. We look up as unbelievers and see written over the outside of the door, 'him that cometh to me I will in no wise cast out', John 6. 37, but once saved, and having entered by faith, we see above the door but on the inside there is written, 'he hath chosen us in him before the foundation of the world', Eph. 1. 4.

October 26th

Deuteronomy 7. 12-26

THOU SHALT BE BLESSED ABOVE ALL PEOPLE

The blessing of the Lord here, as in all scripture, is conditional on obedience to God's revealed word, 'if ye hearken to these judgments', v. 12. Now, as then, we will not receive a blessing unless we are in the right place spiritually.

If they were obedient, the Lord promised them:

1) **Material wealth**, v. 13 – we should be careful not to teach a prosperity gospel based on Old Testament passages which were specific to the people of Israel. Spiritual blessings are far greater and long lasting. 'Blessed be the God and Father of our Lord Jesus Christ, who hath blessed us with all spiritual blessings in heavenly places in Christ', Eph. 1. 3.

2) **Victory over the enemy**, vv. 15-16, 23 – this was not accomplished by their own efforts or strength. They may well have been daunted by the number of foes, v. 17, as it is recorded, 'The fear of man bringeth a snare', Prov. 29. 25. Rather, they were to trust the Lord for victory, v. 19. Our case is exactly the same, for in the spiritual warfare in which we are engaged we have no strength of our own but must trust in the Lord. 'Thanks be to God, which giveth us the victory through our Lord Jesus Christ', 1 Cor. 15. 57. To further encourage them the Lord tells them to remember former victories, v. 18, and that the Lord is on their side. 'If God be for us, who can be against us?', Rom. 8. 31.

Once the enemies around them were defeated the Israelites were commanded to put away anything remotely connected with idolatrous worship; they were not to desire even the seemingly valuable things linked therewith, v. 25. So, the Lord promises them, 'There shall no man be able to stand before thee', v. 24.

As believers, we need to stand for God. We may feel fear as we seek to witness for the Lord. It may be that those who speak against Christ and the gospel use clever arguments and use them skilfully, but if we stick to the simple testimony of salvation in Christ, then perhaps God will speak to them and the stronghold of the enemy will be broken down. May we know the blessing of the Lord, as did those in Israel, as we experience spiritual victory today.

October 27th

Deuteronomy 8. 1-20

FORGET NOT THE LORD THY GOD

The Lord promised His people that He would bring them into a good land, v. 7, 'a land of brooks of water, of fountains and depths that spring out of valleys and hills; a land of wheat, and barley, and vines, and fig trees, and pomegranates; a land of oil olive, and honey; a land wherein thou shalt eat bread without scarceness', vv. 7-9. At the point when they enter into these blessings, He reminds them to remember to be thankful, v. 10. It is at just such points in life, when everything seems to be going right and we are comfortably well off materially, that there is a real danger of forgetting the Lord, v. 11.

How important it is to remember at such times 'that man doth not live by bread only, but by every word that proceedeth out of the mouth of the Lord doth man live', v. 3. Also, that the things which we can taste and touch whilst in this life are but transient and in any case are all His, Ps. 50. 10. It is easy in our present society to let the things of most importance, such as spiritual exercises, the things of God, be pushed out. We must remember at all times that whatever we have, or are, is to be put at His disposal and made available for His use.

There was a danger of evil pride, the most insidious of sins, creeping in at the very point of their prosperity and blessing, vv. 14, 17. All that they had, even their health and strength, was given by Him, v. 18. It was important for them to remember constantly that the Lord was the source of everything they enjoyed and to live in obedience to His revealed word and will, v. 11. They were to remember, too, the former days when the Lord humbled them, v. 3. Trials and testings might seem grievous at the time we pass through them, but as in their case they were to bring them to a fuller realization of the greatness of their Lord, v. 3.

If, as was eventually the case, they should be forgetful and wander astray then judgement would surely follow, v. 19. In the case of the backsliding believer today, although he will never lose his salvation, if genuinely saved, John 10. 28, there will be chastening down here, v. 5, and an awful loss of reward at the judgement seat of Christ, 1 Cor. 3. 15.

October 28th

Deuteronomy 9. 1-14

THE LORD THY GOD GOETH BEFORE THEE

In spite of the overwhelming odds and formidable strength of their enemies the people were comforted by the promise that He would be there with them and fight for them, v. 3. But, at the same time, it is said, 'So shalt thou drive them out', so the role of the people was important, to be there and be willing to fight on the Lord's side. How gracious was the Lord in not only redeeming them, but also accepting the service of His people and rewarding those who were prepared to be faithful.

The victory to be obtained would not be the result of any righteousness or virtue possessed by them, but it would be all of Him, v. 4. 'Every virtue we possess, and every victory won, and every thought of holiness, are His alone', HARRIET AUBER. No room for boasting then, even if we are faithful in service; we must say that it was the Lord who wrought the victory.

The people were stubborn and rebellious in their rejection of the Lord, time and again, vv. 6-7, but, in mercy, He still dealt with them. How gracious is the Lord towards the believer who turns in true repentance and confesses his sin, for there is an advocate with the Father, even when rebellion has been manifested, 1 John 2. 1-2. Whilst Moses was collecting a hard copy of the commandments given verbally at Sinai, the people were already seriously sinning, v. 12. How soon they had forgotten the goodness and glory of the Lord and all that He had done for them! But how like us!

So, we must learn from their experience of the Lord's dealings with them, 'Now all these things happened unto them for ensamples: and they are written for our admonition, upon whom the ends of the world are come', 1 Cor. 10. 11. For those who were marked by disobedience and who had no part with the Lord, there was a severe judgement, for 'there fell of the people that day about three thousand men', Exod. 32. 28.

Let us remember that no matter how formidable the enemy, we can stand in His strength, 'My grace is sufficient for thee: for my strength is made perfect in weakness', 2 Cor. 12. 9, and we can also be assured that He is with us always. 'I will never leave thee, nor forsake thee', Heb. 13. 5.

October 29th

Deuteronomy 9. 15-29

O LORD GOD, DESTROY NOT THY PEOPLE

On returning from the mount and finding the people occupied in idolatry and immorality Moses became involved immediately in deep intercessory prayer. This intercession manifested:

1) **Love** for those for whom he prayed. They had often caused him problems and heartache and at one stage nearly stoned him, Exod. 17. 4, yet he still loved them deeply. Surely this speaks to us today. Many a problem in a local assembly would have been solved, if there was this kind of intercessory prayer. Even for those who are difficult and show disdain for us! The people are reminded of their stubbornness again, in no less than four separate geographic places, vv. 22-23, but still Moses will intercede for them. Love like this, even for our enemies, can break down great barriers. Consider Christ who loved us even whilst we were His enemies, Rom. 5. 8-10.

2) **Humility** – he fell down before the Lord, vv. 18, 25. He did not come to the Lord with any sense of pride in himself, as being the only one who was right, but took the side of the people in deep humility and sorrow for their sin.

3) **Fasting** – v. 18. There was a price to pay; he refrained from even the basic necessities of life, v. 18. This kind of intercessory prayer comes at a cost. Consider Epaphras, who laboured fervently for the Colossians, Col. 4. 12. The believer should be marked by sacrifice in every aspect of his spiritual life. Paul, when speaking to the Philippians, mentions the 'sacrifice and service' of their faith, Phil. 2. 17. This applies even to our praise, 'By him therefore let us offer the sacrifice of praise to God continually', Heb. 13. 15. How can we offer to the Lord that which costs us nothing?

4) **Persistence** – Moses prayed for them for a period of forty days and nights, v. 25. This reminds us of Jacob who, in persistence in his dealings with the Lord, said 'I will not let thee go, except thou bless me', Gen. 32. 26. Moses did not give up easily but waited on the Lord until he had the answer, 'But the Lord hearkened unto me at that time also', v. 19. Moses' intercession was in the will of the Lord – the people were not judged, but shown mercy by the covenant keeping Lord, v. 27.

October 30th

Deuteronomy 10. 1-11

TWO TABLES OF STONE LIKE UNTO THE FIRST

The great need for the people of God was to get back to His word. Only then could they move on with Him. Moses had broken the first tables not only out of righteous anger, but also as a symbolic act of their breaking of the law. But God was not done with them and in mercy He is prepared to replace the tables.

If the people of God are to be recovered, God's word will need to be at the centre of their lives. These second tables were placed in the ark, after a long delay, at the setting up of the tabernacle, Exod. 40. 20. What blessings they had missed out on because of their rejection of His word at the first giving.

God says, 'I will write on the tables', v. 2. This reminds us that the Bible is the inspired word of God. Men wrote it under inspiration and therefore without error. 'All scripture is given by inspiration of God, and is profitable for doctrine, for reproof, for correction, for instruction in righteousness', 2 Tim. 3. 16.

The priesthood and the ministry of the Levites is emphasized, vv. 6-9. The people could not keep close to the Lord by themselves but needed the mediatorial ministry of God's provision. Daily sacrifices for sin would be necessary. All this reminds us of our own case. Had it not been for the one Mediator, 1 Tim 2. 5, we would never have been able to start with God, for only through His one supreme sacrifice for sin can we be brought nigh. As with them, so with us, there is a need for daily cleansing from the defilement of the wilderness journey. Hence, we have the present high priestly ministry of the Lord Jesus as our Advocate, 1 John 2. 1, and Intercessor, Heb. 7. 25.

In view of the renewal of His word they can now move on to possess the land promised to them, v. 11. There are lessons in all this for believers, for we need to move forward to take possession of all that we have in Christ.

'See that ye refuse not him that speaketh. For if they escaped not who refused him that spake on earth, much more shall not we escape, if we turn away from him that speaketh from heaven . . . wherefore we receiving a kingdom which cannot be moved, let us have grace, whereby we may serve God acceptably with reverence and godly fear', Heb. 12. 25, 28.

October 31st

Deuteronomy 10. 12-22

WHAT DOTH THE LORD REQUIRE OF THEE?

Moses will now remind them that the Lord requires something of them, v. 12. Their position of privilege as those whom God had chosen, v. 15, brought with it responsibility. His requirements should be paramount, as He is the Creator and Possessor of all things, v. 14. They were required to:

1) **Fear** the Lord – that is, to have a heart that so honours God that it will not offend Him under any circumstances.

2) To **walk** in all His ways – four times in the book of Deuteronomy they are exhorted to do this. First, there must be an understanding of His word, then, a desire to make it so much part of ourselves as to adjust our practice to conform.

3) To **love** Him – this doesn't just happen, but involves a definite act of the will to set one's affections upon the Lord.

4) To **serve** Him – that is to do all that we do as if doing it for and unto Him.

5) To **keep** His commandments – 'to keep' not only means outward observance but to protect as precious. John later writes, 'For this is the love of God, that we keep his commandments: and his commandments are not grievous', 1 John 5. 3.

So, all this will be 'for thy good', v. 13. His commands are with our best interests in mind, for as our Creator He knows what is best for us.

Circumcision was an external sign of the covenant of Jehovah with His people, v. 16; it signified death to the flesh. It was always essential that it should be accompanied by inward reality, v. 16. Paul, writing to the Roman believers, says, 'But he is a Jew, which is one inwardly; and circumcision is that of the heart, in the spirit, and not in the letter', Rom. 2. 29.

God's essential nature means that He would never be unfair in His treatment of those most needy, but rather will show them unbiased compassion, v. 18. The people were to reflect this in their attitude to strangers, remembering that they too were once strangers in Egypt, v. 19.

'He hath shewed thee, O man, what is good; and what doth the LORD require of thee, but to do justly, and to love mercy, and to walk humbly with thy God?', Mic. 6. 8.

November 1st

Deuteronomy 11. 1-15

BE STRONG, AND GO IN AND POSSESS THE LAND

The people of Israel stood poised on the borders of the Promised Land, ready to invade and occupy. But future prosperity was dependent on learning the lessons of the past and responding to the new conditions of Canaan. Here, Moses constantly underlines the necessity of a love for Jehovah which demonstrates itself in practical obedience to His commands, vv. 1, 8, and 13.

First, Israel had to **remember God's greatness** displayed historically in three crucial experiences: (i) what He did 'unto Pharaoh' and his army in devastating judgement, vv. 3-4; (ii) what He did 'unto you' during the wilderness journey by way of miraculous correction, v. 5; (iii) what He did 'unto Dathan and Abiram', v. 6, in response to their rebellion against God's choice of Levi in Numbers chapter 16. The omnipotence of God is no textbook dogma but a reality attested in His people's experience. Moses pointedly uses the word 'chastisement' at the head of his list of divine activities, v. 2. Because the infinitely great God is a God of discipline, His people must be reverently submissive. Though we have not seen, as Israel did, 'all the great acts of the Lord', v. 7, we have them infallibly recorded in scripture for our learning and encouragement.

Second, Israel had to **look ahead to God's goodness** as it would be demonstrated in the land. Unlike Egypt, watered from the Nile by means of complex irrigation systems, v. 10, Canaan relied upon the divine provision of 'the rain of heaven', v. 11. Material prosperity flowed from national obedience, 'If ye shall hearken . . . I will give you the rain', vv. 13-14. Israel's tenure and enjoyment of the land were therefore directly based on loyalty to Jehovah. Although the Christian's blessings are, by contrast, heavenly, grace-based and inviolable, Eph. 1. 3, they still require practical obedience as the expression of genuine love to the One who saved us.

Day by day, therefore, let us recall God's mighty power and tremble; and let us appreciate His gracious provision in Christ, and trust. To know both the severity and the goodness of God is the recipe for true spiritual strength.

November 2nd

Deuteronomy 11. 16-32

DAYS OF HEAVEN UPON THE EARTH

Today's reading starts with a **warning**, 'Take heed to yourselves', v. 16. If obedience guaranteed Israel's prosperity, departure would provoke judgement, the first sign of which would be crop failure. Elijah must have had this passage in mind when he prayed that God would send a drought in response to Ahab's idolatry, 1 Kgs. 17. 1. The principle remains. Salvation delivers from eternal punishment, but God is so concerned for His people's spiritual well-being that, to draw them back when they go astray, He will visit them with discipline. If we will not listen to the word He will use other means to get our attention.

Israel's safeguard against departure and painful correction was scrupulous obedience to God's **words**, vv. 18-20. Moses' instructions are a model for a biblical education. First, 'ye shall lay up these my words in your heart and in your soul'. The scriptures are to be consciously stored up in the human command and control centre so that they influence the life. Second, the people were to 'bind them' where they could neither be forgotten nor overlooked. Starting the day with the word is the best way to ensure that divine truth is given its prime place. Third, the Israelites were to 'teach them' in the home. Spiritual training starts at home. Those who restrict the teaching of the word to the gatherings of the local assembly are in danger of making an unscriptural division between equally important spheres of life. It is never wrong to open up the word. Fourth, 'thou shalt write them', for nothing gets truth into the mind like copying it out. What we write we remember.

Such a solid foundation would maintain the nation's **welfare**, vv. 21-25. It would preserve her from discipline and anticipate the beneficent characteristics of the millennial kingdom, v. 21, when Israel would be the head of the nations, her land stretching as far as the Euphrates. Those will truly be days of heaven upon earth when Christ reigns in glory from Jerusalem and all are subject to His rule. Yet, the New Testament believers have a greater privilege: as citizens of heaven, Phil. 3. 20, we are commanded to set our affection on things above, Col. 3. 2, enjoying constant access to the throne of grace, Heb. 4. 16.

November 3rd

Deuteronomy 12. 1-16

THE PLACE WHICH THE LORD SHALL CHOOSE

Israel was to be different from all other people, not least in its worship. After all, it was redeemed to be a testimony to the true God in a world immersed in pagan idolatry. False religion spawned a multiplicity of worship centres and rituals, v. 2, but God's people were to have a single centre. What Israel eventually possessed in type at Jerusalem, Christians enjoy now in reality when they gather to the name of the Lord Jesus, Matt. 18. 20.

The place of God's choice was **exclusive**, vv. 2-3. Israel had to destroy everything contrary to God: religious pluralism had no place in a theocracy. When Christ comes in, error must go. It was also a **single** place, vv. 4-5. Many gods generate many places, but the true God has but one gathering centre, His Son, Gen. 49. 10. That is why throughout the world believers content to obey scripture meet in a similar way. Further, the practical unity of each local assembly is crucial – churches are not to divide up into house groups, 1 Cor. 11. 18, 20. A **chosen** place displayed God's sovereign right to dictate the details of His people's lives. Everything we need to know about the local assembly is laid down in the New Testament, 1 Tim. 3. 15. It was a **commanded** place to which 'thou shalt come', v. 5, for obedience was not optional, Heb. 10. 24-25. Called 'his habitation', v. 5, it was God's **dwelling** place among His people, reflecting in its design and activities the nature of the occupant. A local assembly is a standing testimony to what God is and the demeanour of the saints should be a lesson in godliness.

As the location where sacrifice was offered it was a **solemn** place, v. 6. Fires constantly burning in the tabernacle and the temple courts were a reminder of death. The local assembly is eternally linked with the work of Calvary, being 'purchased with his own blood', Acts 20. 28. Therefore, as a **spiritual** place, everything was done 'before the Lord', v. 7, just as each exercise of the church is primarily for the honour of Christ Jesus. At this **joyful** place, v. 7, feasts and offerings expressed the thankfulness of those who had benefited from God's great salvation. The local assembly is meant to be a sphere of holy joy.

November 4th

Deuteronomy 12. 17-32

WHAT THING SOEVER I COMMAND YOU, DO

Israel's laws about tithing, vv. 17-19, diet, vv. 20-25, sacrifices, vv. 26-28, and separation, vv. 29-32, were lucid and direct. What Jehovah said, Israel must do.

But the direction in verse 32 is more than a simple insistence upon obedience: it lays down clear parameters. First, 'thou shalt not add thereto'. The three great statements of biblical authority which occur near the beginning (here in Deuteronomy), in the middle, Prov. 30. 5-6, and at the close, Rev. 22. 18-19, of the canon of scripture highlight the dangers of **supplementing** God's word with human inventions. It would be all too easy for a zealous Israelite leader to go beyond what was written in order to safe-guard the truth. Thus, the Pharisees 'made the commandment of God of none effect' by their traditions, Matt. 15. 6, teaching man-made regulations as though they were divine law. Scripture commands gospel preaching but not the method, the time or the place. When the singing of traditional hymns becomes more important than the proclamation of the word, human custom has usurped divine authority.

Second, 'thou shalt not . . . diminish from it'. If misguided zeal rushes to expand God's word, craven compromise encourages **subtraction** from it. The pressure of godless cultural norms, the increasing wickedness of a hell-bent world, the dwindling number of those with a heart for God's word – all these might persuade Israel's leaders that the more uncomfortable and unfashionable of God's laws could be quietly jettisoned. As Christendom speeds further away from authentic Christianity, assembly leaders may feel embarrassed about maintaining the distinct roles of male and female in the local church, or preserving the simplicity of the Lord's Supper, or resisting the onward sweep of ecumenism. But the God who foreknew all the problems His people would face still commanded simple obedience. The principle applies equally to us, 'Observe and hear all these words', v. 28. Saints cannot select those parts of scripture they would obey. Our rule of life is the 'whole counsel of God', Acts 20. 27 RV, for there alone is our spiritual safety.

November 5th

Deuteronomy 13. 1-18

THOU SHALT NOT CONSENT UNTO HIM

A people trained to expect divine signs and wonders, 1 Cor. 1. 22, were particularly vulnerable to frauds. Therefore, the Lord gave them advance warning of false teachers, their recognition and their removal.

The **false prophet**, vv. 1-5, was particularly dangerous for two reasons: he was no stranger but would arise 'among you', v. 1, and his wonders were absolutely real, v. 2. The reason for his rejection was not his miracles but the message they endorsed: 'Let us go after other gods', v. 2. Miracles in themselves are no guarantee of truth, Matt. 7. 22-23; 2 Thess. 2. 9, nor can they generate saving faith. The many who 'believed' in the Lord Jesus 'when they saw the miracles which he did', John 2. 23, were not acknowledged by the Saviour Himself, for genuine 'faith cometh by hearing, and hearing by the word of God', Rom. 10. 17. The reason God allows false teachers is to test the loyalty of His people, Deut. 13. 3. Would they run after the exciting and new or would they stick with the old and true? Error must not only be resisted but removed.

The **family member**, vv. 6-11, who secretly encouraged departure from God's word, was equally culpable. Of course, it would be painfully distressing to expose, repudiate and execute a relative, vv. 9-10, but in Old Testament Israel, as in the New Testament local assembly, the spiritual must take precedence over the natural. Elders who favour their family at the expense of God's word are failing the flock.

The **idolatrous city**, vv. 12-18, which abandoned God's revealed will for the evils of Gentile religion required even more extreme treatment. Once the departure was clearly demonstrated, v. 14, for hearsay is no substitute for a scrupulous examination of the facts, the city and all its inhabitants were to be blotted out, vv. 15-16.

These solemn passages make clear that flagrant disobedience to God's word cannot be tolerated among His people because it dishonours God and endangers men. Regardless of its power, v. 2, its perpetrator, v. 6, or its popularity, vv. 12-13, it must be put away.

November 6th

Deuteronomy 14. 1-20

THOU ART AN HOLY PEOPLE

Israel's special relationship with Jehovah as His child nation meant they were to be set apart from all other people in how they looked and what they cooked.

Bodily **disfigurement** was a common pagan mourning practice, 1 Kgs. 18. 28; Zech. 13. 6, which involved abusing the body God had created to appease deities which did not exist. Christians will shun the bodily degradation and inane physical decoration which marks modern youth culture, just as they will avoid copying the trivialised funerals of a godless society. Twenty-first century man, obsessed with beauty, youth and vigour, is terrified by the thought of ageing and death. The believer, however, accepts that the tabernacle of the body grows old, and maintains a respect for the elderly, Lev. 19. 32, for there is no attractiveness like that of godly old age, Prov. 16. 31.

The rest of the section is devoted to Israel's **diet**, vv. 3-20, for He who accomplished their redemption, provided their guidance and gave them their landed inheritance had both the right and the wisdom to dictate what they ate. In such matters they could not rely on personal preference but were wholly dependent upon God. As far as Israel was concerned, foods were clean or unclean, not because of any innate quality, but because God said so. Believers today are no longer under the dietary laws of Israel, for Christ Himself taught that defilement was not contracted through the stomach, 'making all meats clean', Mark 7. 19 RV. The final New Testament word is conclusive, 1 Tim. 4. 3-5. Christians can eat what they please. The spiritual lessons, however, must not be missed. What we dwell on, what we spend time over, what dominates our thoughts – that becomes the food of our souls. May God's pure word be our daily spiritual nourishment, Matt. 4. 4. Israel's food laws taught discernment, v. 7: the people had to check carefully whether something was clean or unclean according to precise divine criteria. Believers today check all they read and hear against the immutable standard of the word. A teaching may sound wholesome, may be popular and even come with the endorsement of trusted men, but scripture alone is infallible, Acts 17. 11.

November 7th

Deuteronomy 14. 21-29

THAT THE LORD THY GOD MAY BLESS THEE

God's choice of Israel as His elect nation was like His saving activity today – it was all of grace. Neither their merits nor their might but His uncaused love made them the beneficiaries of His covenant, Deut. 7. 6-8. But practical enjoyment of this privilege was dependent upon obedience to His detailed regulations.

The animal that died naturally, v. 21, was not to be consumed because Israel's livestock had to be slaughtered in a particular way so as to drain out the blood, 12. 23-25. This drove home the lesson that blood was special – the source of life and the price of atonement, Lev. 17. 11. Of course, this was only a foreshadowing of greater events. Christ did not die a natural death, for death had no claim on the sinless One, but gave Himself 'an offering and a sacrifice to God,' Eph. 5. 2.

God's people were to register their loyalty and gratitude by bringing the tenth of their annual agricultural produce to His official gathering centre, vv. 22-26. This taught three lessons. First, all came from God. The Israelite should eat his food joyfully in Jehovah's presence, acknowledging His bounty, v. 24. The Christian holds nothing of his own, but gladly traces every blessing, every gift, and every breath back to the Lord Jesus. Second, God was to be feared. The annual harvest ingathering could never be taken for granted because it was the gracious provision of Jehovah. God's daily mercies should foster an attitude of reverence. Third, difficulty was no excuse for disobedience. The place of God's choosing was non-negotiable, vv. 23-25, and those who might feel their distance from it prohibited them from bringing their cattle and produce were given a special allowance to convert their tithe to money and then purchase the equivalent on arrival. The New Testament believer is expected to arrange his life around the scriptural activities of the local assembly. There is much to be said for living close to the meeting place.

Finally, there should be a concern for others, vv. 27-29. The third year tithe was given over to the Levites and the disadvantaged. God's saints, accountable for what they do with what God gives them, will show practical care for needy brethren.

November 8th

Deuteronomy 15. 1-11

OPEN THINE HAND WIDE

Moses' foreview of life in the Promised Land sometimes looks beyond the Old Testament experience of Israel to the millennial kingdom, when all God's promises to His people will receive perfect fulfilment. This explains the apparent contradiction in today's passage, which speaks of a time 'when there shall be no poor among you', v. 4, while simultaneously insisting that 'the poor shall never cease out of the land', v. 11. The former will certainly be true under the benevolent reign of Messiah when restored Israel will be greatly blessed, v. 4, fully obedient, v. 5, and as a result become the economic mainspring of the millennial earth, v. 6.

In the meantime, however, 'ye have the poor always with you', Matt. 26. 11. The nation was therefore to practise both humanity and generosity: (i) in observing the year of the Lord's **release**, vv. 1-3; and (ii) in providing practical **relief** for fellow-Israelites in genuine need, vv. 7-11. The seven-yearly release guaranteed that no one in real hardship would become permanently overcome by debt, one of the great failings of modern capitalism. Behind the statute lies an unspoken reminder of God's goodness: Israel had benefited from the Lord's release in redemption from Egyptian slavery and the free gift of Canaan. God's grace to us is both the model and the stimulus for gracious dealings with our brethren. But lest any use the proximity of the year of release as an excuse for withholding help from those in need, v. 9, Moses counsels the importance of an outgoing disposition. A hard heart and a closed hand ill suit those who have profited from God's abundance, vv. 7-8.

The lessons in giving are forthright: it is to be from the heart, v. 7, ungrudging, v. 10, and generous, vv. 8, 11, recognising that God has blessed His people 'for this thing', v. 10. The very prosperity Israel enjoyed was entrusted to them that they might display the kindness of God towards others less affluent. This principle is illustrated in the spontaneous open-handedness of the first believers at Pentecost, Acts 2. 44-45, and the unexpected munificence of the poor Macedonian saints, 2 Cor. 8. 1-6. Glad giving is a reflection of God's own grace.

331

THOU SHALT NOT LET HIM GO AWAY EMPTY

The sabbath year involved not only a national cancelling of debts, 15. 1-11, but also a releasing of Israelite slaves, 15. 12-18. The Israelite who through irremediable poverty had to sell himself into servitude was not to endure that humiliation for ever. After all, by divine intervention the entire nation had been redeemed from cruel bondage in Egypt, v. 15, so its social policies were to reflect that glorious freedom.

Two provisions were made. First, the slave who gladly accepted his freedom in the year of release (and this must have been the vast majority) was not to go away empty-handed. His erstwhile master was to help set him up in his new independent life with the provision of foodstuffs to tide him over until his own labours could sustain him, v. 14. The master was not to begrudge him his liberty, bearing in mind the diligent service he had performed over six years, v. 18. The law here assumed both the God-fearing humanity of the master and the assiduous hard work of the slave, Eph. 6. 5-9.

The second provision was for the few who, in response to kind and generous treatment, developed a special bond of affection for their masters and opted to stay where they were, vv. 16-17. Moses laid down a solemn ritual which sealed their perpetual service. But this was no degradation. Rather, it was the ratification of a personal desire. The willing slave voluntarily, happily contracted himself to his master.

Christians will immediately think of the Son of God who, though owning all things as Lord of the universe, freely entered into humanity dedicated to the service of Jehovah, 'taking a bondman's form', Phil. 2. 7 JND. He is His people's pattern. To be tied by bonds of reverence, affection and loyalty to a good master is not base servitude but the opportunity for joyful, fulfilling service. This is now by grace every believer's position. Delivered from sin's bondage, we are the satisfied, lifelong servants of the best of masters. In answer to the sad question, 'Will ye also go away?', John 6. 67, let us identify ourselves with the Hebrew servant and respond, 'I will not go away from thee', Deut. 15. 16.

November 10th

Deuteronomy 16. 1-8

REMEMBER THE DAY

Israel's birthday as a nation was never to be forgotten. It involved a miraculous rescue and a calendar change, v. 1, Exod. 12. 2, and an animal sacrifice, v. 2. The Passover feast was the annual memory-jogger, to remind the people of who they were.

It commemorated a **divine deliverance**, v. 1, for 'the Lord thy God brought thee forth' from terrible slavery into freedom. Similarly, every Christian is a beneficiary of God's sovereign mercy in saving him from the present and the eternal consequences of sin. But this rescue was inseparable from a **solemn sacrifice**, v. 2. It was God's power that broke Egypt's fetters, but the lamb had to die that His people might be sheltered from divine judgement. The death of the Lord Jesus Christ renders to God everything that is due to His holy name on behalf of His elect. Further, the nation was liberated to be distinct for God in a heathen world, vv. 3-4. The ceremonial removal of leaven (one of the Bible's emblems of corruption) teaches **separation from sin**, for a redeemed people are expected to live for the pleasure of their Redeemer.

Since deliverance was a corporate event, its celebration was to be national: Israelites were to travel to God's appointed gathering centre for the Passover, vv. 5-6. Although believers will constantly give thanks for the work of Calvary it is peculiarly in the context of the local assembly that they 'proclaim the Lord's death', 1 Cor. 11. 26 RV. This therefore becomes the great **focus for fellowship**. Further, the Passover (immediately followed by the feast of unleavened bread) was an act of **individual identification**, v. 7, each member of the redeemed community partaking of the roast sacrificial lamb. A merely intellectual grasp of Christ is insufficient: there must be a personal appropriation of His saving work. Finally, the feast period **legislated against labour**, v. 8. Nothing was to dissipate the nation's pleasure in their new status as God's ransomed ones. Israel's cessation from work points forward to the spiritual rest believers enjoy today in Christ. No longer trying to satisfy God by their own efforts, they gladly lean their weight upon the One whose finished work on the cross meets all their needs.

November 11th
Deuteronomy 16. 9-12

REJOICE BEFORE THE LORD THY GOD

Israel's ceremonial calendar was built upon the Passover. Because 'it shall be the first month of the year to you', Exod. 12. 2, it became the starting point for all that followed. The truth of redemption set the tone for every national observance, just as today it colours the believer's entire life.

The **computation** of the 'feast of weeks', also called Pentecost, was exact: seven weeks were counted from the ingathering of first fruits (the early harvest, here described as 'such time as thou beginnest to put the sickle to the corn', v. 9). Yet there seems to be no record of the observance of this festival in the Old Testament. All the emphasis therefore falls upon its fulfilment, 'when the day of Pentecost was fully come', Acts 2. 1. From first fruits to Pentecost was fifty days: and from the resurrection of Christ to the descent of the Holy Spirit to inaugurate the church age was fifty days. God can be relied upon to keep His appointments punctually. Can we?

This feast, like others, involved an **oblation**, but instead of a lamb it was a sample of the harvest God had provided. Israel was educated to understand that all blessings, spiritual and material, came from God and must be acknowledged 'with a tribute of a freewill-offering', v. 10. Whatever we may render in service and worship, God has first given us. The character of the feast was not gloom but **jubilation**, v. 11, yet not the frothy merriment of the world. Israel's joy was always linked with Jehovah's presence among His people, 'Thou shalt rejoice before the Lord', v. 11. It was therefore a delight which was holy, corporate, encompassing the entire family, and out-flowing, a delight which embraced stranger, fatherless and widow. What Israel displayed in measure is now exemplified fully in the body of Christ, for at Pentecost saved Jews and Gentiles were prospectively incorporated into one body through Spirit baptism. God's grace burst the banks of Judaism to bless those who were 'aliens . . . strangers . . . far off', Eph. 2. 12-13. But whatever the season of the year, whatever the circumstances, Israel could never forget its **foundation**, v. 12. Everything looked back to redeeming grace. Christians cannot forget Calvary.

November 12th
Deuteronomy 16. 13-17

A SOLEMN FEAST UNTO THE LORD

The last festival of Israel's religious calendar was the feast of tabernacles. Like the first, it looked in two directions: back to the nation's historical experience, and forward to its ultimate fulfilment in Christ Jesus. The Passover commemorated deliverance from Egypt, but also anticipated the cross where 'Christ our passover is sacrificed for us', 1 Cor. 5. 7. Tabernacles, following the final triumphant harvest ingathering, was a retrospective on the nomadic conditions of the wilderness journey, Lev. 23. 42-43, but also a hint of kingdom blessings to come when Messiah would reign over His people in righteousness and peace. One can understand why Peter, overawed in the company of a glorified Lord flanked by celebrities like Moses and Elijah, thought instinctively of this feast, with its combination of spiritual satisfaction and unalloyed delight, Matt. 17. 4.

Israel's celebrations therefore fell into three groups, v. 16: (i) unleavened bread, which included the feasts of Passover and firstfruits as adjuncts; (ii) weeks; and (iii) tabernacles, which comprehended the adjacent feast of trumpets and the Day of Atonement. These were the annual convocations of the nation, requiring the presence of all males at God's chosen centre. But there were conditions. 'They shall not appear before the Lord empty'. God demanded of His people, first, their physical **presence**. The application to the meetings of the local assembly is obvious, where saints are expected to gather to the name of the Lord Jesus Christ not three times a year but at least every first day of the week, Heb. 10. 25. Second, God looked for **preparation**. To come with something to give involved personal effort in the selection of a suitable offering which adequately reflected Jehovah's material benevolence to His people, for 'every man shall give as he is able', v. 17. At the breaking of bread it is the responsibility of all to come with hearts full of thanksgiving for the Lord Jesus, and the special privilege of the males to express corporate gratitude on behalf of the whole company. Not every prayer need last twenty minutes. 'As he is able' indicates that the God who knows our capacities expects our adoration to be in proportion to our appreciation of His Son.

November 13th

Deuteronomy 16. 18-22

JUDGE THE PEOPLE WITH JUST JUDGEMENT

The chapter which summarizes Israel's religious calendar closes, perhaps surprisingly, with two brief paragraphs about the importance of justice, vv. 18-20, and the danger of idolatry, vv. 21-22.

The people of a righteous God were to behave righteously in daily life. Once they had settled into the land, an administrative system would be set up to ensure the maintenance of justice in their communities. This justice was to be **impartial**: 'thou shalt not respect persons', v. 19. Just as Peter discovered that God has no favourites in the operation of His saving grace, Acts 10. 34, so assembly elders are to be free from family prejudice. It was to be **incorruptible**: 'neither take a gift'. To act scrupulously according to principle rather than personal gain must be the believer's aim in all circumstances. It was to be **invariable**. According to YOUNG's *Literal Translation*, verse 20 begins, 'Righteousness – righteousness thou dost pursue'. The emphasis is unmistakable. Neither personal weariness nor the fluctuation of public opinion could alter the divine requirement of absolute justice. Israel, God's sample of the human race, failed, its history being littered with injustice, Mic. 7. 2-3, but God is the righteous Judge. At Calvary He proved Himself to be both just, in meting out on Christ the full penalty for our sins, and 'the justifier of him which believeth in Jesus', Rom. 3. 26. The debt has been paid in full, and the debtors discharged.

The final warning against idolatry was specifically aimed at the subtle evil of ecumenism. Israel might be tempted to build a Canaanite fertility image near to Jehovah's altar, not in a brazen effort to replace truth with falsehood but in a politically correct toleration of all viewpoints. What could be more reasonable? People could therefore make their own choice, following Jehovah or Baal or both, as it pleased them. Trouble is, the supreme God of the universe will brook no rivals. He must be Lord of all. The solemn words, 'which the Lord thy God hateth', remind us that He who loves truth and justice hates error, Ps. 33. 5; Prov. 15. 9. Whatever the pressure, the local assembly must stand firmly for God's unchangeable truth.

November 14th

Deuteronomy 17. 1-7

HE THAT IS WORTHY OF DEATH

This section warns Israel against two evils which were specifically abominations to Jehovah. The first is **disrespect**, v. 1, offering to God what is unworthy of Him. The second is **disloyalty**, vv. 2-7, abandoning Jehovah's covenant in favour of idol worship.

Since regular sacrifice was built into Israel's daily life, there was always the danger that solemn ceremonial might degenerate into mechanical, heartless ritual. Worse, the Israelite might become so accustomed to bringing his offering to Jehovah's altar that he would cease to marvel at the majesty of the One he worshipped. Malachi berated the people for offering to God what they would never have dared present to an earthly master, 'the blind . . . the lame and sick', Mal. 1. 8. To offer God the rejects was both to insult His infinite greatness and to damage the symbolism of the sacrifices. A perfect God can accept nothing less than perfection. That is why we have nothing of our own with which we can please Him. But the message of the gospel is that what God's holiness required God's own love has supplied. The ultimate offering to which all others pointed was the 'lamb without blemish and without spot', 1 Pet. 1. 19, whose atoning death has eternally satisfied God's demands. When Christians meet for worship, the best they can ever do is return to God their feeble appreciation of the One God has given them. May our worship never be second best!

If an imperfect sacrifice was an abomination, so too was the worship of idols. To adore the creature instead of the Creator, Rom. 1. 25, was insanity. It is sad when those who boast in their learning should be so swift to swallow cunningly devised fables like evolution. But idolatry was also treason, meriting death, v. 6. Once again the importance of strict justice is underlined. No charge could be accepted save on the basis of multiple testimony, as a solitary witness might be prejudiced or mistaken. Further, the witnesses were not sheltered by anonymity: they were held publicly responsible for their evidence by being the first to stone the offender. Israel, like the local assembly, needed to be preserved from the evil of malicious gossip.

November 15th
Deuteronomy 17. 8-13

THE SENTENCE OF THE LAW

Scripture is nothing if not realistic. It frankly recognizes that God's redeemed people can and will have problems with one another. Once established in the land, Israel required a comprehensive local justice system to settle disputes, 16. 18. Cases which proved too difficult for the local magistrates would be transferred to a higher court located at the place of God's choosing, 17. 8. In a theocratic nation the religious and the civil were inseparable, so the ultimate court of appeal consisted of priests and an officiating supreme judge. This tribunal's verdict was final: wilful resistance was liable to the death penalty, 17. 10, 12.

The practical lessons from this aspect of Israel's history are powerful. First, when believers face 'a matter too hard', they are to take it, not to some earthly authority, but to Christ Himself, the personal fulfilment of God's chosen gathering centre in the Old Testament. He, today, is our object of worship, our means of access to God, our focus of unity and our source of guidance. As we prayerfully study the word, we discover His mind in relation to those things which disturb us. Principles for godly behaviour in every circumstance are found in the scriptures.

Second, disputes between brethren, the all too frequent cause of friction in the local assembly, are to be settled internally, Phil. 4. 2. Israel did not turn back to Egypt for civil arbitration; neither will a church of God air its difficulties before a secular court, 1 Cor. 6. 1-3. The God who is sufficient for eternal salvation is well able to organize the day to day lives of His ransomed people through His written word, 2 Tim. 3. 16-17.

But, third, wilful rejection of the teaching of scripture is a serious sin. In Israel such rebellion incurred death, a penalty designed both to maintain God's honour and promote healthy reverence, 17. 13. Today, certain sins may require exclusion from the local church, 1 Cor. 5. 13. Yet while death cut off the presumptuous Israelite from the nation, and excommunication removes the unrepentant believer from local assembly fellowship, nothing can excise a genuine member from the body of Christ, Eph. 5. 30; John 10. 27-29.

November 16th
Deuteronomy 17. 14-20

WHOM THE LORD THY GOD SHALL CHOOSE

More than four hundred years before Saul, son of Kish, the law anticipated a time when the nation of Israel would reject God's rule and demand a king, 'like all the nations that are around me', Deut. 17. 14 NKJV.

This is not to say that the concept of kingship for Israel was not a part of God's divine plan. God had promised both Abraham and Jacob that their descendents would be kings, Gen. 17. 6; 35. 11, and later Jacob prophetically announced that the tribe of Judah would be the royal line, 49. 10. But when Israel demanded a king, they expressed their desire to be like the nations around them; they rejected their holy standing before God, and they rejected God as their shield and defender, 1 Sam. 8. 20.

In anticipating the hardness of their hearts, the law provided regulations for the king in the passage before us. First, the king must be the one whom 'the Lord thy God shall choose', Deut. 17. 15. The book of Deuteronomy is a restatement of God's covenant with the nation. The expression, 'the Lord thy God' appears some 239 times in this book, and was ever a reminder to the people of their covenant relationship with God. Israel was not to be a democracy, but God reserved the right to choose the king for the nation. Second, this king must be an Israelite and not a foreigner.

Four specific prohibitions are given for the king, 17. 16-17. Violation of any of these four prohibitions would indicate a lack of dependence upon the Lord, and would cause both the king and the people to turn their hearts away from the Lord.

The safeguard against disobedience and coldness of heart is devotion to the word of God. Therefore, the king was required to 'write for himself' a copy of the law, to keep it with him, and to read it all the days of his life, 17. 18-20. The history of the nation bears out the need for these royal instructions.

That which was true for the king of Israel holds true for us today. The only safeguard against disobedience and coldness of heart is devotion to the word of God. Let us determine to write the word of God on our hearts, to keep it with us at all times, and to both read and meditate on the scriptures day by day.

November 17th
Deuteronomy 18. 1-8

THE LORD IS THEIR INHERITANCE

God's intention was that the Israelites be 'a kingdom of priests, and an holy nation', Exod. 19. 6, but the people were afraid to approach God and requested that Moses be their mediator, 20. 19. So God established a distinct priesthood, and sovereignly chose Aaron and his sons to fulfil this role, 28. 1.

However, Aaron's tribe, the tribe of Levi, had come under God's judgement because of the cruel, passionate act of Levi and his brother Simeon in avenging their sister Dinah, Gen. 34. 25-31. Jacob prophesied that, as a result of their cruelty, these two tribes would be scattered in Israel, 49. 5-7.

In an agrarian society, where land provides wealth and security, the Lord graciously made provision for the financial security of His people, not only by giving them land but also by establishing inheritance laws that prevented the permanent loss of tribal lands. But Levi's actions had resulted in the forfeiting of his descendant's right to a land inheritance.

When the tenth plague of Egypt brought death to the firstborn of each household, God redeemed the firstborn Israelites through the death of the Passover lamb. So the firstborn belonged to God by redemption. But God took the Levites in exchange for the firstborn of the children of Israel, and gave them to Aaron and his sons to care for them and to minister in the tabernacle, Num. 3. 6-13, 44-51; 8. 16-19.

Then, in His mercy, God provided an inheritance for this scattered tribe of Levi, not an inheritance of land, but, even better, He provided Himself as their inheritance, Deut. 18. 1-2. Although they lacked lands to generate wealth, when sacrifices and offerings were brought to the Lord, a portion was set aside to provide for the Levites. They had the privilege of eating the Lord's portion, Deut. 18. 1, because He had sovereignly chosen them to stand and minister in the name of the Lord, v. 5.

How gracious and merciful is our God! How good to know that we have been given 'an inheritance incorruptible, and undefiled, and that fadeth not away, reserved in heaven for you, who are kept by the power of God through faith unto salvation ready to be revealed in the last time', 1 Pet. 1. 4-5.

November 18th

Deuteronomy 18. 9-14

AN ABOMINATION UNTO THE LORD

When God, in an act of grace, gave the Promised Land to the nation of Israel, He was simultaneously bringing judgement upon the Canaanites, because their practices were morally repulsive to His holiness. Therefore God was insistent that His redeemed people should not 'learn to do after the abominations of those nations', v. 9.

The practices listed here are all related to the occult. With the exception of child sacrifices, these things are very much on the ascendancy in our society today and popular culture is making them increasingly 'mainstream'. Even children's books are popularizing and glamorizing occult practices and we need to be alert to the subtle wiles of the devil.

In an age when many are convinced that the controlling factor of God's character is His love, such words are startling. As believers, we must never forget that some things are absolutely repulsive and disgusting to a thrice holy God. But notice that not only are these practices an abomination but also those who practise them, v. 12. Indeed, 'God is angry with the wicked every day', Ps. 7. 11.

Why is it that these particular things are an abomination to the Lord? They are all efforts to replace God and His revelation. They are not a denial of the supernatural, but they are a denial of God's supremacy. It was because of these things that the nations were being driven from the land, but sadly the Israelites became infected by these sins, Jer. 32. 35.

In addition to these practices, Deuteronomy lists inferior sacrifices, 17. 1, idolatry, vv. 2-5, cross-dressing, 22. 5, and unjust weights, 25. 13-16, as being abominations to the Lord, and Leviticus adds homosexual practices, Lev. 18. 22-30. Most of us would have no problem condemning all the above, and are rightly repulsed by them. But what we may find more convicting is that a proud look, a lying tongue, and sowing discord among brethren are also abominable to the Lord, Prov. 6. 16-19. We tend to overlook and excuse such behaviour, perhaps because in condemning them we would be condemning ourselves. May God help us to view sin as He does.

November 19th
Deuteronomy 18. 15-22
I WILL RAISE THEM UP A PROPHET

The Canaanites used witchcraft, omens, mediums and necromancy for their guidance, v. 10-11, but God had not appointed such for His people, v. 14. Rather, He promised a Prophet like unto Moses, v. 15. Fourteen hundred years later, the Jewish people were still living in anticipation of this coming Prophet, when John the Baptist burst onto the scene and ended 400 years of silence. Many wondered if he was the long anticipated Prophet but he emphatically denied it, John 1. 21.

However, in his sermon in Acts chapter 3, Peter declared that the waiting had come to an end. God had raised up His Son Jesus, v. 26. He was the One like unto Moses, not in every point, but certainly in the fact that He spoke face to face with God and brought God's word to the people. Of course, the Lord Jesus far exceeds Moses as the ultimate and final revelation of God, John 1. 18; Heb. 3. 1-3.

This Prophet would be 'from the midst of thee, of thy brethren', Deut. 18. 15. The humanity of the Lord Jesus, and His descent from Abraham, are both necessary truths, 'it behoved him to be made like unto his brethren', Heb. 2. 17. His humanity fulfilled this ancient prophecy but is also essential for His work as Saviour, High Priest, and Mediator.

'Him you shall hear', Deut. 18. 15 NKJV. This was the obligation of the people. This was also the failure and condemnation of the first-century Jews, who heard the word of God spoken by the Word of God. Some would say, 'Never man spake like this man', John 7. 46. Others would say, 'What need we any further witness? for we ourselves have heard of his own mouth', Luke 22. 71. Having heard the Living Word, they wanted to destroy Him, John 8. 40. Peter's quotation gives God's sentence, 'And it shall come to pass, that every soul, which will not hear that prophet, shall be destroyed from among the people', Acts 3. 23.

Thank God we have a Prophet who has spoken to us the words of eternal life, John 6. 68! 'See that ye refuse not him that speaketh', Heb. 12. 25. Rather, may His words be to us 'the joy and rejoicing' of our hearts, Jer. 15. 16.

November 20th

Deuteronomy 19. 1-13

SEPARATE THREE CITIES FOR THEE

Life is sacred. Therefore, the Lord was concerned that the land He was giving to the people should not be polluted by the shedding of innocent blood, v. 10. This meant that premeditated murder must be punished, without pity, v. 13, life for life, and the responsibility for this was placed upon the kinsman-redeemer in his role as the revenger of blood, Gen. 9. 5; Num. 35. 16-19. But God maintained a clear distinction for accidental manslaughter, and *commanded* that cities of refuge be established where the manslayer could flee for safety, Deut. 19. 10.

While six cities were to be designated as cities of refuge, only the three within the borders of Israel are in view here. The land west of the Jordan was to be measured and divided into three parts (so ESV) with one city of refuge in each part, so that they were readily accessible, with good roads leading to them, v. 3. According to extra-biblical Jewish writings, these roads were to be thirty two cubits wide, well-maintained, and without obstruction, so that the manslayer would face no impediment in reaching safety.

How thankful we are that God has provided a place of refuge for us to flee to, Heb. 6. 18! How wonderful to know that in Christ there is safety and security. If the manslayer ventured out of the city, once again he would be in danger of the avenger of blood. How much better the security we have in Christ, John 10. 28-29! We know that He is readily accessible to all who will come to Him for safety, Rom. 10. 8. But how awful it would be if we were responsible for setting up obstacles that prevented anyone coming to Christ for safety. Ravi Zacharias has likened the ministry of apologetics, 1 Pet. 3. 15, to that of 'brush clearing', removing those intellectual hindrances that stand in the way of people coming to Christ. May we, like John Baptist, be involved in smoothing the path for Christ, Isa. 40. 3-4.

It is interesting to see that this type of Christ made provision not only for the Israelite, but also 'for the stranger, and for the sojourner among them', Num. 35. 15. Truly, the gospel we preach is 'the power of God unto salvation to every one that believeth; to the Jew first, and also to the Greek', Rom. 1 .16.

THE JUDGES SHALL MAKE DILIGENT INQUISITION

God's laws are not arbitrarily given but rather reflect His own nature and character. As a just judge, God desired that right-eousness and justice characterize His theocratic kingdom. One day the Lord Jesus Christ will return to earth to establish His kingdom in perfect righteousness and justice. 'He shall not judge after the sight of his eyes, neither reprove after the hearing of his ears: But with righteousness shall he judge', Isa. 11. 3-4.

Under the Mosaic Law, God's theocratic kingdom was medi-ated through fallen men with limited knowledge who were liable to show favouritism and corruption. So, in His wisdom, God set up safeguards to protect people from false accusation.

First, there was a need for multiple witnesses, Deut. 19. 15. Then, there was a need for a public trial with both parties pres-ent before the Lord and His earthly representatives, the priests and the judges, vv. 16-17. Thirdly, the judges were required to make diligent inquiry into the accusations being brought, v. 18, and the responsibility was theirs to render a verdict. If it was determined that a false accusation had been brought, then the nation must do to the accuser what he wanted done to the accused, v. 19. This would not only serve to purge the nation of evil, but act as a preventative to further false charges.

There is an obligation upon the church today to judge evil in its midst, 1 Cor. 5. 7, 12-13. Paul taught that as those who will one day judge both the world, 1 Cor. 6. 2, and angels, v. 3, we are responsible to judge matters between believers in our assemblies. This is not limited to just 'church' business, but also regarding 'things pertaining to this life', v. 4. How sad when our business affairs threaten to destroy the peace and unity of the assembly. Paul said that in such cases it is better to be wronged and defrauded than to take our affairs to the civil courts, vv. 6-7. Like the Lord Jesus, we can commit ourselves to Him who judges righteously, 1 Pet. 2. 23. But when such issues are brought before the assembly, let us use the safeguards God gave to His ancient covenant people to make sure that righ-teousness, truth and justice prevail.

November 22nd

Deuteronomy 20. 1-9

LET HIM GO AND RETURN UNTO HIS HOUSE

Warfare is here considered to be an accepted part of life for the Israelites. This little nation, Deut. 7. 7, would be involved in both offensive battles to take possession of that which God had promised and defensive battles against the enemies who would seek to destroy them. So the exhortation comes to them, 'Be not afraid of them: for the Lord thy God is with thee', 20. 1.

One of the lesser known functions of the priest is mentioned in verse 2. The scriptures do not provide us with the identity of this particular priest, but according to ALBERT BARNES, the rabbis called him 'the anointed of the war'. He stands before the nation as a spiritual leader and reminds them that God is with them, to fight for them, and to save them, vv. 3-4.

However, the Mosaic law provided several exemptions from military service. Four times over our passage repeats, 'Let him go and return unto his house', vv. 5, 6, 7, 8. The first three demonstrate God's compassion for one who has not yet entered into the enjoyment of some anticipated, legitimate pleasure while the fourth demonstrates God's wisdom in not allowing fearful soldiers to infect the rest of the army with their fear.

It is good to remember that there are legitimate pleasures in this life and that we have a compassionate God who 'giveth us richly all things to enjoy', 1 Tim. 6. 17. But on the other hand, we recognize that we are involved in a spiritual battle and are called upon to 'endure hardship, as a good soldier of Jesus Christ', 2 Tim. 2. 3 NKJV. The apostle Paul was willing to sacrifice legitimate pleasures, such as having a believing wife, 1 Cor. 9. 5, and encouraged the Corinthians to make similar sacrifices in view of the present distress, 7. 26, and shortness of time, v. 29. May God grant us wisdom to determine that which we may legitimately enjoy and that which we should forsake.

But may it not be that any of us 'return unto his house' as a result of fear, 'For God hath not given us the spirit of fear; but of power, and of love, and of a sound mind', 2 Tim. 1. 7. We have God's promise 'I will never leave thee, nor forsake thee. So that we may boldly say, The Lord is my helper, and I will not fear what man shall do unto me', Heb. 13. 5-6.

November 23rd

Deuteronomy 20. 10-20

SAVE ALIVE NOTHING THAT BREATHETH

We are horrified when we hear of genocide taking place in countries such as Rwanda and Serbia, and rightfully so. But many people are also troubled when they read passages such as this, where God commands the nation of Israel to commit genocide against the nations that inhabit the land that God promised to His people. Some would go so far as to distance themselves and say they don't believe in a God who would command such atrocities. But we must not imagine that we are more wise or merciful than God. Rather, we must recognize that God, as our Creator, is entitled to be our Judge, and nothing in scripture says that judgement must be left until the final judgement day.

Notice that God makes a clear distinction between those nations that are near the Promised Land and those that are distant. He did not authorize the Israelites to wipe out just any nation, but limited the 'curse of destruction' to those nations that would be a threat to the purity of His people. God had told Abraham 400 years previously that these nations would be destroyed, but that their iniquities had not yet reached fullness, Gen. 15. 16. Now, that time had come.

These six nations, v. 17, (a seventh is mentioned in Deuteronomy chapter 7 verse 1) were notoriously wicked people who deserved the judgement of God. But when Israel failed to follow God's command, they fell into the very trap that God had warned them of, namely that they were corrupted by the evil practices and religious activities of these wicked people.

Remember that God, who does not change, always responds to repentance, Jer. 18. 8. When the Ninevites repented of their sin, God spared them, just as Jonah feared, Jonah 3. 10; 4. 1-2. Had these nations turned from their wicked ways, they would have been spared destruction; and remember that when the Israelites fell into the same sins as these wicked nations, the judgement of God came upon them also.

The Judge of all the earth does act in perfect justice. He is worthy of our praise, not only for His love and mercy, but also for His wrath and judgement. Let us sing His praises for His exercise of justice and righteousness, Ps. 67. 4.

November 24th

Deuteronomy 21. 1-9

OUR HANDS HAVE NOT SHED THIS BLOOD

An unsolved murder! Fiction writers love to delve into these mysteries and the hero always manages to untangle the web of deceit and catch the perpetrator. But in real life it is not always so easy.

Yet, God's concern was that the nation 'put away the guilt of innocent blood from among you', v. 9. But how could this be accomplished if the murderer couldn't be identified?

The Lord, in His wisdom, provided a means of atoning for the shedding of innocent blood. The town nearest to the crime scene was identified by measurement and this town was to take responsibility for the atonement ceremony. Perhaps this was because the killer was most likely to have come from that town, or perhaps because the defilement of the land was closest to them and most likely to affect them.

The elders of that city were to take a young heifer, that had never been yoked, down to a valley that had never been ploughed or sown and had flowing water, and there break the heifer's neck. The priests were to be there as judicial representatives to settle the case, v. 5. The elders, as representatives of the town, would wash their hands over the heifer and declare their innocence of the murder and request that the Lord provide atonement for the innocent blood that was shed. The promise is then given that atonement would be provided, v. 8.

This ceremony was unusual in that normally atonement or cleansing are accomplished through the shedding of blood, but here the heifer's blood is not shed but rather its neck broken, RV, The heifer was not a sin offering, but rather stood in the place of the unknown murderer and took his punishment so that the land would not be defiled by innocent blood. Forgiveness for the sinner was not accomplished, but the guilt for the sin was diverted from the town onto the heifer. By their hand washing ceremony, the elders declared that they had no complicity in the murder.

By contrast, Pilate's hand washing did not remove his guilt for the murder of our Lord. His was merely a futile attempt to salve a guilty conscience.

November 25th
Deuteronomy 21. 10-17

SHE SHALL BE THY WIFE

The Israelites were forbidden to marry Canaanite women, Deut. 7. 3, so the women spoken of here must be those from distant lands who were allowed to live, 20. 14. The legislation outlined is intended to protect these women from mistreatment by the Israelite soldiers. It is common, even today, to hear reports of soldiers entering villages and humiliating and raping the women. Yet, God knew that not only would this be damaging to these foreign women but that the whole nation of Israel could be corrupted by such a deviant approach to sexuality.

James tells us that pure religion is marked by caring for widows and orphans, Jas. 1. 27. God Himself is described as 'a father of the fatherless, a defender of widows', Ps. 68. 5 NKJV, and expects those in positions of power not to take advantage of those who lack the normal protection of family. So, even those who are foreigners and prisoners of war are offered the protection of the Mosaic law.

If a man was attracted to one of these prisoners of war, he was to bring her to his house and allow her a full month to mourn the death of her parents, accompanied by the Jewish signs of mourning. Then, he could go in to her and be her husband and she would be his wife.

In recognition of the hardness of their hearts, Matt. 19. 8, Moses also made provision for how these prisoners of war should be treated in the event of the husband being displeased with her and wanting a divorce. He could not then treat her as a slave and sell her for money because he had humbled her. He was to let her go as a free woman, without constraint.

The morality of the Mosaic law was greatly superior to that of the surrounding nations in that day, as evidenced by the provision that was made in the law for these women. And, despite the fact that Christianity is often pictured today as being patriarchal and anti-women, the Gospels demonstrate that the Lord Jesus elevated women to an even higher level than Judaism. The apostle Paul, while emphasizing the distinctive roles that men and women have in the home and the assembly, declared that men and women are now one 'in Christ', Gal. 3. 28.

November 26th

Deuteronomy 21. 18-23

THIS OUR SON IS STUBBORN AND REBELLIOUS

The Mosaic Covenant was a contractual agreement between God and the nation of Israel. Deuteronomy is the restatement of that covenant for the second generation of Israelites after their deliverance from Egypt. Virtually all the aspects of the law included with it the penalty of death for failure to comply, so that Paul can describe it as the 'ministry of death, written and engraved on stones', 2 Cor. 3. 7 NKJV.

Unless we are Jews, we were never actually under the Mosaic Covenant, but the law still serves for us the function of revealing God's moral standards and showing us how far short we fall of the glory of God, Rom. 3. 23. Yet, even though we might not have had the written code of the law, our conscience demonstrates that we have the law written on our hearts, Rom. 2. 15, and are without excuse before a holy God.

The law concerning the stoning of a rebellious teenager shocks our moral sensibilities. It is hard for us to imagine a parent who would bring their son before the elders of the city and condemn him to death. Those who think they are standing on higher moral ground by condemning God for this demonstrate only that they don't understand the seriousness of sin and in particular rebellion.

We must keep in mind the words that Samuel spoke to Saul, 'For rebellion is as the sin of witchcraft, and stubbornness is as iniquity and idolatry', 1 Sam. 15. 23. This will help us to understand how seriously God views the sin of rebellion. It is an attack on God's delegated authority and therefore an attack on God's own authority. Under the terms of the Mosaic contract, this was a capital offence.

It is a reminder to us today of the great responsibility that God has placed on parents. We can see around us that the break-down of the family has resulted in the break-down of society. This is an area where we as Christians can shine brightly, if we will follow the biblical instructions for disciplining our children. If we allow rebellion to go unchecked when our children are small, it will only become more difficult as they come to the teen years. May God help us to build strong Christian families.

November 27th

Deuteronomy 22. 1-4

RESTORE IT TO HIM AGAIN

'Finders keepers, losers weepers'. This childhood philosophy is unfortunately not limited to childhood. For many, it is simply a fortuitous opportunity that should not be squandered. I remember as a teenager being at a youth meeting where the speaker was telling about a time of great need in his life when he had nothing to put on the table and driving home in the car was in great prayer about this need. Suddenly a chicken ran out in front of the car! He thanked God for this miraculous provision and took the chicken home for dinner. But it makes you wonder: 'Who lost their chicken?'

This passage shows that theft can take more subtle forms than armed robbery or breaking and entering. Indeed, it is a call to be proactive to prevent your neighbour from loss of property. To 'turn a blind eye' is, in a sense, to be an accomplice to the loss. No punishment is prescribed for this inaction, but it is stressed as a moral obligation.

In the passage we read of an ox or sheep or ass that wanders away, presumably in the absence of the owner. The person who sees this happening must take action to return or safeguard his neighbour's property. And, if someone sees his brother in need of help with an ox or donkey that has fallen in the ditch, there is again a moral obligation to help.

The challenge is how we are to apply this to our times. Within the covenant community of Israel, there was clearly a responsibility for them to assist one another. Similarly, it is clear that within the family of God we should love one another, Gal. 5. 13; and bear one another's burdens, Gal. 6. 2. But if we see a stranger broken down on the side of the road, do we have a moral obligation to act?

The parable of the 'Good Samaritan', Luke 10. 30-37, would show that the Lord believed we do. While care should be exercised, 'As we have therefore opportunity, let us do good unto all men, especially unto them who are of the household of faith', Gal. 6. 10. No doubt the priest and Levite were just being careful, but the Samaritan is praised as the one who showed mercy. Our Lord says: 'Go, and do thou likewise', v. 37.

November 28th

Deuteronomy 22. 5-12

A GARMENT OF DIVERS SORTS

Distinctions are very important to God. As we read a passage like this, teaching some of the distinctions God wanted His covenant people to observe, some of them we find quite unexpected and curious.

The distinction between male and female is fundamental, based on creation, and obvious in God's design. Yet we know society is facing increasing challenges in today's Western culture. Efforts are underway in many countries to redefine marriage, and homosexuality is increasingly portrayed as a normal, alternative lifestyle. This is the end result of the blurring of distinctions that started many years ago. Verse 5 seeks to stop that process by prohibiting cross-dressing. However, we must also recognize that fashion is determined by local cultures, so it is impossible to make a blanket statement covering every culture about what clothing is distinctively male or female as fashions change and none of us wear today what Moses would have considered men's clothing!

We do find it curious that the mixing of materials in garments, v. 11, is included in the Mosaic law, as few of us today would worry about such a distinction. There is nothing of a moral nature here, but rather the point is that the people of God must be people of discernment, learning to make and maintain God-given distinctions. Likewise, the prohibition against sowing a vineyard with different types of seed, v. 9, and ploughing with an ox and donkey, v. 10, are not moral issues *per se* but are object lessons that point to the truth of separation.

Paul takes up the imagery of the unequal yoke, 2 Cor. 6. 14. While this passage has been rightly applied to issues of marriage and business partnerships, the context of the passage points particularly to the dangers of false teaching and idolatry. This is a message that needs to be sounded clearly in days when ecumenical efforts are made to unite all faiths. Paul boldly asks, 'What communion hath light with darkness?', v. 14. And, while we recognize the unity of all true believers, we must not sacrifice truth in the process. May we be discerning believers who hold and speak the truth with grace.

Deuteronomy 22. 13-30

IF ANY MAN TAKE A WIFE

While we often feel uncomfortable talking about issues of sexuality, the Bible does not shrink from tackling these vital concerns. God's covenant with Israel was designed to promote purity and punish evil, as improper attitudes towards sex will defile the people of God.

Six distinct areas of sexual conduct are dealt with: the first has to do with charges of infidelity against a bride; the next has to do with adultery; the next three have to do with rape; and the final is a prohibition against a man marrying his step-mother.

Paul warns us to 'flee fornication. Every sin that a man doeth is without the body; but he that committeth fornication sinneth against his own body', 1 Cor. 6. 18. He also says each one 'should know how to possess his own vessel in sanctification and honour, not in passion of lust', 1 Thes. 4. 4-5 NKJV, and warns that the Lord is the avenger of those who are defrauded through sexual sin, v. 6.

Sexual purity before marriage is vital for all parties concerned. For a person to give their virginity to one other than their marriage partner is to defraud their marriage partner as well as the marriage partner of the other person. Also at stake is the honour of the family, so that unfounded accusations of sexual promiscuity against the bride incur a stiff financial penalty paid to the girl's father and the accuser is obliged to remain with and provide for the accused for the rest of his life.

Adultery with a married woman is an evil that God required be put away from Israel through the death penalty. The depths of the depravity of our society are indicated by adultery being not only accepted but celebrated and made the basis of much that is called entertainment.

Divine wisdom recognizes distinctions between rape in the city and rape in the countryside. A betrothed virgin who is raped in the country is assumed to be innocent as her cries for help could not be heard; her attacker is to be put to death. But a betrothed virgin who is raped in the city is considered to be guilty unless she cries out for help as no cry for help would indicate consent; both parties are to be put to death.

Deuteronomy 23. 1-16

THEREFORE SHALL THY CAMP BE HOLY

One of the great privileges of the Israelite nation was the presence of the Lord in their midst. The camp was centred around the tabernacle, with the Most Holy place housing the ark of the covenant and the mercy seat, representing God's dwelling place among them. The Israelites camped in order around the tabernacle, but the Levites camped immediately around the tabernacle to guard the nation from the wrath of God, Num. 1. 52-53. The presence of a holy God walking in their midst demanded holiness of the people, Deut. 23. 14.

In order to maintain this holiness, certain people were prohibited from entrance into the congregation, or assembly, vv. 1-8, and certain activities would temporarily require soldiers to go outside their camp in times of war, vv. 9-13.

Eunuchs were denied access, most likely because they had mutilated their bodies, v. 1. Those who were born illegitimately were denied access, as were their descendents until the tenth generation, v. 2. Again, the reason is not specified, but demonstrates God's concern for sexual purity among the people.

Verses 3-6 explain why neither an Ammonite nor Moabite was allowed entrance among the people of God until the tenth generation forever; they had failed to respond to the requests of the Israelites during their pilgrimage, and because they had actively sought their harm through the hire of the prophet Balaam.

The difficulty is in understanding what this exclusion involved, because if the prohibition against a Moabite is forever, then Ruth, for example, should have been excluded. It could be that the exclusion was only until the tenth generation; it could be that they were allowed in the camp but not to approach the tabernacle to worship; or it could be taken as a general law that was over-ruled by grace on the exercise of personal faith.

Permission was granted for the Edomites and Egyptians in the third generation because of their filial relationship and their treatment of the Israelites respectively, vv. 7-8.

Finally, guidelines are given for two specific incidents of defiling bodily discharges that would render the camp impure and offend the holiness of their Commander-in-Chief.

December 1st

Deuteronomy 23. 17-25

THE LORD THY GOD WILL SURELY REQUIRE IT.

The only mention in Deuteronomy of the house of God occurs at verse 18. The section of our reading is, therefore, clearly related to how one must behave in the house of God, part of the apostle's purposes as he wrote 1 Timothy chapter 3. Our chapter also notes that being in the land, v. 20, being in the congregation, vv. 1-3, and the camp, vv. 10-14, brought responsibilities upon the Israelite. Greater still was the responsibility of association with the house where God dwelt. And it is so today: where God dwells among His own redeemed people, He requires holiness, as the Corinthian assembly had to learn.

The gross immorality that is associated with both the female and the male prostitute (or 'sodomite') is wholly unacceptable to a holy God, v. 17. God would repel any that would bring the proceeds of immorality into His house, v. 18. The gods of the nations around Israel might find that surprising, but any Israelite knew that they were to be holy as He is holy, Lev. 11. 44; 19. 2; 20. 7; 1 Pet. 1. 16. The same high standards are to be upheld in our day, so that where there was a breach of the divine requirement to be holy, Paul instructs, 'Put away from among yourselves that wicked person', 1 Cor. 5. 13. God would require of them any deviation from His demands.

The second demand in our section relates to vows. In a desire to please God in earnest, honest devotion, the Israelite was permitted to vow a vow of devotion. So untrustworthy is the flesh that even that kind of desire the law hedges around with caution. Ecclesiastes chapter 5 warns against vowing and then trying to retract it by claiming it was a mistake. Heaven heard and heaven would require it. The God of the house of God would require it.

The third requirement relates to how a brother was to be treated. No one was to lend another money at exorbitant rates, vv. 19-20, 'supposing that godliness is a way of gain', 1 Tim. 6. 5 RV. And, although they might eat of, they were not to exploit, a brother's bounty, vv. 24-25. Paul by the Spirit would write that each was to eat his own bread, 2 Thess. 3. 12; otherwise the Lord would require it of any associated with His house.

December 2nd

Deuteronomy 24. 1-4

A BILL OF DIVORCEMENT

The Lord Jesus exposed the background to these verses as the hardness of men's hearts, Matt. 19. 8. Here are emotions so different from those celebrated in popular songs – the husband can find nothing to please in his newly-wed wife, v. 1, and can hate his wife, v. 3. Indeed, the noun 'uncleanness', v. 1, on which the heartless man puts away his wife does not point to her having been immoral but more likely to something ceremonial. So distasteful is the new wife to this hard-hearted man that he is not prepared to wait even a few days until she is no longer unclean, and does not consummate the marriage. The woman would suffer unimaginable pain in being sent away with a bill of divorcement.

The passage indicates that she may marry another man, v. 2. The hardness of his heart is such that he hates her. The Hebrew verb translated 'hate' is not used of strong detestation, but of cold indifference. The case outlined shows the woman has encountered the same problem again – hardness of heart.

What is to become of this poor woman? Will she be subjected to similar treatment again, perhaps at the hand of the man who first suggested that she was unclean, even if he might claim that circumstances have changed and she is no longer defiled, v. 4? The Lord who cared about the widow and the orphan, vv. 19-21; also Deut. 10. 18; 14. 29; 16. 11, also cared about this poor rejected woman. She is not to return to a home where rejection might again be her portion.

Verse 4 indicates that, before Christ came, matters related to home-life were noted by God. If the sins considered here were to happen, Israel would lose their tenure of the land. Today, the New Testament requirement on a husband is that he love his wife, Eph. 5. 25; Col. 3. 19, and give 'honour unto his wife, as unto the weaker vessel', 1 Pet. 3. 7. The Christian has the supreme example in Christ who 'also loved the church, and gave himself for it', Eph. 5. 25. He would not act out of hardness of heart, nor lead him or his wife into an adulterous relationship, Matt. 5. 32; 19. 9. He would ever have before him that 'from the beginning it was not so', Matt. 19. 8.

Deuteronomy 24. 5-13

OBSERVE DILIGENTLY

'Giving all diligence' was a responsibility Peter laid upon Christians, 2 Pet. 1. 5. He required every fibre of the being to be intent on developing in the faith. A similar commitment was expected of those Moses instructed by the Spirit, v. 8.

The obligations upon those first listeners are two: concern for the newly-wed wife, and compassion towards one's brethren especially in respect of one that is poor, perhaps so poor that he has borrowed from his brother. These verses regulate conduct: the conduct of the husband whose wife needs to be *cheered*, v. 5, and the poor who might be *cheated* by the powerful creditor, vv. 6-7, 10-13. Verses 8-9 are a parenthesis, warning against any breach of the fraternal code.

The infinite care of the Creator is evident in verse 5. The young bride is missing family and the home where she had grown up. Whether in times of war or peace, her husband is to attach priority to her happiness. Success in battle might bring the husband recognition as a mighty man of valour. Success in business might also bring prestige. But more important is domestic peace. In a period of marriage breakdowns, how wise the counsel even for the twenty-first century!

The heartless extortioner is also under scrutiny. In verse 6 the prohibition is against taking the millstones that ground the family's corn in case they starved. Other forms of extortion are mentioned: kidnapping, and slave trading would bring the sentence of death. In verses 10-13, the security for a loan could not be taken from the home without the borrower's consent; it might be a man's cloak. After sundown, as the temperature dropped, the lack of that cloak might injure the poor man's health. A caring God would not hold the moneylender guiltless.

But why is Miriam's leprosy mentioned? She did not lend money nor extort high interest rates. She would seem to have been the ringleader in maligning her brother, and consequently she was smitten with leprosy, Num. 12. 10. The rich lender might think he can avoid Israel's court charging him with the sins listed in our verses, but Israel's God is to be feared; He may visit the offender with leprosy. Let him observe diligently.

December 4th

Deuteronomy 24. 14-22

THOU WAST A BONDMAN IN EGYPT

Inscribed in the hearts of succeeding generations was the tragic story of how their fathers had been sorely afflicted in Egypt, when there arose a king that knew not Joseph, Acts 7. 18. How could they forget with the reminders that each Passover season brought? But, in later years, the cries of the bondslaves of 1500 BC were easily drowned out in the circumstances of daily life. The call to remember is, therefore, heard at verses 18 and 22 in respect of employer-employee relationships, and then of good harvests and the increased prosperity they brought the rich.

The examples which Moses was guided to include were not hypothetical. Writing to Christians 1500 years later, James also deals with the oppression of rich men, Jas. 2. 6. He identifies as sin the withholding of day labourers' wages who have reaped the harvest fields, Jas. 5. 4. Indeed, 'the cries of them which have reaped' were reaching the ears of the Lord of hosts. At verse 15, Moses underscores that any such charge would be heard and the guilty landowner pronounced guilty by the court of heaven, whether the labourer was an Israelite or a foreigner. Israel's courts might not choose to intervene in respect of the foreigner or the orphan or the widow, but heaven saw their oppression as sin, vv. 16-17. To avoid such sins, they should remember Egypt and the lash their forefathers smarted under.

For the disadvantaged, the increased prosperity of the oppressing rich would be particularly vexing. But the Spirit does not address their grievances here. Through Moses, He lays upon the landowners increased responsibilities. It would not have been illegal to share the bounty with the poor, but the law now required that needy groups be afforded opportunity to work in the fields within the limits set out in verses 19-21. They would be able to glean after the most of the harvest had been gathered. The memory of Egypt would ensure this charitable attitude would remain.

We too should 'remember that ... in time past' we were 'the servants of sin', but now being 'made free', we 'became the servants of righteousness', Eph. 2. 11; Rom. 6. 17-18. Such reflections should ensure that we remember the poor, Gal. 2. 10.

December 5th
Deuteronomy 25. 1-10

HIM THAT HATH HIS SHOE LOOSED

The chapter deals with the more settled conditions Israel was to know once they entered the land of promise when 'brethren (would) dwell together', v. 5. Verses 1-3 anticipate that controversies may arise and demand that these be disposed of righteously, v. 1. Equally important is the demand that the sentence meted out to the guilty should not be excessive, lest the guilty brother should seem vile in the eyes of the one the court justified – a precept not without its relevance today.

Alongside that precept is one about the treatment of the oxen charged with separating the grain from the chaff by laboriously treading back and forward over the harvested sheaves laid out on hard ground; their wages were to be some of that grain. Paul states that even more important than ensuring the oxen were humanely treated was the lesson for our day. 'For our sakes' it was written that we might see why a servant of the Lord should be supported, that those who 'preach the gospel should live of the gospel', 1 Cor. 9. 14.

When 'brethren (would) dwell together' in the land, childlessness would be a problem. It could lead to land passing out of the family altogether. The institution of Levirate marriage was to address that difficulty. The word 'levirate' is from the Latin word *levir*, 'a husband's brother', who was required to marry his deceased brother's wife that she might bear a son in her deceased husband's name. The practice had continued from the days of the patriarchs, Gen. 38. 8. Ruth was also childless on the death of her first husband. In her case there was no brother-in-law to become her husband, and so the nearest kinsman was sought. Her case was further complicated by the question of debt surrounding the dead man's estate, Ruth 4. 1-13. That record has resonance with us; we see this passage too as being 'for us'. It tells of One who came near to redeem Israel, but, for us Gentiles, it tells of One on whom by nature we had no call. Out of love, and not as required by law, He willingly redeemed us. We honour Him upon whom men spat without cause, and give Him the name above every name, not the name 'him that hath his shoe loosed', v. 10.

Deuteronomy 25. 11-19

REMEMBER WHAT AMALEK DID UNTO THEE

The terms of the Mosaic Law disabused the Israelite of every notion that all would be perfect in the land. There would be strife, v. 11, unfair trading, vv. 13-15, and enemies, perhaps the cruellest of whom is mentioned at verse 17.

The punishment to be meted out on Amalek, that inveterate enemy of Israel, was to be severe: he was to be blotted out, v. 19. But the stern denunciations of evil and the sentences to be passed upon the guilty of Israel in the earlier verses 11-17 remind us that God is no respecter of persons. 'For as many as have sinned without law shall also perish without law: and as many as have sinned in the law shall be judged by the law', Rom. 2. 12. How delighted we are that today Christ receives sinful men, whether they have sinned without law or in the law!

The indecent behaviour of the woman whose husband was wrestling with another fell below the acceptable standards the law expected of a woman. The use of a heavier weight, when buying rather than selling, was wholly unjust against a brother, so much so that the perpetrator might be cut away in early life, v. 15, a punishment worse than losing a hand, v. 12. Amalek's actions also had fallen below the acceptable standards God expected of one nation in conflict with another, for Amalek cut off the stragglers ('the hindmost') when the army was marching, and attacked 'the faint and the weary', v. 18. These crimes were not to be committed in the future; these were the very sins Israel had experienced from Amalek some forty years before this time. Tired of the journey and slackening in their discipline, Israel had suffered much from Amalek, Exod. 17. 8-16.

Israel would have more immediate battles to fight before she would be able to eliminate Amalek; indeed from generation to generation they would be a constant threat. Saul and David faced that foe. But Amalek was no more troublesome than the foe Christians face daily. The flesh is like Amalek in that it is always liable to attack, especially when our zeal and devotion are flagging. We learn from this passage why we are to mercilessly crucify 'the flesh with the affections and lusts', Gal. 5. 24. We dare not forget that lesson, v. 19.

December 7th

Deuteronomy 26. 1-11

THE FIRST OF ALL THE FRUIT OF THE EARTH

Five times in these verses the Israelite is reminded that the land he inhabited was not the fruit of military victory but a gift from God. Gratitude was therefore to be shown fittingly in the basket of firstfruits he was to bring to the priest. But that gratitude was to be rooted even more deeply than in the land gifted and the fruits it produced. It was to be rooted in the mercy once shown to their ancestor Jacob and, supremely, in redemption from Egypt, vv. 5-9.

Clearly, Israel's Creator and Redeemer knew the fickleness of the individuals that would comprise that nation over the years they would occupy Canaan. They would be prone to forget, so each individual male was obliged to bring his basket of firstfruits each year, lest he forget. He was to confess, 'I profess . . . I am come unto the country . . . I have brought (that) which thou, O Lord, hast given me', vv. 3, 10, whilst owning in the plural pronouns that, as a nation, God had richly blessed them. In other ceremonies, national gratitude would be acknowledged, Lev. 23. 1-14. Here, the emphasis is on individual gratitude.

The same God also knew how easily the Christian could forget, and so the Lord Himself initiated the simple remembrance gathering, Luke 22. 19-20. Under the Spirit's guidance, Paul set out in more detail what assemblies of the Lord's people were to do on the first day of the week, 1 Cor. 11. 23-29. Paul also expected that Christians, like himself, would have personal gratitude towards 'the Son of God, who loved me, and gave himself for me', Gal. 2. 20.

In the declaration the offerer made before the Lord, he spoke about his father Jacob as 'a Syrian ready to perish', v. 5. The phrase indicates Jacob's Aramaean links and the perils of his nomadic way of life to which he had been called. In mercy Jehovah had preserved him to the end of his long life; even at that stage, with famine threatening, there was for him provision in Egypt, the land from which ultimately the nation was delivered. How thankful the offerer should have been for the mercy and power that provided for Jacob *in* Egypt, and deliverance to his seed *from* Egypt.

December 8th

Deuteronomy 26. 12-19

LOOK DOWN FROM THY HOLY HABITATION

Even the casual reader of this chapter would observe that Israel's God intended that communion with Himself be sustained. At verses 3, and 5-10, the Israelite was given words to use as he offered his firstfruits, that his God might hear his voice, vv. 13-15. It was not enough to be seen to do, God desired to hear his voice tell what he was doing. Nor is it different today.

The event to which these verses refer is 'the year of tithing', v. 12. It occurred in the third year. Some think that third year was the third year they were in the land, but more likely the statute relates to every third year, cf. Amos 4. 4. They were to take the opportunity to share their inheritance with the Levite, who had no inheritance; to share their home with the stranger away from home; to provide fatherly care to the fatherless, and protection to the widow, who has no recourse to a husband. But they were also to tell their God that they had done so. Surely He would know without being told! He so instructed because He loved to hear their voices.

There may, of course, have been another reason for this commandment, vv. 13, 14, 16, 17. Among the statements the offerer would make was the confirmation that he had kept nothing back that God was claiming, 'I have brought away the hallowed things out of mine house', v. 13; 'I have not eaten thereof', v. 14. Knowing God to be omniscient, it would be unlikely that a man would deliberately lie to God Himself. He might lie to another man, but surely not to God. Sadly, we are able to recall that a lie to a saint in the presence of God is a 'lie to the Holy Ghost', Acts 5. 3. The divine commandment delivered by Moses required them to confirm that they had obeyed and, unlike Ananias and Sapphira, they had kept nothing back that they had given to God. There would be circumstances that might make demands upon them, mourning being one. But would a man rob God to meet his obligations even in a time of mourning, Mal. 3. 8?

Obedience might be costly, if they were to be gracious to others, but there would be recompense, for the Lord would look down from His holy habitation and bless them and their land.

December 9th

Deuteronomy 27. 1-8

WRITE UPON THE STONES THIS LAW

These verses are part of Israel's preparation for the land, a land flowing with milk and honey. They are reminded for the fourth time in this book that it had been promised to their fathers, v. 3. The land was to be one in which the law given by Moses was to be prominent from the moment of entrance. Great stones would be erected on which would be inscribed a permanent and public record of the complete law, v. 3. The record was also to be 'very plain', v. 8.

Israel was not only to see these words as a list of demands upon them; they were also to see them as the terms of a covenant, for which they were to be grateful. For that reason they were to build an altar on Mount Ebal and offer there burnt offerings and peace offerings. They knew from Leviticus 1 and 6 that the burnt offering was wholly for the Lord and so was consumed upon the altar, but that they could share in the peace offering. They were to eat that offering with joy, v. 7. Sadly, as a nation they were to know little of the joy of obedience and much of the bitterness that rebellion against God can bring. The New Testament maintains that link between obedience and joy, so the Philippians who obeyed, even in Paul's absence, could 'rejoice in the Lord alway', Phil. 3. 1; 4. 4.

In providing instruction for activities on Mount Ebal, God instructs how the altar was to be built. Unlike the brazen and golden altars with which at least the nation's priests were familiar, this altar was to be of whole stones, vv. 5, 6. No stonemason's skills were to shape it into an appealing artefact; no 'iron tool' was to be used in the process, v. 5. The thoughtful would acknowledge that the basis of their blessing was not in their own ingenuity or skill, but in the love of their God. All that was required of them was obedience.

Unusually, 'Moses with the elders commanded the people', v. 1. Those elders would outlive Moses and teach that the pathway of obedience begins with writing the law on those stones, thus making it their own. In our case, the Spirit writes on the fleshy tables of our heart that we might be obedient, who 'have renounced the hidden things of dishonesty', 2 Cor. 4. 2.

December 10th
Deuteronomy 27. 9-26
ALL THE PEOPLE SHALL SAY, AMEN

Few passages of scripture are as disturbing as the section before us. The twelve tribes of Israel were to be assembled on two sides of a narrow ravine, so that each group of six would be within earshot of the other. The group descended from Jacob's two principal wives were on Mount Gerizim to bless the people, the other group, the descendants of the maid servants, on Mount Ebal to curse. If both the voices of cursing and blessing could be heard in our chapter, the reader might still have felt uneasy as to the consequences. However, only the curses are heard, 'And all the people shall say, Amen'. The reader is left with the impression that under the law Israel would prove disobedient and experience more of the curses than the blessings, as Paul was to conclude, 'as many as are of the works of the law are under the curse', Gal. 3. 10, quoting verse 26 of this chapter.

It would appear that Moses and 'the priests the Levites', v. 9, took their place in the valley between the two rocky mountains. Doubtless both blessings and curses were uttered, but only the record of the curses is given.

The curses pronounced that day were twelve in number, a further pointer to the future state of that people whose pledge was uttered in those words, 'And all the people shall say, Amen'. The curses, in the main, reflect the Decalogue and other principal commandments. The twelfth sums up the total obedience required by the law, 'Cursed be he that confirmeth not all the words of this law to do them', v. 26. We can understand why James said, 'whosoever shall keep the whole law, and yet offend in one point, he is guilty of all', Jas. 2. 10.

After our Lord's sacrificial death and resurrection, a number of Jews came to own that every conscious act of transgression subjects the sinner to the curse of God, from which none but He who has become a curse for us can possibly deliver us, Acts 13. 39; Gal. 3. 10, 13. The chilling reality of this historical event makes the more evident the hopelessness of law-keeping as a means of salvation. We bless God for a Saviour who saves not by works of righteousness that we have done, but according to His mercy, Titus 3. 5.

December 11th

Deuteronomy 28. 1-14

BLESSED SHALT THOU BE

The securing of the blessings detailed in these verses would have set Israel apart from every nation at any point in history. They would have been 'high above all nations', v. 1; invincible in conflict, v. 7; feared for their identification with the Lord their God, vv. 9-10; the financial support of the poorer nations, and, as the leading nation of the world, the head, the source of counsel, succour and safety to the weaker nations around them, v. 13. What an enviable position to occupy!

The blessings listed were among the benefits the covenant with God would bring them. All of them would be poured out upon them from the very windows of heaven, v. 12, Mal. 3. 10. The covenant into which they had willingly entered was conditional. It required of them hearing diligently the voice of the Lord their God, vv. 1, 13, and keeping His commandments, vv. 9, 13, 14. Hearing and keeping are two parts of the same exercise of obedience. The hearing ear and the consistent walk, that turns not to the right hand or the left, v. 14, are essential to the enjoyment of blessings set out in these verses. Hearing and keeping seem to ask so little in exchange for so much.

That Israel never enjoyed what God intended for them indicates that without a work of God in the soul and the indwelling Spirit to empower, neither nation nor individual can truly say, 'that we keep his commandments: and his commandments are not grievous', 1 John 5. 3. Every child of God today has the potential to be obedient and so enjoy, not the material blessings of these verses, but 'every spiritual blessing in the heavenly places in Christ', Eph. 1. 3 RV. Indeed, says the apostle John, the measure of obedience expected of Israel is the very proof of reality, 'By this we know that we love the children of God, when we love God, and keep his commandments', 1 John 5. 2.

As there were false gods, like the gods of the Amorites they would encounter in the land of Canaan to allure Israel into disobedience, v. 14, so the world today offers much to harden the heart, stop the ears and close the eyes lest there be understanding and obedience. But its riches or popularity never enable any to hear the words of our verses, 'Blessed shalt thou be'.

December 12th

Deuteronomy 28. 15- 24

CURSED SHALT THOU BE

These grave verses tell in unambiguous terms the results of disobedience to the Lord's commandments. Six specific curses are
detailed, each devastating in import, only to be followed by a
series of statements which indicate that the Lord Himself would
be active in bringing to bear upon them for 'every transgression
and disobedience . . . a just recompense of reward', Heb. 2. 2.

The sobering consideration associated with the six specific
curses is not the pain of each but the cumulative effect of all
six upon them, for 'all these curses shall come upon thee, and
overtake thee', v. 15. How very different their portion would
have been, if wholehearted obedience marked them! Obedience
would bring 'all these blessings', v. 2. The six blessings, vv. 3-6,
are not exactly ordered as the corresponding curses, vv. 16-19;
only the second and third are interchanged. The lesson was
plain: obedience brings blessing, disobedience cursing.

God had not been silent. Ringing in their ears was the voice
of the Lord their God, v. 15. How serious to fail to respond when
God speaks! To be obedient demanded diligence, v. 1. However,
the noun 'diligence' does not occur in verse 15. Anything less
than complete diligence would only lead to disobedience with
all its ruinous consequences. Even Christians are expected to
'shew the same diligence to the full assurance of hope unto
the end', Heb. 6. 11, and to add to their faith virtue and other
God-honouring characteristics, 2 Pet. 1. 5-7.

Not only had God spoken, v. 15, but He would act, vv. 20-68.
His dealings would not only be providential, as the six curses
might be indicating, but He would engage personally in sending, v. 20; making, vv. 21, 24; smiting, v. 22; causing them to be
smitten, v. 25, and other activities detailed in the remainder of
the chapter. Indeed, the chapter is demanding an answer to
Joshua's challenge, 'Choose you', Josh. 24. 15. Would they be
wise and choose obedience? Would they say, 'Better to hear,
"Blessed shalt thou be", than "Cursed shalt thou be"'?

It is the same today! God has called us to inherit blessing,
1 Pet. 3. 9. He will not stand idly by while we live below 'the
fulness of the blessing of the gospel', Rom. 15. 29.

THE LORD SHALT SMITE THEE

The covenant that offered to Israel the unparalleled blessings unfolded at the beginning of this chapter was to bring grave penalties in its breach. The hand that was smiting would be unmistakably that of their God. There would be aggressive enemies whose visitations would cause a great loss of life, vv. 25, 48, the dominating immigrant, the nation that would take their king into captivity, v. 36 (as Assyria and Babylon would do), and a particularly terrorizing nation from afar with whom they would have to contend, whose prolonged siege would reduce the nation to cannibalism, vv. 49-58. But each blow they struck would be the Lord's hand in discipline. So too were the various providential judgements, whether the 'botch (or boil) of Egypt', v. 27, cf. Exod. 9. 9-11, or some other disease or drought or famine or marital breakdown, vv. 27-35, 38-42. In Egypt, their distress caused the Lord to bare His arm in deliverance; now that arm is against them because of their disobedience.

What is equally telling is the effect of the nation's distress on the onlooker, whether the nations around them or the exercised soul within their own borders. Israel under blessing would probably arouse jealousy, but under discipline it would be 'an astonishment, a proverb . . . a byword . . . a sign and . . . a wonder', vv. 37, 46. At the height of the nation's achievements, Solomon would be warned in these very terms, 1 Kgs. 9. 7. At the lowest point to which they were to sink, Jeremiah would use similar terms, when Nebuchadnezzar was about to remove them into captivity, Jer. 24. 9. Even David gave 'great occasion to the enemies of the Lord to blaspheme', 2 Sam. 12. 14.

How sad when our conduct causes the name of the Lord to be blasphemed! How sad when men wonder that the hand of the Lord is disciplining us! How much more serious when we fail to be 'exercised thereby', Heb. 12. 11! God's desire for Israel was that they be obedient to Him and so enjoy great blessing at His hand. He has larger designs for our profit – 'that we might be partakers of his holiness' and produce 'the peaceable fruit of righteousness', Heb. 12. 10, 11. We know that His smiting us is the Father dealing in love with His sons.

December 14th

Deuteronomy 28. 49-62

A NATION OF FIERCE COUNTENANCE

Writing almost a thousand years after this chapter was penned, Ezekiel reports that God will send His 'four sore judgements' on Judah – the sword, famine, dangerous beasts and pestilence, Ezek. 14. 21. All of these 'sore judgements' are included in the warnings of the last chapters of Deuteronomy. These verses deal with a particularly ruthless enemy, v. 50, and his use of the sword, but also with long-lasting diseases, vv. 59-62.

Because of Israel's disobedience, a nation would be sent of God to chastize Israel. It would not be Philistia or Egypt, but a nation that would come swiftly from afar, a nation that did not speak one of the Canaanite languages with which Israel was familiar, v. 49. It would not be aware that a divine commission was being undertaken and yet would fulfil its commission without fear or favour. To Israel, it would be 'strong of face', that is, 'pitiless' in the execution of its purpose, v. 50. Jeremiah uses very similar language of Babylon, Jer. 5. 15-17, which nation is probably in view here. Certainly, it devastated the land and laid siege to Jerusalem. However, the Romans also besieged Jerusalem and were even more destructive on entering the city.

The effects of a long siege are presented as a warning to Israel. There would be cannibalism, v. 53, a prophecy fulfilled when Babylon, Rome and Assyria laid siege to Israel's cities, 2 Kgs. 6. 28-29; Lam. 2. 20, 22; 4. 10. The most refined of men and women, who had grown up in luxurious conditions, would stoop to that dreadful sin, vv. 45-57. Within those once-favoured circles, the closest of relationships would be despised and competition for human flesh would arise. The secret sin of the young mother would be eating her own child before a near relative could seize the child.

The threatened sword in the hand of the fierce nation and the threatened pestilences known, v. 60, and unknown, v. 61, were to the end that the 'glorious and fearful name, the Lord thy God' might be feared, v. 58. Only under the shadow of His wing could there be safety from that nation of a fierce countenance and the many diseases that would decimate the nation that once had been as 'the stars of heaven for multitude', v. 62.

December 15th

Deuteronomy 28. 63-68

THY LIFE SHALL HANG IN DOUBT BEFORE THEE

The fear of God is the beginning of knowledge and of wisdom, declared Solomon, Prov. 1. 7; 9. 10. He assures us that this kind of fear is a wholesome emotion. But the fear of man can be a paralysing force; this is the message of these distressing verses. Perhaps no people would be more exposed to that paralysing fear than a people transported to a far-off country.

But why was Israel being confronted with stark warnings about mass exile to a foreign land? They were about to embark on securing the land their God had promised them. They were certain that He would fulfil His promise to their father Abraham, but were now being cautioned about presuming to keep that land. They found great joy in contemplating rest in the land, knowing that, having promised, consistency with His own character would demand that their God give them the land. Now they had to consider that a holy God would not allow the defiling of His land without divine retribution following. Consistency with His own character demanded it. Jehovah had rejoiced in giving them the land; He would rejoice in the governmental removal of sinful Israel from the land, v. 63.

The perils of exile would be immense, as Jehovah would pluck them from the land and deliver them over to the false gods that so bewitched them, v. 64. Their evil influence would affect the heart, the eye and the soul, v. 65. Life would be filled with despair, 'thy life shall hang in doubt before thee', v. 66, like some precious ornament on a slender thread. Constantly, they would fear the thread of life breaking. Inconsolable desolation would rob day and night of purpose. They would sigh, 'Would God it were even . . . Would God it were morning!'

With their sin would return bondage, as the ominous mention of Egypt recalls, v. 68. After Jerusalem's destruction by Rome in AD-70, certainly many thousands of Jews were transported to Egypt, there to be sold as slaves. At least partially, that event recalls the warning issued in these verses. The strange reference to a ship might indicate inescapable punishment, from which no man would redeem them. Once again Israel would need to wait for divine intervention.

368

December 16th

Deuteronomy 29. 1-20

YE STAND THIS DAY BEFORE THE LORD

All Israel gathered in Moab. They took their stand before the Lord. On this momentous day, God was making a fresh covenant with the nation as they entered Canaan. At its heart lay the promise, made to the patriarchs, that Israel would be established as God's people and that God Himself would be their God. That promise will receive its final fulfilment for all the people of God in the new heavens and new earth, Rev. 21. 3. This covenant bound the succeeding generations of Israel.

In making the covenant, Moses recounted the Lord's mighty acts in the past. In their liberation from Egypt, the people had seen His power in action. Yet, at a deeper level they had not seen it. Because of their hardness of heart, God had blinded them to the significance of what they had witnessed. Often we also fail to see God's hand at work. Rarely do we hear His voice in the events of life. Thus, we do not take to heart the lessons the Lord is teaching us.

God then addressed the people directly, reminding them that He had led them through the wilderness. Their clothes and their sandals had not worn out. They had no need for bread when God had provided manna, or for wine when He had supplied water from the smitten rock. His miraculous provision had clearly shown Him to be the Lord their God. Moses recalled that Israel had already defeated mighty kings and possessed their land. We also need to remember what great things God has done for us and thus keep His word, 1 Sam. 12. 24.

Danger loomed ahead in the future. The detestable idolatry of the nations would prove a fatal attraction for Israel. The false gods of the twenty-first century are still alluring. We must keep ourselves from idols, 1 John 5. 21. Those who forsook the Lord would be like noxious plants, poisoning the whole nation. Our wrong actions can impact deeply on others, Heb. 12. 15. A solemn sentence is passed on anyone who dares to think himself safe from judgement while living in defiance of God. This is total self-deception, Gal. 6. 7. It can only lead to utter ruin. Our sins still deeply grieve the Lord. Let us seek by His grace to cleanse ourselves from them.

December 17th

Deuteronomy 29. 21-29

WHAT MEANS THE HEAT OF THIS GREAT ANGER?

Surprisingly, it is the Gentiles who will ask this searching question. The nations around Israel will voice it when they see Canaan reduced to ruin. Israel's land will be despoiled. Its landscape will be devastated Fields once fruitful will lie desolate. Canaan will share the fate of the cities of the plain. It will be reduced to a charred, barren wasteland by God's hand. Even her godless neighbours will sense that these calamities are His work of judgement.

The question will receive a ready response. The Lord's anger blazed against His land because His people had broken His covenant. They had forsaken Him to serve other gods. The curses of the covenant had already been pronounced. Now, the Lord had invoked them against disobedient Israel. The people were carried off into exile from their ravaged land.

The key word of the passage is 'anger'. It is used four times. On each occasion it is attributed to God. The Hebrew word vividly pictures vehement emotion. God's anger is not sinful. It is not spiteful or capricious. It expresses His holy revulsion against anything which offends His perfect purity. Sin displeases God. His deep love for His people is wounded by their transgressions. We dare not dismiss the idea of God's anger from our thinking as a relic of a primitive age. Our God is still a consuming fire, Heb. 12. 29.

Our passage ends with some fundamental assertions. All spiritual truth falls into two categories, revealed and unrevealed. God has chosen not to disclose everything about Himself. The element of mystery always remains when we seek to fathom His being and His ways. Nonetheless, He has graciously unveiled to us a vast store of priceless truth in His word. Nothing which we need to understand has been kept covered. Revealed truths 'are ours to value, share and obey', RAYMOND BROWN. We must value the treasures of revelation, they are of infinite worth. We must share them, especially with children and young people. Each succeeding generation should be taught God's word. Above all, we must obey everything that God has commanded us. Divine truth is revealed to be practised.

December 18th

Deuteronomy 30. 1-10

THE LORD THY GOD WILL TURN THY CAPTIVITY

God foresaw that Israel would forsake Him and suffer exile as a result. However, scattering would not be the end of their history. God here gives His people a tremendous promise, which is still unfulfilled. He will bring them back from captivity. He Himself will fetch them home and completely restore their fortunes. Their exile ended, Israel will enjoy blessing and possess their land. This will flow from the Lord's heart of compassion for His people.

The promise is conditional on Israel's genuine repentance. They will reflect on all their bitter experiences and then return to the Lord. This will involve sorrow for the past and a new resolve for the future. They will seek to obey all that God had commanded them with inward sincerity and true commitment.

The promise is reliable because it is made by the Lord Himself. He is utterly dependable and fully able to carry it out. The Lord assumes responsibility for the fulfilment of His own promise entirely. He speaks as the Sovereign One who takes the initiative. He, Himself, will re-gather Israel. Distance is no obstacle and geography no barrier to the Creator of the world. However far His people have been scattered, even to the ends of the earth, He will bring them back to their land. Israel's future restoration will be accomplished by God's mighty power.

The promise is glorious because of the blessings it secures. God will multiply His people more than ever before in their long history. He promises them far more than material benefits. He will grant them inward spiritual cleansing and renewal, the circumcision of the heart. This radical work of grace will change the centre of their whole moral being. They will be fully consecrated to the Lord, loving Him with true devotion and enjoying spiritual vitality. The passage thus anticipates and parallels the glowing prophecies of the new covenant, cf. Jer. 31. 33-34; Ezek. 36. 24-38. God will remove His curses from Israel and place them on their persecutors. He will delight in His people and will rejoice to prosper them. What a wonderful prospect is revealed in this ancient prediction of Israel's future blessing by the Lord their God!

Deuteronomy 30. 11-20

LIFE AND GOOD, AND DEATH AND EVIL

Moses reaches the climax of his address. As the herald of God, he appeals to Israel. He pleads for their wholehearted commitment to the Lord's covenant. He leaves them in no doubt about God's message.

God's message was accessible. It could be easily understood. The Lord's revelation to Israel was not hidden away in some unreachable place. Nor was it placed behind some insuperable barrier. Rather, it was very near them, in their mouth and in their heart. Paul quotes this passage in Romans chapter 10 verses 6 to 8 to show that God asks men and women 'not for some superhuman effort but only for a glad acceptance of His grace in Christ', THOMPSON. Many hearers of the gospel would prefer, like Naaman, to do 'some great thing', 2 Kgs. 5. 13. All that God requires is personal trust in the living Lord Jesus. God's messengers today must ensure that their message is intelligible and relevant to their hearers.

God's message was challenging. It demanded a choice. Moses called for a verdict. In a tender appeal, Moses implored Israel to love the Lord their God, walk in His ways and keep His commandments. 'Choose life', was his soul-stirring call. Today's preachers must also bring their audiences to the point of decision. The aim of Moses' message was that the people should cling to the Lord, holding fast to Him in affection and loyalty. Clinging to the Lord was vital to Israel because He was their life. So, too, Christ is our life, Col. 3. 4. We must hold fast to Him with a steadfast purpose.

God's message was crucial. It had eternal consequences. Israel's destiny hung on their response to this proclamation. Moses laid the stark contrasts of life or death, good or evil and blessing or cursing before them. He called heaven and earth to attest that he had faithfully discharged his trust. Titanic issues turn on the preaching of the gospel today, eternal life or eternal death, 2 Cor. 2. 14-16. Every preacher must seek to be free from the blood of all men by declaring the whole counsel of God, Acts 20. 26-27, and making it clear how much depends on the response to the message.

December 20th

Deuteronomy 31. 1-13

HE WILL NOT FAIL, THEE NOR FORSAKE THEE

Israel faced days of challenge and change. Moses was about to leave the scene. His eventful career, in the palace and the wilderness, was about to end. Ruefully, he recalled that God had barred him from entering Canaan. He would never lead Israel over the Jordan. The people had never known life without Moses. Fear and doubt must have filled their minds. In our passage, the Lord twice gives this outstanding promise. He addresses the nation in verse 6. Then, He addresses Joshua as His chosen successor to Moses in verse 8.

God was not going to abandon His people. As the divine Warrior, He would lead them into Canaan. He would be their Supreme Commander in a campaign of conquest. Israel, then, must be strong and encouraged. They had nothing to fear from the Canaanites. God was to be their companion and their champion. Likewise, the Lord Jesus promised His disciples His presence and protection throughout this present age, Matt. 28. 20.

No doubt Joshua trembled at the thought of standing in the place of Moses. God graciously gave him a personal reassurance of His presence with him. He reminded Joshua that He had called him to lead Israel into their inheritance. The Lord would be by his side in all his endeavours. From such a promise, we too can still take courage and defy our enemies, Rom. 8. 31; Heb. 13. 5-6. Paul knew the strengthening granted by the presence of the Lord Jesus when he stood before Nero, abandoned by his friends, 2 Tim. 4. 16-17.

Not only did Israel have God's presence. They also had His written word. We have the same divine resources. Moses deposited the scrolls of the law with the priests and elders. The law had to be read to all Israel once every seven years. Male and female, old and young, home-born and stranger, all had to gather to hear it proclaimed. The aim of this public reading was that all Israel should fear the Lord and observe what He had taught them. It is still God's desire that all His people should attentively hear and faithfully practice all His word. Thus, our lives will be moulded by Him for His glory.

BE STRONG AND OF A GOOD COURAGE

The Lord makes it clear to Moses that his death was very imminent. At this point, he had to bring Joshua with him to the
tabernacle as there God Himself would inaugurate him as the
new leader of His people. As the successor to Moses, the Lord
was going to commission Joshua publicly.

Joshua faced a demanding task. However, he had been well
trained for his new role by the experiences of life. He had served
with devotion as Moses' right-hand man. With God's help he
had already gained the victory for Israel over Amalek. Along
with Caleb, he had stood for God against the other ten spies, and
indeed the whole nation. All of this preparation was not enough
to qualify him to take the place of Moses. God had also marked
Joshua out publicly as the man of His choice. Moses had just
reminded him of his future task and had assured him of the
divine presence.

Before Joshua was inaugurated, the Lord appeared in the
pillar of cloud. Then, He gave a solemn prediction of Israel's
defection from Himself. After the death of Moses, the people
would ally themselves with the idols of Canaan and bring upon
them God's holy anger. Disaster upon disaster would befall
them. The Lord knew all too well the evil inclination of Israel's
heart before they set foot in Canaan, the land of God's promise
and yet of their coming disloyalty.

These tragic events lay in the future. In the present, the Lord
commissioned Joshua to lead Israel into the land He had sworn
to give them as their own. With all his preparation behind him
and conscious of God's calling, Joshua is encouraged to be strong
and courageous. He needed that word from God with all the
dangers which faced him, not least the character of the people
he was to lead. God gives us the same summons today. To fulfil
our ministry, we must be strong in His power and grace, Eph.
6. 10; 2 Tim. 2. 1. We are called to watch, stand fast and quit
ourselves like men. 1 Cor. 16. 13. We must realize our weakness
in order to draw on the strength which God supplies. Like
Joshua, may each of us know God's hand of blessing upon us,
enabling us to accomplish our own unique service for Him.

December 22nd
Deuteronomy 31. 24-30

THE LAW IS A WITNESS AGAINST THEE

Moses had yet more to do before his ministry was finally over. He had carried out God's charge to write the song of witness and teach it to the people, v. 22. Now, he must arrange to deposit the written law of God with the Levites. The sacred scrolls were to be laid beside the Ark of the Covenant. The tables of the Ten Commandments had already been deposited inside that sacred chest, Exod. 40. 20. The ark was God's throne, the symbol of His sovereign rule. Thus, the royal law was closely linked with the throne of God in Israel.

That law, inside the ark and beside it, stood as a witness against Israel. The nation is addressed as an individual to emphasize its unity. The law's true function was always negative. It was given to demonstrate that men sin and are, by nature, sinners. It stamps the label of transgression on all evil and reveals sin in its true colours as manifest rebellion against the Sovereign Ruler. In itself, the law is holy, just and good, Rom. 7. 12. However, it was weak through the flesh, Rom. 8. 3. The material on which it had to work, sinful human nature, was radically defective. The law could not communicate the spiritual power needed to fulfil its demands, Gal. 3. 21. All that it could do was to condemn. It could neither justify nor sanctify. How grateful we should be that justification comes through faith alone, apart from the works of the law, Rom. 3. 28. How important to grasp that it is only through the Holy Spirit's empowering that the righteous requirement of the law can be fulfilled, Rom. 8. 4.

Moses was only too aware, from his own bitter experience, of Israel's tragic record of rebellion against the Lord. Time and time again that spirit had been manifest in the wilderness. Their opposition to Moses was truly opposition to the God who had appointed him. They had been stubborn in resisting God's demands and unresponsive to His grace. Moses warned Israel that all of this would become more evident after his death. The song he had written would confirm the witness of the law against them by showing that they would abandon God's ways and provoke Him to anger. We cannot defy God with impunity.

AS THE APPLE OF HIS EYE

The song of Moses presents a panorama of Israel's history. The aged leader begins by calling heaven and earth to hear his words of spiritual refreshment. He proclaims the name of the Lord, His revelation of Himself, as he calls his hearers to celebrate God's greatness. The Lord is perfect in His attributes and all His ways. He is utterly faithful, wholly just and totally truthful. Yet Israel, in their perversity and foolishness, had already rejected Him despite all His fatherly care.

Moses reminds them of God's election. His entire programme for the nations centres on Israel. He rules the world with their interests in mind. He settled earth's boundaries to secure sufficient territory for them. Best of all, they were His special treasure and distinctive inheritance.

Because Israel was so precious to Him, the Lord had protected them throughout the wilderness journey. He had enclosed them like a walled garden. He had taught them by His law. In the striking simile of our text, He had kept them as the 'apple of his eye'. In Hebrew, the apple, or pupil, is termed 'the little man' because we see a miniature of ourselves in another person's eye. The pupil is the most sensitive part of the eye, in itself our most precious organ. The body has an instinctive mechanism to defend the pupil from all harm. So the Lord shields His people. Centuries later, He declared that he who dared to touch Israel touched the apple of His own eye, Zech. 2. 8. Individually, David claimed the same protection, Ps. 17. 8. So can we!

In the desert, Israel had often seen the mother eagle, stirring up her nest, encouraging her young to fly and gently saving the eaglets from falling as they learned to soar. So God had used the trials of their wanderings to train them for their destiny as His people. The Lord had been their Shepherd as He had led them towards Canaan. Moses looks forward to the conquest of the land. He recounts that God's care for His people would not cease when they reached their inheritance. There, God would shower prosperity upon them. All that Israel would enjoy resulted from the protection and provision of her God.

December 24th
Deuteronomy 32. 15-44

THEIR ROCK IS NOT AS OUR ROCK

The Lord lavishly showered prosperity on Israel in Canaan. The nation, described by their name Jeshurun, the upright one, responded in rebellion. They became self-sufficient. They used the gifts but scorned the Giver. Worse, they embraced novel deities in place of the Lord. They began to worship the demons whose sinister power lay behind their lifeless idols. God, the loving parent of the nation, was forgotten. Grieved and provoked, He hid His face from Israel. In judgement, He brought disasters upon them. Famine, pestilence, wild animals and massacre were His arrows of destruction. Indeed their idolatry merited their obliteration from the earth. In grace, God refrained from utterly destroying Israel, lest their foes claimed the credit for their ruin. God thus hints that His final purpose is their preservation and deliverance.

Humiliating defeat was often the fate of Israel's armies, even when they out-numbered their enemies. Lacking all insight, they did not discern that it was the Lord's hand that had surrendered them to disaster. Sadly, they did not grasp that their calamities were the judgements of their offended God. They put their trust in the false gods of their neighbours. Idols became their rock of defence. They were not even pebbles, far less rocks. The true Rock of Israel was the Lord Himself. He is totally dependable and grants impregnable security to those who trust Him. The gods on whom apostate Israel relied were nothing in comparison to Him. So are the God substitutes of the twenty-first century. They cannot deliver in life's crises. Israel's defeats foreshadowed greater disasters in the future. The Lord would unleash His holy vengeance upon them.

Yet, that will not be the end of their story. At the last God will vindicate His people. He will have compassion on them when they abandon their self-reliance. As the unique Sovereign, He will heal and restore the remnant of Israel and pour out dreadful judgement on all His enemies. As the song concludes, Moses invites the nations to join Israel in praising the Lord who provides atonement for His land and His people. His purposes of grace and government will be fulfilled.

December 25th

Deuteronomy 32. 45-52

THOU SHALT SEE THE LAND

His song concluded, Moses charged Israel to set their hearts on all the words that he had taught them and to teach them to their children. God demands whole-hearted obedience to His word from His people. This is the message of Deuteronomy. We do not live by bread alone, but by every word which proceeds from the mouth of God, Deut. 8. 3. Scripture is certainly not a futile word. The Lord Himself is the life of His people, Deut. 30. 20. So is His word. The words of scripture are our spiritual bloodstream. Our chief aim should be to know and obey God, through knowing and obeying His word. Only then can we know spiritual prosperity.

On the very same day, God gave Moses his final instructions. He had to climb Mount Nebo, overlooking the Dead Sea, to view Canaan from afar and to die on the summit. God's government did not permit Moses to enter the land of promise. His grace did permit him to see it 'from a distance', v. 52 NIV. Unknown to Moses, he was going to stand on its soil in the distant future. On the Mount of Transfiguration, he would appear beside the promised Prophet like himself, Deut. 18. 15, to whom his writings faithfully witnessed, John 5. 46.

God had passed this tragic sentence on Moses because of disobedience to His word. At Meribah Kadesh, the Lord had expressly commanded Moses to speak to a rock, so that water could flow abundantly from it to meet the needs of Israel. Moses did not carry out God's instruction to the letter. Instead, frustrated by the rebellion of the people, he struck the rock twice with his rod, Num. 20. 7-13. He did what he thought best, not what God had directed. There and then, the solemn judgement was pronounced which was now being executed. Moses had failed to honour the holiness of God. He had not reverenced Him as He deserved. What a price he paid! We too will suffer loss at the judgement seat of Christ for our disobedience.

God prizes obedience above all else we can give Him, 1 Sam. 15. 22. May we carry out all He requires of us, empowered by His Spirit, seeking to honour and please Him in everything by obeying His word.

December 26th

Deuteronomy 33. 1-7

YEA, HE LOVED THE PEOPLE

The benedictions on the tribes form the testament of Moses. These are blessings 'flowing from the very heart of the God of Israel', C. H. MACKINTOSH. Jacob had blessed his sons, the ancestors of the tribes, almost 500 years earlier. He had dwelt on their failures. Moses entirely omits them. God's grace had triumphed over human sin. The central declaration of these last words of Moses is that God loves His people, v. 3. Divine love is timeless and unchanging. One of the great themes of Deuteronomy is God's love for Israel. It lay behind their election and the exodus, Deut. 4. 37. It was unconditional. The Lord had loved His people, simply because He had chosen to do so, Deut. 7. 6-8. The Lord's love for the patriarchs continued to their descendants, and made them His own people, Deut. 10. 15. It was God's love which had turned the curse of Balaam into a blessing, Deut. 23. 5. The tribes were reminded of God's abiding love, as they prepared to enter Canaan. We can have no greater encouragement than to know that God loves us with an everlasting love.

The Lord had displayed His glory at Sinai. His majesty had blazed like the rising sun of a desert dawn when He came down to meet His people. Accompanied by hosts of angels, He had communicated His law to Moses. In turn, he entrusted the divine word to Israel. That word had become their prized possession. They had sat at the Lord's feet, receiving His instruction. As His holy ones, the people were in God's mighty hands, secure in the grasp of the Lord. At the great assembly of Israel's tribes, the Lord had manifested Himself as their King, the only ruler of His people. The glorious God who was the lover of Israel had become their instructor, guardian, and sovereign.

Reuben and Judah were the first tribes blessed by Moses. He implored God that Reuben would remain as an independent tribe and not fall into extinction. For the warrior tribe of Judah, he sought the Lord's help when they cried to Him in battle and strength for their hands. In the wars of Canaan to come, Moses knew his people would need God's help. Have we sought His help today in the spiritual conflict?

December 27th
Deuteronomy 33. 8-11

BLESS, LORD, HIS SUBSTANCE

Moses now blesses his own tribe of Levi. They were 'devoted to the Lord's service', RAYMOND BROWN. The priesthood belonged exclusively to Levi. The rest of the tribe had other duties in the tabernacle and its worship. Levi was entitled to look to the nation as a whole for material support.

The Lord had entrusted the Urim and the Thummim to the high priest. He carried them in his breastplate, Exod. 28. 30; Lev. 8. 8. These lights and perfections were an oracle by which God made His will known to Israel, Num. 27. 21. Today, such miraculous guidance is neither needed nor provided. Christians are indwelt by the Holy Spirit. God has given us His completed word in scripture. His Spirit leads us primarily through that word. In the choices which life presents, we are called to make mature decisions, prayerfully and wisely. We must patiently wait for the leading of God's providence and seek His glory in everything.

The priests and Levites had to live with the Lord's interests as their chief concern, above the closest earthly ties. In one of Israel's darkest days, the men of Levi had faithfully displayed that spirit by carrying out God's judgement on idolaters despite family relationships, Exod. 32. 26-29. That service had gained them the priesthood, Deut. 10. 8. The Lord Jesus calls us to recognize His supremacy over the closest family ties, Luke 14. 26.

The priests had to present instruction from the Lord to the people. They had to keep His word safe and teach it faithfully, Lev. 10. 11. Israel looked to them for direction and example, Mal. 2. 5-6. Christians also need to be taught the content of their belief and the behaviour it demands. The priests also presented worship from the people to the Lord by offering incense and placing the sacrifices on His altar. All Christians are privileged to be priests to God, 1 Pet. 2. 5. We are called to offer Him the continual sacrifices of praise and prayer with our lips and service in our lives, Heb. 13. 15-16. Above all, we must present our bodies to Him as living sacrifices, Rom. 12. 1. Moses invoked the Lord's blessing on the substance and service of Levi. May He bless the holy and royal priesthood of today.

December 28th

Deuteronomy 33. 12-17

HIM THAT WAS SEPARATED FROM HIS BRETHREN

God's blessings on the descendents of Rachel are now presented. The benediction on the tribe of Benjamin is exquisite. Benjamin was never a populous tribe. David calls them 'little Benjamin', Ps. 68. 27. Nonetheless, they are 'the beloved of the Lord', v. 12. We can have no greater privilege than a personal assurance that God Himself loves us. Benjamin would enjoy daily safety and constant shelter by remaining in the Lord's presence. He would dwell between His shoulders. This is 'a memorable picture of a loving and thoughtful father carrying his exhausted child home on his shoulders', RAYMOND BROWN. Tenderly, our Father delights to carry us through the dark experiences of life. He will never let us fall as His support is unfailing.

God's blessing is then invoked on the descendents of the one who was separated from his brethren, v. 16. Joseph knew the bitterness of rejection, exile, false accusation and imprisonment. These costly sufferings paved the way for his elevation as a prince in Egypt, Gen. 41. 39-44. On the throne, he delivered Egypt and his brothers from the disaster of famine.

Jacob had celebrated Joseph as 'a fruitful bough', Gen. 49. 22. Fruitfulness was to be the experience of his tribe. Moses rehearses the bountiful blessings that God would bestow on the tribal territories of Ephraim and Manasseh. Joseph's descendents would enjoy the very best natural resources. Gifts of the very highest quality would be lavished upon them: reviving rain and dew, refreshing springs of water, plentiful harvests, security from ancient mountains and all the fullness of the soil. Such a land would be a tempting target for marauders. Ephraim and Manasseh would also be granted military strength and prowess to defend what they had received. These populous tribes would push off invaders from their bountiful land with the strength and fierceness of the bull and the wild ox.

Israel's neighbours saw prosperity as coming from the Baals. The tribes of Joseph are reminded that their good land was the gift of 'him who dwelt in the bush', v. 16. The great I AM is the source of all fruitfulness.

December 29th

Deuteronomy 33. 18-25

AS THY DAYS, SO SHALL THY STRENGTH BE

The benedictions on six tribes are pronounced in this passage. With the entire nation, these tribes looked forward to entering Canaan with a mixture of apprehension and expectation. As he blessed them, Moses gave them a two-fold prediction. Bounty and battle both lay ahead. In their allotments in the north of the land, the Lord would amply provide for them. However, to gain and hold these territories would demand struggle and conflict.

Zebulun and Issachar are called to rejoice in God's plans for them. One tribe would venture abroad in trade while the other remained settled at home. With easy access to the Mediterranean Sea and the Lake of Galilee, they would enjoy maritime wealth. God's own hand would enlarge the tribe of Gad. Naphtali would experience the manifest favour of the Lord. Asher would be the most blessed of all the tribes. Abundant resources would be theirs. We are blessed with every spiritual blessing in Christ, Eph. 1. 3. The heavenlies are our Canaan.

In that same sphere we face mighty foes, Eph. 6. 12 NKJV. These tribes would engage in warfare in Canaan. God would empower them for the battles ahead. Gad will be like a lion in its strength and prowess. Dan will bound with the energy of a fearless lion cub. Indeed, Gad would selflessly fight with the whole nation until all Israel's territory was secured although its own lot lay east of Jordan. Metaphorically, Asher receives sandals of iron and bronze to hold their prosperous domain. We too must wear the boots provided by the gospel of peace to stand our ground for God, Eph. 6. 15.

In verse 25, God's great promise to Asher glows against this background of conflict. 'Physical strength would be miraculously renewed with every fresh sunrise', RAYMOND BROWN. The Lord Jesus declared that sufficient for the day is its own trouble, Matt. 6. 34, NKJV. More than sufficient for that trouble is the strength promised by our gracious God. The Lord's mercies are 'new every morning', Lam. 3. 23. He will provide daily strength for daily needs throughout our pilgrimage, whatever the difficulties may be. Let us wait on Him today to have our strength renewed, Isa. 40. 31.

December 30th

Deuteronomy 33. 26-29

WHO IS LIKE UNTO THEE, SAVED BY THE LORD?

Moses began his testament with God. He ends it with God. As he commenced, he had celebrated God's appearance at Sinai. He reaches the finale by rejoicing in God's future victories.

The God who had entered a close relationship with Israel has no equal, far less a rival. The Canaanites portrayed Baal as a heavenly charioteer. That was only imagination. In reality, the heavens and the clouds will be the chariot of Israel's God, as He flies to their aid. The Lord is the Creator of the universe. Rain and dew, wind and tempest are all at His command. He is the Master of sun, moon and stars. He is the eternal One, the mighty bulwark of His people and their sure recourse in every peril. His everlasting arms of almighty strength would be underneath them to protect them from all danger and lift them up from every failure. No one can stand against this mighty warrior. He will drive out all of Israel's enemies before them. His word of command is enough to bring about their destruction. God still defends His people. Greater is He who is in us than he that is in the world, 1 John 4. 4.

The strength of the Lord's arm will grant Israel security. Undisturbed by any aggression, they will enjoy to the full God's plentiful provision in their land. These predictions were partially fulfilled under Joshua and later under the better kings. Their complete fulfilment will be when Israel is restored to God in the millennial reign of Christ. Then, the Lord Himself will be their Protector, Zech. 2. 5.

No wonder that Moses exclaims that all Israel was truly happy, blessed indeed by the Lord. In our passage, he issues a challenge. There is only one answer to the question he poses. No other nation is like Israel, simply because they have been delivered by the Lord in His grace and power. 'No one is like them because no one is like Him', RAYMOND BROWN. The peerless God is the shield and sword of His people who gains the victory for them. Their foes will cringe before them. The strongholds of the enemy will be laid waste by God's power. May we rejoice that we are more than conquerors through Him who loved us, Rom. 8. 37.

December 31st

Deuteronomy 34. 1-12

HIS EYE WAS NOT DIM

This 'inspired postscript to the book of Deuteronomy', C. H. MACKINTOSH, records Moses death on Mount Nebo. There, the Lord showed him a vista of Canaan. The undimmed eyes of the aged leader swept over a circle from north to south as God brought before him the delights of Israel's future home. His ears heard the Lord's own voice declare that what he had seen was the territory which He had sworn to give to His people. Thus, their title was secure. God had kept His promise to Moses by allowing him to see the glory of the land which he was forbidden to enter. He would also keep His promise to Israel.

So Moses left the scene. His body was buried by God's own hand in an unmarked grave. In his long life, he had experienced personally the blessing he pronounced on Asher, Deut. 33. 25. His strength had equalled his days. Moses far exceeded his own inspired record of the normal human life span, Ps. 90. 10. His life had been demanding yet, at its end, his eyes were clear and his physical strength unabated. The closing chapters of Deuteronomy are more than enough to demonstrate that his spiritual vision and vigour were equally undiminished.

Israel mourned their great leader for thirty days. Yet, Moses was replaced by Joshua. He was God's man for the new situation. He now steps into leadership, richly endowed with wisdom by the Holy Spirit for the tasks before him.

The ministry of Moses was unparalleled in the Old Testament. Supremely, he was the servant of the Lord. Biblical leadership is always servant leadership, Mark 10. 43. Moses' chief desire had been to know, obey and please God. 'That three-fold longing provided the essential motivation for Moses' entire life', RAYMOND BROWN. He had worked outstanding signs and wonders in Egypt and prevailed over Pharaoh and his magicians. He had demonstrated God's power at the Red Sea and in the wilderness. Yet, the outstanding line in his inspired epitaph is that he was the prophet whom the Lord knew face to face. Beyond all else, Moses was an outstanding man of prayer. He knew daily intimate communion with God. That was the secret of his greatness.